BAE SYSTEMS
Advanced Technology Centres
Sowerby

CAIRS No.	11344
CLASS No.	159.99
HELD BY	~~C Neary~~ (255) Library.
Order No. 505-04	Price £43.95
Copy No. 1	Date Jan '05

PASSENGER BEHAVIOUR

Passenger Behaviour

Edited by
ROBERT BOR
*Royal Free Hospital
London, UK*

ASHGATE

© Robert Bor 2003

All rights reserved. No part of this publication may be reproduced, stored in a retrieval system, or transmitted in any form or by any means, electronic, mechanical, photocopying, recording or otherwise without the prior permission of the publisher.

The editor has asserted his moral right under the Copyright, Designs and Patents Act, 1988, to be identified as the author of this work.

Published by
Ashgate Publishing Limited
Gower House
Croft Road
Aldershot
Hants GU11 3HR
England

Ashgate Publishing Company
Suite 420
101 Cherry Street
Burlington, VT 05401-4405
USA

Ashgate website: http://www.ashgate.com

British Library Cataloguing in Publication Data
Passenger behaviour
   1. Aviation psychology 2. Aeronautics, Commercial - Passenger
   traffic 3. Aviation medicine
   I. Bor, Robert
   155.9'65

Library of Congress Cataloging-in-Publication Data
Passenger behaviour / edited by Robert Bor.
     p. cm.
   Includes bibliographical references.
   ISBN 0-7546-0936-7 (alk. paper)
   1. Air rage. 2. Aeronautics, Commercial--Passenger traffic. I. Title: Passenger behavior.
II. Bor, Robert.

HE9787.3.A4P37 2003
155.9'65--dc21

2002043701

ISBN 0 7546 0936 7

Printed and bound in Great Britain by MPG Books Ltd, Bodmin, Cornwall

Contents

List of Boxes and Tables	*vii*
List of Figures	*ix*
List of Contributors	*xi*
Acknowledgements	*xviii*

Introduction   1
Robert Bor

1   Legal Aspects of Passenger Behaviour   11
    Glenvil Smith

2   Flying-related Stress   17
    Iain B. McIntosh

3   The Evolution of the Airline Industry and Impact on Passenger Behaviour   32
    Alex Cruz and Linda Papadopoulos

4   Just Plane Scared? An Overview of Fear of Flying   45
    Elaine Iljon Foreman

5   Psychological and Psychiatric Difficulties among Airline Passengers   60
    Julia Heller

6   Air Travel and the Implications for Relationships   66
    Olga Levitt and Robert Bor

7   Homesickness and Air Travel   81
    Susanne Robbins

8   Air Rage Post-9/11   95
    Angela Dahlberg

9   Passenger Attention to Safety Information   118
    Lauren J. Thomas

10	Passenger Behaviour in Emergency Situations *Ed Galea*	128
11	The Psychological Impact of Aircraft Disasters *Man Cheung Chung*	183
12	Hostage Behaviour in Aircraft Hijacking: A Script-based Analysis of Resistance Strategies *Margaret A. Wilson*	201
13	Physiology of Flying: Effects and Consequences of the Cabin Environment *Richard Dawood*	223
14	Health and Illness among Airline Passengers *Jane N. Zuckerman*	232
15	Long-haul Flights, Travel Fatigue and Jet Lag *Jim Waterhouse, Thomas Reilly and Ben Edwards*	246
16	Appetite and In-flight Catering *Peter Jones and Margaret Lumbers*	261
17	Sex and International Travel: Behaviour, Health and Human Rights *Stephen Clift*	276
18	Civil Aviation? *Simon Calder*	300
Index		*307*

List of Boxes and Tables

Box 1.1	Specimen parts of IATA Resolution, RRP 1724	14
Box 2.1	Case history 1	19
Box 2.2	Case history 2	23
Box 2.3	Case history 3	25
Table 3.1	Evolution of in-flight food from the 1970s/1980s to the 1990s	40
Table 3.2	Evolution of certain aviation variables over time	43
Table 4.1	Danger of flying in relation to other modes of transport or situations in the US	48
Table 7.1	Symptoms of homesickness	82
Table 10.1	Summary of serious accident statistics for the US	132
Table 10.2	Average distance to exit as measured in units of seat rows, for survivors and fatalities	137
Table 10.3	Passenger use of nearest exit	146
Table 10.4	Reasons for exit choice given by those passengers NOT using nearest exit	147
Table 10.5	Direction of travel and distance travelled in seat rows for passengers where starting locations and exit usage is known or inferred	148
Table 10.6	Exit usage in terms of percentage of passengers using each generalised exit position	149
Table 10.7	Generalised passenger exit usage for aircraft with three exit pairs in 90-second certification trials	150
Table 14.1	Guidelines for medical fitness to travel	239
Table 14.2	Common medical events aboard commercial aircraft	243
Table 15.1	Check list for travel fatigue	248
Table 15.2	The use of bright light to adjust the body clock after time-zone transitions	257
Table 15.3	Check list for dealing with jet lag	259
Box 17.1	Reports of sexual incidents in the course of air travel	280
Box 17.2	Imported syphilis in Finland	282
Table 17.1	Details of six recent British studies on sexual behaviour and risk among travellers/tourists	284
Box 17.3	Two sex tourism websites	288

Box 17.4 At risk profile for unaccompanied minors arriving in the UK and seeking asylum (West Sussex Social Services) 297

List of Figures

Figure 5.1	Interplay of cognitive and physical symptoms of anxiety	62
Figure 10.1	Survival statistics as a function of all serious accidents in the US during the period 1983–2000: (a) overall survival rates and (b) specific survival rates	130
Figure 10.2	Survival statistics as a function of all survivable serious accidents in the US during the period 1983–2000: (a) overall survival rates and (b) specific survival rates	131
Figure 10.3	The four main interacting aspects that govern evacuation	136
Figure 10.4	Over-wing Type-III emergency exits: (a) of the type typically found on aircraft that must be manually operated; (b) open Type-III with hatch thrown out; and (c) new hinged type found on Boeing new generation 737 aircraft	140
Figure 10.5	Age distribution of passengers in the AASK database	146
Figure 10.6	The division of the cabin into three general areas	149
Figure 10.7	Images from certification type trials showing: (a) action of an assertive crew member making physical contact with passengers; (b) passengers jumping onto a Type-A slide; and (c) passengers sitting down onto a slide at a Type-A exit	155
Figure 10.8	Passenger exit delay time distribution for main deck Type-A exits with assertive crew	159
Figure 10.9	CAMI narrow body test facility: (a) passengers exiting a smoke filled simulator via a Type-I exit; and (b) internal passenger behaviour during a simulated evacuation	162
Figure 10.10	Cranfield B737 simulator: (a) interior view; and (b) Type-I exit in use	164
Figure 10.11	View down the main stair in the Cranfield VLES showing a possible dual lane stair configuration with central handrail	167
Figure 10.12	Cranfield VLES showing: (a) model view of the entire simulator with upper deck slide deployed; (b) modular nature of structure; (c) interior view of upper deck; and (d) upper deck slide in use	174

Figure 10.13 CAMI B747 facility: (a) aircraft exterior; and (b) artist's impression of completed facility 175

Figure 10.14 vrEXODUS generated scene from an airEXODUS evacuation simulation 178

Figure 15.1 Mean circadian changes in core (rectal) temperature measured hourly in eight subjects: living normally and sleeping from 24:00 to 08:00h (solid line); and then woken at 04:00h and spending the next 24 hours on a 'constant routine' (dashed line) 250

List of Contributors

Robert Bor has worked as both a clinical and academic psychologist. He is presently a consultant clinical psychologist at the Royal Free Hospital, London and prior to this, has held Chairs in psychology at London Metropolitan University and City University, London. He is Visiting Professor at City University, London, where he teaches on the MSc course in Air Transport Management. He also contributes to the Diploma in Travel Health and Medicine at the Royal Free and University College Medical School in the Academic Department of Travel Medicine and Vaccines. He is a Chartered Clinical, Counselling and Health Psychologist, an Associate Fellow of the British Psychological Society, as well as a UKCP Registered Family Therapist. He provides a specialist psychological consultation service for air crew and their families and airline managers, as well as for passengers. He has set up a treatment service for passengers who have a fear of flying at two London travel health clinics. He is frequently interviewed for television and newspaper features on the psychology of travel. He serves on the editorial board of several leading international academic journals and has authored and co-authored numerous books and papers. He holds an Honours degree in psychology from the University of the Witwatersrand, Johannesburg, and a Clinical Psychology Masters and Doctorate from the University of South Africa. He is a Fellow of the Royal Aeronautical Society and a Member of the European Association for Aviation Psychology and British Travel Health Association. He has a pilot's licence. Robert Bor is also Churchill Fellow.

Simon Calder was born two miles from the runway at Gatwick Airport. He first flew in October 1962, as a result of the Cuban Missile Crisis, when his parents took the whole family to the Channel Islands to lessen the risk of obliteration in the event of a nuclear conflict.

Ten years later he began his career in travel at Gatwick airport, as a cleaner for British Airways and, later, Laker Airways. He then became a security guard, frisking passengers. It was during the gaps between flights that he began to write budget travel guidebooks, starting with the first hitch-hiker's manual to Britain and encompassing destinations from Amsterdam to Cuba.

He became travel editor for *The Independent* in 1994, and shortly afterwards began presenting for BBC2's *Travel Show*. He now reports for BBC1's *Heaven and Earth Show* and the *Travel Channel*, and for BBC radio.

His latest book – *No Frills, the Truth behind the Low-Cost Revolution in the Skies* (Virgin, 2002) – explains the history of no-frills airlines.

Man Cheung Chung earned his BA in psychology and sociology at the University of Guelph, Canada, and PhD at the University of Sheffield. He worked as a Research Psychologist at University College London. He then embarked on a Research Fellowship at the University of Birmingham and subsequently held lectureships at the Universities of Wolverhampton and Sheffield. He is now a Principal Lecturer in the Department of Psychology at the University of Plymouth. He is also an Associate Fellow of the British Psychological Society. He was an honorary therapist at Uffculme Clinic in South Birmingham Health Authority, a Visiting Lecturer for the International Centre for Advanced Studies in Hong Kong and an honorary lecturer at University College London. His main research interests focus on post-traumatic stress disorder and the history and philosophy of psychology. He has published numerous articles and chapters, and has delivered many conference papers related to the above, as well as other topics, such as challenging behaviour, schizophrenia, court diversion scheme and stress and burnout.

Stephen Clift is Professor of Health Education in the Department of Health and Social Welfare Studies, Faculty of Health at Canterbury Christ Church University College. He is editor of several books on international tourism and health, and has recently published an edited collection entitled *Gay Tourism: Culture, Identity and Sex* (Continuum Press, 2002) with Michael Luongo and Carry Callister. His current research interests have moved in the direction of the role of the arts in health promotion and healthcare. He has undertaken research on the health benefits of choral singing and is currently evaluating the Sound Start project, based on the Isle of Wight, which is encouraging mothers to sing to their babies before and after birth.

Alex Cruz is founder of Alnad Ltd, a consultancy that focuses on providing core travel expertise to travel providers and their suppliers. Previously, he was a partner at Arthur D. Little management consultancy and a senior manager at Sabre, the travel distribution company. He has worked with many airlines worldwide in commercial, marketing and technology issues. He is an associate at the Center for Advanced Studies in Telecommunications. He earned a MS in Industrial Engineering from The Ohio State University and a BS in Computer Integrated Manufacturing and Math from the Central Michigan University.

List of Contributors

Angela Dahlberg is president of Dahlberg & Associates, an aviation management consultancy located in Calgary, Alberta, with 25 years experience in aviation management, training, station operations control management, cabin safety policies and procedures. She has researched the phenomenon of disruptive passengers since 1995. She is the author of *Air Rage – The Underestimated Safety Risk* (Ashgate, 2001), the first comprehensive investigation of its kind, and her papers have been published regularly. Considered an expert, she is frequently consulted and her work is used as source material, especially for training. She is an accomplished speaker at aviation conferences and has appeared on media shows in Canada.

Richard Dawood, BSc, MD, DTM&H is a specialist in travel medicine at the Fleet Street Travel Clinic and looks after large numbers of frequent air travellers, flying on business as well as pleasure. He is the editor of *Travellers' Health: How to stay healthy abroad*, the fourth edition of which has just been published.

Ben Edwards is a Lecturer at the Research Institute for Sports and Exercise Sciences, Liverpool John Moores University. His main research interest is in the measurement of physical performance and general physiology in exercise in humans, with particular reference to problems associated with changed sleep-wake schedules, including jet lag, and ways to alleviate this. He has a PhD and has published several research papers on these topics.

Ed Galea is a professor and the founding director of the Fire Safety Engineering Group (FSEG) at the University of Greenwich where has worked in fire safety research since 1986. His chair at the University of Greenwich is supported by the UK CAA. His work in fire safety began with his analysis of the tragic Manchester Boeing 737 fire. Since then, it has expanded to include the modelling of human behaviour and evacuation, fire/smoke spread, combustion and fire suppression. In addition to his interests in aviation safety, his work is applied to buildings, rail and marine environments. He the author of over 100 academic publications and serves on a number of national and international standards and safety committees concerned with fire and evacuation including BSI, ISO, IMO and SFPE.

Julia Heller is a Consultant Clinical Forensic Psychologist and has worked for the last eight years at the Dene Hospital in East Sussex which is a medium secure hospital for female offenders. She currently works at Parkside Hospital which is a general hospital where she runs a psychology outpatient service. She also consults to some airlines and is involved in psychological testing of pilots. She holds an Honours Degree in Psychology from Bristol University, an MSc in Clinical Psychology from Surrey University and a PhD from the University of London.

Elaine Iljon Foreman is a Chartered Clinical Psychologist who specialises in the treatment of fear of flying and other anxiety related problems. She holds an Honours Degree from Durham University and a Masters Degree from Aberdeen University. Her highly specialised treatment programme for fear of flying is based on over 20 years of clinical experience and on her ongoing research and development of cognitive behaviour therapy. She researched the treatment of anxiety at Middlesex Hospital Medical School, London and has created a brief, intensive therapy course for the fear of flying based on cognitive behavioural techniques. As well as being an invited expert on radio and TV programmes, her research results have been presented at international conferences in Europe, North America, the Far East and Australia.

Peter Jones is the IFCA Professor of Production and Operations Management, and Director of the Travel Catering Research Centre at the University of Surrey. He is the author or editor of nine textbooks relating to operations management in service industries in general, and the hospitality industry in particular. He is currently leading a DTI-funded Industry Forum Adaptation Programme research team, investigating UK best practice in hotels, restaurants, leisure operations, the licensed trade and visitor attractions.

Olga Levitt currently works as an independent systemic psychotherapist. She consults to individuals, couples and families as well as to groups who work together in organisations. She is a trainer and supervisor of therapists, psychologists and social workers and is a regular lecturer on the postgraduate Counselling Psychology programme at London Guildhall University. She worked for many years in Child, Adolescent and Family Mental Health Services. In her clinical as well as her personal life, she is interested in the creative ways in which we all strive to maintain stability while simultaneously embracing change, particularly that involving travel and the repeated separations and reunions which this brings.

Margaret Lumbers is Senior Lecturer in Food Science and a Registered Public Health Nutritionist and member of the Travel Catering and Food,

Consumer Behaviour and Health Research Centres at the University of Surrey. She has worked in both industry and education and has research interests in food choice, food access and procurement, cross cultural studies and food risk perception.

Iain B. McIntosh is a family doctor. He initiated a travel health clinic in his group practice and accumulated research data over a decade on travel related anxieties and phobias which has been presented at international medical conferences. Extensive global travel and professional duties as an in-flight medical repatriation doctor have provided practical experience of travel stressors related to air transportation. He is a co-founder of the British Travel Health Association, editor of the *British Travel Health Journal* and is committed to promoting physical and psychological health among world travellers.

Linda Papadopoulos is a Chartered Counselling and Health Psychologist and a Reader in Psychology and Course Director at London Guildhall University. She has published widely in the field of counselling and medical psychology, and more recently in aviation psychology. She has been invited to give specialist lectures at numerous universities and medical schools both in England and abroad. She is Course Director of the MSc in Counselling Psychology at London Guildhall University and holds several research grants. She has worked in numerous treatment settings, both NHS and private, and has extensive experience in working with individuals, couples and families. She has an extensive publication record.

Thomas Reilly is Professor and Director of the Research Institute for Sports and Exercise Sciences, Liverpool John Moores University. He has spent much of his research career (about 35 years) investigating circadian rhythms in humans, with particular reference to the rhythms of physical performance at rest and during exercise, and the problems associated with changed sleep-wake schedules, including jet lag. He has published many research papers and reviews, and been author, co-author and co-editor of several books. He is chairman of the Physiological Committee of the British Olympic Association.

Susanne Robbins trained as a Counselling Psychologist at London Guildhall University. She now practices in the NHS in both primary care and in a district hospital, and is particularly interested in counselling people with medical problems. She is also a registered nurse and has worked in a variety of clinical settings.

Glenvil Smith is a graduate of Trinity College, Cambridge and qualified with Norton Rose in 1976. He was formerly in-house counsel to a leading 'incoming' tour operator, to the Crown Agents and to Dan-Air, at the time the UK's second largest airline. From 1986 to 1997 he was a partner, then consultant to the Oxford solicitors' practice of Dallas Brett. He currently advises airline clients of Aviation and Tourism Law Consultants Ltd on all aspects of aviation law. He is a member of the European Air Law Association and the Travel and Tourism Lawyers' Association and a lecturer in air law and route negotiation on the MSc course in Air Transport Management at City University.

Lauren J. Thomas read for a BA in Psychology at the University of Liverpool, and an MSc in Applied Psychology at Cranfield University. She then joined the Defence Evaluation Research Agency, where she worked on a range of human factors projects in occupational psychology. She returned to the Human Factors Group at Cranfield University as a Teaching Fellow in Aviation Psychology. A chartered occupational psychologist, she teaches on various postgraduate courses. Her research interests include selection, training and cabin safety, and she also supervises MSc student research in these areas. A Chartered Occupational Psychologist, she is currently completing her PhD on the factors influencing passenger evacuation from very large transport aircraft.

Jim Waterhouse is a Senior Lecturer at the Research Institute for Sports and Exercise Sciences, Liverpool John Moores University. He holds a PhD and has spent his research career (over 30 years) investigating circadian rhythms in humans, with particular reference to the problems associated with changed sleep-wake schedules (including jet lag) and methods of assessing the body clock from measurements of core temperature. He has published many research papers and reviews, and been co-author and co-editor of several books. He has been President of the European Society for Chronobiology (1989–93) and President of the International Society of Chronobiology (1997–2001).

Margaret A. Wilson is an applied psychologist who has been teaching forensic psychology in the UK for many years. She has conducted a great deal of research on the psychology of terrorism and lectured extensively on the subject worldwide. She holds an honorary academic post at The University of Kent at Canterbury.

Jane N. Zuckerman is Director of the Academic Centre for Travel Medicine and Vaccines, and holds the positions of Elective Tutor and Senior Lecturer and Honorary Consultant at the Royal Free and University College Medical School and the Royal Free Hampstead NHS Trust, London. She is also the Medical Director of the Royal Free Travel Health Centre and the Medical Director of the Royal Free Clinical Trials Centre. Her major fields of interest include the evaluation of new travel related and more general vaccines including those of hepatitis A and B. Her other interests include research into different aspects of travel health and medicine, including issues of staying well when travelling, and occupational risks of exposure to health hazards particularly blood-borne viruses. She is also involved in developing postgraduate education within the speciality of travel medicine. She is the course organiser for the Diploma Course in Travel Health and Medicine (University of London), an Introductory Short Course in Travel Medicine (University of London) and an Annual Study in Travel Health. She is a member of the International Society of Medicine and the British Travel Health Association. She is the editor-in-chief of *Travel Medicine in Practice*, a recently launched journal for healthcare professionals and has contributed to several peer-reviewed journals on topics related to travel medicine, the medical student elective period and new developments within the field of vaccines. She also holds the position of Chair of the European Travel Health Advisory Board. She received the award of Hospital Doctor of the Year 2001 and also received the Hospital Doctor Innovation Award for 2001.

Acknowledgements

I am enormously grateful to the following people who have helped at the various stages of this project and in the production of the book: John Hindley and Carolyn Court of Ashgate Publishing helped to develop the original idea and have been supportive throughout; Brandon Storey provided extensive editorial assistance; Pat FitzGerald's hard work converted the original text into camera-ready copy in record time.

Lastly, this book would not have come about without the many conversations I have had with pilots, cabin crew, airline managers and others involved in aviation, as well as passengers, and I thank everyone for the time they have given and the interest they have shown.

Introduction

Robert Bor

Air transportation is the world's largest industry. The aerospace industry is wholly dependent upon people – pilots, cabin crew, air traffic controllers, maintenance engineers, airport personnel and, of course, passengers. It is increasingly recognised that it is vital to understand human factors in order to improve safety and security, and manage the ever-growing number of passengers. Surprisingly little has been published on the psychological aspects of air travel, although, where available, literature appears across a range of specialist publications. There is no single authoritative modern text on passenger behaviour. This book seeks to remedy this.

The principal foci of recent published literature in the field of aviation psychology have been safety and the selection of aircrew. Emerging issues and problems such as terrorism, unruly passenger behaviour, the advent of low-cost no-frills carriers and longer non-stop flights have broadened the agenda of aviation psychologists. This new volume will, one hopes, contribute a psychological perspective to passenger behaviour and help the reader to acquire an understanding of how air travel disrupts human relationships and behaviour patterns, as well as bodily functions.

This book is written mainly for flight crew and cabin crew, as well as others who work professionally in commercial aviation who share an interest in passenger behaviour. This includes ground staff, airline and airport managers, airline safety experts, aviation psychologists, human factors specialists, aerospace medical and nursing specialists, and aircraft designers and manufacturers. A further audience includes researchers, the media, and social and occupational psychologists. It is hoped that some 'frequent flyers' will also be interested in this book.

The development of commercial air travel was one of the defining achievements of the last century. The impact that modern civil aviation has had on our lives is far-reaching. It has completely altered how we relate to others and do business, since almost anywhere on earth can now be reached in little more than 24 hours. Air travel brings us into contact with others and has therefore altered and increased possibilities in our lives. Our horizons for holidays can be much further than ever before and consequently air travel has an impact on lifestyle and expectations. Of course, aircraft are used for far more than moving people from place to place. Humanitarian aid can be delivered more rapidly to inaccessible populations. Aircraft are also used for geopolitical purposes, especially during conflicts, to move troops, observe movements on the ground and to bomb, and serve as a platform for learning more about the challenges for astronauts of space travel.

The airline industry has moved through a number of phases since brothers Orville and Wilbur Wright pioneered the Age of Flight on 17 December 1903. Their fragile aircraft, *Flyer*, lifted off the ground for 12 seconds. Many modern passenger aircraft are longer than the 120ft they flew! World War I highlighted the strategic value of aircraft as a method of transport, observation and as a weapon. After the war, aircraft were increasingly used to carry mail and goods, but in those days, aviation was considered more entertainment for curious and sometimes bewildered audiences on the ground than regarded as an industry. Commercial air travel only took off in the late 1920s and early 1930s. In the early days, it was only accessible to those who were wealthy enough to afford it. Air travel was perceived as glamorous, yet dangerous. After World War II, there were vast numbers of surplus aircraft and pilots, as well as a whole manufacturing industry in aviation, all of which served to launch modern commercial aviation. Jet aircraft, growth in aviation infrastructure (e.g. construction of airports), longer non-stop sectors, the advent of larger passenger aircraft and lower fares made air travel increasingly accessible and attractive. Modern commercial aviation is characterised by its size as well as its complexity. There are several discernible sectors, including short-haul, long-haul, low-cost, no-frills, business, holiday, package and supersonic, among others. Passengers come from all walks of life, every nationality and culture and are anything but an homogenous group.

Most air travellers encounter a number of similar challenges in the course of their journeys. Humans have not evolved naturally to fly. We are arguably best suited to terrestrial activity, possibly as an evolved form of hunter-gatherer and almost certainly as a self-propelling species. We encounter evolutionary barriers when we exceed what we are best designed to do. These include a range of familiar, though arguably noxious, symptoms or 'penalties' including jet lag, motion sickness and fear, among others. While developments in air travel have been spectacular and rapid, from an evolutionary point of view, our species has a certain amount of catching-up to do in order to cope better with the demands of air travel.

Even the most seasoned air travellers appear to carry an 'emotional charge' when they fly. They may experience a range of both pleasant and unpleasant feelings, ranging from claustrophobia, frustration, fear and elation to anxiety stemming from separation from a loved one, relief, disorientation or a sense of anticipation and adventure. The scientific study of passenger behaviour is, however, in its infancy. Surprisingly little is known about the psychological impact of air travel. This underdeveloped understanding of how and why passengers are prone to behave in certain ways may be due, in part, to an outdated belief that passengers are tolerant and compliant, and that most appear to adjust effortlessly to the unique and specific demands of air travel. While this is generally the case, certain prominent exceptions, highlighted in the media, have raised questions about what it is that leads some passengers to react to air travel or to conduct themselves in a way that deviates from the norm.

Many people travel in order to relax on holiday and reduce stress in their lives yet, ironically, air travel seems in itself to expose passengers to stress. Some sources of stress may seem mundane, such as having to cope with a short delay, but nonetheless can trigger intense emotional reactions. The absence of any information or an acceptable explanation from airline employees or crew simply exacerbates the situation. Away from the familiarity and security of their accustomed environment, there is increased risk to passengers of suffering psychological problems, as well as greater exposure to a range of hazards and health risks. Air travel can induce depression, anxiety, panic attacks or even psychosis in vulnerable individuals.

Air travel affects how people behave. Some become demanding; regress to an infantile stage of development; are difficult to please; appear to have scant regard for the needs (and rights) of fellow passengers; confide the most personal and intimate details of their life to a complete stranger; become clingy, rowdy or anxious; withdraw into themselves; commit acts of 'air rage'; drink too much alcohol; ignore the rules and smoke on board aircraft even where this is expressly prohibited; or even sexually molest the passenger seated adjacent to them. Most passengers, of course, adapt to the unique challenges of the experience. It is unclear, however, whether these patterns of behaviour could be observed in the same people in a different context, or whether being on board an aircraft at 35,000ft specifically triggers them. The so-called 'causes' or triggers of passenger behaviour are clearly multifactorial. A number of factors may affect how airline passengers behave, although the relevance and strength of each is difficult to determine. These factors include some of the following:

1 what happens to passengers in the time leading up to boarding the aircraft (e.g. the journey to the airport, delays, stress, check-in formalities, seat

allocation, etc.). Their emotional state may be primed or aroused by a number of unwelcome or stressful experiences and encounters. Underlying fears, such as being in an enclosed space, a fear of heights, a fear of dying or being separated from a loved one can add to the practical challenges that most passengers may endure;

2   what passengers experience on board aircraft also affects how they behave. This ranges from the quality of in-flight entertainment and service to the meal service, tenor of crew/passenger relationships, how they relate to those around them, extent of a delay (if any), among many other factors;

3   the personality of the passenger also affects his or her capacity to cope with change, stress, crowds, enclosure, separation from loved ones and fatigue as well as other features of modern air travel;

4   the physical and mental health status of the traveller is also relevant to an understanding of passenger behaviour. This includes the effects on the passenger of prescribed medication, recreational drugs and/or alcohol, any of which may affect cognitive capacities and behaviour. The physical effects of air travel have psychological consequences and these apply especially to transmeridian long-haul flights, which may produce irritability, claustrophobia, sleep disturbance, boredom, restlessness from excessive 'seat belts on' conditions and other problems in passengers. These reactions may be intensified and prolonged by excessive alcohol consumption or the effects of certain prescribed or illicit drugs;

5   the unique cabin environment directly affects passenger behaviour. The air inside the aircraft cabin is low in humidity and deviations from usual ambient conditions have been found to produce stress and irritability, while lowered air pressure can lead to mild hypoxia and impairment of cognitive tasks, such as reasoning. Noise levels from the engines and outside air rushing past the aircraft are an additional source of stress. Loud noise also results in people having to raise their voices when communicating which can be misconstrued as aggressive behaviour thereby increasing tension between people. Cramped conditions on board aircraft may exacerbate stress and may trigger acts of violence. Passengers may seek to establish dominance over an empty seat, a shared arm rest or to reserve overhead locker space. Emotional reactions intensify when personal space is invaded by strangers. Crowded and cramped conditions can lead to feelings of deindividuation which is linked to less restrained behaviour;

6   cultural background, gender, age and other demographic variables mediate how people cope with stress and the travel experience;

7 passengers' attitudes towards and expectations of air travel and the airline also affect how they behave. These may be shaped by airline advertisements, class of travel, membership of frequent flyer programmes which may arouse a sense of entitlement, price paid for their ticket relative to other passengers and past experiences of air travel with which comparisons may be made. Expectations may also be shaped by the purpose of the trip. A business passenger may value privacy, quality of service, physical space and amenities above some other criteria and may feel annoyed if these are jeopardised. A family travelling on holiday, on the other hand, may attach higher value to being seated together and on-board amenities for children and may therefore express annoyance if their expectations are not adequately met. While flight delays and separation from luggage affect everyone, actual responses vary between people;
8 the social context of the traveller is also relevant to an understanding of passenger behaviour. A rowdy group of sportsmen or a group travelling abroad for a hen weekend may present a greater challenge to cabin crew and fellow passengers in terms of their behaviour than a fearful, withdrawn passenger travelling alone. Research within the field of social psychology has highlighted the effects of being within or apart from a group, the impact of separation on one's emotional state and behaviour patterns within hierarchically organised social systems (i.e. where crew members carry authority and passengers are duty bound to comply with their instructions). This may lead to resentment where passengers judge airline employees to have fallen short of their expectations;
9 the legal consequences of antisocial behaviour on board aircraft also influence passenger behaviour (e.g. being drunk and disorderly, ignoring a smoking ban or behaving in an aggressive or threatening manner towards other passengers or crew). How passengers behave may be further linked to the likelihood that they perceive of crew, other passengers or the airline taking action where rules are broken or safety threatened;
10 perceptions of air travel within an era. In recent years, given hijackings, air rage and the 11 September 2001 attacks, passengers might view being on board an aircraft as a more dangerous or violent milieu than was previously the case. This may in turn affect how they manage or respond to threats or general risk with regard to personal safety and security.

The chapters that follow address a range of topics concerning passenger behaviour and have been arranged around certain themes. In Chapter 1, Glenvil Smith, one of the world's leading lawyers specialising in aviation, sets the scene by highlighting the range of laws that govern passenger behaviour, including both rights and obligations. In spite of the complex issues relating to jurisdiction, it is reassuring that the law pertaining to passenger behaviour aims to protect aircraft, crew, fellow passengers and people on the ground wherever they may be. In Chapter 2, Iain McIntosh describes the range of stressful situations and encounters that passengers must endure. Drawing on his clinical experience and illustrated through case vignettes, he also points out a number of practical steps that passengers can take in order to cope better with air travel and personal stress. This is followed in Chapter 3 by Alex Cruz and Linda Papadopoulos' historical account of developments in commercial aviation and the reciprocal relationship between these and passenger behaviour. They recognise that the industry is constantly evolving and highlight some developments that are likely to occur in the near future and the likely impact these will have on passengers.

In spite of the fact that commercial aviation remains one of the safest forms of public transport, readers may be interested to learn that a fear of flying affects a large percentage of passengers, estimated to be in the region of 40 per cent in some studies. Images of the 11 September 2001 terrorist atrocities in the USA where passenger aircraft were deliberately crashed into the Twin Towers, the Pentagon and into a field in New Jersey are indelibly seared in many people's minds and affect their perception of airline safety. Indeed, a fear of flying can no longer be lightly dismissed as irrational. However, as Elaine Iljon Foreman points out in Chapter 4, a fear of flying can be treated by psychological therapy and modern approaches to therapy tend to be brief and effective. For some passengers, however, air travel either exacerbates or triggers psychiatric symptoms. In Chapter 5, Julia Heller describes the range of psychiatric problems that passengers may exhibit on board aircraft. She also stresses the need to prevent those who appear agitated or mentally unstable from boarding aircraft in the first place, as specialist treatment can more readily be afforded on the ground. Furthermore, psychiatric problems within the confines of an aircraft cabin can jeopardise safety and passenger comfort.

Psychologists have intensively studied the impact of separation from loved ones over the years. The implications of attachment behaviour, as it is termed, for air travellers are discussed by Olga Levitt and Robert Bor in Chapter 6. They describe the ebb and flow of relationship dynamics and how passengers are affected emotionally by the disruption brought about by air travel. Through illustrative vignettes, they also explore the challenges to relationships of the 'intermittent spouse syndrome'. Susanne Robbins elaborates on some of the issues raised in a chapter on homesickness. This and the previous chapter stress that passenger behaviour on board aircraft and in airport terminals should be interpreted and understood in the context of the traveller's emotional state: although they may not display obvious signs of distress, they may feel isolated, frightened and/or lonely.

The next five chapters cover topics relating to safety and passenger behaviour. Recent media reports have highlighted the problem of disruptive passenger behaviour, or 'air rage' as it is commonly termed. In Chapter 8 Angela Dahlberg addresses some of the possible causes or triggers of air rage and what airlines can do to prevent such incidents. She stresses the need for crew selection and training in order to improve management of the problem. Safety is paramount in the airline industry. In the following chapter, Lauren Thomas addresses the issue of passenger attention to safety information and the relationship this has to survivability in the event of an incident or accident. Her recommendations are based on the results of systemic research into this problem. How passengers behave in emergency situations is the topic of Chapter 10. Ed Galea provides a thorough analysis of the relevant issues and highlights the different ways in which passengers tend to react during an emergency. It is encouraging for readers to learn that most incidents are survivable, though passenger and crew behaviour rather than the extent of the accident often mediate survivability. This chapter clearly illustrates how the scientific approach to an understanding of passenger behaviour can be put to practical use and benefit both passengers and crew.

In spite of the excellent safety record of the airline industry, accidents do sometimes occur and the emotional consequences for the surviving passengers and crew, as well as the impact on relatives, other airline employees and members of the rescue services are important to understand. In Chapter 11, Man Cheung Chung reviews published research on this sensitive topic and highlights the lessons that can be drawn from previous disasters in order to ensure that compassionate and appropriate help and support is offered to those who may be affected.

The unlawful commandeering of an aircraft, commonly termed 'a hijacking', is of considerable interest in an era of global terrorism. Margaret Wilson's chapter on hostage behaviour in aircraft hijackings provides a fascinating account of how passengers, crew and hijackers behave in these situations. Drawing on actual examples, she highlights discernible patterns in behaviour and makes some speculative comments about the nature of the threat in the post-September 11 era.

The final collection of chapters examines passenger health issues and how these affect behaviour. In Chapter 13, Richard Dawood discusses the physiology of flying and the effects of air travel on the passenger and his or her behaviour. This chapter also highlights the unique problems and challenges posed by air travel generally and the aircraft cabin specifically. Jane Zuckerman points out in Chapter 14 that travel increases the risk of contracting an illness. She also points out that passengers and health care staff are increasingly conscious of these risks and more is now known about how to prevent or reduce risk in some cases. Useful health-related information is provided in this chapter.

Many travellers who have experienced long-haul flights, especially those involving a transmeridian journey, will be familiar with the term 'jet lag' and may have experienced travel fatigue. This is an important topic because the effects of fatigue and jet lag may persist well beyond the actual journey and continue to disrupt routines and behaviour for several weeks. Jim Waterhouse and his colleagues provide a detailed account of this problem in Chapter 15 and suggest ways in which to prepare for and cope better with the effects of jet lag. Passenger behaviour – especially mood – is affected by appetite. Peter Jones and Margaret Lumbers offer an overview of the logistics of catering within the airline industry and how, over the years, airlines have responded to the challenge of feeding vast numbers of passengers. The use and effects of alcohol on board aircraft and at altitude are also covered in their chapter.

A book about passenger behaviour would not be complete without some reference to sexual activity among travellers. However, having sexual relations on board aircraft has not, to the best of my knowledge, been the subject of serious academic study even though it has been linked to cases of disruptive passenger behaviour. In Chapter 17, Stephen Clift offers a fascinating insight into the subculture of sex tourism. This chapter facilitates an awareness of sexual behaviour and risk-taking among travellers as well as the trafficking of women and children for sexual purposes, both of which are relevant to an understanding of passenger behaviour.

Finally, few are as well qualified to comment on the experience of modern air travel from the point of view of a passenger as Simon Calder, who is both a leading travel journalist as well as an avid traveller. His insightful and wry account of modern air travel must surely strike a chord with everyone who reads this book and who has travelled on an aircraft as a passenger within the last few years.

Each of the contributors approached was enthusiastic about the project right from the start. This enthusiasm was quickly translated into hard work. I was fortunate in that all contributions were received well before the final submission date and my colleagues very ably produced chapters that synthesise current research and thinking in their specialist areas, as well as highlighting their own unique contributions to this field. I am enormously grateful to all of them for their contributions and support.

The aim of this text is to bring together, in one authoritative source, a selection of specialist topics that contribute to a contemporary understanding of passenger behaviour. At first glance the study of passenger behaviour may appear a simple and straightforward undertaking. As many researchers in this field will attest, this is anything but the case. While airline passengers are a captive population, it is difficult to undertake naturalistic research in an aircraft due to a combination of factors. These include a reluctance by airlines to permit research to be undertaken in a commercial and customer-sensitive environment, ethical considerations, the exceptional cost of such research and possible safety implications of some research. Precise replication of some conditions in an aircraft cabin is also not always possible. Understandably, the extent of knowledge about passenger behaviour is not uniform across a range of topics. More is known about certain issues than others and this imbalance is, in part, reflected in the content of this book. Some chapters are longer than others, while others are more descriptive when compared to those where the topic is more amenable to empirical study. Readers will recognise some overlap between chapters. This is unavoidable as there are multiple perspectives on some themes. For example, the topic of air rage can be approached from both legal and psychological perspectives.

The book does not offer an exhaustive list of topics on passenger behaviour nor do the contents prescribe how best to address some of the problems that are highlighted. Instead, through invited specialist contributions, it seeks to raise awareness and establish the important benefits of learning more about passenger behaviour. I am aware that there are gaps in this text and that many other topics could have been included. I hope that readers will provide feedback about the book and that future editions will incorporate and reflect their ideas and suggestions.

The global travel industry has expanded rapidly over the past 25 years and the ever-increasing number of airline passengers – now approaching 2 billion per year – prompts the need for greater awareness and appreciation of the psychological needs and reactions of air travellers. Psychology is not a precise science, however, and it is not possible to predict behaviour across the range of situations and contexts that passengers experience. There are too many factors and variables that elude methodological control. In spite of these limitations, there is increasing recognition of the importance of understanding more about passenger behaviour not only for technical, safety, health, legal and practical reasons, but also to ensure the relative comfort of passengers in an increasingly stressful and complex travel environment. It is exactly 100 years since the Wright brothers 'invented' modern aviation, and it is fitting that publication of this book should mark this important milestone. It is hoped that this book will help to reflect what is already known about passenger behaviour and also point the way forward for future research.

Chapter 1

Legal Aspects of Passenger Behaviour

Glenvil Smith

'Why should I "behave"? I've paid my (extortionate) fare to the airline, am headed off on business and I can do what I please on the flight! Or can I?'

Fortunately for the rest of us, he can't. Not only do criminal sanctions regulate whole areas of passenger behaviour but an airline's Conditions of Contract and General Conditions of Carriage for Passengers and Baggage govern the contractual relationship between an airline and its passengers, and these have a good deal to say on what a passenger may and may not do. There is also the theoretical possibility of a potential claim being brought directly by fellow passengers if damage (in its widest sense) is caused to others.

Article 17 of the Chicago Convention of 1944 states that 'Aircraft have the nationality of the State in which they are registered' with Article 18 preventing dual registration (the former Concorde service from London-Heathrow to Dallas, Texas via Washington, DC involved de-registration of the aircraft from the British register and re-registration onto the U.S. register (or vice versa) every time the flight transited Washington). Accordingly, there can be no ambiguity as to 'whose law' governs in-flight behaviour, although as most nations have ascribed to various international conventions, a wide measure of uniformity exists worldwide. In the case of a UK registered aircraft, the Carriage by Air Act 1961 – which imports into English law the Warsaw Convention 1929 as amended at the Hague in 1955, but which is shortly to be updated by the implementation of the Montreal Convention 1999 – applies, together with various EU Directives and Regulations, although these tend to deal more with 'passengers' rights' and 'carrier's obligations'.

In order to protect civil aviation from anti-social (or worse) passenger behaviour, the Tokyo Convention 1963 governs 'offences against penal law' or 'acts which, whether or not they are offences, may or do jeopardise the safety of the aircraft or of persons or property therein or which jeopardise good order and discipline on board' and which are committed on board aircraft registered in contracting states. The Tokyo Convention forms the bedrock of legislative protection across the world devolving, in accordance with Article 3(1), jurisdiction over offences and acts committed on board to the state of registration. Article 6 permits the aircraft commander, when he has reasonable grounds to believe that a person has committed, or is about to commit, such an offence or act on board the aircraft to use:

reasonable measures including restraint which are necessary:

(a) to protect the safety of the aircraft, or of persons or property therein; or
(b) to maintain good order and discipline on board; or
(c) to enable him to deliver such person to the competent authorities or to disembark him.

Fortunately for the commander (and his or her crew), the aircraft owner, operator, any charterer and indeed any passenger who gets involved, Article 10 exonerates all from responsibility for the 'treatment undergone by the person against whom the action was taken' under the Convention. A rare bit of 'carte blanche' indeed!

The principles of the Tokyo Convention and the later Hague Convention of 1970 (which is primarily directed against the unlawful seizure of aircraft) are imported into English law as regards British registered aircraft through sections 91, 92 and 94 of the Civil Aviation Act 1982 and are bolstered by the Aviation Security Act 1982 and the Aviation and Maritime Security Act 1990. Extra-territorial jurisdiction is claimed by virtue of the important Civil Aviation (Amendment) Act 1996, covering any 'act or omission which takes place on a board a foreign aircraft ... where ... the next landing of the aircraft is in the United Kingdom and [if] the act or omission would, if taking place [in the country of registration of the aircraft] also constitute an offence under the law in force in that country'.

Day-to-day regulation of British registered aircraft (and passengers travelling in them) is to be found in the Air Navigation Order 2000 and related instruments. This Order (which is likely to have a near equivalent in most other countries) includes provisions such as:

63. A person shall not recklessly or negligently act in a manner likely to endanger an aircraft, or any person therein.
64. A person shall not recklessly or negligently cause or permit an aircraft to endanger any person or property.
65. A person shall not enter any aircraft when drunk, or be drunk in any aircraft.
66(2). A person shall not smoke in any compartment of an aircraft registered in the United Kingdom at a time when smoking is prohibited in that

compartment by a notice to that effect exhibited by or on behalf of the commander of the aircraft.
67. Every person in an aircraft shall obey all lawful commands which the commander of that aircraft may give for the purpose of securing the safety of the aircraft and of persons or property carried therein, or the safety, efficiency or regularity of air navigation.
68. No person shall while in an aircraft:
   (a) use any threatening, abusive or insulting words towards a member of the crew of the aircraft;
   (b) behave in a threatening, abusive, insulting or disorderly manner towards a member of the crew of the aircraft; or
   (c) intentionally interfere with the performance by a member of the crew of the aircraft of his duties.

The above provisions obviously give the airline, and the applicable authorities, a fairly broad armoury in case of need. Criminal penalties (from fines to imprisonment) apply to anyone who is shown to have broken any of these stipulations.

As regards the civil law of contract, almost all international carriers worldwide have adopted IATA Resolution 724 ('Passenger Ticket – Notices and Conditions of Contract'): most feature the standard 'Eleven Conditions' printed on their own form of tickets (or e-tickets) and/or IATA travel agents' neutral ticketing stock. Within Standard Condition 3, the passenger is advised that, amongst other things, his contract of carriage by air is subject to 'carrier's conditions of carriage and related regulations which are made part hereof (and are available on application at the offices of carrier) ...', which means that a passenger is bound by each carrier's published General Conditions of Carriage.

Carriers all have their own set of General Conditions, but are likely broadly to follow another IATA Resolution, RRP 1724, which is expressed as 'Recommended Practice' and which is therefore up to any carrier to adopt, or amend in whole or in part. Articles of particular interest here are Art. 7 ('Refusal and Limitation of Carriage') and Art.11 ('Conduct aboard Aircraft') and specimen parts of these are reproduced in full at the foot of this chapter. Whilst RRP 1724 has recently been amended after 'discussions' with consumer bodies across the world to be 'fairer' and more 'user friendly' to passengers, even in their current form it provides an airline with a useful, and specific, course of dealing with obstreperous travellers.

Box 1.1   Specimen parts of IATA Resolution, RRP 1724

1.1.1 RIGHT TO REFUSE CARRIAGE

1.1.2   In the reasonable exercise of our discretion, we may refuse to carry you or your Baggage if we have notified you in writing that we would not at any time after the date of such notice carry you on our flights. You will not be entitled to a refund for any Tickets purchased by you or on your behalf following such notice being given.

1.1.3   We may also refuse to carry you or your Baggage if one or more of the following have occurred or we reasonably believe may occur:

    1.1.3.1   such action is necessary in order to comply with any applicable government laws, regulations, or orders;

    1.1.3.2   the carriage of you or your Baggage may endanger or affect the safety, health, or materially affect the comfort of other passengers or crew;

    1.1.3.3   your mental or physical state or attitude or demeanour, including your impairment from alcohol or drugs, presents a hazard or risk to yourself, to passengers, to crew, or to property;

    1.1.3.4   you have committed misconduct on a previous flight, and we have reason to believe that such conduct may be repeated;

    1.1.3.5   you have refused to submit to a security check;

    1.1.3.6   you have not paid the applicable fare, taxes, fees or charges;

    1.1.3.7   you owe us any money in respect of a previous flight owing to payment having been dishonoured, denied or recharged against us;

    1.1.3.8   you do not appear to have valid travel documents, may seek to enter a country through which you may be in transit, or for which you do not have valid travel documents, destroy your travel documents during flight or refuse to surrender your travel documents to the flight crew, against receipt, when so requested;

    1.1.3.9   you cannot prove that you are the person named in the Ticket;

> **1.1.3.10** you have failed to comply with the requirements set forth in Article 3.3 above concerning coupon sequence and use;
>
> **1.1.3.11** you fail to observe our instructions with respect to safety or security;
>
> If we have, in the reasonable exercise of our discretion under this Article 7.1.2 refused to carry you on the basis of any of the above, or have removed you en route, we may cancel the remaining unused portion of your Ticket and you will not be entitled to further carriage or to a refund in respect of the sector(s) covered by the Ticket. We will not be liable for any consequential loss or damage alleged due to any such refusal to carry or removal en route.
>
> 11.1 GENERAL
>
> If, in our reasonable opinion, you conduct yourself aboard the aircraft so as to endanger the aircraft or any person or property on board, or obstruct the crew in the performance of their duties, or fail to comply with any instructions of the crew including but not limited to those with respect to smoking, alcohol or drug consumption, or behave in a manner which causes discomfort, inconvenience, damage or injury to other passengers or the crew, we may take such measures as we deem reasonably necessary to prevent continuation of such conduct, including restraint. You may be disembarked and refused onward carriage at any point, and may be prosecuted for offences committed on board the aircraft.

It is indeed quite possible, as a matter of contract, for an airline to declare to a passenger, in specified circumstances, 'Please never travel with us again'. Each airline has its own policy for 'policing' passengers who have been considered unruly. British Airways and Cathay Pacific have both had to deal with rampaging members of pop groups and have banned them from flying again with their airline. More formally, KLM has introduced a 'Watchlist on Unruly Passengers' which is linked to their worldwide reservations system; this is sub-divided into a 'No Fly' (in cases of previous 'gross misconduct') and 'Selectee' (where further flights may be permitted subject to certain conditions). KLM has stressed that passengers only go on these lists on the grounds of clear reports submitted by frontline personnel using 'stipulated procedures'.

One airline has gone so far as to introduce a contractually agreed 'disruption charge' of €1,000 (or equivalent) for smoking on board. The formal message is 'You may not smoke in any part of an aircraft operated by us' (which is clearly stated in the airline's General Conditions of Carriage and announced in flight) ... but should you dare to do so, we are going to incur clean-up charges, may have to discharge fire extinguishers and fresh air sprays and the costs we incur will be 'liquidated damages' (which we will charge to your credit card if we have the details). In addition, of course, applicable criminal penalties for breach of the relevant Air Navigation Order could apply. It is therefore, within limits, open to any airline to 'agree', through its conditions of carriage with its passengers, that financial consequences can flow from specified actions. The 'hit them in their wallet' message can prove powerful too.

The main chapters of this book point at why passengers can behave in the way they do, but if they do, and they disrupt operations, the law is far from toothless!

Chapter 2

Flying-related Stress

Iain B.McIntosh

International travel alters routine and can markedly affect mental state (Bar-El, 1991). Relocation is a recognised stressor (Lucas, 1987). Vocational, leisure and relocation activities involving road, rail and air travel are a routine of modern life. All modes of transport can be anxiety provoking. However, airborne travel appears to create more psychological upset than other transportation (McIntosh et al., 1998).

> Be near us Lord. We know that flight,
> Is but a challenge to thy might,
> A privilege and not a right.
> Lord, whose mercy we revere,
> We know we should not be up here
> (Harding, 1993).

This rhyme expresses the inner feelings of some air travellers. Despite recent terrorist tragedies affecting aircraft and airports, the number of people using this mode of travel continues to increase. Many air travellers however, suffer some measure of anxiety relating to air travel and one in 10 may be seriously disturbed (ibid.).

Anxiety is a response that is learned when a 'danger signal' is perceived. The 'danger signal' is previously paired with a situation which naturally produces a negative reaction, either through direct exposure, modelling or vicarious learning (Rachman, 1977). The individual responds through a process of operant conditioning, to either reduce personal anxiety levels or achieve a state of safety (Mohrer, 1939). Fear of flying is considered a form of aversive conditioning, maintained by avoidance behaviours (Bor et al., 2001).

With air travel having become increasingly common, more people are exposed to associated stress. Many travellers are close to their stress tolerance levels before they board the flight (McIntosh, 1996). Between 10 to 40 per cent of air travellers experience some kind of fear response to the air travel process (Foreman and Borrill, 1994; Van Gerwen et al., 2000). Enjoyment of air travel may depend upon a predisposition to cope well with a variety of physical and psychological stressors of some complexity (Nahrwold, 1990).

In a random sample of 1,771 world travellers, 63 per cent admitted to travel-associated worries. Flying anxieties were prominent. Women suffered more worries than men, but men were more seriously worried about their concerns. A larger proportion of non-travellers expressed fears of flying than those who had flown in the previous year, suggesting this anxiety may prevent people from flying at all (McIntosh, 1996). Men had more travel experience in the previous three years than women but significantly more women than men were worried about flying (McIntosh et al., 1998). There may, however, be a greater willingness for women to report certain kinds of anxiety (Chambless, 1985), particularly as this has not been shown to correspond to physiological differences in reactivity (Wilson, 1966).

The prevalence of pre-flight, in-transit and in-flight worries, levels of situational anxiety generated in the air travel process, frequency of anxiety problems and coping strategies have been studied (Swanson et al., 1999). On boarding the flight, 49 per cent of participants reported anxiety 'sometimes, often or always' and 70 per cent admitted anxiety during the flight. Take-off and landing procedures were the most frequently quoted sources of anxiety. Flight delays, which are particularly stressful, were also highly rated by a high proportion (Stradling, 1994).

Arrival and travel through the airport and baggage reclaim is also anxiety-provoking. In some people the level of anxiety is associated with in-flight physical components of stress, such as dyspnoea and palpitations. Those reporting greater anxiety reported significantly more in-flight health problems, in particular breathlessness and palpitations.

Panic attacks in passengers are the most frequent medical occurrence to be reported by airlines (Harding, 1993). They involve cabin crew who are routinely given special instructions on handling them. Severe panic attacks or phobic avoidance reactions at the time of aeroplane boarding can delay flight departures if the passenger and their luggage has to be off-loaded. This can provoke anxiety in other passengers on the flight. Inability to control a situation may lead to anxiety, but in some it may be the precursor of panic. This is a non-psychotic manifestation of stress, associated with an intense feeling of dread, which may prevent passengers actually boarding the flight.

> **Box 2.1 Case history 1**
> On a holiday charter flight a panic-stricken teenager refused to exit the entry steps and enter the cabin. She clung desperately to hand-rails, ultimately screaming and shoving at parents and crew trying to calm her and encourage boarding. Her panic reaction triggered an asthmatic attack. Airport medical staff advised that she discontinue her journey. Baggage retrieval and loss of departure slot resulted in a three-hour delay to take–off, to the disadvantage and angst of family and fellow travellers.

Hypoxia

People are very sensitive to lack of oxygen. There can be physiological and psychological consequences to oxygen lack in-flight. The effects of hypoxia include personality change, loss of judgement and feelings of unreality and worry. Hypobaric hypoxia can cause hyperventilation.

Hyperventilation

Hyperventilation is another commonly reported incident on commercial aircraft. Over-breathing can occur as part of the classic 'fight or flight' response to perceived threat. It should not be regarded as a syndrome in its own right, but as a symptom of anxiety causing additional problems. The over-breathing results in hypocapnia – fall in the level of carbon monoxide in the blood – and a change in body sensations. The resulting emotional arousal causes more over-breathing and the cycle continues (Nias, 1998). Hyperventilation creates feelings of dizziness, apprehension, light-headedness and anxiety. The commonest cause of hyperventilation in flight is emotional stress and particularly anxiety (Harding, 1993). A vicious circle of symptoms can be produced in anxious passengers.

Air travel-related anxieties can be divided into pre-, post- and in-flight categories, with each having recognised stressors. Many people express anxiety not just about the flight, most hazardous part of their journey, but to in-transit occurrences where formerly there was little direct threat to health. Airport concourses are now a target for terrorist action and sites for the rare presence in UK of armed police. Many of the public now experience disquiet when in transit through them, at a time of maximum personal psychological vulnerability (Pollitt, 1986). They may be affected by a number of factors:

- changed environment,;
- loss of family support;
- exposure to cultural and social change;
- fear of the unknown;
- loss of control of one's destiny;
- powerlessness (Lucas, 1987);
- deindividuation (Diener, 1989).

These impositions are additional to *just experienced*, or *about to be exposed to*, flying-related anxieties e.g. fear of heights, fear of enclosed spaces, close proximity to others, and limitations on toilet access (Harding, 1993). These features, singly and combined, can promote the anxiety experienced by air travellers (Steptoe, 1988).

Personal Control and Powerlessness

Passengers have problems in adjusting to the perceived loss of personal control involved in air transit. Western society embraces a philosophy that individuals endeavour to structure and control their lives. Many people try to avoid the unexpected, exert control over surroundings and expect things to proceed in a specific direction. Coping with situations beyond personal control in airport or aeroplane may be a novel experience, creating cognitive dissonance and considerable stress in some. There is internal pressure for the individual to be assertive to bring change and control – an unachievable objective in the airport milieu, where events often appear to be beyond anyone's control.

Passengers who can accept limitations and work within new systems as they are encountered (Pandey, 1998) adapt most successfully to these demands upon the person. Air travel may be an accelerated learning course for some people to accept things beyond their control. For instance, what in Europe is a problem to solve in Asia may be a limitation to accept. This philosophy, if applied to air transit pressures, might defuse much accumulated anxiety.

In reality, air travel for most travellers has become increasingly stressful and unpleasant. For some people, coping strategies prove inadequate (Lucas, 1987; McIntosh, 1996; Rayman, 1997). Prolonged sitting in cramped, crowded and impersonal conditions can promote a feeling of deindividuation which has been linked with the appearance of less restrained personal behaviour (Diener, 1980).

Pre-flight Anxieties

People of varying age, culture, intelligence and socioeconomic status are herded together in anonymity and in a manner unparalleled elsewhere in society (Lucas, 1987). This melange of individuals with widely differing expectations and needs can cause friction. Air travel industry operatives are at the interface of complex group dynamics. They do not always demonstrate the sound organisation and awareness of human needs and sensitivities which the location merits (Bor, 1999). The stressors relating to commercial air transportation can be difficult for the young and enabled, but can have a more adverse impact on the elderly and disabled (McIntosh, 1992).

Potential stressors in air transit often operate prior to arrival at the airport. Deadlines for check-in, gate closure and take-off are a feature of air travel. A punctual journey to the airport becomes ever more uncertain with road congestion and rail network inadequacy creating delay. Missing a bus or train may be an inconvenience. Missing a flight with infrequently served destinations often thousands of miles away may ruin the business or holiday trip. Ticket and baggage check-in brings queues and doubts about luggage, safety and worries about passengers being 'bumped' off flights.

Airport transit is divided into land and airside demarcation, with the latter an alien scene for some. Fifty years ago one could arrive at the airport, have person and luggage weighed, complete ticket formalities, enter the airfield and board the aircraft to depart within minutes. Security precautions and surveillance have added hours to pre-flight requirements, with security checks themselves intimidating, a personal intrusion and constant reminder of terrorist threat. Frisking of person and hand baggage for weapons draws attention to the vulnerability of air travel and the potential threat to the individual of related morbidity and mortality.

Passport controls are stressful encounters for those with documents or a mien viewed with suspicion by authorities. Language differences create problems in spoken and signed communications, stressful even for those with normal hearing and sight. Those of advanced years, or with visual or hearing impairment, or ethnic disadvantage, are exposed to greater stress when transiting these locations (McIntosh, 1992). Once checked-in for the flight, the individual becomes a pawn in the system, reduced to a seat number, one among many in an anonymous crowd of strangers. With prolonged pre-departure times there is ample opportunity for worry about flight safety. Environmental stressors affect the passenger whose coping skills may be hard-pressed. Basic personality traits such as anxiety, obsessionality, irritability and aggression can come to the fore.

Apparently seemingly well-integrated married couples and partners may develop acute interpersonal tension due to different reactions to unpredictable circumstances in this situation (Lucas, 1987). Unclear public announcements, poor acoustics, misleading direction signs, erroneous flight displays and strange environs psychologically disturb transit passengers. They are cut off from the outside world by customs and security barriers.

Uncaring airline and airport staff can heighten anxieties at this vulnerable time. There may be a breakdown in relationships between passengers and airline staff (Bor, 1999). Inside the airport, in the mêlée of departing travellers, feelings of isolation, frustration, irritability and anger can easily develop. Delayed departures with little justification for the delay and scant explanation of reason and duration add to frustration and the feeling of loss of control. Loss of the sense of individual control calls for a difficult adjustment in some people. Some travellers are unable to adapt to the situation (Pandey, 1998). People are at the mercy of an uncaring system. They are treated as objects, processed and transported *en masse*, in a noisy often congested, alien environment. This is a unique situation in which people are effectively trapped; they cannot move on and they cannot go back. They are dependent on service providers and an impersonal service.

Larger airports and aircraft squeeze more and more people through this transit system, with airport authorities and airlines giving little thought to diminishing potential stressors. There is scant consideration of the psychological impact of transit through the airport and the mental effects on the traveller once aboard the aeroplane. Except for the chapel, there are few quiet places accessible to the economy class air passenger. Other than food and drink, there are few distractions to fill waiting hours, when the anxious can brood about their worries. Cinemas, libraries, bingo halls, swimming pools and gymnasia should perhaps be future design features of all airports, destressing alternatives to the profit-making shopping diversions currently on offer.

Jet Lag and Stress Malaise

Many transit passengers in hub airports will also be affected by change in

> **Box 2.2 Case history 2**
>
> A 74-year-old healthy widower, arrived back from visiting Australia jetlagged and disorientated and wandered about Heathrow from morning until early evening. He had become confused from anoxia, sleeplessness and conflicting advice from travel staff. He was very stressed when he finally attracted the attention of security staff and required sedation and overnight care before returning home.

circadian rhythm as a result of their travels and will be trying to adjust to jet lag. This may diminish their mental competence and make them more psychologically vulnerable (Nicholson et al., 1986). Stress malaise has been described (Chapman, 1995), when air travellers complain of faintness and light-headedness, manifestations of travel-related stress, due to a combination of worry and apprehension about movement through a strange environment and the effects of jet lag and fatigue.

Travel stressors can result in severe degrees of anxiety and panic, but they are also associated with other emotive states. In the elderly and the cognitively impaired they can create confusion which will promote further anxiety. Elderly travellers can become disorientated and very anxious when transiting a large air terminal. Other events and factors in a person's life causing stress, such as relationship problems, work difficulties and financial problems, can increase susceptibility to anxiety (Doctor et al., 1990).

Management of In-transit Stressors

Flying-associated worries and anxieties should not be dismissed lightly by health care professionals, as the effects may have a considerable impact on the affected person's life and on their family. Health professionals and airport and airline authorities need to address these problems. Organisational and design changes to the flow of people in transit areas need attention. The depersonalising of the air traveller and the psychological impact on flyer and transit passenger needs to be studied and changes implemented to humanise the air travel scene.

Many stressors could be diminished or eliminated by more considered design, furnishing and decor of air terminals and improved communications. Airport planners and airline managers should consider factors that compound the effects of stress on their clientele. Land-, air-side and cabin crew should be given training to identify and manage the stressed (Bor, 1999).

Easy access to free and duty-free alcohol and its ingestion on and before the flight may prove to be a causative component in air rage incidents. Commercial objectives encourage passengers to drink alcohol before and during the flight, but the closed confines of an aircraft cabin is a dangerous place for the disinhibited. The banning of alcohol on aeroplanes may prove a more effective safety measure than the exclusion of scissors and knives from the cabin. The reason for and likely duration of delay should be communicated immediately and honestly to travellers, who find this one of the most stressful parts of the travel scene (McIntosh, 1996).

In-flight Anxieties

Air travellers have worries, anxieties, apprehension and fears about flying and many enter an aircraft with the thought that they may be chancing their luck, a feeling much more universal since the events of 11 September 2001 in the US. Air travel itself, although relatively safe per mile of travel compared to car and train journeys, contributes several additional factors to the in-transit angst already felt by many passengers. Although aeroplanes can fly faster, further and safer than when the industry was in its infancy, new features of this travel mode have recently increased the hassle and stress of relocation by air. Air travel-related anxieties are at the bottom end of a continuum, at the top of which are phobias.

Pre-flight psychological pressures can increase the actual stress of travel within the aircraft. Some air travellers overcome pre-flight ordeals but can barely cope with the actual air journey. Others, aware that the most dangerous part of an air trip is at take-off, when wings are full of fuel, become calmer with the jet off the ground and *en route*.

Air transport users cover a broad spectrum, with the seasoned vocational and business traveller at one end and those making one-off emergency journeys or their first flight at the other. In between are the mass of occasional travellers. All at some time experience some apprehension about leaving *terra firma* on an airborne journey. Most cope with the eventualities of normal flight but any anomaly can swing emotions from apprehension to a state of severe stress and fear and panic. Flight anxieties are associated with a constellation of four fundamental fears:

a) heights;
b) crashing;

> **Box 2.3 Case history 3**
> On a scheduled flight, the aeroplane took off on time. As it lifted off the runway, at the point of maximal engine rotation and with wheels inches off the tarmac, a seagull was sucked into the engine intake. A thump was felt through the aircraft and to the horror of passengers sitting by the wings, a shower of feathers thrust out from one of the engine nacelles. The pilot had moments to abort or continue the flight. He opted to land with very heavy braking and stopped the aircraft 2 metres from the end of the runway. Fire engines and ambulances were in attendance. Four hours later the flight was cleared again for take-off but, by then, two passengers had been so psychologically disturbed by the incident that they refused to recommence their flight.

c) instability; and
d) confinement (Howard et al., 1983).

There are often associations with agoraphobia and claustrophobia (Dean and Whittaker, 1982). People with a high degree of emotional reactivity are more at risk of acquiring phobias (Wolpe, 1956).

Frequency of flying may condition regular air travellers to aerial transit, but terrorist attacks, crashes, near misses, weather inclemency, labour disputes and air traffic control disorganisation can trigger anxiety in the most hardened air traveller. These features can promote even more anxiety in those only occasionally exposed to the frenetic air travel scene. For those who have steeled themselves for the flight and activated all their coping skills, extended delay in departure can take them over the 'just coping' threshold to a stressed state.

Studies show that, although some people react with mild concern about air relocation, many are moderately to seriously concerned, with some exhibiting mild fear symptoms and others frank phobia (see, for example, McIntosh, 1996). Some are overtaken by panic and others exhibit behaviour which can result in air rage.

Coping Strategies

Distractions used by passengers include reading, creative writing and listening to music. Concentration on a task divorced from the reality of the scene is an effective means of coping with anxiety. Recourse to a good book or productive writing are useful distractions, of particular value at take-off and landing. Music lovers can turn to favoured music programmes from personal CD players. The airlines take advantage of the calming effect of music when they relay it through the cabin while the seat belt sign is illuminated.

While cigarette smoking is no longer socially acceptable on the aircraft, many travellers still turn to the white sticks with the filter ends in the departure lounge to reduce their tension. A pre-boarding unit or two of alcohol may calm the traveller, but over-indulgence brings the risk of disinhibition of behaviour and the possibility of air rage. The combined use of a tranquilliser or sleeping pill and alcohol is a dangerous in-flight habit to be avoided.

Hypnotherapy, including self-hypnosis, and relaxation techniques help many air travellers to cope with associated anxieties. These are effective coping strategies, but intending travellers need to learn the procedures and practise them in the weeks before departure. Anxiolytic medications are still prescribed by many GPs for aircraft-related anxieties and phobias (Swanson et al., 1999). These may be of value as a one-off response to treat the symptoms but the underlying condition merits referral to a psychologist or hypnotherapist, and therapy to change the unwanted behavioral response will bring permanent cure.

The non-smoking environment of most aircraft denies the smoker a coping support at a time of maximal need, generating frustration, irritability and more anxiety. The passenger may see this as an infringement of personal liberty. This situation places the cabin crew, who monitor breaches in regulations, in a parental/command role with passengers. This authoritarian approach can subsequently trigger an air rage incident.

A study of British people six months after the New York Twin Towers disaster showed that the public was more worried about travel by air than previously: many were flying less and some were refusing to consider air travel at all (Swanson, 2002). Former dominant concerns about the air worthiness of aircraft – perhaps legitimate when so many of the jumbo air fleet are now at least 25 years old – have been replaced with fear of an in-flight explosion, terrorist attack and security lapses (Swanson et al., 1999). These anxieties are unlikely to be allayed until the terrorist threat no longer exists or authorities can assure the public that security measures are effective.

Many travellers worry about their health while abroad (McIntosh, 1994). Recent publicity has been given to the possibility that long-haul aeroplane travel may be a cause of deep vein thrombosis (DVT), although this remains unproven (Walker and McIntosh, 2002). This is, however, another source of anxiety for air travellers (Swanson and McIntosh, 2002), who find themselves encouraged by health professionals to exercise limbs while on long flights and constrained by flight attendants who do not want passengers wandering in the aisles. This can promote cognitive dissonance in the air traveller and further anxiety. This conflict will remain until research reveals cause and effect and remedial measures are implemented to diminish risk and health worry.

People with considerable travel anxieties or fear of flying may acknowledge that they may cause difficulties in relationships during pre- and post-travel. They may threaten career advancement when there is a business travel requirement. Many non-travellers who desire to travel abroad remain at home because of psychological concerns about flying. These anxieties are rarely addressed by health professionals and may not even receive attention at specially organised travel health clinics (Hill and Behrens, 1996). Travel agents rarely address such issues with clients (Gorman and Smythe, 1992). The travel industry's role in promoting good health in travellers is recognised, and collaboration between industry and community travel health clinics recommended (Steffen and Dupont, 1994). A combined effort to minimise known travel-related stressors might lead to healthier travel. Failure to identify these travel-related problems condemns many non-travellers to Britain's shores. Doctors and travel health clinic personnel often fail to provide appropriate advice (Keystone et al., 1994). They should consider the effects of travel stressors and coping strategies in travel health consultations. Advice and counselling should be provided on all aspects of travel and travel-related anxieties, and fears and phobias identified and addressed. Pre-travel health assessments should inquire about travel-related psychological problems.

Treatment of Air Transit-related Anxieties and Fears

Many travel-related fears and anxieties can be effectively, and often quite quickly, treated by cognitive behavioural therapies (Bor et al., 2001), hypnotherapy using behavioural techniques (McIntosh, 1991) and neurolinguistic programming (McDermott, 1997). No-one should be denied access to treatment. Treatment should be offered to the non-traveller and the potential traveller, or referral made to those skilled in treatment. Effective therapy brings cure and self-dependence. Provision of an anxiolytic may temporarily relieve the symptoms but does not cure the individual of severe phobic anxiety. With the help of alcohol or a sedative, many anxious travellers brave the air journey then worry over the vacation about how they can manage the return journey.

Health professional pre-travel assessment should, perhaps, include:

- use of the Flight Anxiety Situations questionnaire (Van Gerwen and Diekstra, 1999), which can provide an indication of anxiety components specific to the individual's anxieties about flying;
- identification of target behaviour to be changed and maintaining factors;
- the person's social and personal resources and coping skills;
- factors limiting and/or inhibiting treatment to be identified;
- objectives to capitalise on useful strategies and, introduce more appropriate skills;
- identification of interventions most likely to be adopted by the individual according to circumstance (Cautela and Upper, 1977).

All treatments should be directed towards improving patient ability to manage anticipatory anxiety as well as fears encountered at airports and on-board aircraft (Bor et al., 2001). The use of alcohol as a coping strategy is significantly correlated with breathlessness and palpitations (McIntosh et al., 1998). It should be discouraged and other coping strategies encouraged. Over-ingestion of alcohol and tranquillisers and the resultant disinhibition of normal behaviour leads to hostility and aggression. Air rage may threaten even before the flight is called.

Poor adaptive mechanisms can create emotional disequilibrium. Frustration, irritability and aggression during travel may be elements involved in air rage (Bor, 1999).

Countermeasures to Diminish Pre-flight and Flight Stress

Strategies can be employed to reduce the stress of air travel, e.g.;

- timely airport arrival;
- pre- or post-flight stay at the airport hotel;
- pre-booked seating;
- if possible, travel on daytime flights;
- travel west to east on long-haul flights;
- purchase the highest category of seating affordable;
- use executive airport lounges in transit;
- avoid alcohol drinking on the flight;
- avoid anxiolytic use on the flight;
- take a 75mg aspirin on the day of a long-haul flight. Exercise the legs and feet on the journey. This may reduce the risk of DVT and associated worry;

- adhere strictly to security regulations to avoid unnecessary security screening;
- take advantage of available therapies and relaxation techniques for existing anxieties and fears. Seek these as early as possible when making flight and vacation arrangements.

Conclusion

Air travel-related anxieties and fears are common. They can be severe and lead to panic and avoidance behaviour. Adaptive coping strategies are effective but some can result in antisocial behaviour. Countermeasures to decrease stress in transit can be useful. The anxiety-prone, the elderly, and the phobic in particular should consider countermeasures to avoid unnecessary hassle and stress. Airport and airline management should consider stressful elements in air travel. These should be investigated and countered where possible. Travel health professionals should consider psychological factors likely to affect the traveller at a pre-travel health consultation. This should be part of routine assessment. Health professionals should be aware that travel-related anxieties; fears and phobias respond well to cognitive behavioural techniques and anxiolytic prescriptions are best avoided for people with these problems.

References

Bar-El, I. (1991), 'Psychiatric Hospitalisation of Tourists in Jerusalem', *Comprehensive Psychiatry*, Vol. 32, pp. 23–44.
Bor, R. (1999), 'Unruly Passenger Behaviour and In-flight Violence', *Travel Medicine International*, Vol. 17, pp. 1–6.
Bor, R., Parker, J. and Papadopoulos, L. (2001), 'Psychological Treatment of a Fear of Flying', *Journal of the British Travel Health Association*, Vol. 1, pp. 21–6.
Cautela, K. and Upper, D. (1977), 'Behavioural Analysis, Assessment and Diagnosis', in *Perspectives in Behaviour Therapy*, Kalamazoo, Michigan: Behaviourdelia, pp. 3–27.
Chambless, D. (1985), 'The Relationship of the Severity of Agoraphobia to Associated Psychopathology', *Behaviour Research and Therapy*, Vol. 23, No. 3, pp. 305–10.
Chapman, P. (1995), 'In-flight Emergencies', *Travel Medicine International*, Vol. 13, No. 3, pp. 171–173.
Dean, R. and Whittaker, K. (1982), 'Fear of Flying', *Journal of Travel Research*, Vol. 21, pp. 7–17.
Diener, E. (1989), 'Deindividuation: The absence of self-awareness and self-regulation in group members', in P. Paulus (ed.), *The Psychology of Group Influence*, Hillsdale, New Jersey: Lawrence Erlbaum.

Doctor, R., McVarish, C. and Bione, R. (1990), 'Long-term Behavioural Treatment Effects for the Fear of Flying', *Phobia Practice and Research Journal*, Vol. 3, pp. 33–42.

Foreman, E. and Borrill, J. (1994), 'The Freedom to Fly', *Journal of Travel Medicine*, Vol. 1, No. 1, pp. 30–35.

Gorman, D. and Smythe, B. (1992), 'Travel Agents and Health Advice given to Travellers', *Travel Medicine International*, Vol. 1, No. 3, pp. 111–15.

Harding, R. (1993), 'Aeromedical Aspects of Commercial Air Travel', *Journal of Travel Medicine*, Vol. 1, No. 4, pp. 21–4.

Harding, R. and Mills, J. (1993), *Aviation Medicine* (3rd edn), London: British Medical Journal Publishing.

Hill, D. and Behrens, R. (1996), 'A Survey of Travel Clinics throughout the World', *Journal of Travel Medicine*, Vol. 3, No. 1, pp. 46–7.

Howard, W., Murphy, S. and Clarke, J. (1983), 'The Nature and Treatment of Fear of Flying', *Behavioural Therapy*, Vol. 14, pp. 557–67.

Keystone, J., Dismukas, R. and Sawyer, L. (1994), 'Inadequacies in Health Recommendations for Travellers', *Journal of Travel Medicine*, Vol. 1, pp. 72–8.

Lucas, J. (1987), 'Psychological Aspects of Travel', *Travel Medicine International*, Vol. l, No. 5, pp. 99–104.

McDermott, P. (1977), 'Fears, Phobias and Neurolinguistic Programming', *Journal of British Society Medical Dental Hypnosis (Scotland)*, Vol. 17, pp. 47–9.

McIntosh, I. (1980), 'Incidence, Management and Treatment of Phobias in a Group Medical Practice', *Pharmaceutical Medicine*, Vol. 1, No. 2, pp. 77–82.

McIntosh, I. (1991), 'Treating Travel Phobias with Hypnotherapy', *Journal of the British Society Medical and Dental Hypnosis*, Vol. 7, No. 5, pp. 18–20.

McIntosh, I. (1992), *Travel and Health in the Elderly*, Dinton, Somerset: Mark Allan Publishing, Quay Book Division.

McIntosh, I. (1996), 'The Psychological Trauma of Foreign Travel', *Psychiatry in Practice*, Vol. 15, No. 2, pp. 6–8.

McIntosh, I., Power, K. and Reed, J. (1996), 'Prevalence, Intensity and Sexual Differences in Travel Related Stressors', *Journal of Travel Medicine*, Vol. 3, pp. 96–102.

McIntosh, I., Reed, J. and Power, K. (1994), 'The Impact of Travel Acquired Illness on the World Traveller', *Scottish Medical Journal*, Vol. 39, pp. 40–44.

McIntosh, I., Swanson, V., Power, K., Raeside, F. and Dempster, C. (1998), 'Anxiety and Health Problems Related to Air Travel', *Journal Travel Medicine*, Vol. 5, No. 4, pp. 198–204.

Mohrer, O. (1939), 'A Stimulus Response Theory of Anxiety and its Role as a Reinforcing Agent', *Psychology Review*, Vol. 46, pp. 553–65.

Nahrwold, M. (1990), 'Fear of Flying, or an Unaesthetised Person is not an Aeroplane', *Anaesthetiology Review*, Vol. 14, No. 5, pp. 68–72.

Nias, D. (1998), 'Addressing the Causes of Hyperventilation', *The Practitioner*, Vol. 242, pp. 187–92.

Nicholson, A.N., Pascoe, P.A., Spencer, M.B., Stone, B.M. and Green, R.L. (1986), 'Nocturnal Sleep and Daytime Alertness of Aircrew after Transmeridian Flights', *Aviation Space and Environmental Medicine*, Vol. 57 (Suppl.), pp. B42–B52.

Pandey, P. (1998), Editorial', *Clinic Health News*, 1–2 August.

Pollit, J. (1986), 'The Mind in Travel', *Travel Medicine International*, Vol. 4, pp. 72–4.

Rachman, S. (1977), 'The Conditioning Theory of Fear Acquisition', *Behaviour Research and Therapy*, Vol. 14, pp. 125–34.

Rayman, R. (1997), 'Passenger Safety Health and Comfort; A review', *Aviation, Space and Environmental Medicine*, Vol. 68, No. 5, pp. 432–40.

Steffen, R. and Du Pont, H. (1994), 'Travel Medicine, What is That?', *Journal of Travel Medicine*, Vol. 1, No. 1, pp. 1–3.

Steptoe, A. (1988), 'Managing Flying Phobia', *British Medical Journal*, Vol. 296, p. 25.

Stradling H. (1994), 'A Travel Clinic Audit', *Travel Medicine International*, Vol. 12, No. 3, pp. 83–8.

Swanson, V., McIntosh, I. and Karatzias, A. (1999), 'Travel Phobic Anxiety and its Management', *Scottish Medicine*, Vol. 18, No. 2, pp. 6–9.

Swanson, V. and McIntosh, I. (forthcoming 2002), 'A Study of People's Attitudes to Flying and the Relationship of Flying and Deep Vein Thrombosis', *Journal of the British Travel Health Association*.

Van Gerwen, L. and Diekstra, R. (1999), 'Construction and Psychometric Characteristics of Two Self Report Questionnaires for the Assessment of the Fear of Flying', *Psychological Assessment*, Vol. 11, No. 2, pp. 146–58.

Van Gerwen, L., Spinhoven, P. and Van Dyeck, R. (2000), 'Fear of Flying Treatment Programmes for Passengers', *Aviation, Space and Environmental Medicine*, Vol. 71, No. 4, pp. 430–37.

Walker, E. and McIntosh, I. (2002), 'Travellers Thrombosis', *Journal of the British Travel Health Association*, Vol. 2, pp. 10–16.

Wilson, G. (1966), 'An Electrodermal Technique for the Study of Phobias', *New Zealand Journal of Psychology*, Vol. 65, pp. 696–8.

Wolpe, G. (1956), *Psychotherapy by Reciprocal Inhibition*, Stanford, California: Stanford University Press.

Chapter 3

The Evolution of the Airline Industry and Impact on Passenger Behaviour

Alex Cruz and Linda Papadopoulos

Introduction

The evolution of air travel since the early 1930s not only presents us with an incredible collection of technological achievements but also demonstrates significant changes in the attitude and profile of passengers and businesses towards travel. From the large cabins, hot meals and exclusive service of propeller-based aircraft in the 1940s and 1950s, to the crowded cabins of low-cost carriers of the twenty-first century, passengers and their behaviour towards the air travel experience has evolved considerably. This chapter examines how the air travel experience has evolved since it became a viable transportation means until today, looking at a set of specific aspects such as seating and service and how they have influenced travellers.

In order to study the evolution of passenger behaviour, we will divide our reflections into three distinct stages of aviation in the last 70 years:

- *Propeller-based aircraft*: while the actual timing of this stage in aviation history could be debated, it clearly represents the time when commercial air travel became a reality. Aviation was becoming more than just a mail delivery service, a farming aid or a converted instrument of war. Although exclusive, commercial airlines committed to destinations, large fleets and a diverse scheduled service.
- *Jet-based aircraft*: commercial aviation had become a reality in the late 1950s but it received a significant and irreversible boost when a de Havilland Comet took off from London for Johannesburg in May 1952, the first commercial jet. It was soon followed by the Boeing 707, a much larger aircraft, of which, more than 1,000 were eventually built. Easily recognisable aircraft such as the Boeing 747 were introduced in this era, marked by the beginning of deregulation in the US.

- *Air travel now means mass transport*: with several established aircraft manufacturers and newer, more efficient models becoming available every three to four years, the air travel industry has reached every corner of the world. Economics in aviation have changed as various public subsidies begin to disappear. The pressure to make airlines viable begins to surface.

The Era of Propeller-based Aircraft

> **We hope that you enjoy DC-3 Airways' very special 'Custom Service'. No other airline offers these first-class amenities at coach fares:**
>
> - Deep-cushioned, reclining chairs.
> - Meals prepared by world-renown chefs.
> - Complimentary beverages including the finest-label wines.
> - Wine and cheese baskets served in-between mealtimes. (Sorry, not available on morning flights.)
> - Breakfast eggs cooked to order right on board and served to you piping hot on heated plates.
> - Hot towels to refresh before and after meals.
>
> *No wonder so many customers insist on DC-3 Airways when their plans call for air travel. Shouldn't you, too?* (Mock-up from an airline brochure about their DC-3 Service).

If we examine today's air travel standards, flying in the 1930s and 1940s was by comparison slow and noisy. However, it was clearly expensive, exclusive and luxurious. The aircraft of those times were led by the PanAm Clippers and the DC-3. The aircraft themselves were significantly smaller when compared to those used today. In order to travel from the US East Coast to the West Coast, a flight required multiple stops and overnight rests.

The cabins of the larger aircraft were large and divided into compartments as in train coaches; some aircraft included a stateroom, a dressing room and men's and women's restrooms. Seats provided ample legroom and space, room to stand up and walk around; separate sitting/dining areas and, on night flights, airlines offered sleeper beds. The food offered to passengers was carefully prepared; clearly, those who could afford to fly were used to sophisticated dining. Meals were hot and in some places served in a separate cabin. Non-smoking areas in the cabin were not relevant as the awareness of the dangers of smoking generally and on-board aircraft specifically, had not emerged.

The service staff were formally called air hostesses and initially they were required to be nurses, single, younger than 25 years in age; weigh less than 115 pounds; and stand less than 5 feet, 4 inches tall. While they were trained to provide an exclusive service, their typical duties also included some baggage handling and even refuelling aircraft.

The volume of commercial passenger flights at that time was small even between some large cities. It was common to offer long-haul routes with multiple stops. In addition, aircraft at that time were much more weather-dependent for their navigation and many could not fly above adverse atmospheric conditions. As a consequence, delays were common. However, the event of flying was so exclusive and the journeys so long, that passengers allocated longer 'blocks' of time to travel – delays were normal and part of the adventure of air travel.

Checked-in baggage was common for most passengers and many travellers did not carry more than one carry-on item on board the aircraft; indeed, the cabins were not prepared to accommodate many items. The relatively low volume of flights and the large crews working on flights resulted in fewer cases of baggage mishandling.

However, building and operating reliable aircraft able to take people across long distances comfortably was a science in learning – there were multiple air-related incidents, including mid-air collisions. These accidents discouraged some travellers but they did not stop the passion of a few leaders to continue researching and building new machines. Overall, the flying experience was luxurious and for the privileged.

The passenger profile during this era was marked by the following:

- mixture of business and pleasure, with air passengers considered wealthy and educated;
- white and mostly male;
- interested in the speed and romance of travel that air afforded.

This profile of aircraft cabins, in-flight service and passenger types resulted in clearly 'good' passenger behaviour on board. Interestingly, when social scientists have tried to explore passenger behaviour, rarely do they find a coherent set of personality indicators that are predictive of either 'good' or 'bad' behaviour. Rather, factors that are related to the passengers' surroundings, the social make-up of the situation, or passenger expectations are much better indicators of behaviour. The flying experience of the first few years of the commercial airline industry not only met passengers' expectations but often far exceeded them, thus limiting the possibility of agitation or stress. This is not to suggest that all service was necessarily better at that time, but that passengers' demands, and to some extent their sense of entitlement, were not as high as they are today. In addition, travellers at this time 'chose' to fly rather than being obliged to. Air travel was driven by social class – a status symbol considered sophisticated for the times, an exclusive club for only the most successful or most privileged. As such passengers felt much more in control than their present day counterparts, who are often forced to fly in order to meet the demands of their business. Further, travellers at that time were very similar to each other socially, thus fostering an 'in-club' mentality during flights and promoting it towards other passengers and crew.

The Era of Jet Aircraft

> The first time I flew to Florida they served eggs and pancakes,' said the woman '... how much this industry has changed since I started flying in the 1960s. Jumbo jets were still on the drawing board. The Cadillac of the industry was the Convair 880. Pilots said it practically flew itself, and that was before cruise control. The new plane of the 1960s for crossing the ocean and coast-to-coast flying was the Boeing 707. We referred to it as the Starlight Express, because it was the mode of transportation for many celebrities. On a long flight we often had live entertainment when a small group would take out their guitars and lead the entire cabin in a sing-along. Trays featuring piping hot stuffed chicken breasts and wild rice were hand-carried from the galley to your seat on flights scheduled with 45 minutes of flying time. Planes often landed at airports with food trays under passenger seats because there wasn't time to pick them up. Bridge games spontaneously started in the small lounge area. Flight attendants were called 'hostesses' because they wanted the passengers to feel like guests in their homes. They passed out cigarettes and gum before every takeoff. Everybody smoked' (Gail Todd, a freelance writer and a flight attendant for more than 30 years).

Although the UK pioneered the introduction of commercial jet service through the de Havilland Comet in 1952, two fatal accidents due to metal fatigue paved the way for Boeing's introduction of the first large jetliner to be manufactured in large numbers, the 707. Jets constituted a revolution to aviation in many respects. They not only provided 50 to 80 per cent faster trips but they were able to fly larger number of passengers faster, evading turbulence that is common at lower altitudes. Shortly after their introduction, many 'firsts' in aviation were achieved in terms of distance, time and number of passengers flown: the Boeing 707 was able to fly 119 passengers non-stop from London to New York within eight hours, travelling at speeds of over 550 miles per hour.

The aircraft flown in this era became bigger and faster, culminating with the introduction of the 747 in 1969, followed by the McDonnell Douglas DC-10, the Lockheed L1011, the first Airbus and the spectacular Concorde in 1976. Some of these aircraft are still in operation and most have served as basic design for newer models. Travellers' expectations began to change as it was possible to conduct business in two cities on the same day, to travel somewhere for the weekend (and return in time for work) and to conduct return intercontinental travel within a week. Anywhere on earth could now be reached within 24 hours.

The interior of jetliners changed dramatically: compartments, dressing rooms, staterooms and sleeping berths disappeared altogether. Indeed, the shock was so considerable to passengers that most airlines introduced redesigned 'premium' services a couple of years after large cabins were introduced in order to remedy the increasing sense of loss of exclusivity. The only remnants of the earlier generation were popular lounges at the front or back of the cabin that were intended to allow passengers to relax with coffee or drinks and socialise with other passengers.

Food was still considered a perk of flying and hot meals were expected even in short segments. Indeed, this aspect of air travel service remained during this period. Two fundamental differences appeared in the delivery of on-board dining with respect to prior travelling experiences: the food began to be brought to passengers using catering trolleys rather than individually, and the food was pre-prepared – both defining features of air travel since.

Air hostesses aimed to provide an exclusive service; however, larger numbers of passengers made this more difficult. At the same time, as each airline grew and the number of flight attendants increased to the thousands, some began to unionise in the 1980s. As a consequence, the requirements to become a flight attendant were still demanding in terms of physical aptitude but being a nurse was no longer required and other restrictions fell away.

Leading up to the deregulation of the US skies in the 1970s, air traffic volumes began to increase significantly. Jet service was now mature and passengers had become used to the provision of multiple flights between the different destinations. As a consequence, traffic-related delays became a reality. Indeed, it was in the late 1970s and early 1980s that airlines were confronted with the problem of on-time performance.

The era of jet aviation removed some of the exclusivity associated with flying; it opened up aviation as a safe mode of transport and facilitated a significant increase in the number of both leisure and business passengers. But while many people used air transport, there were still many more who did not. The era of mass air transport was not to take hold until the 1980s.

The perceived end of the era of exclusivity was marked by the introduction in the US of an airline called People's Express. People's Express eliminated first class, in-flight meals and employee unions, and increased aircraft utilisation, number of passengers per aircraft and frequencies between cities. While it was highly successful for the first three years, it eventually went bankrupt – some people arguing it was over-visionary for the times. However, it proved that air passengers would easily exchange 'exclusivity' for 'price', a concept that took off in the late 1990s.

The spectrum of traveller profile widened considerably with respect to previous times: there were more business, government and military passengers, and more middle-class vacationers. Families travelling were more common; indeed, terms like 'infant' and 'child' were given formal definitions and procedures in aircraft operating manuals. Income levels of average passengers were those of middle class and upwards. This was an era in which many passengers were flying for the first time.

This period heralded the end of flying as an 'elite' experience, as more people enjoyed air travel from wider social backgrounds. Air travel became more egalitarian and accessible. Politicians might be seated next to plumbers, and business flyers next to babies. As a consequence, the trip was a challenge for everyone on board and tempers and resentments began to be displayed. Other problems, such as fear of flying, also became more prominent issues. Restrictions started to be placed on passengers such as amount of carry-on baggage, security checks and nonsmoking rules, reducing a sense of control for the passenger. The first incidents of passenger behaviour relating to abuse by passengers were noted through alcohol; these tended to be overlooked and unrecorded. The potential for antisocial passenger behaviour began to emerge but, clearly, it was not fully understood.

The Era of Aviation as a Means of Mass Transport

> Then came the glitz and the Boeing 747. Piano bars replaced bridge games. Hand-carried chicken breasts turned into a choice of chicken or beef served from an aisle cart that often did a better job of warming the tossed salad than it did the meat. The gum and cigarettes gave way to rented headsets. Smoking was limited to the back section of the plane, where the smoke became so thick you

could hardly see the in-flight meal. And America discovered Europe and everyone wanted to cross The Pond. That's when one airline developed the concept of cheap air travel. People's Express grabbed the imagination of the flying public. It cut costs, filled planes and lowered prices. No movie. No first-class section. Instead of a meal service, travellers received a paper bag with a sandwich and an apple. People's Express went belly up, but its concept now flies with nearly every airline. The question is, will air travel go through another transformation? (Gail Todd).

No meals. No tickets. No seat pre-assignment. No refunds. Minimum compensation when something goes wrong. Low prices. I am there (new generation traveller).

People's Express' revolutionary concept of mass travel at low prices did not save the airline from failing at the end of the early jet era but it certainly inspired many other low-cost start-ups and it proved that there was a market for no-frills service and prices. The 1980s and 1990s were marked by a boom in air travel at all levels: aircraft types, airlines, markets and types of passengers. This era saw the introduction of aircraft such as the Boeing 757, 767 and 777 and the development of the Airbus 3XX family. These aircraft are large, fast and efficient, providing air carriers with many options in terms of destinations and traffic mix. While the basic speed of travel did not evolve with respect to the previous era, the evolution of airlines and air traffic provided more travel options for passengers, including multiple price options for similar routes. This confirmed air travel as an accessible means of transport for large segments of the worldwide population.

Two clear types of airline appeared in the marketplace during the 1990s:

- *Full service airlines*: the traditional national carriers continued to provide multiple services to destinations, meals, baggage handling, direct reservation options, etc. These airlines also attracted business passengers. Most of the airlines in this category steadily upgraded their business and first class cabins in what seemed to be a race for luxury; indeed, the initial exclusivity of 180° bed seats was soon extended to business class for many carriers. Many full service airlines gradually downgraded certain aspects of short-haul service in an effort to save costs and compete against low-cost carriers, but still provided significantly more services than other carriers. Other characteristics of full service airlines included:

    o   ticketing and check-in flexibility;

o passenger loyalty programmes;
o prompt, and sometimes generous, compensation for delays/ cancellations;
o cabin upgrades;
o free drinks;
o less aircraft utilisation with the possibility of improved on-time arrival rates.

- *Charter airlines and low-cost carriers*: the charter airline industry began as an extension of tour operators. Soon many of these operators started to offer flight-only packages, in essence becoming semi-scheduled, low-frills airlines travelling to holiday destinations. They all shared certain common characteristics:

    o passengers were on holiday, ready to forget the stresses of their everyday daily work lives;
    o seat pitch and recline were the least generous in the industry in order to increase seat numbers and generate more revenue;
    o limits on the number of free drinks served sometimes by crews in casual uniforms;
    o cabins were mostly configured in single economy class ;
    o passengers typically received a fraction of delay/cancellation compensation compared to that offered by full service airlines;
    o passengers did not have any other amenities such as flexible check-in, ticket changes, lounges, airmiles, etc.;
    o passengers tolerated these inconveniences mostly because of the low price of the package.

The basic concept of the interior of aircraft changed only slightly in this period with respect to the previous one. The only significant difference made was to reconfigure the cabin layout to fit more passengers. This was achieved by removing premium class rows by full service airlines, and galleys and baggage compartments by low-cost airlines. Indeed, at the beginning of the period, cabin lounges were still common, then they disappeared completely, but by 2000 they began to reappear again in premium classes.

The most significant evolution in the aircraft cabin in this period was the smoking ban in nearly all flights and routes, regardless of length of flight or destination. US airlines led this change under pressure from the strong anti-smoking lobby. Most major international airlines gradually implemented that ban during the mid- to late-1990s, with a few minor carriers still permitting smoking on some longer routes.

Catering evolved in different ways depending on class of service and segments of travel (see Table 3.1).

Table 3.1   Evolution of in-flight food from the 1970s/1980s to the 1990s

	Short-haul	**Mid- and long-haul**
Economy class	Reduced Removed hot meals Introduced third party brands	One hot meal Served in standard meal trays Increased offer of water
Business and first class	Minimalised appearance Small hot components at certain times of the day	Evolved from trolley service to individually served meals, at the passenger's request

This tendency to minimise food and beverage service was a result of the airlines' struggle to keep their full service status while controlling costs, and it affected many passengers who paid and were seeking full service.

Flight attendants' unions and subsequent actions become a reality. Flight attendants lobbied for a multitude of changes in their service regarding physical aptitude for recruitment, line of operational responsibilities, type of in-flight service, rest time, overnight hotels, seniority benefits, etc. At the same time, air travel across many air segments became a commodity; certain cities enjoyed more than 50 flights per day between them and most were full. These factors slowly removed the exclusivity of air travel launching well-known comparisons to coach travel. Airports continued a programme of expansion of terminals and runways and air space became more congested. Technology and evolution of traffic control methodologies evolved at a slower pace than terminal and runway space developments.

The profile of passengers in the 1980s and 1990s constituted a natural evolution from that witnessed in the 1960s and 1970s.

- The spectrum of passengers broadened further: most businesses, however small, assumed air travel as an accepted and required means of transport. Similarly, a much larger proportion of the population became passengers who considered air travel as transport for leisure trips.
- Race, gender and nationality profiles were less relevant when studying passengers; rather, spending power, salaries and professional groups

became more relevant, in an effort to forge long relationships through targeted flight offers.
- Some other interesting trends surfaced:
  o a gradual shift of business passengers from full service to low-cost airlines;
  o increasing use of the Internet to plan air travel events;
  o a move by airlines to customise the relationship with the clients;
  o the appearance of airline alliances;
  o the resurgence of terrorism as a threat in the skies;
  o a move by airlines to save fuel costs by managing the intake of reprocessed air and oxygen in aircraft cabins.

Air passenger behaviour changed considerably, influenced by the evolution of cabin service, cabin crew profile, smoking bans, flight delays and the profile of the air passengers themselves. Air passenger behaviour grew as a very relevant issue in the aviation industry after air rage incidents became very frequent and well publicised. The subject became the focus of attention of airlines, governments and research agencies which began to understand all the new behaviour drivers.[1] We have a clearer understanding for example, that the structural make-up of the cabin itself is not the best designed for either decision-making or acting under stressful situations. Research has demonstrated that the unique environment of the aircraft cabin can directly affect behaviour. The air inside the cabin is dry and low in humidity, and such environments have been found to produce stress, irritability and to reduce one's ability to make sound judgements. The loud noise from the engines also results in people having to raise their voices, which can be wrongly perceived as aggressive behaviour thus leading to difficult social interactions between people. The cramped conditions on new aircraft may also make people feel more agitated. People may feel that they have to aggressively seek or protect their territory especially when strangers are invading their personal space. This, of course, can be further aggravated when passengers share their space with a wide cultural, ethnic and social diversity of strangers. The fact that many travellers these days may be emotionally aroused either due to leaving a loved one, worrying about a business trip or even resentment about having to fly means that they are likely to feel vulnerable, decreasing their sense of power and control and potentially leading to unplanned, irrational and sometimes violent reactions (Bor, 1999).

Undoubtedly, these conditions are compounded by the changing face of the airline service providers. Airlines are now less service oriented and more impersonal. As a consequence, passengers are less likely to relate personally to air crew and more likely to see them as representatives of an airline that has emphasised cost rather than service, and consequently someone that they can vent their anger on. Interestingly, challenging passenger behaviour in the form of air rage is not just an economy class phenomenon, but is seen increasingly with business class passengers and those on frequent flier programmes, who are often more demanding and aggressive as they have higher expectations of the service.

Many analysts are already speculating as to how the next era in aviation will unfold and what its main feature will be: whether this will see a complete shift of passengers from full service to low-frills carriers remains to be seen. All low-cost carriers in the world survived the fluctuation in passenger numbers after 11 September 2001 and most announced large fleet expansions shortly thereafter. Across the US and Europe, these carriers have also announced significant plans for route expansions, supported by profits earned through hard market conditions.

Summarising the Evolution

When we examine the evolution of commercial air travel across a set of variables, we can see how passenger behaviour will undoubtedly be affected (see Table 3.2)

During the first period, passenger behaviour was probably marked by the status that flyers had associated with flying. Passengers were under pressure to 'behave' according to the principles that were promoted by the airlines themselves; indeed, while there are a few recorded incidents about alcohol-related incidents, it is believed that they were the exception.

When jet service was introduced, exclusivity of travel began to fade although passenger expectations remained unchanged.

What Does the Future Hold?

Only one aspect of aviation can be predicted with a certain degree of conviction: the number of passengers will continue to grow at around 3 per cent to 4 per cent per year. If we extrapolate from existing data, we should expect the market to develop in one or more of the following ways:

Table 3.2   Evolution of certain aviation variables over time

	Propeller-based	Jet service	Modern era of mass transport
Smoking	Freely allowed	Back of cabin	Banned
Food*	High standards, hot	Lower standards, hot	Few hot
Cost of flying	High	Medium	Low
Cabin service*	High quality	High/medium quality	Medium/low quality
Cabin design*	Ample space	Less space	Cramped
Status of travellers	Exclusive	Less exclusive	Popular
Speed of travel	Fast	Very fast	Very fast
Carry-on baggage*	Nearly none	Some	A lot, but restricted
Flight delays	Some, unnoticed	Increasing, noticed	Many, noticed
Baggage service*	No issues	Some lost baggage	Some lost baggage

*   Aspects affected by airlines' economic pressures.

- more airport and runway expansion programmes;
- more flight services to more destinations;
- air traffic management systems and processes improving at a slower rate;
- low-cost airlines continuing to develop and grow throughout Europe and the US;
- full-service airlines trying to emulate low-cost airlines; just a few appear as economically viable;
- more affordable travel, providing access to air travel to even more people;
- the Internet becoming the preferred method for booking flights and conducting air travel-related transactions.

These trends point towards an increase in the stressing factors that affect air passenger behaviour, mixed with a clear acknowledgement that passenger behaviour itself is a significant factor in the design of aircraft cabin and cabin service.

The traditional slow rate of change in some parts of the aviation industry is likely to be driven by successful litigation as a result of more serious air rage incidents (many alcohol-related), deep vein thrombosis (as a consequence of reduced seat leg room in long-haul flights) and/or hypoxia (lack of oxygen to the brain, as a consequence of excessive recycling of on-board air). Any subsequent changes are more likely to take place in the aircraft cabins of full service airlines, who maintain travellers' high expectations. From the beginnings of the PanAm Clipper and the luxury of live entertainment and freshly cooked meals, to the cramped conditions of no-frills carriers, civil aviation has truly become more accessible. Passenger behaviour will have to undergo yet another transformation as air travellers' expectations are reshaped by airline changes that will focus on increased security, health safety and less on-board service.

Note

1 An interesting evolution of passenger behaviour also arose after the 11 September 2001 attacks: US air passengers have expressed, through multiple media interviews, their willingness to get involved in any possible future on-board incidents, following the example of the passengers in flight AA 93 that crashed outside Pittsburgh. In that respect, there has been a growing camaraderie between passengers in the US which is likely to surface in any other future incidents, and may perhaps influence other passenger behaviour.

Reference

Bor, R. (1999), 'Unruly Passenger Behaviour and In-flight Violence', *Travel Medicine International*, Vol. 17, pp. 1–6.

Chapter 4

Just Plane Scared? An Overview of Fear of Flying

Elaine Iljon Foreman

Two caterpillars were crawling laboriously through the undergrowth, when a butterfly fluttered by. Watching in horror, the first caterpillar exclaimed to the second 'No way would you ever get *me* up in one of those things!' People who suffer from a fear of flying will frequently resort to the 'it's not natural' argument – 'If man were meant to fly, he would have been born with wings'. Countering this with 'If man were meant to go at 70 miles per hour on the motorway, he would have been born with spots, four legs and a furry tail', does little to shake the conviction.

Searching for agreement on the nature of fear of flying, let alone the causes and the best form of treatment, reveals a myriad of often contradictory opinions. In this chapter, the major prevailing perspectives from the published clinical literature will be presented. It will not be possible to provide a comprehensive summary of the whole field – one Internet search on 'fear of flying' yielded 728,000 sites alone!

The range of people who can be affected by a fear of flying extends from those who have never flown before to frequent flyers, including civilian and even military aircrew (Dyregrov et al., 1992, Goorney 1970). The consequences of the fear can be far-reaching. It can limit the person's professional opportunities, affect leisure options, and even mean that one person may decide to take holidays without their partner on a regular basis, if the partner will not fly. There are implications for long-term relationships, and likewise difficulties in family holidays if children refuse to travel. The problem can have a substantial impact on professional, social and family life (Van Gerwen, 1988 in Van Gerwen et al., 1997), and can affect marital or relationship satisfaction because fear of flying hampers or restricts either partner's freedom of movement. When considering the range of the population who suffer from fear of flying, Ekeberg, Seeberg and Ellertsen (1989) propose that individuals affected can be divided into three groups: those who avoid all flights; those who restrict flying to an absolute minimum, and experience considerable discomfort prior to and/or during each flight; and those who display continuous mild or moderate apprehension about flying, but do not avoid it, even though it remains an unpleasant experience.

Epidemiological studies have reported a wide range of point prevalence, from 10–25 per cent of the population (Dean and Whitaker, 1980), 10–20 per cent (Agras et al., 1969), to 2.6 per cent (Frederikson et al., 1996), with the disorder being found in the latter study to be twice as common in women as in men. Expanding the range still further, it has been reported by Capafons, Sosa and Vina (1999) that 45–50 per cent of the population suffer anything from a slight discomfort or apprehension to a very intense fear, and about 10 per cent suffer from such a high degree of fear or anxiety that they avoid flying. Despite the oft-cited belief that if someone is afraid of doing something they will avoid it, Greco (1989) quoted from a study indicating that one in every four flyers shows a significant degree of fear or anxiety. This high prevalence is extended still further by the report of Van Gerwen (1993) who suggested that 30 per cent of the Dutch population are afraid of flying. In a recent survey of travellers in Scotland, McIntosh and his colleagues (1998) found that 40 per cent of their sample were worried by take-off and landing. One can also ponder what proportion of the 50 per cent of a random sample of a Norwegian population who have never flown reported by Blomkvist (1987) have not done so because of their fear. The high prevalence seems to be an international phenomenon, remaining high up to the present time, a view which is supported by the finding of Ost, Brandberg and Alm (1997), who found that 10 per cent of their Scandinavian sample totally avoided flying, and 25 per cent said they would avoid it where possible, and use tranquillisers and/or alcohol where flying was unavoidable.

Looking at the people who do fly despite their fear, Greist and Greist (1981) report that 20 per cent of fearful flyers who travel by air use alcohol or sedatives to cope with severe anxiety, and this view prevails within the vast majority of the literature reviewed. Substantial costs are incurred through the fear of flying; in 1982, average revenue loss for the airline industry through fear of flying was estimated at $1.6 billion by Roberts (1989).

However, despite the high levels of reported fear cited in the studies of prevalence, Spilka et al. (1977) asserted that, apart from the automobile, the aeroplane is the most popular form of transport. The increasing popularity is shown in that overseas flights by British residents rose from 5.9 million in 1971 to 16.5 million in 1986 (Iljon Foreman and Iljon, 1994). In 2001, the Civil Aviation Authority reported that 180 million passengers used UK airports. These figures are reflected internationally, with a report from the European

Airline Association stating that 2 billion people travelled by air in the year 2000. Looking at the recent growth in air travel, David Henderson (2002) of the European Airline Association (EAA) states that in the last 40 years the European air travel market has doubled in size five times – that is to say, in 2000 it was 32 times bigger than in 1960. The last doubling cycle – to the year 2000 – took 10 years; the previous one, 12 years. While there were two periods of a marked downturn, at the time of the Gulf War in 1991 and in 1986, following the Chernobyl disaster and the bombing of Tripoli, in both cases growth resumed quite quickly and the lost market was recaptured. It has not all been steady growth, however. Any study of air travel cannot fail to refer, as Henderson does, to the 'shocking, savage events' of 11 September 2001. In the following 24 weeks EAA carriers lost over one-quarter of their North Atlantic and more than 10 per cent of their short-haul traffic, with overall volume down 15 per cent compared to the previous year. By February 2002, North Atlantic air travel was 10 per cent below the expected norm, while European routes gradually produced a small growth for the first time, and even Asia-Pacific routes rose from 23 per cent down in passenger traffic to near-previous year levels. Were the losses to be sustained over 12 months the cost to the industry would amount to €12 billion. The previous worst-ever annual loss, in 1992, was US$2.4 billion. Six months after the 11 September attacks, at least two airlines – Sabena and Swissair – both of which had encountered some economic problems before the terrorist attack, were no longer in existence. As Henderson states, that is respectively, 78 and 71 years of aviation history swept away. The differential recovery of air travel implies that people are reaching alternative conclusions on the risks associated with air travel, depending on the route and the airline. Another factor is that of cost, with the 'no-frills' airlines being the ones to have profited from the difficulties of the larger, full service carriers.

This all seems to reflect that a key factor in people's judgement is that, as emotional beings, we formulate responses on the basis of the 'perceived' and not the 'true' risk of an activity. Gewertz (1996) refers to the hackneyed statistical construct that one has a greater chance of dying in a car crash on the way to the airport than during the flight itself. I have actually been on a flight where the Captain's greeting to the passengers began: 'Congratulations, ladies and gentlemen. You have just completed the most dangerous part of your journey – getting to the airport!' The following table, compiled by Greco (1989), on the probability of coming to harm in different situations makes for fascinating reading.

Table 4.1 Danger of flying in relation to other modes of transport or situations in the US

Mode of transport/situation	Number of deaths per year in US	Comparative safety of airline travel
Car	45,000	29 times safer
Walking/being a pedestrian	8,000	8 times safer
Staying at home	20,000 accidental deaths	18 times safer
Working on the job	11,000 accidental fatalities	10 times safer
Homicide by spouse or relative	7,000 homicides	6 times safer
Bus		4 times safer per mile
Train		4 times safer
Boating		8 times safer

Source: USA Department of Transport document (Greco, 1989).

As can be seen, one has a greater statistical chance of dying if one *avoids* flying and stays at home, than of being killed in a plane crash. Given the odds of one in 14 million of winning the UK National Lottery, it is sobering to realise that one is more likely to be dead by the end of the week than to have won the lottery. It would be interesting to see if this bet was ever featured in the bookies' odds!

Jones (2000) suggests that in the early years a reluctance to fly was regarded as a normal human response and not as evidence of a mental disorder. Those who *wanted* to fly were regarded as the ones whose sanity might be doubted. Reference is made to such diagnostic categories as 'aeroneurosis' and 'aerophobia' (Anderson, 1919; Gotch, 1919). Fear of flying can be a symptom that may be a product of an acute or post-traumatic stress disorder, a generalised or phobic anxiety disorder or part of some other major or minor psychiatric condition. Fear of flying is classified in the *Diagnostic and Statistical Manual of Mental Disorders* (American Psychiatric Association, 1994) as a specific phobia, situational type. It is characterised by a marked, persistent, excessive fear that is precipitated by the experience or immediate prospect of air travel. Exposure to this phobic stimulus almost invariably provokes an anxiety response – sometimes to the point of a panic attack – which the individual recognises as unreasonable, and which produces significant interference or distress. It is in a different category to the other non-situational phobias, which are categorised as 'social' or 'agoraphobias'. In the previous edition of DSM (American Psychiatric Association, 1987), fear of flying was classified as a simple phobia, akin to spider or needle phobias.

People suffering from a fear of flying frequently report the presence of other psychological difficulties. Wilhelm and Roth (1997) found that 44 per cent of their sample had met criteria for current panic disorder with agoraphobia, or had done so in the past. This group was more concerned with internal or social anxiety. The simple phobics in this study did not have this worry, but both groups were equally concerned regarding the worry about 'external danger'. Iljon Foreman and Borrill (1994) found that 60 per cent of their sample reported 'other fears', besides that of flying. These included a diverse range such as a fear of spiders, swimming, agoraphobia, claustrophobia, heights, falling, social embarrassment, crowds, collapsing and 'being under some one else's control'. Dean and Whitaker (1982) examined the association between fear of flying and psychiatric disorders and suggest that 46 per cent of travellers with a fear of flying have other phobias; 33 per cent present with agoraphobia and 25 per cent with claustrophobia.

It is generally agreed that fear of flying is not a unitary phenomena, but consists of various underlying fears. These may meet the criteria of identifiable psychological disorders, or may just be factors which apply only to the situation of air travel. Howard, Murphy and Clarke (1983) identified six separate 'source' fear categories, in the following order of significance: crashing, 51.8 per cent; heights, 23.2 per cent; confinement, 17.9 per cent; instability, 11.1 per cent; panicking, 5.4 per cent; and lack of control, 5.4 per cent. In their sample of 38 fearful flyers, Walder et al. (1987) found that 37 per cent were afraid of 'being enclosed', 34 per cent were afraid of crashing, and 13 per cent were afraid of heights. The remaining 16 per cent were afraid of losing control, air sickness, or had a multitude of worries. Dean and Whitaker (1982) reported that out of 562 responses by fearful flyers, 29 per cent were associated with a fear of dying, 24 per cent with a fear of heights, and 7 per cent with fears of bad weather. Beck, Emery and Greenberg (1985) also emphasised the heterogeneous nature of fear of flying, and highlighted the following fears: fear of suffocation due to deprivation of air; fear of subjective tension and loss of control; fear of crashing and death; fear of loss of control in social situations; fear of vomiting or fainting and the subsequent humiliation; agoraphobia; fear of being trapped in an enclosed space; and fear of being separated from a caretaker and experiencing a serious disorder such as a heart attack. Heller (1993) suggested that people are less bothered by a fear of heights, the plane crashing, or even dying, than they are about experiencing negative feelings, perceived loss of control, and what others may think of them. Howard, Murphy and Clarke (1983) identified four underlying categories for the fear of flying: heights, crashing, instability and confinement.

Rosenhan and Seligman (1989) suggested that specific phobias can be grouped into three categories – situational phobias, animal phobias and mutilation phobias. The difficulty with classifying fear of flying as a 'specific phobia' is that this does not clarify what it is about flying which frightens the person. It could as easily fit into the 'situational' as the 'mutilation' categories, depending on what it was that the person feared. As one person seeking help for their fear of flying succinctly put it: 'Flying? That doesn't bother me at all! *Crashing*? Now *that* bothers me!'. Another person said that he was so terrified that he might make a fool of himself if he could not escape that he found himself almost wishing the plane would crash.

Perhaps the most parsimonious proposal is that of Iljon Foreman and Borrill (1993). Based on clinical assessment and standard questionnaires, analysis indicated that the fears could be conceptualised as two separate categories, with some people experiencing fears from both categories. The first group reported fears that concerned a 'loss of internal control'. These subsumed all those fears relating to social anxiety, panic disorder, claustrophobia and agoraphobia. In this first group, the person fears some form of internal catastrophe, where in some way they will go 'out of control'. They are unable to employ the strategy of escape, and therefore remain terrified of the frightening prospect. The second group report a fear of a 'loss of external control' – something happening to the plane. The latter fear encapsulates heights, turbulence, bad weather, and all of the precursors to crashing. The third group have both fears – a loss of internal and of external control.

This view fits neatly with the findings of McNally and Louro (1992), who looked at fear of flying, agoraphobia and simple phobia in 34 people. They concluded that the distinguishing features were that danger expectancies (loss of external control) motivate flight avoidance in simple phobia, whereas anxiety expectancies (loss of internal control) motivate flight avoidance in agoraphobia. This view builds on the earlier findings of Reiss and McNally (1985). It is therefore not so much panic *per se* that differentiates simple phobias from agoraphobia, but rather the fear of panic (Goldstein and Chambless, 1978). This view is supported by the findings of Wilhelm and Roth (1997), who found that those with panic disorder and agoraphobia were more concerned with internal or social anxiety, while simple phobics did not have this worry, but all were equally concerned regarding external danger. Likewise, it was reported by Howard, Murphy and Clarke (1983) that specific flying phobics fear crashing, while agoraphobics fear panic attacks.

Van Gerwen and Diekstra (2000) suggested that treatment of fear of flying can generalise to other phobias. This is consistent with the findings reported by Iljon Foreman and Borrill (1994). There is considerable concern that the existing diagnostic and classification systems such as DSM IV and ICD–10 do not appropriately acknowledge the diverse nature, aetiology and types of fear of flying. It is a heterogeneous, not a unitary phenomena (Van Gerwen et al., 1997).

One of the most detailed studies in the literature is that of Van Gerwen et al. (1997) who carried out an analysis of data from 419 patients who were referred to a treatment agency because of fear of flying. They examined in depth the nature of the fear, and found that female patients stated 'fear of being involved in an accident' as their primary fear, while males stated 'not being in control'. Given the conceptualisation of Iljon Foreman and Borrill (1993), rather than this indicating a difference between males and females, both genders can be seen to be reporting the same thing – a fear of an external loss of control. When considering the second reason given for the fears, women reported a 'fear of confined spaces/claustrophobia (lifts, underground travel, tunnels)' while men cited a 'fear of losing control over themselves (crying, fainting, going mad, heart attack or heart palpitations)'. Once again, rather than a gender difference, both of these fears neatly fall into the same category of a fear of a loss of internal control. The phobic fears that are most specifically associated with high levels of flight anxiety are claustrophobia, fear of water, and fear of heights. This is intuitively likely, as these are central to the experience of flying – one is trapped, does fly over water, and it is a long way down! Thus it seems logical that anyone fearing these will be highly likely to fear flying as well. Claustrophobia is also moderately related to agoraphobia, and once again this is intuitively logical, given that those suffering from claustrophobia often worry about panicking in public and the difficulty of escaping. Van Gerwen et al. (1997) add that while people have come forward with specific fear of flying, it may be accompanied by other phobic reactions such as death, travel, heights, confined spaces (lifts, subways, tunnels) crowds, going crazy, darkness, fire, thunderstorms, illness, heart attack, palpitations, blood, wounds, hospitals and bad weather. It would therefore seem that all of the above, while appearing at first glance to be totally heterogeneous, can be neatly divided into the two categories of 'loss of control' fears previously described. The current consensus is best summarised by Moller, Nortje and Helders (1998) who conclude that while there is agreement on the heterogeneous nature of the fear of flying, there is at the present time no clear understanding as to the nature of the underlying and the associated fears.

While it has not been possible from the literature review to find a consensus on the reasons why people are afraid of flying, some authors have grappled with the underlying causes of the fear. Early writings on fear of flying from 1920–66 emphasise the internal, unconscious processes and mechanisms behind the fears. Morgenstern (1966) states that it is a reflection of the pervasive dualism and of man's feelings when neurotic illness causes the metamorphosis of an intense need to fly into an equally strong dread of flight. Freud's (1960) writings also suggest an underlying cause, whereby the aeroplane itself might represent the displacement of a strong figure of threat or desire in the person's internal world. Shneck (1989) refers to 'separation anxiety' as an underlying cause of the fear. From an early behavioural perspective, other authors have proposed that the fears can be seen as a conditioned response to an aversive experience (Watson and Rayner, 1920). Taking the cognitive behavioural perspective, a pattern of avoidance behaviour is set up which reinforces the anxiety and prevents the possibility of testing, and invalidating, the feared predictions of future catastrophes (Marks, 1987; Greenberger and Padesky, 1995; Clark, 1999; Salkovskis and Clark, 1992; Wells, 1997). Building on this view, Wilhelm and Roth (1997) propose that their results support a 'vulnerability-stress' model, with flying phobia developing in people who were more susceptible to events that had little impact on non-phobics. They suggest that flight phobia began for many of the sample by a rise in anxiety while flying, either triggered internally, or by a transitory over-reaction to a minor external event. This resulted in direct conditioning of a phobic response to flight stimuli. They further propose that specific vulnerabilities of various kinds present at phobia onset may have promoted this process, and add that cognitive biases could have played an important role particularly in the initial progression and maintenance of the phobia.

Returning to the search for the underlying causes of the fear, Williams (1982) proposed that fear of flying actually represented a difficulty in communication. He hypothesised that the phobic person is expressing a different message by refusing to fly. Examples could be the child who does not want to return to boarding school, or the partner who resents being uprooted yet again to follow their spouse's promotion trail.

The way in which a treatment type is linked to the conceptualisation of the fear of flying is highlighted by Goorney (1970). In the case of Williams' (1982) theory, treatment can in some cases be a matter of validating the refusal to fly, rather than trying to change the person's behaviour. Looking at the psychodynamic perspective, the hypothesis of an underlying, unconscious cause implies that it is clinically necessary to obtain insight into this, in order for the unconscious to be brought into consciousness, and processed in a new and more productive manner. The treatment of choice from this theoretical perspective would therefore be one of the forms of psychodynamic psychotherapy. Carr (1978) reported that before 1965, the treatment of choice was indeed psychodynamic psychotherapy and the success rate of treatments was on average 18 per cent. After the development of behavioural treatment, however, the success rate rose to 77 per cent. In a review of psychological treatment of a fear of flying Bor, Parker and Papadopoulos (2001) confirm that long-term explorative psychoanalytic therapy has not been shown to be effective in the treatment of a fear of flying.

An interesting meta-view of the relationship between psychodynamic, cognitive behavioural and even virtual reality therapies is propounded by Vincelli (1999). He suggests that starting from the interpretation of dreams until the most up-to-date procedures of cognitive restructuring, the common goal has been to intervene on the internal representations of reality that prove to be nonfunctional with respect to the required adaptation to the environment.

More recent results from treatments based on cognitive behavioural principles have shown success in 70–98 per cent of cases (Van Gerwen and Diekstra, 2000). Cognitive behaviour therapy proposes that it is not events *per se* but rather a person's interpretation of them that is responsible for the production of feelings such as anxiety and/or depression. In the case of anxiety, it is hypothesised, the interpretations relate to an exaggerated perception of danger. It is not only the external events that can be seen as a source of danger, but also internal events such as the physiological symptoms of anxiety themselves. There is also a reciprocal relationship between the external event and the perception of danger, such that once individuals have labelled a situation as dangerous, they tend to selectively scan and interpret situations in ways that augment their sense of being in danger. Specific techniques to modify cognitions, and thus affect the interaction between thoughts, feelings and behaviours, form the predominant core of the cognitive behavioural approach.

A closer examination of the different forms of psychological therapy by Iljon Foreman (in press) highlights the range to show such a breadth that it can make even the experienced clinician wonder whether all of these can indeed be subsumed under the same heading. Of these different forms of psychological therapy, a vast number have been utilised specifically to enable people to overcome their fear of flying. Psychoanalytic therapy, systemic therapy, hypnosis, virtual reality, reattributional training, systematic desensitisation, stress inoculation training, coping self-talk, cognitive preparation, flooding, implosion, *in vivo* exposure and relaxation training and cognitive behaviour therapy have all been described in the literature (Denholtz and Mann, 1975; Haug et al., 1987; Roberts, 1989; Beckham et al., 1990; Rothbaum, Hodges and Kooper, 1997; Capafons, Sosa and Vina, 1999). Comparisons between treatments reveals that systematic desensitisation, flooding, implosive therapy and relaxation training, are all equally effective compared to no treatment control (Howard et al., 1983). In a more recent randomised controlled trial, Anderson, Rothbaum and Hodges (2001) carried out a study comparing virtual reality (VR), a technique which allows individuals to become active participants, interacting through sight, sound and touch, in a computer generated three-dimensional world, to standard exposure and to a control group. They found that VR and standard exposure were better than controls, with no difference between the two treatment groups at two and six month follow up.

Given that, to date, a single effective treatment component responsible for improvement in all cases has yet to be established, there is disagreement within the literature on whether to employ a multifaceted package of interventions (Sidley, 1990). Greco (1989) supports the proposal that a multi-modal treatment programme is the most effective. This view is further supported by Agras, Sylvester and Oliveau (1993) who suggests that combinations of medication and exposure therapy may be the optimal approach to treatment. They cite the work of Mavissakalian, Michelson and Dealy (1983) and of Mavissakalian and Michelson (1986) in support of this, noting that this hypothesis requires further testing in controlled trials. Following on from this, a trial by Wilhelm and Roth (1997) raises concerns about the efficacy of such a combination in the treatment of fear of flying. They found that using a combination of medication and cognitive behavioural interventions produced a poorer result than the cognitive behavioural treatment alone.

Considering established treatment programmes for fear of flying rather than individual research studies which are of a more academic nature, Jones (2000) highlights the concerns raised by Van Gerwen and Diekstra (2000) that there can be a 'one size fits all' approach. In addition, concerns are expressed that the treatment of fear of flying may be undertaken by anyone, whether or not trained as a therapist, whether or not licensed to treat patients. Jones concludes that the Tarrytown study highlights the need for differential diagnosis. This is based on the premise that those whose fears derive from underlying anxiety processes respond best to a different therapeutic approach than those whose fears derive from a specific traumatic experience. As one would perhaps expect with such a 'fascinating and complex problem' as the treatment of fear of flying, a consensus on this issue has yet to be reached by those working in this field.

The most parsimonious treatment study published to date appears to be that of Ost, Brandberg and Alm (1997). A single three-hour session of massed treatment, including a return domestic flight was compared to five sessions of exposure and cognitive restructuring for 28 randomly assigned patients. The former group were more successful immediately post-treatment. At one year follow up, there was a reduction in the number who took the behavioural test with immediate post-treatment results of 93 per cent of the one session group and 79 per cent of the five session group falling to 64 per cent of both groups. The patients studied fulfilled the DSM–IV criteria for specific phobia, but were excluded if they had 'other psychiatric problems requiring immediate treatment'. It is thus unclear whether people with panic disorder, claustrophobia and social phobia were included in the study, and therefore one cannot tell if this treatment is of the 'one size fits all' variety.

The results of Iljon Foreman and Borrill's study (1994) indicated that employing the conceptualisation of the two types of fears – a 'loss of internal control' (subsuming panic disorder, social anxiety, claustrophobia and agoraphobia) and 'loss of external control' (subsuming fears of heights, turbulence, and all the elements which ultimately can be reduced to a fear of crashing) can enable a treatment programme to be successfully employed in which one size does indeed fit all.

No clinician or researcher would ever be likely to claim a 100 per cent success rate, however. The next challenge is to examine in more detail both people for whom treatment of whichever form has been successful, and also those who could be considered as 'failures'. The latter terminology may be seen as somewhat harsh, and alternative terminology that published articles have employed are 'negative outcomes, therapeutic drop outs, change resistant, treatment resistant, lack of success', and finally people who indicate 'lack of treatment related progress'. Published research has often been criticised for a reluctance to examine the group showing 'lack of treatment related progress'. This must be viewed in the context of 8 per cent of British clinical psychologists being responsible for 50 per cent of the published work. Understandably, perhaps, the choice is to focus on the factors implicated in 'success', especially as negative findings are substantially less likely to accepted for publication. The modal number of journal articles and conference papers published by British clinical psychologists is zero, and it is therefore important to bear in mind that published articles are likely to be atypical of normal clinical practice. The challenge therefore is one of trying to apply these research findings in a meaningful way to normal clinical practice. Concentrating on both the negative as well as the positive research findings, it should be possible to identify the critical factors that make for therapeutic efficacy.

A model to elucidate the process of cognitive change in the treatment of fear of flying which could prove valuable in the search for agreement of the key elements of treatment efficacy has been proposed by Borrill and Iljon Foreman (1996). Given that at long-term follow-up many studies have reported a decrease in the level of treatment effects, employing the model may also enable clinicians to account for this decrease, and to develop relapse prevention strategies that would help to maintain the therapeutic gains achieved.

For those who currently see themselves as 'just plane scared', there is the option in the future not to be grounded by fear. Once that fear is conquered – and given the pending arrival in 2006 of the new Airbus 380, whose maximum passenger load is 840 people – literally thousands more people will be taking off because, for them, the sky will no longer be the limit – they will be free to fly.

References

Agras, S. (1993), 'The Diagnosis and Treatment of Panic Disorder', *Annual Review of Medicine*, Vol. 44, pp. 39–51.

Agras, S., Sylvester, D. and Oliveau, D. (1969), 'The Epidemiology of Common Fears and Phobias', *Comparative Psychiatry*, Vol. 10, pp. 151–6.

American Psychiatric Association (1987), *Diagnostic and Statistical Manual of Mental Disorders,* 3rd edn, revised, Washington, DC: APA.

American Psychiatric Association (1994), *Diagnostic and Statistical Manual of Mental Disorders*, 4th edn, Washington, DC: APA.

Anderson, H. (1919), 'The Psychology of Aviation', in *The Medical and Surgical Aspects of Aviation*, London: Oxford University Press.

Anderson, P., Rothbaum, B. and Hodges, L. (2001), 'Virtual Reality: Using the virtual world to improve quality of life in the real world', *Bulletin of the Menninger Clinic*, Vol. 65, No. 1, pp. 78–91.

Beck, A., Emery, G., Greenberg, R. (1985), 'Anxiety and its Disorders: A cognitive perspective', New York: Basic Books.

Beckham, J., Vrana, S., May, J., Gustafson, D. and Smith, G. (1990), 'Emotional Processing and Fear Measurement Synchrony as Indicators of Treatment Outcome in Fear of Flying', *Journal of Behavior Therapy and Experimental Psychiatry*, Vol. 21, No. 3, pp. 153–62.

Blomkvist, A. (1987), 'Public Transportation Fears and Risks', in Lennart Sjoberg (ed.), *Risk and Society: Studies of risk generation and reactions to risks, The Risks and Hazards, Series 3*, London: Unwin Hyman, pp. 35–45.

Bor, R., Parker, J. and Papadopoulos, L. (2001), 'Psychological Treatment of a Fear of Flying: A review', *Journal of the British Travel Health Association*, Vol. 1, pp. 21–6.

Borrill, J. and Iljon Foreman, E. (1996), 'Understanding Cognitive Change: A qualitative study of the impact of cognitive-behavioural therapy on fear of flying', *Clinical Psychology and Psychotherapy*, Vol. 3, No. 1, pp. 62–74.

Capafons, J., Sosa, C. and Vina, C. (1999), 'A Reattributional Training Program as a Therapeutic Strategy for Fear of Flying', *Journal of Behavior Therapy and Experimental Psychiatry*, Vol. 30, pp. 259–72.

Carr, J. (1978), 'Behaviour Therapy and the Treatment of Flight Phobia', *Aviation, Space and Environmental Medicine*, September, pp. 115–18.

Clark, D. (1999), 'Anxiety Disorders: Why they persist and how to treat them', *Behavior Research and Therapy*, Vol. 37, No. 1, S5–27.

Dean, R. and Whitaker, K. (1980), 'Fear of Flying: Impact on the US air travel industry', Boeing Company Document BCS–00009–RO/OM, Seattle: Boeing.

Dean, R. and Whitaker, K. (1982), 'Fear of Flying', *Journal of Travel Research*, Vol. 21, pp. 7–17.

Denholtz, M. and Mann, E. (1975), 'An Automated Audiovisual Treatment of Phobias Administered by Non-professionals', *Journal of Behavior Therapy and Experimental Psychiatry*, Vol. 4, pp. 111–15.

Dyregrov, A., Skogstad, A., Hellesoy, O. and Haugli, L. (1992), 'Fear of Flying in Civil Aviation Personnel', *Aviation, Space and Environmental Medicine*, Vol. 63, No. 9, pp. 831–8.

Ekeberg, O., Seeberg, I. and Ellertsen, B. (1989), 'The Prevalence of Flight Anxiety in Norway', *Norsk Psykiatrisk Tidsskrist*, Vol. 43, pp. 443–8.

Frederickson, M., Annas, P., Fischer, H. and Wik, G. (1996), 'Gender and Age Differences in the Prevalence of Specific Fears and Phobias', *Behavior Research and Therapy*, Vol. 34, No. 1, pp. 33–9.

Freud, S. (1960), *The Standard Edition of the Complete Psychological Works of Sigmund Freud*, The Hogarth Press, London.

Gewertz, B. (1996), 'Presidential Address: Overcoming our Fear of Flying – Vascular Surgery in the Next Decade', *Journal of Vascular Surgery*, Vol. 23, No. 5, pp. 745–8.

Goldstein, A. and Chambless, D. (1978), 'A Reanalysis of Agoraphobia', *Behavior Therapy*, Vol. 9, pp. 47–59.

Goorney, A. (1970), 'Psychological Measures in Aircrew – Normative Data', *Aerospace Medicine*, Vol. 41, pp. 87–91.

Gotch, O. (1919), 'The Aeroneurosis of War Pilots', in *The Medical and Surgical Aspects of Aviation*, London: Oxford University Press, pp. 109–49.

Greco, T. (1989), 'A Cognitive-behavioural Approach to Fear of Flying: A practitioner's guide', *Phobia Practice and Research Journal*, Vol. 2, No. 1, pp. 3–15.

Greenberger, D. and Padesky, C. (1995), *Mind Over Mood*, New York: The Guilford Press.

Greist, J. and Greist, G. (1981), *Fearless Flying: A passenger's guide to modern air travel*, Chicago: Nelson Hall.

Haug, T., Brenne, L., Johnson, B., Bentzen, D., Gotestam, K. and Hugdahl, K. (1987), 'A Three System Analysis of Fear of Flying: A comparison of a consonant versus a nonconsonant treatment method', *Behavior Research and Therapy*, Vol. 25, pp. 187–94.

Heller, F. (1993), 'Overcoming the Fear of Flying', in W. Dryden and L.K. Hill (eds), *Innovations in Rational Emotive Therapy*, Newbury Park: Sage Publications, pp. 238–52.

Henderson, D. (2002), 'Uncertainty and the Outlook for World Air Travel – Europe and the North Atlantic', paper given at the *FAA Commercial Aviation Forecast Conference*, Washington, 12–13 March 2002.

Howard, W., Murphy, S. and Clarke, J. (1983), 'The Nature and Treatment of Fear of Flying', *Behavioural Therapy*, Vol. 14, pp. 557–67.

Iljon Foreman, E. (in press), 'Putting Fear to Flight: Cases in psychological treatment', in R. Bor and L. Van Gerwen (eds), *Psychological Perspectives on the Fear of Flying*, Aldershot: Ashgate.

Iljon Foreman, E. and Borrill, J. (1993), 'Plane Scared – Brief Cognitive Therapy for Fear of Flying', *Scottish Medicine*, Vol. 13, No. 4, pp. 6–8.

Iljon Foreman, E. and Borrill, J. (1994), 'Long-term Follow-up of Cognitive Behavioural Treatment for Three Cases of Fear of Flying', *Journal of Travel Medicine*, Vol. 1, No. 1, pp. 30–34.

Iljon Foreman, E. and Iljon, Z. (1994), 'Highwaymen to Hijackers: A survey of travel fears', *Travel Medicine International*, Vol. 12, No. 4, pp. 145–52.

Jones, D. (2000), 'Fear of Flying: No longer a symptom without a disease', *Aviation Space and Environmental Medicine*, Vol. 71, No. 4, pp. 438–40.

Marks, I. (1987), *Fears, Phobias and Rituals: Panic, Anxiety and their Disorders*, New York: Oxford University Press.

Mavissakalian, M. and Michelson, L. (1986), 'Agoraphobia: Relative and combined effectiveness of therapist-assisted *in vivo* exposure and Imipramine', *Journal of Clinical Psychiatry*, Vol. 47, pp. 117–22.

Mavissakalian, M., Michelson, L. and Dealy, R. (1983), 'Pharmacological Treatment of Agoraphobia: Imipramine versus Imipramine with programmed practice', *British Journal of Psychiatry*, Vol. 143, pp. 348–55.

McIntosh, I., Swanson, V., Power, K., Raeside, F. and Dempster, C. (1998), 'Anxiety and Health Problems Related to Air Travel', *Journal Travel Medicine*, Vol. 5, No. 4, pp. 198–204.

McNally, R. and Louro, C. (1992), 'Fear of Flying in Agoraphobia and Simple Phobia: Distinguishing features', *Journal of Anxiety Disorders*, Vol. 6, No. 4, pp. 319–24.

Moller, A., Nortje, C. and Helders, S. (1998), 'Irrational Cognitions and the Fear of Flying', *Journal of Rational, Emotive and Cognitive Behavior Therapy*, Vol. 16, No. 2, pp. 135–48.

Morgenstern, A. (1966), 'Fear of Flying and the Counterphobic Personality', *Clinical Aviation and Aerospace Medicine*, Vol. 37, pp. 404–7.

Ost, L., Brandberg, M. and Alm, T. (1997), 'One versus Five Sessions of Exposure in the Treatment of Flying Phobia', *Behavior Research and Therapy*, Vol. 35, No. 1, pp. 987–96.

Reiss, S. and McNally, R. (1985), 'Expectancy Model of Fear', in S. Reiss and R.R. Bootzin (eds), *Theoretical Issues in Behavior Therapy*, San Diego, California: Academic Press, pp. 107–21.

Roberts, R. (1989), 'Passenger Fear of Flying: Behavioral treatment with extensive *in-vivo* exposure and group support', *Aviation, Space and Environmental Medicine*, Vol. 60, pp. 342–8.

Rothbaum, B., Hodges, L. and Kooper, R. (1997), 'Virtual Reality Exposure Therapy', *Journal of Psychotherapy Practice and Research*, Vol. 6, No. 3, pp. 219–26.

Rosenhan, D. and Seligman, M. (1989), *Abnormal Psychology*, Norton, New York.

Salkovskis, P. and Clark, D. (1992), 'Cognitive Therapy for Panic Attacks', *Journal of Cognitive Psychotherapy*, Vol. 5, No. 3, pp. 215–26.

Shneck, J. (1989), 'Separation Anxiety and Fear or Avoidance of Flying', *Journal of Clinical Psychiatry*, Vol. 50, No. 1, p. 474.

Sidley, G. (1990), 'Brief Clinical Reports: A multi-component intervention with a lady displaying an intense fear of flying – a case study', *Behavioural Psychotherapy*, Vol. 18, pp. 307–10.

Spilka, B., Loeb, N., Weldon, L., Markel, T. and Albi, L. (1977), 'Those who are about to Fly: Death concerns and feelings and behaviour about air travel', *Omega*, Vol. 8, No. 2, pp. 107–16.

Van Gerwen, L. (1993), Director, VALK Foundation, Leiden, personal communication.

Van Gerwen, L. and Diekstra, R.(2000), 'Fear of Flying Treatment Programs for Passengers: An international review', *Aviation, Space and Environmental Medicine*, Vol. 71, No. 4, pp. 430–37.

Van Gerwen, L., Spinhoven, P., Diekstra, R. and Van Dyck, R. (1997), 'People who Seek Help for Fear of Flying: Typology of flying phobics', *Behavior Therapy*, Vol. 28, pp. 237–51.

Vincelli, F. (1999), 'From Imagination to Virtual Reality: The future of clinical psychology', *Cyber Psychology and Behaviour*, Vol. 2, No. 3, pp. 241–8.

Walder, C., McCracken, J., Herbert, M., James, P. and Brewitt, N. (1987), 'Psychological Intervention in Civilian Flying Phobia', *British Journal of Psychiatry*, Vol. 151, pp. 494–8.

Watson, J. and Rayner, R. (1920), 'Conditioned Emotional Reactions', *Journal of Experimental Psychology*, Vol. 3, pp. 1–14.

Wells, A. (1997), *Cognitive Therapy of Anxiety Disorders: A Practical Manual and Conceptual Guide*, Chichester: John Wiley.

Wilhelm, F. and Roth, W. (1997), 'Acute and Delayed Effects of Alprazolam on Flight Phobics during Exposure', *Behavior Research and Therapy*, Vol. 35, No. 9, pp. 831–41.

Williams, M. (1982), 'Fear of Flight: Behaviour therapy versus a systems approach', *The Journal of Psychology*, Vol. 111, pp. 193–203.

Chapter 5

Psychological and Psychiatric Difficulties among Airline Passengers

Julia Heller

Relatively little is known about the psychological and psychiatric sequelae of air travel. This is because the field itself is relatively new and there has been little substantial research in the area. Psychological problems, understandably, have taken a back seat to the perceived more pressing issues of general safety and more strictly 'medical' problems. However, it is now timely that there is more acknowledgement of how air travel impacts on psychological well-being not only for its own sake but also because, as will be demonstrated below, this can also have a bearing on passenger safety.

There are likely to be at least three ways in which air travel can precipitate or contribute to psychological difficulties. First, there is the general stress of travelling. Secondly, there is the specific stress of air travel. Thirdly, there are individual factors that are known to induce physical symptoms in the air that will have a 'psychological' impact. It is an established finding that the stress of getting to and through a modern airport may be considerable (see Chapter 2). There may be concerns for some inexperienced travellers about getting through the system, there may be anxieties about delays, and there may be anxieties about issues of safety (McIntosh et al., 1998). It has been reported that three-quarters of medical emergencies happen while travellers are still on the ground (Goodwin, 2000).

The specific anxieties about air travel have been relatively well researched. What seems to emerge is that a small, but significant, proportion of travellers do experience distressing anxiety and panic in flight (see Chapter 4). For example, it is reported that 5 per cent of all medical emergencies on board all Qantas international flights in 1993 were related to anxiety conditions (Donaldson and Pearn, 1996). In a more recent comprehensive study by Matsumoto and Goebert (2001), information about psychological/psychiatric conditions was obtained by Medlink. This is a 24-hour service used by commercial airlines to obtain medical consultation by physicians. It was estimated that a medical consultation was sought on approximately 24 per cent of US flights. Of the 1,375 in flight calls to Medlink, 3.1 per cent were accounted for by passengers suffering from an anxiety condition. They also established that nearly half the total number of passengers were in their 20s and 30s and that the majority were females. The fact that in-flight anxiety appears to be predominantly a younger female phenomenon has also been confirmed in other related studies (McIntosh et al., 1998) and is consistent with the pattern of anxiety disorders in the general population.

The third mechanism for psychological symptoms is the specific conditions at altitude that may indirectly exacerbate physical symptoms that may then contribute to psychological instability or distress. For example, the primary factor contributing to medical problems is reduced cabin pressure (Kay, 1994). Although this is generally well tolerated in healthy individuals, those with compromised circulatory and/or pulmonary function may experience hypoxaemia (a condition in which the blood contains too little oxygen). Similarly, it is well known that reduced cabin pressure can produce minor abdominal discomfort. Other environmental factors include low cabin humidity causing dehydration and air turbulence causing nausea and vomiting. These physical symptoms are likely to cause, at the very least, a degree of distress and anxiety in some passengers (not least because they may signal the potential for a more severe physical condition), but it is speculative as to how they contribute to more generalised anxiety.

People who are anxious about air travel will also experience some typical physical symptoms that are common in all anxiety states, such as heart palpitations, stomach cramps, dizziness, nausea, and breathlessness, so that there may be some overlap with the symptoms caused by the *specific* conditions in air travel. In a similar way, people experiencing hypoxaemia are likely to hyperventilate. It is well established that anxiety and panic states can similarly result in hyperventilation which itself induces feelings of dizziness, weakness, headache and nausea.

It is known from other areas of psychological research that the cognitive experience of anxiety (thinking processes) contributes to such physical symptoms which then increases the feelings of lack of control and anxiety, thus resulting in a vicious circle. Likewise, the experience of physical symptoms (whether or not resulting from initial anxiety) may then serve to increase the perception that one is feeling anxious and indeed losing some control. This is illustrated in Figure 5.1. In other words, for some passengers it may not be very clear what has been the primary cause of some physical symptoms and or hyperventilation – the direct result of hypoxaemia or other environmental factors or anxiety *per se*.

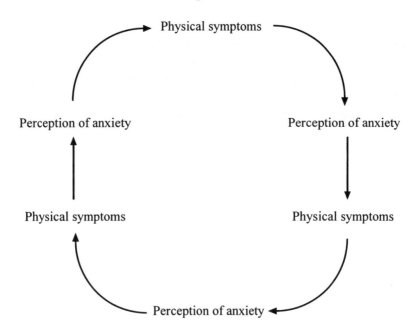

Figure 5.1   Interplay of cognitive and physical symptoms of anxiety

There are very few studies suggesting an association between actual air travel and psychiatric pathology, although a few isolated cases have attracted media attention. In the study by Matsumoto and Goebert (2001), which analysed in-flight calls to Medlink, two passengers (out of 48 calls in one year) were hospitalised on landing in local psychiatric hospitals (following emergency landings) and given a 'psychiatric' diagnosis (psychosis and attention-deficit/hyperactivity disorder). However, these diagnoses were made without seeing the person and on the basis of descriptions alone.

Another recent study assessed time zone changes and major psychiatric morbidity among passengers hospitalised in a mental health centre of a hospital in Israel between 1993 and 1998 (Katz et al., 2001). The authors divided patients into two groups depending on the number of time zones crossed in flight to Israel. The two groups were then controlled for past psychiatric history and other factors. The researchers found a similar number of first episodes of psychotic and major affective episodes in both groups but a higher number of relapses of these illnesses in the bigger time zone group. They concluded that jet lag triggered or exacerbated major psychiatric disorders. What is unclear from this study is whether it is the specific effects of some of the time zone changes such as fatigue, sleep disturbance, impairment of cognitive functions or the more general stress of air travel (particularly long flights) which contribute to relapses of mental illness. It is well known that 'stress', as a general factor, is a major contributor to relapse of mental illness.

Results from an early study (Jauhar and Weller, 1982) lend weight to the theory that rapid time zone changes act as a precipitant to affective illness in predisposed people, in that depression was diagnosed significantly more often on flights from east to west. There are some major methodological difficulties, however, with this study and one must exercise a degree of caution in interpreting and applying their results.

On 29 December 2000, a Kenyan man on a Nairobi-bound British Airways flight burst onto the flight deck, lunged for the controls and caused the aircraft to plunge 10,000 feet. Incidents of this nature are extremely rare. This situation was very different from a growing number of air rage cases. The particular incident was related to the passenger in question having a paranoid psychotic illness. This translated into a highly volatile state of being convinced that people at the controls or on the flight were about to harm him. People experiencing such thoughts are naturally very agitated and anxious and are also likely to be very distressed. It would be extremely difficult, if not impossible, to have a rational dialogue with such a person and quick acting medication to sedate such a person would probably be necessary. It is also probable that people suffering from this problem will present with some bizarre symptoms of marked suspiciousness and distress prior to their flight. In this case, it seems that this particular man did, in fact, talk to airport personnel before boarding about his fears that he was being persecuted and followed. His presentation would have been one of severe agitation and probably distress. He is likely to have been somewhat incoherent and his style of conversation may have jumped from one subject to another without making 'normal' logical steps. Preventing such an obviously distressed passenger from travelling is clearly preferable to having to manage the symptoms of his psychiatric condition at 35,000 feet.

The available information from the Civil Aviation Authority and the Write Partnership Ltd (who have collated data on air rage incidents) suggest, however, that, as expected, the majority of people who are involved in air rage incidents are not mentally ill. What is undisputed is that the small number of cases where severe mental illness is implicated can be particularly devastating, as in the above example.

The vast number of air rage incidents are related to people who are likely to have either a formal personality disorder or at least personality difficulties. The personality disorders most implicated are termed antisocial personality disorder (or in more common usage, psychopathy) or borderline personality disorder. Both disorders have traits and features in common and in particular a difficulty in managing appropriate boundaries and impulsivity – i.e. a tendency to act quickly without due thought and consideration to the consequences. People who warrant either of these diagnoses may have problems in managing their anger and they tend to have a pervasive pattern of disregard for the rights of others. Those with a personality disorder of these types are also likely to drink alcohol irresponsibly. Alcohol misuse is considered to be implicated in about 25 per cent of air rage incidents (Bor et al., 2001). It is therefore a significant factor either on its own, or in combination with a mental illness or more commonly a personality disorder. Drug misuse seems, from the limited data available, to be less implicated in incidents of air rage.

Some recent examples of the above are available from the Write Partnership Ltd. In one such case, a 34-year-old passenger who was on board an Air France flight en route from San Francisco to Paris was taken into custody on arrival for alleged assault of a crew member. The passenger was said to have punched a cabin crew member when the crew announced to him that they were not prepared to serve him any more alcoholic drinks. His behaviour prior to this was said to be loud, unruly and arrogant.

In another example, a Continental Airlines flight en route from Anchorage to Seattle was forced to return when a 38-year-old passenger began causing a disturbance. The incident began when the passenger started to argue with her boyfriend. It escalated when a member of the cabin crew asked her to calm down. The passenger threw a can of beer, hitting the crew member and spilling beer on several passengers and a small baby. The First Officer left the flight deck to help but when he tried to restrain the woman he was badly bitten on the wrist. These examples are typical of the more common incidents of unruly behaviour on board all airlines and are likely to be due to a combination of the person's disturbed personality make-up and alcohol misuse. The vast majority of air rage incidents are committed by men in their 20s and 30s, and this conforms to other forms of aggressive or violent behaviour in the community.

The last example is therefore rather atypical in terms of gender but does highlight the fact that knowing the more likely types and groups of people who are going to be disruptive is useful but not sufficient.

It is evident that one of the major challenges for ground and airline staff is the prevention and management of such incidents. Some incidents can be prevented. In the Nairobi case, for example, some greater knowledge of the risks posed by paranoid and persecuted individuals should have alerted ground staff (who were aware of his feelings of persecution) to the dangers of this man being allowed to board. Knowing what to look for and refining the criteria for people fit to board are key to preventing similar incidents. It is inevitable that some cases will be missed and the onus then is on airline crew to manage the situation to the best of their abilities. This requires training in conflict management, i.e. when and how to de-escalate a situation (using psychological techniques) or when medication and or physical restraint are the only viable options. This does not, of course, guarantee successful outcomes, but there is considerable evidence from forensic psychiatric hospital research that such training does reduce the risks of violence and aggression and that staff are more confident in handling difficult situations.

In conclusion, there are a few but significant studies on the psychological or psychiatric behaviour of air passengers. Future research should probably focus on: a) how to minimise general anxiety in flight and enhanced training for cabin crew in dealing with this; b) the prediction of the few but important cases of the 'mentally ill' passenger prior to boarding and management in air; and c) psychological and environmental strategies for minimising and coping with air rage incidents. The field of clinical psychology and the specialist branch of forensic psychology could play a major role in developing such projects.

References

Bor, R., Russell, M., Parker, J. and Papadopoulos, L. (2001), 'Survey of the World's Airlines about Managing Disruptive Passengers', *International Civil Aviation Organisation Journal*, Vol. 56, No. 2, pp. 21–30.
Donaldson, E. and Pearn, J. (1996), 'First Aid in the Air', *Australian and New Zealand Journal of Surgery*, Vol. 66, pp. 431–4.
Goodwin, T. (2000), 'In-flight Medical Emergencies: An overview', *British Medical Journal*, Vol. 321, pp. 1338–1341.
Jauhar, P. and Weller, M. (1982), 'Psychiatric Morbidity and Time Zone Changes: A study of patients from Heathrow Airport', *British Journal of Psychiatry*, Vol. 140, pp. 231–5.
Katz, G., Durst, R., Zislin, Y., Barel, Y. and Knobler, H. (2001), 'Psychiatric Aspects of Jet Lag: Review and hypothesis,' *Medical Hypotheses*, Vol. 56, No. 1, pp. 20–23.
Kay, R. (1994), 'Safe Air Travel: Preventing in-flight medical problems', *Nurse Practitioner*, May, pp. 39–44.
Matsumoto, K. and Goebert, P. (2001), 'In-flight Psychiatric Emergencies', *Aviation, Space and Environmental Medicine*, Vol. 72, No. 10, pp. 919–23.
McIntosh, I., Swanson, V., Power, K., Raeside, F. and Dempster, C. (1998), 'Anxiety and Health Problems Related to Air Rravel', *Journal of Travel Medicine*, Vol. 5, No. 4, pp. 198–204.

Chapter 6

Air Travel and the Implications for Relationships

Olga Levitt and Robert Bor

Air travel disrupts normal patterns of relationships. Interaction on board aircraft, both with known fellow travellers and strangers, the relationship with those left behind and those at the point of destination are all affected by the particular context. Anyone observing the greetings of arriving travellers at an airport will quickly become aware of the different and powerful emotions being expressed. Transitions perturb people. The perturbation may be exciting and welcomed or distressing and feared, or somewhere inbetween, but it will almost certainly take people out of their normal routines and away from their usual systems of support. Fears associated with flying, air rage, hijacking, bombs on planes and airline incidents and accidents, as well as the dramatic events of 11 September 2001, have contributed to anxiety about safety, both for travellers and those who care about them, as well as for the general public.

The ease and speed of air transport has made it possible, and increasingly imperative, that people travel great distances in the pursuit of their careers and to maintain and develop relationships. Indeed, air travel has changed the way people conduct their relationships. Air travel, together with frequent and prolonged absences from home, have become part of the routine for an increasing number and variety of careers including pilots and aircrew, bankers, businessmen and -women, travel agents, members of the armed forces, journalists, entertainers, sports people, international charity workers and many more. Cheap fares and the introduction of 'no-frills' airlines has also made air travel more accessible to people who previously may not have considered it as a means of transport. It is also used more frequently for brief visits, where formerly it would have been considered uneconomical to make the journey.

Any journey has a special quality – it is the time and space 'between'. On an aeroplane, one is bound together with strangers, each traveller having a story or a reason for making the particular journey from the departure point to their destination. Air travel also provides particular opportunities and constraints as to what one can do while on the journey. The feeling of being out of contact with the ground contributes to the 'time out of time' and difference from normal routines and activities which many people experience, especially on long flights.

Passengers seated next to one another, who start out as perfect strangers, may become emotionally closely connected with the person sitting next to them. Usually, this temporary bond between fellow passengers is brought about by a combination of factors including physical proximity, a less threatening side-by-side seating pattern (rather than face-to-face), boredom, fear and loneliness. Emotional arousal is commonly exhibited through either social withdrawal and detachment (resisting social advances of other passengers) or close engagement through a confessional relationship (making new temporary bonds). Some passengers seek out flight attendants for social interaction in order to ease their sense of detachment. Attachment behaviour is often more visible and intense in airport arrivals and departure halls where primitive fears and raw emotions are displayed (Fraley and Shaver, 1998).

This chapter focuses on frequent travel by air and the ways in which people who repeatedly separate and reunite struggle to develop and maintain intimacy, where patterns are continually being disrupted. This chapter also examines the relationship implications for these frequent travellers and those closest to them – their partners, parents and children. It also looks at the effect on other aspects of their social lives.

The ideas presented are based on relevant psychological and sociological theory, published research as well as the authors' clinical experience. In providing an educative, preparatory and clinical service for those whose work involves travel, as well as in a general counselling practice, the authors meet with people for whom frequent travel and regular separations are seen to disrupt their relationships. While some of those who have sought help have presented with the clear idea that their difficulties were related to work stress, including frequent travel, others present with seemingly unrelated symptoms such as depression, anxiety or marital discord which, on further exploration, are clearly identified as being related to the unwelcome changes brought about by frequent air travel. This is not to suggest that frequent travel is necessarily problematic. Most people cope reasonably well with the dynamics of relationships in which travel plays a part. For some, the repeated absences and reunions become an integral part of the way of managing the dance of intimacy and distance, independence and dependence which all couples and families have to negotiate. Indeed, some seek work and careers that involve them in frequent travel and in 'intermittent spouse relationships' (Rigg and Cosgrove, 1994).

While this chapter does not specifically address passenger behaviour directly, it is hoped that the reader will gain a better understanding of the emotional 'charge' that passengers carry when they travel due to disruption in their personal lives as well as changing patterns of attachment. These can all expose them and others to primitive fears, giving rise to both predictable as well as unexpected reactions to stressful situations, both at home and during travel.

Travel, Relationships and Psychological Health

Travel can be seen as exciting and providing opportunities. It also interrupts both office and domestic routines. In relation to family life, it can be a relief from coping with a fretful toddler or simply a break from loading the dishwasher. There is increasing research evidence, however, which highlights that frequent travellers and their partners are at increased risk of mental health problems which can require medical and/or psychological intervention and affect work performance (Curley, 2001). Some common symptoms include depression and anxiety. There is also evidence that these difficulties are mirrored in the families of travellers. Couple relationships are at increased risk and children display more emotional and behavioural difficulties.

Jet lag, with travellers returning home tired, irritable and experiencing disruption to their sleep pattern, is one of the factors that contributes to strained relationships. The effects of jet lag may not be obvious, especially to the traveller him/herself, but may affect relationships with the rest of the family through contributing to a lack of patience, a high level of distractibility and a general inability to join in with the normal rhythm of family life.

In a survey carried out by Striker et al. (1998) for the Health Services Department of The World Bank, self-report questionnaires from returning staff who had been travelling showed that more than one-third of employees reported high levels of stress. These were mainly attributed to the impact of travel on the family and a sense of isolation, followed by health factors and workload on return from travel. Interestingly, time zone differences did not contribute to the self-reported stress of these travellers. Insurance claims for treatment of psychological disorders of World Bank staff were also far higher for frequent travellers than for a comparable group of non-travellers. These findings were unanticipated, because the popular view is that travel is seen as a good thing, relieving stress, providing a break from office routine and allowing people to work in less bureaucratic ways. Those selected to travel were seen as committed, competent and creative employees who gained satisfaction from their overseas assignments. They were often so diligent in their work that they were seen as their own worst enemies. Most were also highly committed to their families and found balancing home and work an enormous pressure. Those who were unattached were worse off emotionally. While partner and family can be an added stress, these relationships can also be an enormous source of support and provide a buffer against emotional upheaval. Friendship ties tend not to be as strong as family ties and can be more easily broken through lack of communication and long periods of separation.

In a survey comparing the experiences of spouses, aircrew wives when compared to ground crew wives revealed a lower sense of well-being in the aircrew families. They reported feeling like a one-parent family and found it difficult to involve their husbands in things they had missed while away. They described feeling isolated when their husbands were away and feeling upset and rejected when their husbands returned and were tired (Rigg and Cosgrove, 1994).

Theoretical Orientation/Conceptual Framework

We have embraced an approach of practical theory – that is, theory which we have found is of use to people engaged in travelling and those who remain behind – in making sense of their thoughts, feelings and behaviour. This theory may find a place in staff training, both for those whose jobs directly involve flying, such as aircrew, as well as those for whom flying and travel are more a means to an end, in the sense that they travel because their job needs to be done in different locations. This may include business, sport and entertainment. This is an important area of study as the effect of travel can be more comprehensively understood and these findings translated into affording people more resources for managing their lives. This conceptual framework may be of use to managers who plan work rosters and make decisions involving travel, irrespective of the nature of the work involved. This understanding may also be useful to those consultants to whom people come when there are personal difficulties – GPs, human resource and occupational health officers, psychologists, counsellors as well as individual, couple and family therapists.

(a) Systems Theory

In formulating an understanding of what happens to people when they travel and the ways in which they act and react, systems theory has a natural fit as it connects the individual to family and to work and other systems. This approach helps us to examine the interdependence of ideas and thoughts on the one hand and behaviour and action on the other. It is also a neutral approach that recognises the uniqueness of each situation and is not prescriptive (Dallos and Draper, 2000). Changes that lead to difficulties in the family may occur outside the family in other systems, such as in the workplace. A new manager or falling profits in the company will have an impact on the family as well as work relationships, for instance, through changes in work hours and levels of stress. Companies' policies about travel have also changed since 11 September 2001, as have social and political systems and these have affected peoples' everyday lives and their relationships. Aircrew and others whose jobs are dependent on the airlines and tourism industries have experienced periods of uncertainty and vulnerability and many employees have lost their jobs, with far-reaching implications for family life and individual mental health. Those who have continued to fly, as well as their loved ones, may have felt more anxious before and during flights. Many factors, therefore, affect peoples' attitude to flying and to separation. Relationships are continually and inevitably changing in light of these changing circumstances. Changes in one part of a family or social system inevitably affect another part of that system. Similarly, changes at the wider socio-political and economic levels of system affect family and individual functioning.

> Brian was referred to a therapist by his GP following his presentation at the surgery with what seemed to be a panic attack. He had apparently suffered a similar episode a week before. Among many other issues explored, the therapist asked him about his family and relationships and whether there had been any recent changes at home. He described an increasing wave of anxiety that peaked every time his wife, a First Officer on a major international carrier, left home for her next flight. Brian had previously shared in all his wife's achievements, but since 11 September his anxieties for her safety had intensified. Brian had not recognised the strength of his own feelings and his loyalty to his wife's career had prevented him from acknowledging his fears, even to himself. He also spoke about the couple's plans to start a family. Talking openly enabled Brian to recognise his feelings and they could then be addressed rather than manifesting in debilitating panic attacks.

(b) Attachment Theory

The actions that people engage in are informed both by what is happening in the moment and by their own previous experience, particularly the patterns of interaction developed in childhood. For example:

> John and Paula, a young married couple, came for counselling because Paula was anxious and depressed and there were frequent arguments between them. After each argument, Paula would question whether the couple should stay together. Both were professionals with successful careers. John's job involved frequent travel and spending time away from home. One of the patterns that was identified through counselling was that arguments almost inevitably occurred immediately before a trip and frequently just after John returned. While John was away he usually telephoned home on the Skyphone from the aircraft as soon as he landed and several times a day thereafter to try to reconcile after the argument and to reassure Paula that he loved her. Paula acknowledged that she became very anxious when John flew and Paula and John both described Paula's feelings and behaviour as causing 'the problem'. The arguments seemed to have a powerful effect in that they led to John calling home more frequently than he would otherwise have done and telling Paula more frequently and more openly how much she meant to him. The behaviour therefore seemed to serve an important function. The danger, however, was that it led both of them to feel that Paula had a problem with managing her anxiety and that the marriage was in trouble.

When examining the continual separations that air travel necessitates, attachment theory is highly relevant. This theory postulates that the way in which we attach ourselves to others in adult life, i.e. form intimate relationships, is informed by our attachments in earliest childhood, particularly to a maternal figure. It is concerned with separations from the mother or main caregiver, the short- and long-term effects of these separations and how they may influence our ability to manage attachments and separations in later life (Bowlby, 1988).

Attachment theory helps us to understand more about how patterns in relationships evolve. When children who have been separated from their mothers are reunited, they initially show detached behaviour for a period of hours or days. After that they again revert to more attached behaviour and may become excessively clingy and may not want to let their mother out of their sight. This extreme behaviour usually disappears relatively quickly and

> John described himself as coming from a close family, with each family member living in close proximity to one another and always in and out of each other's homes. Everyone knew they were loved, but both verbal and physical demonstrations of affection would have felt quite overwhelming and out of place. Paula described significant episodes of disruption to attachment in her childhood. At different times both her parents had been seriously ill and consequently physically and emotionally unavailable to her. Anxiety about her parents' health continued throughout her childhood. Separation for Paula was associated with danger and anxiety. In her family, they told each other frequently how much they loved one another, as there was a constant fear that they would not see each other again.

the child is then able to go on being curious and exploring the world. However, this is not always the case and the distinction is made between 'secure' and 'insecure' attachments. In a secure attachment, the participants in the relationship feel safe and secure and this enables them to be relaxed and get on with doing things. By contrast, an insecurely attached person may be overcome by a mixture of feelings such that they are unable to carry on with normal developmental tasks. Feelings towards their attachment figure may swing between intense love and dependency, accompanied by a fear of rejection, to irritability and an angry vigilance. Insecurity therefore seems to provoke a strong need to be physically close as well as a desire to punish the loved one for any tiny suggestion of perceived abandonment (Holmes, 1993).

Mary Ainsworth (1982) first used the phrase 'secure base' to describe the meaning created by the attachment figure for the attached person. The essence of the secure base is that it provides a springboard for curiosity and exploration. When there is danger, people cling to their attachment figures. Once danger is passed, their presence enables the other to go on with work and play but only if there is some certainty that they will be there again, i.e. that their base is secure. John Bowlby saw marriage and other intimate relationships as the adult manifestation of attachment. This relationship provides a secure base from which one can go out and work and travel, safe in the knowledge that one is cared for and held in mind even when one is not physically present, and to which one can return as if to a protective shelter. Separation anxiety is thus seen as the inevitable consequence of a loving relationship, of caring for someone (Bowlby, 1973).

If the secure base is safe and accessible, attachment behaviour can be minimal and relaxed. If the base becomes unreliable or the limits of exploration are reached, a tension develops and attachment behaviour is displayed. As we grow up, most of us can tolerate longer periods of absence and greater distance from those who provide our 'secure base'. While there is considerable variation in peoples' tolerance of separation, everyone will have a point at which the separation feels too long, the distance between them too great or the absences too frequent to feel secure and comfortable. At this point, we may begin to experience emotions ranging from irritability, anxiety, fear, anger, self-doubt and lack of trust, to detachment, despair and depression (Van Tilburg, Vingerhoets and Van Heck, 1996). There is often a complex mix of feelings and behaviours resulting from individual experiences of attachment and separation in past as well as in current relationships.

There is an intricate and reciprocal relationship between intimacy and distance. With new technologies, geographical distance may not be directly related to psychological distance. Some couples find they have intimate supportive and meaningful conversations during long-distance phone calls and by e-mails but are so anxious or angry, perhaps anticipating the next separation, that they cannot engage in the same level of intimacy when they are together.

There is abundant evidence that children will habitually go to one parent in preference to all other adults when distressed but that in the absence of that preferred person, they will go to others, preferably someone they know well (Bowlby, 1988). This observation has implications for adult relationships. Most people find it helpful to have a network of supportive friends and family when a partner is away and this has implications for couples who work abroad and where one of them travels frequently leaving the partner in a new and possibly unfamiliar environment. By way of contrast, some people try to cope with separation by rapidly replacing the absent attachment figure with another. This may result in a series of relationships or even in social or sexual promiscuity where there is an inability to bear separation or even to face the possibility thereof.

Attachment behaviour can be construed as an effort to maintain equilibrium or homeostasis in an individual's physiological and psychological state. Threats of abandonment in relationships are seen as terrifying and increase separation anxiety; they may also arouse intense anger. This may explain the frequently reported tensions and arguments couples have both before an anticipated trip away or on return. Separation anxiety can lead to complex patterns of behaviour with the person showing the most anxious behaviour not necessarily being the one experiencing the greater difficulty. Anxious attachment behaviour may be provoked in another in order to confirm his/her attachment and love. For example, some young people preparing to go on an adventurous gap year journey may feel that it is not 'cool' to express their anxieties about being away from home. They may unconsciously elicit fearful, protective behaviour in parents by being irresponsible in the weeks leading up to their departure. While separation anxiety is the usual response to the threat or anticipation of loss, mourning is the usual response to a loss after it has occurred. We know that both adults and children feel grief which can include intense feelings of mental pain and longing, misery, anger, despair, apathy and withdrawal (Holmes, 1993).

(c) Developmental Theory

Relationships are never static. While most people engage in relationships displaying fairly predictable patterns, we also change in the way that we relate. This may be for many reasons, but most obviously because our experience of previous situations and relationship patterns prompts this, as does simple maturation. Furthermore, roles change within families. Adults may become parents and children grow to become adolescents and so on.

What is adaptive in terms of family and relationship patterns at one time may be problematic at another. One way to understand this is that relationships continually evolve and are affected by changes in any of the systems in which we live our lives. For instance, a new person entering the family system, such as the birth of a baby, will affect the way travel is perceived. A woman who previously had her own busy career and who enjoyed the change her husband's absences afforded, may feel isolated and resentful if she feels 'stuck at home minding the baby'. Other family members describe coping well during children's early years but find the frequent absence of a parent causes resentment in the early teenage years when the challenges that adolescents bring to families may require the attention of both parents more than previously.

(d) Beliefs and Narratives

There is no doubt that the stress associated with air travel increases pressure on the traveller and the family, whether it be from the absences from home, disruption of routines, effects of jet lag, unpredictability of schedules or other causes. The way in which family members respond is partly determined by the interaction of the external stressors and the network of beliefs concerning work and family relationships in which the people involved live their lives.

Peoples' past experience in intimate relationships is only one variable that affects how we respond to separations and reunions, whether they be for

> David, a professional footballer, sought counselling as he became physically unwell every time he was due to board a flight home from playing football abroad. He described his marriage as 'good' but further discussion revealed that he felt undermined by the strong alliance which had developed between his wife and 11-year-old daughter. David was frequently away from home in pursuit of his career and his daughter had become his wife's confidante especially in his absence. His daughter then resented her father's return home which disrupted her close relationship with her mother and put her back on an equal footing with her two younger brothers. The family were referred for family therapy to help them to manage the different relationship patterns that developed when David was either at home or away.

> Alan travelled on an almost weekly basis all over the world for his work. His employer expected him to travel economy class, to work over weekends if necessary and to stay in low budget accommodation. He was content in his work because his employer was a charity in whose work he passionately believed. While his wife supported him in his career, knowing how important the cause was to him, she also made attempts to encourage him to protect himself better from the backache caused by long hours sleeping on aeroplanes, frequent changes in time zones and other strains caused by long-distance travel.

business or pleasure. Many other personal beliefs will also determine the way in which travellers, their partners, friends and family respond to the demands of air travel. For instance, whether the job is seen as worthwhile, the division of travel commitments is perceived as 'fair', the rewards to both the traveller and the family are experienced as commensurate, the employee is viewed as appreciated by his/her employer, how safe the means of travel is considered to be and how family members balance beliefs about independence and family closeness. Beliefs of others in the wider family and community such as whether travel is seen as a working norm, 'hard luck' or a glamorous option, are also important in supporting or undermining the family's ability to cope effectively.

(e) Beliefs about Sex and Gender

Beliefs and expectations about gender roles and sex have implications for behaviour and impact on relationships when people travel. Historically men have travelled more for work than women. Mothers, wives and girlfriends were left behind 'to keep the home fires burning' – to provide a 'secure base'. With increasing opportunities for work opening up for women, these patterns are changing. Furthermore, both partners, whether in a hetero- or homosexual relationship, travel separately as a part of their working lives. Many couples find this exciting and enjoyable, enhancing both their careers and personal lives. The 'secure base' comes to reside not in the knowledge that someone is in a fixed place waiting for them, but that they are held in the mind and heart of another and can establish contact at any time. The introduction of children into some of these relationships usually means that at least one partner, or a reliable substitute, has to be at home at any one time. While it is still usually women who give up the travel elements of their jobs to care for children, this is not always the case. It is now increasingly common for women to retain their careers, particularly when it is seen as being at a more lucrative or critical point than her male partner's, and he may opt to take on the greater responsibility for childcare, with the attendant career and travel sacrifices. Many parents share childcare responsibilities, taking turns while partners travel. This may be combined with the help of nurseries and nannies, who may become 'the secure base'. Air travel thereby highlights the difficult decisions of balancing home and career for both men and women, as well as for some same sex relationships.

For male partners travelling away from home, there is a common belief or myth that it is an opportunity for sexual exploration outside their primary relationship. The belief that being geographically removed gives freedom from fidelity to wives and partners is commonly held. A double standard may apply in that the partner who remains at home is expected to be sexually faithful. Many factors have contributed to changes in these beliefs. These include changes in travel patterns for women, the risks of HIV and other sexual infections, greater acceptance of same sex relationships and women's changing expectations about their own sexual fulfilment. Separation, as a consequence of travel draws attention to the possibility of sexual infidelity, irrespective of whether this is actually happening. Suspicion and secrecy are two dynamics that introduce complexity into intimate relationships. It is unclear what the implications are for changes in women's sexual behaviour and the impact this is having on ongoing relationships.

Some couples find that travel and absences from one another continually renew their sex lives while others have difficulty in re-establishing sexual intimacy after an extended break. For some, it is a way to physically and symbolically reunite after a separation due to travel while for others feelings such as anger, distress and despair make a satisfying sexual encounter impossible. Some combine these emotions by falling into a pattern of having an argument on a traveller's return and reconciling in a passionate sexual encounter.

> Mark, a successful website designer, and his partner, Peter, came for help as their relationship was breaking down although they both cared deeply about each other. They described the cause of their difficulties as Peter engaging in 'one night stands' whenever Mark was away. Peter clearly believed that Mark was 'having a good time' on his business trips abroad and would use the opportunity to have casual sexual encounters. He was therefore 'evening the score'. Mark strongly believed in sexual fidelity having witnessed his father's affairs causing his mother tremendous emotional suffering throughout his childhood. On the other hand, Peter, was devastated when he had found out about the cheating of his previous partner and vowed that he would never be that vulnerable again. Mark and Peter's previous experiences and the beliefs which arose from them made it difficult for them to develop trust especially around separations.

For a seemingly small proportion, having sexual relations on board an aircraft is a necessary goal. This may be motivated by the apparent ease of availability, the liberal use of alcohol which is a factor in lowering one's inhibition threshold, boredom, anxiety or the need for physical intimacy to counter loneliness. For some, it is a pure challenge and a necessary rite of passage. Below we have summarised some hints and suggestions for enhancing coping abilities to manage the emotional challenges posed by air travel.

What Airlines, Businesses, Travellers and Families can do to Cope Better with the Emotional Challenges posed by Air Travel

Travellers

- Call or e-mail home frequently – the traveller may not be able to be there for every occasion but can let them know they are in his/her thoughts.
- Take a day off to recuperate and spend time with family before returning to work.

- Arrange a special meal or outing with the family before, or on returning from a trip.
- Share experiences with family members – store particular anecdotes that will appeal to different family members, especially children.
- Bring home gifts! However, there is a danger here, especially for children, of learning to welcome the present and not the person.
- Ensure that the family has an itinerary and a way of contacting the traveller.
- Encourage open communication about feelings and negotiating things like the changes from a matriarchal to a patriarchal family.
- Minimise stress while on the road so that travellers don't arrive back exhausted and irritable.
- Have a form of relaxation while travelling. Some people find jogging or going to the gym a great stress reliever, others attend classical music concerts while one reported a passion for going to athletic meetings around the world. Others will attend religious services.
- Allow families to benefit from any accumulated frequent flyer miles as a perk.
- Encourage employees to get help early – before stress develops into clinical depression – destigmatise going for counselling.
- Educate people on the psychological impact of travel.

Companies

Several suggestions arise from the research with World Bank employees (Kleinman, in Curley, 2001).

- Establish and enforce policies on the maximum number of days people can travel.
- Raise awareness about the impact on families of last-minute changes in travel plans.
- Allow travellers to rest and recuperate following trips.
- Allow travellers to make free daily calls to their families.
- Allow travellers to make their own travel arrangements.
- Allow spouses to come along on trips where appropriate.
- Use new technologies, such as video conferencing to limit the number of trips.
- Lower expectations about completion of office work when travellers are on the road.
- Avoid weekend departures whenever possible.

- Compensate employees for required weekend travel.
- Limit trips to two weeks in duration.

Conclusion

Air travel has become increasingly accessible to more people and is a normal part of life for many. The actual journey and the separation from familiar routines and ongoing relationships and the exposure to different environments and relationships have implications for peoples' psychological and social lives. For every individual who travels, whether alone or with others, there is a family or network of relationships that is affected by changes in existing attachment patterns. All relationships are in a constant state of evolution and development. Changes in relationships are actually and symbolically changed by air travel as people separate from and connect to others in their social network. Even where families travel as a unit, each family member, individually and as part of a unit, has to cope with the changes. Given the sense of dislocation which this kind of change engenders, some passengers might exhibit behaviour which in another context would be atypical. We have examined some of the implications but there are many different reasons for travelling and an infinite variety of couple, family and cultural structures in which these journeys take place. All of these affect the impact of travel at a particular time. It is because air travel is so common and such an accepted part of our everyday lives that it is so often taken for granted. However, research has demonstrated that unless the effects of travel, and particularly the cumulative effects of repeated journeys, are recognised, there is an increased likelihood of psychological difficulties arising for travellers and their families. These problems may occur well before the journey has started or long after the journey has ended. Recognition of the impact of travel helps all those concerned to acknowledge the difficulties and provides an opportunity to prevent or minimise the potentially disruptive effects on relationships.

References

Ainsworth, M. (1982), 'Attachment: Retrospect and prospect', in C. Parks and J. Stevenson-Hinde (eds), *The Place of Attachment in Human Behaviour*, London: Tavistock.

Bowlby, J. (1973), *Attachment and Loss: Vol. 2. Separation, Anxiety and Anger*, London: Hogarth Press.

Bowlby, J. (1988), *A Secure Base: Clinical applications of attachment theory*, London: Tavistock/Routledge.
Curley, R. (2001), 'Blue Skies', *Business Traveler*, December 2000/January2001.
Dallos, R. and Draper, R. (2000), *An Introduction to Family Therapy: Systemic Theory and Practice*, Buckingham and Philadelphia: Open University Press.
Fraley, R. and Shaver, P. (1998), 'Airport Separations: A naturalistic study of adult attachment dynamics in separating couples', *Journal of Personality and Social Psychology*, Vol. 75, pp. 1198–212.
Holmes, J. (1993), *John Bowlby and Attachment Theory*, London and New York: Routledge.
Rigg, R. and Cosgrove, M. (1994), 'Aircrew Wives and the Intermittent Husband Syndrome', *Aviation, Space and Environmental Medicine*, Vol. 65, pp. 654–60.
Striker, J., Luippold, R., Nagy, L., Liese, B., Bigelow, C. and Mundt, K. (1998), *Risk Factors for Psychological Stress among International Business Travelers*, Washington, DC: Health Services Department, The World Bank.
Van Tilburg, M., Vingerhoets, A. and Van Heck, G. (1996), 'Homesickness: A review of the literature', *Psychological Medicine*, Vol. 26, pp. 899–912.

Chapter 7

Homesickness and Air Travel

Susanne Robbins

Introduction

Travelling by air can be both enjoyable and exciting. However, air passengers can also find that the experience includes periods of boredom, frustration, tiredness, anxiety or a combination of these emotions. Passengers on the same flight will typically be flying for very different reasons and will experience the flight in very different ways, but one thing that all the passengers will have in common is that they are away from home. Even the most seasoned traveller probably understands the stresses that this can bring and could describe homesickness. In this chapter, the reader will be introduced to homesickness, its effects and what can be done to alleviate it.

In today's hectic world routine is important, providing stability and security. But disruption to routine and important relationships is increasingly common. Although this disruption is an accepted part of our modern life it is not a trivial matter, and many of us are sensitive to the breaking, even for a short time, of the strong connections that are part of our life. For some, these attachments revolve around home and family. Home represents security and normality, a place where it is possible to unwind in familiar surroundings with family and friends. Perhaps it is not surprising, then, that being away from home can be traumatic for some, causing a longing for the distant home and family. Even frequent and hardened travellers often breathe a sigh of relief when they get home after a long or difficult journey. The feeling is one that many would recognise and have experienced, perhaps most often after a tiring day when it is great to sit down and relax.

Missing home and loved ones can affect the emotions of air travellers in particular ways, making them susceptible to stress and distress. While there is little apparent connection between homesickness and passenger behaviour, travellers may behave out of character as a result of homesickness. They may, for example, be:

- withdrawn;
- disinterested;
- angry;
- hostile;
- claustrophobic;
- agoraphobic;
- upset/crying;
- attention seeking.

There is evidence to suggest that in its most severe form, homesickness can lead to the onset of physical illness. In the case of air travellers we might reasonably expect the symptoms to be less severe, although some travellers might find that these symptoms include some unwelcome emotional and physical problems.

Table 7.1   Symptoms of homesickness

Loss of appetite	Stomach ache	Nausea
Headache	Sleep disturbance	Disorientation
Memory Problems	Anxiety	Insecurity
Depression	Apathy	Fatigue

Sources: Eurelings-Bontekoe et al., 1994; Baier and Welch, 1992; Fisher 1989.

What is Homesickness and How does it Apply to Air Travel?

'Homesickness' has come into common usage as a term that describes the feelings of sadness and anxiety experienced by those who are separated from home and from loved ones. Many dictionaries include the term and the definitions follow a common theme. For example, *Collins English Dictionary and Thesaurus* describes homesickness as 'melancholy at being away from home' while the *Oxford English Dictionary* describes a 'depressed state of mind and body caused by a longing for home'. Definitions of homesickness given by individuals are also remarkably consistent and are characterised by a preoccupation with and an intense longing for home. There is very little variation in the descriptions given by sufferers compared with non-sufferers, and the experience of homesickness is also consistent irrespective of age, culture or gender (e.g. Porritt and Taylor, 1981; Carden and Feicht, 1991; Fisher and Hood, 1987, 1988; Hojat and Herman 1985).

We associate homesickness with staying away from home, but, of course, being away from home does not just mean the stay at the end destination. The experience also includes:

- preparation for the journey;
- travel to the destination, maybe in multiple steps;
- the return trip home;
- getting back into the normal routine when back at home.

The journey can take many forms and involve different modes of transport. However, for the traveller suffering from homesickness air travel is an environment that is potentially particularly inimical because:

- air passengers find themselves constrained both in terms of movement and available opportunities to distract themselves;
- there is plenty of opportunity to mull over problems, dwell on the missing home environment and let negative thoughts develop;
- other sources of stress such as fear of flying, delays, queues or more personal problems will exacerbate the situation.

While opportunities to improve the experience are restricted by the mode of travel, consideration should be given to ways in which the difficulties faced by travellers suffering from homesickness might be addressed, in however limited a fashion.

Who gets Homesick and How Big is the Problem?

While we may feel that we know what homesickness is, should it be something we worry about? Surely it is a relatively inconsequential problem experienced by a minority of children who quickly grow out of it? Since it is such a personal thing it is true that it is difficult to quantify objectively. Many sufferers might arguably grin and bear it, considering it a sign of weakness to admit to feeling homesick (Fisher, 1989).

Understanding the extent of the problem is therefore difficult. Researchers seeking to quantify the problem have tended to work with groups of people who are going through the experiencing of separation from home together. In these situations, homesickness can be explored and understood in greater detail, with individual experiences, influences and behaviours examined. Moreover, by working with groups of people who are away from home for some time it is possible to study the development of homesickness over time and to both identify and examine the factors that influence that development. Such studies have included university students, boarding school pupils, army draftees, children on summer camp and holiday-makers, as well as those suffering more prolonged and forced separation such as refugees and migrants.

While this might not seem to have much bearing on air travel, such studies do provide a good indication of the true extent of the problem, and are reasonably consistent in their findings. For example, studies conducted with university students and boarding school pupils showed that 60 to 70 per cent of first year students were suffering from homesickness shortly after their arrival (Fisher et al., 1985, 1986). While the number of students affected by homesickness declined over time, between 18 and 30 per cent were still homesick in their fourth year of study.

If the homesickness experience varies over time, it is also varies in terms of severity. In the same study some 10 to 15 per cent of the homesick first year students reported themselves as being continuously homesick. This relatively high proportion of students suffered fairly significantly in their first year. In fact, the negative emotions associated with homesickness are much worse for some than for others. While for all sufferers the focus is on 'missing home', feelings vary from periodic thoughts of home to a preoccupation with the separation from home and feelings of misery and grief.

How does Homesickness Affect Travellers?

In a study of homesickness among Dutch adults it was found that the most frequently reported homesickness contexts were holidays and stay-overs, with some travellers reporting feelings of homesickness even before leaving home (Van Tilburg et al., 1996). A possible explanation for this is that since the travel is inevitable but unavoidable, the traveller develops depressed or anxious feelings prior to travel (Thurber, 1995). The emotions experienced in this anticipatory response may continue while away or be limited to the pre-travel period.

In the student study mentioned earlier the incidence of homesickness was shown to decline over the four-year period, while the severity of suffering varied from individual to individual. This pattern is also consistent with the experience of those on shorter duration trips. Generally the experience is that:

- the majority of those feeling homesick do so during the first few days in a new location and then the feeling reduces;
- for some the symptoms continue unabated or even worsen;
- the most severely affected may not get better while away and may feel consistently bad for the duration of the trip.

However, the anticipation of a return home and therefore an end to the separation can cause a reduction in homesickness (Fisher and Hood, 1987; Thurber, 1995). While this is typical, it is by no means always the case and some sufferers find that the prospect of an imminent return home makes them more anxious. These travellers will find that even minor hiccups in their travel plans result in an increase in anxiety. However, even those who suffer very badly find that their symptoms reduce or disappear when returning home or at the latest within a few hours of reaching home (Van Tilburg et al., 1996).

If homesickness is commonly experienced, it follows that a number of passengers and perhaps even crew are likely to be feeling the symptoms of homesickness on any given flight. It therefore makes sense to understand the causes and effects of this condition in greater depth so that we might see what action we can take to alleviate the effects of homesickness on travellers.

What Causes Homesickness?

Different models of homesickness have been proposed (Fisher, 1989), each of which provides an explanation of the cause of homesickness:

- loss;
- interruption of lifestyle;
- reduced control;
- role change;
- conflict.

Each of these models is described below. While any one model might provide an accurate explanation of the cause of homesickness for a particular individual, multiple explanations might also apply. Someone experiencing a reduced level of control in a new situation, separated from loved ones and with normal routine interrupted might find the new situation threatening and want to return home. Yet this situation might easily describe a businessman relocating to a job in a new country and company ahead of his family.

Loss and Grief Caused by Separation from the Family

One way of viewing homesickness is in terms of the grief experienced following separation and loss. From this perspective, homesickness is a similar but less intense experience to that of someone who grieves over the death of a loved one. The low emotions experienced by homesickness sufferers are often grief-like in nature and similar to the feelings experienced by those suffering other forms of loss and separation. Homesickness sufferers often define their feelings in terms of loss (Archer et al., 1998), describing:

- missing parents or family;
- missing friends or familiar faces;
- missing familiar surroundings;
- missing home comforts;
- feeling insecure.

In young children, the level of distress shown when separated from primary 'attachment' figures (Bowlby, 1969) depends on the security of the attachment and the extent to which primary care-givers are perceived as available and responsive. Separation can result in anxious, distressed and searching behaviour and later in helplessness and depression. Adult relationships have been shown to have similar features to the attachment patterns between a mother and a child (Weiss, 1982). These attachment patterns affect both the closeness and security of adult relationships and the extent to which separations are bearable. In fact, observations of the behaviours of couples saying goodbye at an international airport have revealed a similarity to the behaviours seen in children being parted from their primary care-givers (Fraley and Shaver, 1998).

Research into homesickness and the personality of the sufferer has, perhaps not surprisingly, concluded that such a link exists (Van Tilburg, 1999). In particular, individuals lacking self-reliance and self-confidence are viewed as more likely to be homesick, removed as they are from the support of their family. A predisposition to homesickness in an individual might be indicated by:

- an extreme fondness for home, people and social functions;
- a strong feeling of belonging to and sharing in home life;

- the habit of confiding in family and depending on their advice and guidance.

In general, a high level of family cohesion leads to dependence within the family unit and this cohesion is a significant predictor of separation anxiety and homesickness (Kazantzis and Flett, 1998). Removed from the close support of family, lacking self-confidence in social relationships and feeling insecure in the new social surroundings, individuals can find it difficult to form relationships that would replace those left behind.

While separation anxiety and homesickness might be experienced by all cultures, the way that homesickness is experienced may vary. For example, comparisons of the experiences of first year Turkish and American college students found that Turkish students rated themselves significantly more homesick than American students during the first three weeks of school. This finding may have its foundations in Turkish culture, which encourages the unity of the family and discourages the emotional independence of young adults (Carden and Feicht, 1991).

Lack of Control

While anxiety caused by separation from the family is one way of explaining homesickness, an alternative perspective states that homesickness occurs because the individual has significantly reduced control in the new location and circumstances. The lack of control is perceived as a threat and the challenges faced cause the individual to feel a need to 'escape' the environment. Since escape is not a reasonable response, the individual stays in the situation and experiences stress accompanied by a longing for the home environment and the return of control that this represents. From this perspective, the travel experience as well as the environment at the destination location can represent a threat and can cause anxiety.

It is a feature of air travel that the passenger has limited control from the moment of arrival at the point of departure, to leaving the destination airport. There is a very necessary focus on process and observance of regulation:

- bags are taken away;
- property and the person are scanned;
- seats are allocated;
- boarding times are decided;
- once on board the passenger cannot disembark;

- on the plane there is limited choice and mobility.

All of this reduces the passenger's perceived control, potentially adding to the problems of the homesick traveller.

Of course, it can be argued that the feeling of reduced control is the result of feeling homesick, rather than the cause. However, there is evidence to suggest that it is the lack of control that is the primary cause of the wish to return home (Fisher, 1985; Archer et al., 1998). This evidence arises from studies showing that for some individuals, homesickness does not start when they first arrive in a new location but some time afterwards, when the requirements of the new location make themselves felt. Of course, if an individual is feeling homesick and then finds that they have reduced control in the new location, then the low emotions are likely to be exacerbated.

Interruption in Routine

A further model of homesickness proposes that increased anxiety and thoughts of home may follow interruption of normal routine and way of life (Fisher, 1984). Experimental studies have shown that interruption of on-going tasks leads to both increased tension and a determination to continue with the interrupted activity (Mandler and Watson, 1966). The persistence in memory of old routines and ideas can contaminate the new environment by competing for attention. Since they are at the forefront of memory, such routines become a continual reminder of home, causing the home to be more easily missed.

The supremacy of old routines in memory may have an evolutionary origin, since consideration of past ideas and activities may be essential for the development of new, perhaps more effective, plans for future survival (Fisher, 1984). However, continual reminders of home make it more difficult to forget. This can be illustrated by considering that someone who wants to give up smoking will find it much more difficult if they regularly see advertisements for cigarettes and see other people smoking them.

Change in Role

A change in environment also brings a change in perceived role and responsibilities. New tasks need to be performed, requiring an adjustment in self-concept and increased self-focus, leading to increased anxiety. The greater the change in environment, the more self-focus increases (Wickland, 1975), and the greater the potential for raised anxiety. In addition, since a sense of role is reinforced by the way others respond and reciprocate, any lack of such reinforcement leads to increased worry and self-focus, reducing ability to adjust to the new environment.

Conflict

This model refers to the confusion experienced by the homesick person, who is torn between the desire to gain new experiences and a longing to return home, creating anxiety and homesickness.

Multiple Causality

In fact, it is likely that separation from home, the interruption of routine and the challenges of the new situation are all factors in homesickness. Separation anxiety and the strain of the new situation have been found to coexist, demonstrating that homesickness can be multifaceted (Archer et al., 1998). Moreover, if homesickness takes the form of stress, anxiety or depression, it is likely that the condition can be aggravated by any other sources of stress that the individual might be experiencing at the same time.

This latter point can best be illustrated by considering 'Life-Event Inventories' that attempt to define the amount of stress that an individual is experiencing at a given time. Typically these inventories list known stressful events, such as death of a spouse, marriage, relocation, etc., with related point values. Anyone suffering several concurrent events accumulates a greater number of points. The higher the number of points the greater the risk. So the traveller who suffers from mild homesickness, but who also gets slightly nervous flying and is worrying about a daughter's wedding could be suffering as much as another traveller who has a single but more significant issue. In a similar way, those who are suffering other psychological conditions such as depression may find that homesickness exacerbates that existing condition.

Does Familiarity Help?

So far we have considered situations where the subject is typically on their first trip away from home. Studies with closed populations have tended to focus on that environment as one in which there is a richer material to study. But what happens on repeat visits – does familiarity with the experience reduce homesickness? This was indeed what happened in the study referred to earlier, where, after four years, the number of students reporting feelings of homesickness had reduced significantly. However, previous experience does not always inoculate against future experience (Thurber, 1995) and for some the experience is repeated and may be worse for being anticipated. For business travellers, for example, frequent travel can increase the likelihood of depression and other psychological disorders (Curley, 2000). However, for the majority the first trip will be the worst and further trips will see a steady improvement. The individual becomes less dependent on home, the new environment becomes less fearful, and travel itself becomes part of the routine.

Which Travellers Might be Affected by Homesickness?

When considering air travel the only common experience that the passengers and crew share is that they are all travelling by air. A flight might have children and adults; first-time and experienced flyers; nationals of different countries; individuals of different cultures and religions. In addition some may be flying away from home, some returning and some on a leg of a multi-point trip. The psychological make-up of the individuals will vary, as will the stresses that they are under.

We might theorise that a charter flight of holiday-makers or a group of scouts travelling to a jamboree might contain more sufferers than a scheduled flight full of frequent flying businessmen and -women, but, given the multiplicity of factors, would we be correct? The scouts might have all been on many camps away from home and be used to separation. Some of the business travellers might be suffering additional stress from work-related problems, compounded by not being able to talk about their problems. While we might be able to characterise the sort of individual who will suffer from homesickness, carrying out the characterisation would be impractical, apart from being intrusive and time-consuming.

How can Homesickness be Alleviated?

So how can we plan to reduce the effect of homesickness on airline passengers and crew if we cannot easily identify who is at risk? Interventions recommended by practitioners are typically oriented at dealing with the more severe cases. Such interventions might include, for example, counselling aimed at reducing stress or helping the subject adjust to the new environment. These approaches require intervention at a personal level and are therefore not practical in the situation we are considering. However, research has indicated that the symptoms of homesickness can be ameliorated in certain ways, some of which have applicability for passengers; for example:

- provide activities/games to divert attention;
- foster opportunities to develop social relationships;
- increase choices and feeling of control;
- give information about flight and destination;
- allow movement around the cabin;
- offer chances to communicate with loved ones.

Perhaps the most obvious intervention is to create a competing demand for the individual's attention. The more attention an alternative task requires, the less attention can be given to intrusive feelings of home. Passive activities such as reading or watching a film have some efficacy, but unless full concentration is required the thought process is still open to intrusive thoughts, which can also be triggered by something in the subject matter itself that is a reminder of home. Activities that require active physical activity are more successful at diverting attention than activities that are passive or require purely mental attention, since they demand more concentration, particularly if they involve interaction with others. So playing physical sports, visiting interesting places or going to clubs will all tend to demand attention. This might not be practical for airline passengers; however, it might be useful when considering activity options for crew when away from home.

If these activities can be undertaken with a friend or colleague, so much the better. Seeking social support is a preferred coping strategy of many homesick individuals. As a minimum, the social interaction requires concentration and diverts attention. In the destination environment it can allow personal relationships to be formed that can act as replacements for the missing relationships.

A further factor in the predisposition of an individual to homesickness is their commitment to the journey being undertaken. If an individual feels positive and committed to the new environment they are less prone to negative thoughts and to feelings of homesickness. To put this another way, if an individual is having depressive thoughts about the new environment they are more likely to extend these thoughts to what they are missing at home so that a 'circle of causality' develops, with one negative thought leading to another. Commitment cannot be engendered easily: however, providing information related to interesting aspects of the new environment can increase interest and provide a focus on the more positive aspects.

Making the decision to travel and feeling in control of events also makes an individual less likely to feel homesick. While these decisions are made some time in advance of the journey's start, it is possible to give the traveller the feeling of control by increasing available choices and minimising the incidence of problems over which the traveller has no control. Clearly this latter point is an objective of all airlines, it being good operationally as well as for customer satisfaction if things go smoothly. The provision of choices and the involvement of the traveller in making those choices wherever possible would, however, have a positive effect. Providing the opportunity for communication with home should also be considered. The ability to communicate itself provides an element of choice and control. Where contact can be had with loved ones and the contact is positive, this would also tend to alleviate low emotions (Chartoff, 1975).

Conclusion

There is ample evidence that homesickness is a real complaint that a significant proportion of people will suffer from at one time or another. For some the symptoms can be quite distressing and will manifest themselves physically as well as emotionally. The experience might be exacerbated by other problems of an emotional, personal or physical nature. For some individuals air travel itself might contribute stress which is additive to their homesickness. While outbound travellers are perhaps most likely to be suffering from homesickness, inbound travellers may also find that their anxiety to return home results in frustration when delays are encountered.

Identifying those who might be sufferers is not straightforward, and is certainly not practical within the limitations imposed on operators. Understanding the causes and effects of the problem will allow homesickness to be considered as a factor in planning. However, there are also some generic actions that can be taken to help homesickness sufferers get more enjoyment from the travel experience.

Suggested areas for deliberation should include those that offer the ability to generate interest, provide distraction or generate social contact. Consideration could be given to increasing the choice of available in-flight entertainment and interactive media. The inclusion of electronic games provides diversion. Making available interesting information regarding the destination, in a form where the passenger could chose a particular subject and get a depth of information would be very positive, as would the ability to book venues, send e-mails, browse the Internet or conduct telephone conversations. Consideration could also be given to offering choices, both on the ground and in the air. Menu choices are available on many flights, but choosing when to eat might offer further choice. The provision of 'goodie bags' to younger passengers generates interest and items such as colouring books offer distractions while in the air. The ability to move around the cabin and interact with others, while difficult on flights, would also provide useful stimuli.

Of course, many of these areas are considerations in air travel for reasons other than their applicability to homesickness sufferers, and would not be developed or further implemented for their use alone. However, it is hoped that describing the experience of homesickness sufferers, their symptoms and the factors that affect these symptoms, will assist airlines in making decisions regarding the introduction and execution of such services.

References

Archer, J., Ireland, J., Amos, S., Broad, H. and Currid, L. (1998), 'Derivation of a Homesickness Scale', *British Journal of Psychology*, Vol. 89, pp. 205–21.
Baier, M. and Welch, M. (1992), 'An Analysis of the Concept of Homesickness', *Archives of Psychiatric Nursing*, Vol. 6, No. 1, pp. 54–60.
Bowlby, J. (1969), *Attachment and Loss. Vol 1: Attachment*, New York: Basic Books.
Carden, A. and Feicht, R. (1991), 'Homesickness among American and Turkish College Students', *Journal of Cross Cultural Psychology*, Vol. 22, No. 3, pp. 418–28.
Chartoff, M. (1975), 'A School Psychologist goes to Camp', *Psychology in the School*, Vol. 12, pp. 200–201.
Collins English Dictionary and Thesaurus: 21st Century Edition (1993), London: HarperCollins.
Curley, R. (2000), 'Blue Skies', *Business Traveler*, December 2000/January 2001, pp. 42–4.
Eurelings-Bontekoe, E.H.M., Vingerhoets, A. and Fontijn, T. (1994), 'Personality and Behavioral Antecendents of Homesickness', *Personality and Individual Differences*, Vol. 16, No. 2, pp. 229–35.
Fisher, S. (1984), *Stress and the Perception of Control*, London: Lawrence Erlbaum Associates Ltd.
Fisher, S. (1989), *Homesickness, Cognition and Health*, London: Lawrence Erlbaum Associates Ltd.
Fisher, S., Murray, K. and Frazer, N. (1985), 'Homesickness, Health and Efficiency in First Year Students', *Journal of Environmental Psychology*, Vol. 5, pp. 181–95.
Fisher, S., Frazer, N. and Murray, K. (1986), 'Homesickness and Health in Boarding School Children', *Journal of Environmental Psychology*, Vol. 6, pp. 35–47.
Fisher, S. and Hood, B. (1987), 'The Stress of the Transition to University: A longitudinal study of psychological disturbance, absent-mindedness and vulnerability to homesickness', *British Journal of Psychology*, Vol. 78, pp. 425–41.

Fisher, S., and Hood, B. (1988), 'Vulnerability Factors in the Transition to University: A longitudinal study of psychological disturbance, absent-mindedness and vulnerability to homesickness', *British Journal of Psychology*, Vol. 78, pp. 425–41.

Fraley, R. and Shaver, P. (1998), 'Airport Separation: A naturalistic study of adult attachment dynamics in separating couples', *Journal of Personality and Social Psychology*, Vol. 78, No. 1, pp. 1198–212.

Hojat, M. and Herman, M.W. (1985), 'Adjustment and Psychological Problems of Iranian and Filipino Physicians in the US', *Journal of Clinical Psychology*, Vol. 41, No. 1, pp. 130–36.

Kazantzis, N. and Flett, R. (1998), 'Family Cohesion and Age as Determinants of Homesickness in University Students', *Social Behavior and Personality*, Vol. 26, No. 2, pp. 195–202.

Mandler, G. and Watson, D.L. (1966), 'Anxiety and Interruption of Behaviour', in C.D. Spielberger (ed.), *Anxiety and Behaviour*, New York: Academic Press.

Porritt, D. and Taylor, D. (1981), 'An Exploration of Homesickness among Student Nurses', *Australian and New Zealand Journal of Psychiatry*, Vol. 15, pp. 57–62.

Thurber, C. (1995), 'The Experience and Expression of Homesickness in Preadolescent and Adolescent Boys', *Child Development*, Vol. 66, pp. 1162–78.

Van Tilburg, M., Vingerhoets, A. and Van Heck, G. (1996), 'Homesickness: A review of the literature', *Psychological Medicine*, Vol. 26, pp. 899–912.

Van Tilburg, M., Vingerhoets, A. and Van Heck, G. (1999), 'Determinants of Homesickness Chronicity: Coping and personality', *Personality and Individual Differences*, Vol. 27, pp. 531–9.

Van Tilburg, M., Vingerhoets, A., Van Heck, G. and Kirschbaum, C. (1996), 'Mood Changes in Homesick Persons during a Holiday Trip', *Psychotherapy and Psychosomatics*, Vol. 65, pp. 91–6.

Weiss, R. (1982), 'Attachment in Adult Life', in C.M. Parkes and J. Stevenson-Hinde (eds), *The Place of Attachment and Loss in Human Behaviour*, London: Tavistock Press.

Wickland, R. (1975), 'Objective Self-awareness', in L. Berkowitz (ed.), *Advances in Experimental Social Psychology*, New York: Academic Press, pp. 233–75.

Chapter 8

Air Rage Post-9/11

Angela Dahlberg

Introduction

The shock of the 11 September 2001 terrorist suicide attacks on the World Trade Towers in New York and the Pentagon put the United States and global aviation to a severe test. The US government declared war on terrorism and triggered a host of security regulations aimed at preventing similar attacks. According to statistics (BTS, 2002) security concerns, which dominate government agendas, continue to affect economies and behaviour, especially as it relates to air travel.

This chapter examines how legislation, compounded by the trauma of the terrorist attacks, affects the attitudes and behaviour of those working in and using the aviation system. Of special interest are the cabin crews and passengers who ultimately face life or death decisions when on-board violence erupts. Real or perceived competence becomes a critical issue when, so far, on-board intervention has mostly been left to chance.

Air travel, already in a service crisis prior to 11 September, has yet to recover, with business travel in the United States showing a 25 per cent decline year over year. Airport security measures designed to reassure the public have introduced a new area of friction, deterring passengers from flying, especially on short-haul routes. Many passengers opt for ground transportation rather than experience the inconsistencies and increased processing times, compounded as they are by airport security fees.

Air Safety and Reality

The costs of upgrading air safety are staggering. President Bush and Congress moved swiftly to respond to the ailing airport security system that enabled the terrorists to achieve their mission. A deadline for screening all checked baggage was set for 31 December 2002, with costs escalating from $2.4 billion to an estimated $6.8 billion, including funds to increase security employees from 32,000 to 72,000.

Logistical issues surrounding the determination to achieve and availability of the most efficient baggage screening system are part of the problem, despite the impressive security tools offered by the technology sector. Predominantly aimed at improving state of the art screening devices at major airports, they are designed to keeping potential perpetrators – and especially terrorists – out of and away from the aircraft. Kenneth M. Mead, the Transportation Department's inspector general, acknowledged to Congress that the Transportation Security Administration was not able to explain how it had spent the US$2.4 billion that Congress already appropriated. The agency's only two clerks handled monthly invoices totaling US$250 million. The biggest financial and security problem that the agency faces, however, is deciding what kind of baggage-checking system to construct.

Proponents of the most sophisticated machines – which, at a cost of US$1 million each, use a process called computed tomography to check for explosives – acknowledge, however, that not enough of these machines can be manufactured in time to meet the 31 December deadline. Apart from requiring extensive remodelling of airports and strengthening floors, screeners would need intensive training or the error rate soars. No matter what decision on systems to be deployed is reached, economic and operational considerations will be part of the process, while organisational and management issues plague implementation.

The expense of C$2.2 billion in air security measures announced by the Canadian government on 10 December 2001, and the creation of the Canadian Air Transportation Security Authority (CATSA), mirror US attempts to make air travel appear safer. Effective from 1 April 2002, the government imposed a much-opposed fee of C$24.00 per return flight, regardless of length of flight, causing some airlines to cut short-haul routes. The majority of the C$2.2 billion in air security initiatives is earmarked for improved airport screening equipment, but does it improve passengers' physical protection in flight, and will it remove the onus on passengers to play the last line of defence?

Since CATSA took over on 1 April 2002, negotiations with screeners for salaries and benefits highlight old issues contributing to existing problems with performance deficiencies. With low wages ranging from C$8.00 to C$10.79 an hour, screeners at Calgary International Airport reportedly rejected the latest offer by their employer, Group 4 Securitas (Canada) Ltd in a 99 per cent vote (*Calgary Herald*, 2002).

With the introduction of the new security measures, job responsibilities have increased significantly. Based on the low wages, recruitment attracts mostly immigrant workers unable to qualify for higher paid jobs. Only 14 per cent of the screeners have more than five years' experience, making turnover of staff and training a constant preoccupation. Ultimately, critics point to Transport Canada for this long-standing problem, one that continues despite assurances on the health of the security system. Section 4 of The Transport Canada Airport Security Working Group tabled some of these issues in an interim report for further discussions:

Human Factors:

- Training.
- Selection criteria.
- Remuneration and working conditions.
- Security culture.
- Motivation.
- Communication and coordination.
- Successor provisions (protection of incumbents).

Perception of Security

Despite the billions of dollars spent on home security measures and the trend to look for regulations and hardware to guarantee security, incidents of security breaches continue to disrupt airport operations and passengers' travel plans. A survey conducted by University of Michigan political scientist Michael Traugott in March 2002 confirms that the majority of Americans do not feel any safer. Of the 613 people surveyed immediately after the attacks and again in March, 75 per cent reported no increase in their sense of personal security. Although 84 per cent felt that similar attacks were somewhat or very likely to occur in the near future, only 25 per cent thought that such attacks were likely to occur close to where they lived. The majority of respondents (70 per cent) confirmed their willingness to sacrifice some civil rights such as requiring all adults to carry a national identification card with their picture and Social Security number.

Placebo or Reality?

In a move to create the perception of security, President Bush has revived and expanded the air marshal programme, originally created by President Nixon in 1970, after a series of hijackings shook the nation and undermined air travellers' confidence. Advocates of the programme believe it plays an effective part of a multilayered security strategy and acts as a deterrent. Critics point to the dangers of on-board confrontations using arms, with the potential for lethal misunderstandings. Douglas Laird, a former security director for Northwest Airlines, reportedly stated: 'With the attitude present in today's fliers, I don't think there is any real need for marshals.' While the public has stated its willingness to assist cabin crews, it should not be taken as an effective means to address this issue, as I will address later in this chapter.

According to Ricardo Alonso-Zaldivar (*Los Angeles Times*, 2002), the number of air marshals had been reduced from a high of 2,000 to 32 at the time of the 11 September attacks. His research indicates that it 'would take 120,000 marshals or more men and women who usually work in teams, to cover the 30,000-plus daily flights in the United States'. Such a programme could easily cost more than $10 billion a year. Any expectations that this type of sweeping coverage will be instituted are unrealistic. Some security experts believe that taxpayers' money is better spent on airport security, while aircrew labour associations still press for an extended air marshal programme and better training.

Airport Screening

The new Transportation Security Administration (TSA), created in November 2001, assumed responsibility for security at US airports, including the screeners, in February 2002. Federal law requires same-sex screeners to pat down passengers, who should be subject to physical searches only if they trigger metal detector alarms. Random checks are part of the screening process and include flight crews. Any additional checks include the use of a wand and may result in further physical searches. A sense of safety and security eludes passengers confronted with inconsistent screening processes. Torn between the intangible of absolute security and laws intended to govern safe social behaviour lies the unpredictability of human motivation and processes that drive individuals to take or not to take appropriate action based on a complex set of psychological and physiological factors. The type of incidents since 11

September illustrates the shift from a premise of de-escalation to escalation, causing nonsensical and absurd situations in the name of security measures.

Civil Rights

The FAA reiterates the continued validity of civil rights and protection of passengers against discrimination on the basis of race, colour, national origin, sex or creed under the new security laws. Addressing the traveling public, the FAA (Fact Sheet, 2001) offers the following advice:

> However, everyone may experience some inconveniences and delays while the nation adjusts to the new security reality. You may be asked to exhibit an increased level of cooperation in security searches with today's new security regulations. Please assist the security staff in accomplishing their required tasks. Private security screenings requests should be accommodated when possible. Just as there can be no discrimination against people on the basis of race, color, national origin, sex, or creed, there can be no compromise to the commitment and enforcement of safety and security standards in the aviation community.

Such assurances offer little comfort when screeners, freshly empowered and ill-trained, abuse their authority and engage in gross transgressions. These are new dangers that some passengers face while travelling, and are the more repugnant since the perpetrators are representatives of a system intended to protect the public. One such experience reported by passenger Sharon Schmidt (Associated Press, 2002) travelling from Phoenix to Sacramento illustrates what appears to be a wider-spread occurrence.

- According to Schmidt, she was pulled aside by a male screener who conducted a body search by sliding his hands under her sweater.
- Cathleen Reinke, a 29-year-old executive was reportedly (*Philadelphia Daily News*, 2002) called aside for a pat down when she passed through Philadelphia International Airport. The male screener allegedly rubbed the wand all over her body, and then proceeded with a manual rubdown over her waist, hips, backside, and inside her legs, despite her request for a female screener. Distressed about the indecent assault, she immediately complained to security officials and Philadelphia police where the special victim unit proceeded to investigate the incident.

While no reliable statistics are available on the total number of such incidents to date, Arizona Attorney General Janet Napolitano said her office has received more than 50 complaints. Steps taken by passengers to report incidents of inappropriate screening experiences are important in curbing blatant misuse of power resulting in sexual assault.

Unwanted fondling has also plagued female cabin crew members, resulting in two letters of complaint by Pat Friend, president of the Association of Flight Attendants, who lodged official complaints to federal Transportation Secretary Norman Mineta on 9 November 2001 and again on 7 February 2002 about 'illicit touching' and 'unprofessional and abusive behaviour' by airport security screeners. Friend cited a number of examples:

- One female flight attendant passing through security at San Francisco International Airport 'was repeatedly rubbed all over her body with a screening wand wielded by a male security guard'. In Portland, a pregnant flight attendant set off a metal detector with the buttons of her maternity blouse. The screener then subjected her to a body search and in the process pressed against her belly.
- A male flight attendant in Boston was ordered to 'open his belt and the top of his pants and to shake them in front of passengers in the boarding area'. His anger and public humiliation only increased after discovering a passenger on his flight knitting with two long needles, items that were supposedly banned.

Flight crew members experience similar abuses, while believing they are being subjected to more searches than the passengers, or airport workers with access to commercial airliners. Mounting frustration has been evident in reported confrontations with screeners (*Philadelphia Inquirer*, 2002) that have led to the arrests of at least three pilots. Demands for special treatment by crew member labour associations reveal sensitivity to an apparent assault on their professionalism; however, they are are inconsistent with demands for an equally-administered security system nationwide. Pointing to El Al Airlines as having the best aviation security system in the world, they fail to acknowledge that it requires its flight crews, even its company president, to go through the same checks as its passengers. No exceptions are made, something that can be readily accommodated by the airline culture and operational size.

The alleged abuses by some airport security screeners at a number of airports in the US are being investigated as announced by the Secretary of Transportation Norman Mineta. So far, his office could only confirm four complaints about guards groping female fliers, while 18 passengers called a Federal Aviation Administration hotline between mid-October 2001 and 31

January 2002 to complain about treatment they received from security screeners nationwide, including improper touching.

Erring on the side of caution delayed various flights on 28 April 2002, when the FBI investigated suspiciously-acting passengers of Pakistani, Saudi Arabian and Middle Eastern descent, who were detained for questioning. Suspicions were raised due to a variety of alerts caused by cash payments for tickets, lack of luggage, and one-way ticket purchases. In all cases, these passengers were eventually cleared to continue their travel as reported by the press (Associated Press, 2002; Reuters, 2002; *Washington Post*, 2002).

According to reports (*New York Times*, 2002), the Transportation Department received more than 130 complaints about discrimination at airports, 30 involving passengers who were refused permission to board. The number of discrimination complaints reached a peak of 13 during the week of 21 October 2001. Since February 2002, complaints have fallen to about one per week. Mohamed Nimer, research director for the Council on American-Islamic Relations, indicated in an interview that most of the discrimination cases brought to the attention of the council involve 'outright prejudice'. Despite civil rights, in the climate of fear prevailing after the terrorist attacks of 11 September, some people are not comfortable flying in an aeroplane that has people of Middle Eastern, Arab or Muslim backgrounds. Civil rights groups have already filed lawsuits against four American airlines (Reuters, 2002).

Security Breaches

The types of security breaches, including some hoaxes, are wide-ranging:

- The most bizarre case making news headlines (*New York Times*, 2002) involved a French cabin crew member operating a Virgin Atlantic Airways flight en route from London to Orlando on 19 January 2002. Writing bogus bomb threats on the lavatory mirror and a sickness bag, he claimed to have found these messages. Following his report to the flight crew, the captain diverted the aircraft to Iceland. Charged with interference with crew members and endangering the lives of crew members and passengers, the young man could face up to 20 years in prison and $250,000 in fines.
- At Boston's Logan International Airport, a man reportedly set off a metal detector (Associated Press, 2002). However, he was not rescreened due to an apparent shift change, resulting in the evacuation of the United Airlines concourse, affecting three flights and 300 passengers. A

maintenance worker prompted the evacuation of the same concourse on 26 March by mistakenly shutting off the metal detector.
- According to reports (Associated Press, 2002), on 14 April 2002, a picture of Osama bin Laden found inside an overhead bin on American Flight 312 to Dallas resulted in both delaying the flight and a search of McAllen-Miller International Airport terminal.
- In another incident at Louis Armstrong International Airport on 6 May, a man was reportedly (Associated Press, 2002) arrested after two loaded handguns were discovered in his backpack during a random check.

Passenger Attitudes

Passengers' heroic attempts on United Airlines Flight 93 – hijacked on 11 September and which ultimately crashed in Pennsylvania, killing all on board – created a new resolve in the travelling public. Inspired by the desperate attempts to subdue the hijackers, passenger behaviour signals a new respect for crew members and a willingness to come to the rescue.

Supporting this current trend are findings of a survey conducted by culture change group MSB and an Internet research group myvoice.co.uk in the United Kingdom. Of more than 400 respondents, nearly 50 per cent expressed their willingness to take action in case of a hijacking. A further 40 per cent indicated that they would conspire with fellow passengers to subdue hijackers, while 6 per cent confirmed that they would act on their own.

A total of 56 per cent of respondents confirmed that they are now more suspicious of fellow passengers, with 70 per cent prepared to report their observations to the cabin crew. Regarding the state of airport security post-11 September, 65 per cent feel that security is not stringent enough, while 46 per cent believe airport security has already returned to previous standards. Rating the importance of deterrents to hijackings, on-board air marshals were considered the most effective strategy, followed by reinforced cockpit doors, more thorough security checks and banning sharp instruments on board.

These attitudes are not surprising, following the events of 11 September. Positive passenger/cabin crew relations are key to on-board safety and social peace (Dahlberg, 2001). However, passenger intervention in cases of on-board incidents cannot be taken for granted nor is it necessarily effective. Following a luncheon speech on 21 March 2002, I asked the audience (members of the Aircrew Association of Southern Alberta) for their response. Their answer was resoundingly negative. Questions that the aviation industry has to address, rather than promoting or taking effective passenger intervention for granted, are:

- will passengers' current willingness to comply with cabin crews be a permanent change for the better, or will the cooperative mood to assist eventually subside;
- is it the travelling public's role to fill the gap;
- do fellow passengers boarding a flight secretly search out a physical fit, and ethnical neutral male in his prime, hoping that he can be relied on for in-flight emergencies;
- are cabin crew members, once selected for their physical charms and ability to communicate in several languages, haunted by their professional and physical inadequacies, and would training overcome the competency gaps?

Weary of causing suspicion and attracting special attention, passengers' cooperative attitude may well be a psychological overhang eight months after the terrorist attacks. Firstly, passenger interventions on United Airlines Flight 93 were not successful, when considering the total loss of the aircraft and its occupants. As addressed in my book *Air Rage – The Underestimated Safety Risk*, vigilante-type intervention by passengers has already resulted in two unnecessary deaths, although no criminal charges have ever been laid. Arguing that a call for onboard medical assistance by a doctor is no different than calling on passenger intervention during an on-board incident is unconvincing. A doctor has certified expertise in diagnostic and treatment skills, whereas passengers intervening in subduing an out-of-control passenger have not. This poses significant problems for cabin crews, untrained in controlling perpetrators, and passengers, whose violent defence actions can lead to tragedy.

The Role of Cabin Crew

The terrorist attacks of 11 September have caused a paradigm shift. With the increased reliance on passenger involvement to back up cabin crews, the meaning of 'we are here for your safety' might well be the battle cry of passengers coming to the defence of airline workers. The public should voice its thoughts on the role of cabin crews (Dahlberg, 2002) in the new millennium, and which physical and psychological attributes would instil public confidence. What does the travelling public expect of cabin crews, based on the clear understanding that:

- flight crews no longer can provide physical back-up;
- air marshals are not assigned to every flight;
- the role of the air marshal is restricted to hijacking and terrorist events on board;
- cabin crews are not trained in self-protection methods;
- cabin crews are not trained to protect passengers from physical assaults;
- airlines expect passengers to assist cabin crews in case of a major onboard incident.

Current regulations do not require cabin crew members to be capable of managing passenger incidents involving violence on board. As per Annex 6, Part I – Provisions Relating to Cabin Crew – ICAO, cabin crews are assigned by the operator *'in order to effect a safe and expeditious evacuation of the aeroplane, and the necessary functions to be performed in an emergency or a situation requiring emergency evacuation'*. Regulators and enforcement have progressed in responding to the threat of passenger interference with crew members since 1996. As a consequence, the perception of cabin crews' role has changed, and requires an amendment to Annex 6, Part I. Acknowledging the new reality, the legislation should be broadened to reflect not only safe evacuation but should also reflect a threat to the safety of the aircraft in flight and its occupants.

Cabin crew members should be capable of addressing what occurs in the cabin without the incidental and fortuitous assistance of passengers (Dahlberg, 2002). Calling on passengers as a last resort is not in line with the promises of safe transportation. Leaving the role and responsibilities of cabin crews at status quo is irresponsible and playing roulette with fate, hoping that some passengers are willing to risk their lives in defence of the professionals who are supposedly selected and trained to secure passenger safety (Dahlberg, 2001).

Improved security costs the airlines: cockpit door modification, additional training, delays incurred due to hoax security threats and inadvertent security breaches, affect the bottom line. Regardless of the additional threat of on-board terrorism, passenger health, both physical and mental, are of continued concern (Lucas, 2002), requiring greater cabin crew awareness and psychological skills in diagnosing symptoms to choose appropriate intervention.

Training does not conclusively guarantee performance, but it may instil greater confidence.

The incident of the 'shoe bomber' on American Airlines' Flight 63, Paris to Miami on 22 December 2001, once again threatened any sense of security, however spurious. At a first glance, there might be just another security problem, quickly responded to by new requirements for random checks of footwear by airport security personnel. This was also the case on American Airlines' Flight 1238, 8 October 2001, when a man with a history of mental illness stormed the cockpit and was subdued by passengers and crew members. The majority of cases requiring passenger intervention occurs when mentally disturbed passengers or passengers heavily under the influence of alcohol, engage in physical violence on board. Again, security screening prior to boarding was not an effective means of identifying the potential perpetrator prior to the flight. The fact remains that, regardless of expense, systems and people are fallible.

At second glance, however, there might also be a problem with the role and selection criteria of cabin crew, if passengers are to be relied upon to come to the rescue of flight attendants incapable of subduing a dangerous passenger. The frequency of passenger intervention in serious incidents suggests that they are performing defence tasks that cabin crews are clearly incapable of performing themselves. The basic premises have changed.

In the US, discussions point in a new direction. On 27 November Patricia Friend, International President of the Association of Flight Attendants (AFA), addressed a number of on-board safety issues in her testimony before the House Committee on Government Reform on Federal Regulations Needed to Ensure Aviation Security. Two issues raised are of particular interest. On flight attendants' access to non-lethal defensive devices in the passenger cabin, Friend states:

> But the new law fails to require flight attendant access to non-lethal devices in the cabin. Flight attendants are the first and last line of defense for passengers. We are responsible for ensuring that a security threat doesn't reach the cockpit. To effectively meet that responsibility, we must be given the means to defend ourselves, our passengers, and the flight deck from intruders. You can accomplish this by ensuring that flight attendants will be trained and qualified in the use of an appropriate non-lethal weapon stored in a sealed or locked compartment somewhere on the aircraft.

Secondly, there is the issue of licensing flight attendants 'in order to ascertain control and a level of proficiency'. The Association believes that licensing flight attendants will ensure the public that its front line workers are trained and capable of handling the wide range of their responsibilities.

The call for arms indicates cabin crews in the US are facing up to a fundamental shift in their role, leading to behaviour requirements completely opposed to their traditional roles of service providers, care-givers and safety professionals. Without a doubt, a new set of behaviour markers needs to be developed for selecting new recruits.

Cabin Crew Selection

Cabin crews are the airlines most critical resource for achieving a safe and secure cabin environment. Friend, representing more than 50,000 flight attendants in the USA, called on American carriers to 'provide the workers on the plane with the proper training and defensive capabilities we need'. This underlines the fundamental change in the perception of their role. At the heart of the matter are selection criteria in line with the changed social and security environment. They require long-term considerations, since the demographics and aptitudes of the current cabin crew labour force are largely based on an outdated set of marketing criteria (Dahlberg, 1997).

Considering the lifestyle appeal of easy access to free travel and other benefits, the fun factor for prospective cabin crew members has been eliminated. The possibility of facing a terrorist is chilling. Appropriate response capabilities are of a different nature than those required to respond to an aircraft emergency or accident. Not previously addressed in cabin crew selection, mental and physical predisposing factors will play a significant part in handling these types of situations on board. Based on history, one can only deduce that self-interest silenced previous proposals to ICAO for licensing flight attendants, which met with significant opposition from IATA and IFALPA.

Historically, the labour pool supplying female candidates for cabin crews was registered nurses, clearly addressing the effects of the physical cabin environment of the early aircrafts used for passenger transport (Dahlberg, 2001). Males, on the other hand, were chosen for their past experience as stewards on railways and cruise ships. With the introduction of large jet aircrafts in the late 1960s, international air travel prompted the need for multilingual language capabilities to communicate with the increasingly global customer. Airline marketing treated cabin crews as part of the overall commercial product and its image.

The impact of the 11 September terrorist suicide attacks, heightened by governments' resolve to deal with the problem worldwide, clearly points to a long-term and very difficult battle with no victory in sight. Considering the facts that airport security and the declared war on terrorism will not guarantee the safety of innocent citizens and that the sky marshal programmes are limited, the role of cabin crews will have to be considered in the overall strategy to deter terrorist attacks on board.

New Behavioural Markers

With these prospects, new behavioural markers for cabin crews become even more important. A background in security-related professions should be considered. But is it possible to achieve quality service with a staff coming from the military or security-related professions? I discussed this issue with Don Porter, joint managing director of culture change specialist MSB Ltd, based in the United Kingdom. Since airline service in the traditional sense is not easily reconciled with characteristics of security-related behaviours, I was looking for evidence that it is unusual however not impossible to achieve. Don Porter cited the successful service quality training conducted for the Yeomen Wardens, the permanent custodians of the crown jewels in London as such a case in point.

Customer perceptions of quality service (Dahlberg, 2001, 1997) include safety (Kracj and Pausch, 1998; Polak, 1997; Becker, 1992). The five quality dimensions of reliability, assurance, tangibles, empathy and responsiveness do not only relate to service activities but also to all aspects of safety-related duties. At the core are assurance and the ability to convey trust and confidence (Dahlberg, 2001). Trust and confidence stem from contact and connection with passengers. Easing on-board tension, handling irregular situations, dealing with disruptive passengers, or violence due to hijacking and terrorist situations are situations when cabin crews are put to the test. In the post-11 September environment, reliability includes security and the way in which passengers experience cabin crews' abilities to perform security-related activities in-flight. At large, the quality service movement has been poorly translated by the airline industry by failing to achieve synergy between service and safety (Dahlberg, 1997). This is the deciding moment for a new understanding and for closing the gap.

In the early days of air travel, passengers felt reassured that registered nurses in the capacity of 'stewardesses' were able to attend to the physical side effects of air travel plaguing passengers. The knowledge that cabin crews with military or security background are at the service of today's passenger would undoubtedly have an equally positive effect and be a deterrent for passenger misconduct. The marketing value of the traditional cabin crew member has experienced a slow and long-standing decline. It is urgent that airlines wake up to this reality. The old strategies to buy back customer confidence with superficial and short-lived gimmicks at great cost are missing the target. Understanding the fundamental changes in society, airlines have a unique opportunity to address core issues and at the same time fill a marketing gap (Dahlberg, 1997).

Opposition to such thinking will come from two major platforms. It will be argued that airlines are not in the security business but rather in the service and safety business. Security is a national issue and therefore the government's responsibility. This position is unconvincing since, up to the recent changes, airlines in the US and Canada were responsible for airport screening and obviously did a poor job at that. Furthermore, security is a responsibility encompassing all players in civil aviation. Not addressing the mute but vast gap created by the traditional conflict of service and safety perpetuates the insular vision and dangerous self-deception of the airline industry.

The second argument surrounds the logistics of such an approach. Large, established airlines operating within the context of mature labour contracts will have to consider the potential for greater wage demands as one of the dominant issues. Unable to change the demographics of their labour force at will these airlines will be less inclined to consider a massive cultural change over a short period of time.

As already discussed in my book *Air Rage – The Underestimated Safety Risk*, cabin crew commitment to the profession is predominantly based on fulfilling self-interests (Dahlberg, 2001) rather than altruism. In my 25 years experience in in-flight services management, improving cabin crew assertiveness was far less likely to succeed than toning down assertiveness.

Faced with this reality, finding new alternatives is not easy and holds no guarantees. But then again, when it comes to managing the human aspects of air travel, airlines need to address the societal risks on board with a fresh perspective. Drawing recruits as prospective cabin crew members from the untapped labour market of the military, enforcement or security profession would lead to new opportunities, although an unfamiliar one for the airlines. Nevertheless, a more suitable mindset, a proven commitment to putting their lives on the line and training in assessing and dealing with dangerous situations would be worthy assets to build on.

Training

Airline workers confronted with potential terrorists or deranged individuals should be able to handle these situations on their own. In the interim, revised training standards, as defined by the FAA with regard to hijacking and self-defence, will address some of the new realities. Although demanded by crew labour associations, some cabin crew members are uncomfortable when faced with the possibility of defending themselves against the brutal force of a physical attack. Comments such as 'I was not hired for this' express the deep-seated anxieties shaking their confidence.

With the self-defence industry flourishing in the aftermath of 11 September, new problems will arise. Assessing the suitability of these approaches on board is essential, considering the range of different methods available. Only a select few would be considered appropriate on board, while rigorous selection criteria would severely limit the pool of potential cabin crew applicants. Enforcement agencies and experts in tactical training warn that competency is not achieved by once-a-year training. They argue that it requires extensive mental and physical training for months, and continuing on-going practice thereafter.

Building on this view supports my earlier contention that new behavioural markers in line with the emerging security demands on cabin crews are needed. The most appropriate candidates for this job would be those offering traits, and experience in line with traits, favoured by military, enforcement and security professionals. On that basis, job-specific training has a greater chance of succeeding and reducing the risk of inappropriate responses, including vigilante type actions by well-meaning passengers.

Regardless of what airlines determine to be the ideal candidate, key components of any training dealing with on-board violence, (be it passenger misconduct, hijacking or terrorism) are decision-making criteria leading to strategies of escalation or de-escalation.

The current training approaches are less effective with an established workforce because negative attitudes and counterproductive behaviours are well entrenched. In a largely autonomous work environment, little opportunity exists to reinforce new behaviours such as diffusing on-board conflict or engaging in tactical responses. Achieving a culture change is costly and requires significant management commitment, resources and a meaningful reward system.

Security, Contact and Connection

At the core, a sense of security comes from contact and connection with people. If the contact between the airline representative and the customer is nonexistent or fails, the outcome might be physical, psychological, or financial (Dahlberg, 2001). Illustrating the former is a lawsuit filed by a Montreal businessman against Air France. According to reports (*Calgary Herald*, 2002), he was denied his religious rights to pray en route to Paris. The in-charge cabin crew member, a male, allegedly told him in French: 'This is an airplane and not a place for occult practices; return to your seat immediately.' The incident reportedly occurred two hours prior to arrival while the Jewish businessman was praying 'in a barely audible and unobtrusive fashion' in the back of the aircraft.

The failure of cabin crews to relate appropriately to those under their care is also revealed in a report (*The Financial Post*, 2002) involving excessive alcohol consumption. Under the headline 'Nicholson's Former Lover Arrested in Winnipeg', the incident culminated in an alleged assault on one cabin crew member and resulted in an unscheduled landing of a Virgin Airlines' flight en route from Los Angeles to London, England, in Winnipeg, Canada. Because of the woman's background, the reporter played much emphasis on her long-term affair with actor Jack Nicholson but provided little detail on what preceded the incident. It appears she became intoxicated and later fell unconscious. The questions are, how did the cabin crew contribute to her deteriorating condition and what was being done to prevent her to becoming verbally and physically abusive? Locked in a simplistic interpretation of their role, emotionally-disconnected staff frequently fail to diffuse such situations, thereby increasing the risk (Dahlberg, 2001).

The trend for escalated responses in cases of passenger noncompliance certainly sends a message to the public while underscoring the legal position of airline employees. What defines this response is the shadow of a self-righteous attitude where power means more than professional integrity. Training can make a difference in appropriately choosing between de-escalated and escalated responses. First, it needs to clearly identify how to recognise symptoms of stress leading to noncompliance (Dahlberg, 2001) versus high-level security risks.

As discussed in depth in my book *Air Rage – The Underestimated Safety Risk*, passenger misconduct is a complex and multidimensional issue. Chapter 6, 'Passenger Risk Management', presents the *interactive model*, a framework for understanding and managing causes and contributing factors to passenger misconduct. The model describes four key elements: individual risk factors associated with the perpetrator and the victim; workplace risk factors; and outcome of abuse or violent acts. First, there is the perpetrator's predisposition to violence based on individual risk factors. These include:

- history of violent behaviour;
- alcohol and drug abuse;
- mental health;
- temperament;
- stress tolerance;
- coping skills.

Since violence does not occur in isolation but is triggered during interaction with the victim, the successful outcome of these situations depends on the traits that make an individual more vulnerable to becoming a victim:

- age;
- appearance;
- experience;
- health;
- skills;
- gender;
- personality;
- attitudes;
- expectations.

Airlines need to recruit individuals who are not predisposed to being a victim and train them how to use contact and connection with passengers to increase a sense of security onboard. Redefined by the new social and political reality, traditional airline marketing criteria for cabin crew recruits are outdated and simply add unnecessary risks into the workplace. On the other hand, skills, personality, attitudes and expectations of recruits with experience in the military, enforcement or security professions would possibly reduce such risks. Workplace risk factors (Dahlberg, 2001) focus on specific aspects such as:

- physical cabin environment;
- aircraft type and length of flight;
- day versus night flights;
- charter flights;
- operational irregularities;
- compliance.

Contributing to these risks are organisational factors. Corporate policies and procedures, role conflict, service product design and communication (Dahlberg, 2002) are failing in acknowledging their contribution to increasing risks. Unless airlines are willing to address these issues, training efforts will continue to be undermined and credibility sacrificed.

Effects on Air Rage

Driven by events, new anti-terrorist laws and economic consequences increasingly regulate behaviour. Since they are forced to make adjustments, a surge of unwanted behaviours erupts in the process while passengers, together with the aviation community, face new stresses. The trauma of the terrorist attacks is still fresh and nerves are raw, especially in the United States.

According to statistics posted by the FAA for 2001 involving enforcement actions, a total of 317 incidents of interference with the duties of a crew member (violations of 14 CFR 91.11, 121.580 and 135.120) were noted compared to a total of 321 for 2000. For the period of 1 January to 26 June 2002, a total of 83 incidents were reported. Considering these figures, little has changed, at least in the US.

Air rage as a media headline has all but disappeared in the eight months following the attacks, only to be replaced by almost daily news headlines focusing on security issues. Shifting incidents from interference with crew members from the aircraft cabin to the ground, on-board passenger behaviour appeared to be more compliant. According to reports (CNN, 2002) one of a few exceptions involved a Delta Airline flight en route from Atlanta to Madrid that diverted to St John's, Newfoundland. In another incident, a passenger suspected to be suffering from medical or drug problems was reportedly restrained after an altercation with crew members (kansascity.com, 2002). In another case reported by the media (*Boston Globe*, 2002), a passenger with a history of mental illness demanded to be taken off a Delta Airlines flight from Logan, prompting the flight to return to the gate.

Although anti-terrorist legislation has initially curbed on-board incidents of passenger misconduct, the long-term countermeasures aimed at hijackings and terrorist attacks do not eliminate the need to deal with incidents caused by other factors contributing to on-board violence. The experience of 11 September has proved that escalation should determine tactical responses to such threats while, in most cases of passenger misconduct, de-escalation is preferable.

The differences lie in crucial ideological opposites. Without extending the discussion from the narrow perspective of fear and, at worst, paranoia, the scope of the security measures defined by the airline industry and regulatory authorities will remain dangerously myopic.

Next Steps

Roles and Responsibilities

Clearly, the role and responsibilities of cabin crews deserve redefinition. They are the single largest group of airline professionals who share the same on-board space with passengers and are horrified when some of them reveal themselves as terrorists. An armed pilot in the cockpit is of little value when such a situation occurs. Arguments in favour of flight crews carrying guns use *self*-defence as the major issue, not the defence of their team members, the cabin crew or the passengers. This leaves cabin crews as the greatest on-board resource but also the most vulnerable and tactically useless, considering the need for an all-encompassing strategy to combat terrorism.

Selecting new recruits should be conducted by professionals, not cabin crew members on special assignment, a common practice in the industry. A process may include psychological testing to ascertain the most suitable attitudes for dealing with the new reality of complex workplace risks.

Joint Training

Joint training with flight crews, so far a rather *ad hoc* affair, should be mandatory, especially with regard to security measures. With the vote by the House Transportation Committee's aviation subcommittee endorsing legislation on 19 June 2002 that could result in arming more than 1,000 US pilots in the next two years, crew coordination and communication are more crucial than ever. In the meantime, this development does little either to encourage on-board teamwork or to protect passengers and cabin crews from imminent harm.

Assessing the need for de-escalated versus escalated responses is at the core of maintaining social peace on board. Strategising their service activities to reduce passenger stress and using their heightened observation skills to assess abnormal behaviour, cabin crews maximise the opportunity for early and targeted intervention (Dahlberg, 2001). Poor diagnostic skills and deficient passenger relations lead to over-reaction and costly measures. Such was likely to be the case on a reported incident of post-11 September jitters (*New York Times*, 2002). A passenger aboard an American Trans Air flight from Chicago to New York's La Guardia airport became suspicious of a group of people from India when they allegedly switched seats and passed each other notes. The concerned passenger alerted a cabin crew member who in turn advised the captain. According to the information received, authorities called in two F16 fighter jets to accompany the flight to its destination. The FBI and the NYDP terrorism task force subsequently interviewed the group. It turned out that there were no grounds for any concerns since the group simply was excited about their first trip to New York, where they were scheduled to perform. Had information on the manifest concerning these passengers alerted the cabin crew or had they made some personal contact with these passengers earlier on, this type of incident could have been avoided.

Complacency is the silent enemy of maintaining a safe aviation system. In the case of cabin crews, routine tasks dull situational awareness. It takes significant creativity and ingenuity to keep cabin crews motivated after they have completed their training. From personal observation, it takes an average of six to eight weeks after initial training for cabin crew members to settle into a state of comfort and complacency, unless they are self-motivated and high performance oriented.

Cabin Crew Leadership

Cabin crew leadership plays a key role in counteracting complacency and requires intelligent and consistent management support for long-term success. Lead cabin crew members should be selected based on newly-defined leadership criteria and should undergo a rigorous qualification programme. Long-standing contractual obstacles should be examined and addressed.

In line with effective leadership, crew briefings need to be focused on safety and security, especially related to productive passenger relations. The passenger manifest facilitates the anticipation of special needs or service requirements. Team members should be expected to know technical service procedures associated with their position on board in order to free up valuable briefing time. Detailed strategies to use service, including service downtimes to establish passenger relations, require constant effort to address the dangers of complacency. Addressed in detail in the training programme developed by Dahlberg & Associates, complementary modules focus on cabin crew motivation based on self-protection models for mental preparation. Planning, organising and follow-up by the lead cabin crew member is the most effective way to ensure that symptoms of potential passenger misconduct are dealt with in a timely and efficient manner.

Product Design and Delivery

- Eliminate frivolous service design that creates unreasonable passenger expectations.
- Focus on physical needs based on the length of flight, time of departure and passenger demographics.
- Clearly communicate what to expect on scheduled flights and pay attention to irregular operations.
- In short, identify associated risks with less than responsible decisions, especially complimentary on-board alcohol service.
- Design the on-board product with two things in mind, physical comfort and stress reduction.

Service delivery should be timely but unhurried. Too much service is equally detrimental to cabin crews' ability to maintain a high level of situational awareness as is too little service resulting in unattended passengers (Dahlberg, 2001). Night flights are particularly vulnerable, with cabin crews taking lengthy breaks. Similarly, movie times often lack cabin monitoring of any kind.

Conclusions

The curb of disruptive on-board passenger behaviour is a result of sweeping legal, regulatory and economic engineering during the post-11 September period. Counteracting these current improvements are incidents of airport security breaches during the eight months following the implementation of these measures. Apart from any nuisance factors and their associated cost, progress is being made. Although it is too early to measure the long-term effects on disruptive behaviour prevalent in civil aviation, escalated response on the ground has temporarily benefited cabin crews.

A false sense of competency and complacency will continue to be the major threat to aviation security. Once security measures have been fully implemented and accepted as routine, stagnating cabin crew roles, lack of vigilance and threat fatigue will be a fertile combination for greater numbers of incidents to occur.

Air traffic numbers are unlikely to return to pre-11 September levels soon and play a factor in reducing on-board incidents. Inconsistent security measures, friction at screening points and increased check-in times have added to passenger discontent with air travel. With the government now in charge of airport security in the US and Canada, airlines absolve themselves of criticism against long delays and passenger complaints. As Don Porter states:

> Passengers rarely see what goes on behind the scenes at airport terminals and it is therefore imperative that all customer facing security staff deliver convincing and reassuring service to passengers. Staff in any industry can only be expected to deliver high levels of service if they are well trained, motivated and rewarded.

Adding to the traditional conflict of service and safety, security-related issues are now the dominating source of complaints. Passengers need to experience a feeling of safety, reassured by efficient, courteous and competent staff respectful of civil rights in a convenient system. This is far from reality.

Looking for new opportunities to re-establish trust in civil aviation, airlines need to consider more than periodic improvements to the tangible service product. The widening scope of challenges facing cabin crews cannot be simply addressed with training but requires a fresh and bold look at new requirements for selection and recruiting. Industry's continuous resistance to considering safety and security as a potential for marketing (Dahlberg, 1997, 1995) fails to connect with the traveling public's readiness to respond favourably.

References

Associated Press (2002), 'Air Marshals' Future Full of Questions', 14 January.
Associated Press (2002), 'When Hands-on Security gets out of Hand, Where's the Recourse?', 28 February.
Associated Press (2002), 'Boston's Logan Airport Evacuated Again', 29 March.
Associated Press (2002), 'Feds Probe bin Laden Photo on Jet', 18 April.
Associated Press (2002), 'Man Passes Airport Security with Guns', 7 May.
Becker, T.A. (1992), 'Passenger Perceptions and the Marketing of Airline Safety – The Awakening of Airline Safety', White Paper, San Diego.
Boston Globe (2002), 'Flight Crews say Checks Unfairly Target Them – Claim Overkill, and Groping of Attendants', 4 February.
Boston Globe (2002), 'Delta Flight Passenger Arrested', 29 March.
BTS Press release (2002), 7 May.
Calgary Herald (2002), 'Screeners Reject Offer over Money, Recognition', 1 May.
CNN (2002), 'Delta Jet Diverted to Newfoundland', 3 April.
Dahlberg, A. (2001), *Air Rage – The Underestimated Safety Risk*, Aldershot: Ashgate.
Dahlberg, A. (2001), 'Air Rage – A Human Factors Issue – Managing For Prevention', in *Proceedings of the Tenth International Symposium on Aviation Psychology*, Columbus, Ohio, March 5-8.
Dahlberg, A. (2001), 'Airlines Need to Turn more of their Attention to Passenger-related Human Factors', *ICAO JOURNAL*, Vol. 56, No. 5, pp. 15–17, 28.

Dahlberg, A. (2001), 'Les devoirs des passagers – En avion, les voyageurs ont aussi un role à jouer pour assurer leur sécurité', *La Press*, 15 September, p. A24.
Dahlberg, A. (2002), 'Coffee, Tea or Martial Arts?', *Calgary Herald*, 6 January, p. A13.
Dahlberg, A. (2002), 'Autodefense à bord', *La Press*, 12 January, p. A9.
Dahlberg, A. (1997), 'Selling Safety', *Insight IATA*, Vol. 5, Issue 1, January/February, pp. 10, 42–4.
Dahlberg, A. (1997), 'Flyer's Rage', *Insight IATA*, Vol. 5, Issue 4, July/August, pp. 30–31, 46.
Dahlberg, A. (1997), 'Customer Perceptions of Cabin Safety Management', *Proceedings of the 14th Annual International Aircraft Cabin Safety Symposium*.
FAA Fact Sheet (2001), 11 November.
Financial Post (2002), 'Nicholson's Former Lover Arrested in Winnipeg', 22 June, p. A6.
Kansascity.com (2002), 'Kansas Man Charged with Threatening Flight Crew', 4 June.
Krajc, T. and Pausch, R. (1998), *The Perception and Significance of Flight Safety from the Customer's Point of View in the Deregulated Market*, Darmstadt: Technische University Darmstadt.
Los Angeles Times (2002), 'Air Marshals' Future Full of Questions', 14 January.
Lucas, G. (2002), 'Mental Health on board. Flights of Hazard', Royal Society of Medicine Conference.
New York Times (2002), 'Charges of Airport Groping Continue', 20 March.
New York Times (2002), 'Flight Attendant Ordered Held for Threats Made Aboard Plane', 29 March.
New York Times (2002), 'Bolliwood Farce: Indian actress and family detained', 18 July.
New York Times (2002), 'Military Jets Escort Plane to La Guardia', 17 July.
Philadelphia Daily News (2002), 'Touched by a "Pervert"', 26 February.
Philadelphia Inquirer (2002), 'Unions Blame Security Problems in Firing of Pilot after Confrontation', 30 January.
Polak, J. (1997), *Sicherheit als Entscheidungsfactor fuer die Wahl der Fluggesellschaft*, Munich: Fachhochschule Muenchen.
Reuters (2002), 'Muslim Girl had to Remove Headscarf at US Airport', 8 January.
Transport Canada Airport Security Working Group (2002), Interim Report, 7 May.
Washington Post (2002), 'Crew to Guards: Lighten up – airline employees, screeners often at odds over procedures', 2 February.

Chapter 9

Passenger Attention to Safety Information

Lauren J. Thomas

The way that passengers will behave in an emergency is often dependent on how well they have prepared for the situation in which they find themselves. Passenger preparedness can be a significant factor in survivability, evacuation efficiency and injury rates should an emergency arise. For example, the National Transportation Safety Board investigated 21 accidents that occurred between 1962 and 1984. They found that:

> passenger's risk of injury or death in these accidents could have been reduced had they: 1) paid attention to the flight attendant's oral safety briefings and demonstrations; 2) read the safety card to familiarize themselves with the location and operation of safety equipment; and 3) been better motivated and thus better prepared to act correctly during an emergency situation (NTSB, 1985, p. 5).

In some of these cases, not only were passengers generally very poorly prepared, but sometimes they behaved inappropriately, or even contrary to cabin crew instructions.

Because of the association between paying attention to the safety information and passenger survival, the regulatory authorities require all operators to brief passengers on emergency procedures. In the United Kingdom, the Air Navigation Order requires operators to provide a briefing to passengers on the position and method of use of emergency exits, safety belts, oxygen equipment, lifejackets, floor path lighting systems and any other equipment intended for use by passengers in the event of an emergency (ANO, 1997). Similarly, in the United States, Federal Aviation Regulations require passengers to receive a briefing on smoking, emergency exits, seat belts and flotation devices (FAR 121).

Although the operators are required to provide this safety information, it is often disregarded by passengers. The reasons why passengers fail to pay attention to potentially life-saving information are many and varied. For example, passengers may believe that the probability of survival in the event of a crash is so low that paying attention to the safety information is a waste of time. In fact, the vast majority of accidents are survivable. One recent study showed that, of all accidents to Part 121 carriers during the period 1983 to 2000, the overall survivability rate was 95.7 per cent (NTSB, 2001). Several research studies have been conducted to examine why passengers do not pay attention to the safety information provided.

One study investigated the differences between people who paid attention to passenger safety information, and those who did not (Johnson, 1979). Using a structured interview schedule, researchers conducted telephone interviews with a selection of 231 people who had flown on commercial aircraft at least twice in the previous two years. The researchers defined 'attenders' as people who had said that they had previously paid attention to safety briefings, and who also said that they intended to pay attention to the information on future flights. The 'non-attenders' were defined as people who said that they did not pay attention to the safety information, and who expressed no intention of doing so in the future. The results indicated that the non-attenders were more likely than attenders to be male. Non-attenders were also younger and more highly educated than the attenders. Non-attenders were more likely to have flown more often, usually flying alone and on business trips, while those who paid attention to the safety information were more likely to fly in the company of someone they knew, and were more likely to fly for pleasure. Finally, non-attenders were also more likely to report that paying attention to the safety information was a waste of time.

In another study, Fennell and Muir (1992) sent questionnaires, via travel agents, to a sample of air passengers. The questionnaire asked respondents about the pre-departure safety briefing, and the role of the cabin crew on board the aircraft. One of the main findings was that passengers thought the pre-departure safety information would be more effective if it was introduced appropriately, perhaps by telling passengers that the safety equipment on all aircraft differs, and that it is therefore in their own best interests to pay attention to the safety information. Passengers also thought that the cabin crew should appear to be more interested in presenting the information, perhaps reminding people that the information could save lives. While operators may be reluctant to include such information in their safety briefings, perhaps arguing that such an introduction would be likely to cause passengers unnecessary anxiety and alarm, this is not backed up by the research evidence.

Passengers in this research also ranked various cabin crew tasks in order of importance. The responses indicated that passengers thought the three most important cabin crew tasks were responsibility for passenger safety in an emergency situation, helping passengers in an emergency, and informing passengers of the safety procedures. The service aspects of the cabin crew role, such as looking after passengers who become ill, being pleasant to passengers, serving meals and drinks and selling duty-free goods, were not deemed to be so important. Thus, passenger perceptions of the cabin crew role appeared to match the perspective of the regulatory authorities. Legally, cabin crew are required to be on board the aircraft for safety, rather than service, reasons.

As safety professionals, cabin crew are indeed best placed to manage and assist the passengers in an emergency situation. For example, experimental research has shown that the behaviour of the cabin crew is critical in ensuring a smooth and efficient evacuation (Cobbett and Muir, 1996). Assertive cabin crew who provided concise, positive commands and instruction, and used physical gestures and contact when appropriate, achieved significantly faster passenger evacuation rates than non-assertive cabin crew. When the cabin crew left the cabin at the start of the evacuation, to simulate situations where the cabin crew are incapacitated, the passenger evacuation rates obtained were similar to those achieved by non-assertive crew.

However, the fact that passengers appear to acknowledge this may be something of a double-edged sword. Passengers who believe that the cabin crew are responsible for passenger safety may be less likely to take responsibility for their own safety in an emergency situation. The duties and workload of the cabin crew in an emergency may make it impossible for them to provide individual assistance to every passenger. In addition, there is always the risk that, should an emergency situation arise, the cabin crew themselves may be incapacitated.

The National Transportation Safety Board recently completed a study of 46 evacuations that occurred between September 1997 and June 1999 (NTSB, 2000). As part of this study, questionnaires were sent to all passengers involved in the 30 most serious evacuations, which were defined as those involving suspected fire, actual fire, or use of the evacuation slides. Of the 457 passengers who returned their questionnaires, 54 per cent said that they had not watched the entire safety briefing because they had seen it before. Another 15 per cent said that they had not watched the entire briefing because the information it contained was common knowledge. Passengers were also divided on how effective the briefing had been. Over half of the respondents said that the briefing had not contained information specific to their evacuation. They reported that they would have liked more information on exit routes, how to use the slides, and how to get off the wing after leaving the cabin via an overwing exit.

There are no regulations which state the methods to be used in providing the most effective pre-departure briefing, although guidance supplied by the Federal Aviation Administration may be regarded as best practice (FAA, 1999). Cabin crew who conduct live briefings and demonstrations should use their own initiative to attract passenger attention, making eye contact with passengers, being animated, and using clear and distinct diction. They should also ensure that they and their colleagues are distributed evenly throughout the cabin, and that their briefings and demonstrations can be clearly seen and heard by all passengers.

The FAA also acknowledge that some operators may opt to use video recorded pre-departure safety briefings, to ensure consistency of delivery on every flight. Video recordings allow passengers to be shown safety tasks where a live demonstration is not possible, such as the correct manner of using the evacuation slide. Video technology also means that the pre-departure briefing can be given in multiple languages, including, for example, sign language. Video recorded briefings may also increase the variety and the novelty value of the briefing, by using different faces and voiceovers. Rapidly changing images may also assist in attracting, and keeping, passenger attention.

One important issue with regard to pre-departure briefings is that they should present information which is consistent both with passenger expectations, and with what will actually occur in a given emergency situation. In one study, airlines were first asked what commands the crew would use in the event of an emergency or crash landing, where passengers would be required to assume the brace position. Common responses were that the crew would instruct passengers to 'brace', 'grab your ankles', or 'go head down and stay down'. Later, passengers were asked which commands they would expect to hear, they said that they would expect to hear commands such as 'get into an emergency/crash position', 'head down', 'lean forward' or 'we're going to crash'. Approximately 30 per cent of the research participants would not have realised that a crash was about to occur if they had heard the command 'brace, brace' (Johnson, 1998). Hence, the information provided in pre-departure briefings should be consistent with passenger expectations, and with the commands and procedures that will actually be used in a given emergency situation.

As well as the pre-departure briefing, passenger safety information can be imparted via a safety card. Safety cards are used to supplement the information provided in the pre-departure briefing. A card should be available for every passenger seat, so, unlike the information contained within a pre-departure briefing, the information on the safety card remains available for reference throughout the duration of the flight. However, the evidence again suggests that passengers fail to pay attention to the safety information provided.

The NTSB (2000) safety study found that, of 431 passengers who answered the question, 68 per cent said that they did not read the safety card. A large proportion (89 per cent) of these passengers said that they had read the card provided on previous flights. Worryingly, of 399 passengers who answered the question about paying attention to both the safety briefing and the safety card, 44 per cent said that they had not paid attention to either. However, most passengers who did read the safety cards said that they found them useful, particularly with regard to identifying the location of exits. Passengers also reported that the safety cards had provided information on which exits had slides, how to use the slides, and the location of emergency lighting.

To investigate the safety cards further, the NTSB collected a sample of 22 safety cards from the operators who were involved in the case evacuations (NTSB, 2000). They found that the cards in use varied widely: 60 per cent had used coloured drawings, 8 per cent had used coloured photos, and 8 per cent had used black, red and white drawings. All of the cards contained information on the brace position and the operation of emergency exits, although some did not include information on the location of exits. The remaining information provided on the cards varied widely. Some used high quality enlargements to clearly depict the operation of the exit, while others did not. Information on how to move through the exits, use the slides, and get off the wing outside an over-wing exit was also inconsistently provided.

There are industry standards which provide an indication of the types of information that should be included on safety cards, such as the recommended practice guidelines published by the Society of Automotive Engineers (SAE, 1991). However, the presentation of such information does not necessarily guarantee that passengers will pay attention to the information, or understand it fully. The NTSB has recommended that the Federal Aviation Administration set a standard for the minimum acceptable comprehension level for safety cards (NTSB, 1985, 2000). Currently, decisions regarding the suitability of safety cards in fulfilling their intended purpose are made at the discretion and judgment of the regulator.

Safety cards often use pictorials to convey safety information to passengers. A series of related pictorials is known as a pictogram. The underlying assumption is that pictorials and pictograms, unlike text, will be universally understood. This is, of course, important considering that air travel is international in nature. Safety cards ideally need to be understood by everybody, regardless of their language, culture or country of origin. Published standards are available which provide methodologies for assessing the comprehension level of such information. For example, there is an International Standard for judging the comprehensibility of graphical symbols (ISO, 2001). The use of such methods is likely to assist in ensuring consistent levels of passenger comprehension, so that safety cards will be understood by the widest possible audience.

In a study of safety card pictorials, participants were asked to discuss which safety cards, of a sample of 50, were most likely to aid or hinder comprehension (Caird, Wheat, McIntosh and Dewar, 1997). Thirty-six pictorials from nine safety cards were used in comprehension tests, where 113 participants were asked the meaning of the pictorials. The responses were rated as incorrect, partially correct, or correct. Only 16 of the pictorials had comprehension scores of above 50 per cent. The authors concluded that 'safety card pictorials appear to represent a less than optimal universal safety language' (p. 803). This is of particular concern given that all pictorials would need to be understood before a pictogram could be interpreted correctly.

Safety card pictograms have also been evaluated. One such study was undertaken to investigate the extent to which people understood 13 black and white safety card pictograms. Among the 150 English, French and German research participants, the general comprehension levels were generally high. Comprehension was judged by deciding whether the interpretations given by participants were 'correct and complete', 'incomplete but safe', or 'wrong or unsafe'. However, the study also found that while participants were able to make general interpretations of the pictograms, they were often unable to correctly determine the specific details of the information provided (Jentsch, 1996).

Where text is used on safety cards to supplement pictorials and pictograms, careful consideration should be given to the phrases chosen. One study manipulated the phrases that were used on safety cards, and investigated the effect that this had on passenger behaviour on the evacuation slide (Johnson and Altman, 1973). To use the slide effectively, passengers should jump onto it; passengers who sit on the sill take longer to evacuate. The researchers found that safety cards that included the instruction to 'Jump – don't sit' resulted in 73.5 per cent of passengers using the slide correctly. When the cards included the instruction to 'Jump', 67.8 per cent of passengers used the slide correctly. When passengers received no briefing card, only 59.9 per cent of the passengers used the slide correctly. A passenger who sits takes approximately one-third of a second longer to evacuate than a passenger who jumps. This time differential could have a significant impact on the evacuation of 200 or 300 passengers.

There are some general principles or guidelines for the presentation of information on safety cards. For instance, it has been suggested that the information should integrate words with diagrams, and present pictograms in meaningful sequences. Pictorials are preferable to photographs, as they reduce visual clutter (Johnson, 1980). The safety cards that receive poor effectiveness ratings tend to be those that contain more text than pictorial information, and that are somewhat disorganised in their presentation of information (Schmidt and Kysor, 1987). However, because the design and information content of safety cards is known to vary so widely, the only way to be sure that a safety card will be easily understood is to conduct comprehension tests.

The issue of passenger attention to safety information is particularly important where passengers are expected to perform specific duties in the event of an emergency situation. For example, passengers seated in exit rows may be required to open the Type III exit if an evacuation of the aircraft is necessary. Such a situation occurred at Manchester in 1985. A Boeing 737 with 131 passengers and six crew on board was departing for Corfu. On take-off, the left engine suffered an uncontained failure, and a wing fuel tank access panel was penetrated. Leaking fuel rapidly ignited, and by the time the aircraft came to a complete stop, the cabin was filled with black, acrid smoke, which rapidly instilled fear and alarm among passengers.

At the instigation of other passengers, the passenger seated adjacent to the right-hand Type III exit attempted to open it as the aircraft came to a stop. She pulled on the armrest that was mounted on the hatch, in the mistaken belief that it was the hatch handle. The passenger seated next to her reached over and pulled the operating handle, and the hatch, weighting 48lbs, fell inwards, trapping them both in their seats. They were freed by a male passenger in the row behind, who lifted the hatch, and placed it on a vacant seat. It took approximately 45 seconds to make the Type III exit available, by which time many passengers had been overcome by the toxic smoke and fumes. The evacuation delays contributed to 55 fatalities (King, 1988).

The Type III exit hatch is not attached or hinged to the airframe. The hatch, once released, has to be brought back into the cabin, rotated, and disposed of. This mode of operation is counterintuitive in a self-help exit, since the hatch is intended to be operated by passengers. The hatches may weigh as much as 65lbs, and this makes handling particularly cumbersome. Many passengers have reported great difficulty in making Type III exits available in emergency situations. In one case reported by the NTSB (2000), a passenger who attempted to open the Type III exit pulled the operating handle, and put his shoulder to the hatch to push. He had not realised that the design of the hatch meant that it had to be brought into the cabin first. In another case, a passenger operated the hatch, and then had to jump through fire to get away from the aeroplane. Passengers do not always check conditions outside the aircraft before operating the exit.

Although passengers seated in the exit row are screened for their suitability to sit adjacent to the exit, screening provides no guarantee that passengers will pay attention to the safety information. At most, passengers seated in the exit row may be instructed by the cabin crew to read the safety card and ensure that they are familiar with the manner in which the exit operates. However, the type of briefing and the level of detail provided can have a significant influence on the time it takes to make the exit available, and on the way in which passengers dispose of the hatch. If the hatch is left inside the cabin, it becomes an obstacle in the passageway to the exit, and this creates delays for evacuating passengers.

Cobbett, Liston and Muir (2001) investigated the influence of four different types of briefing on the performance of Type III exit operators. Fifty-six groups of three participants were recruited to evacuate a Boeing 737 cabin simulator. All groups received a pre-flight safety briefing and safety card. Fourteen groups received no additional information, while fourteen groups received a minimum Type III exit briefing. The minimum briefing informed the participants that they were seated next to an emergency exit that they may be required to open, and that they should therefore read the instructions on the safety card and seat-back placards.

The last two groups of 14 received detailed briefings, which included the information in the minimum briefing. Additionally, these briefings instructed passengers on when and how to operate the exit. Participants in these conditions were explicitly told the weight of the hatch, and were informed that the hatch was not hinged or attached to the airframe. The operating handles were also pointed out by cabin crew, and participants were told that the hatch should be disposed of outside the cabin. These detailed briefings were presented orally to fourteen groups, and in writing to the remaining participants.

The results indicated that passengers who had received the detailed oral or written briefings reacted to the call to evacuate significantly more quickly than participants in the no Type III briefing or minimum briefing conditions. The overall time taken to make the exit available for evacuation was significantly quicker for participants who had received the detailed written briefing than it was for participants in the other three groups. In addition, a disproportionately high number of participants from the no Type III briefing condition left the Type III exit hatch inside the cabin. Providing the participants with such detailed briefings did take significantly more time, but the evidence suggests that if cabin crew are able to explain safety duties to exit row passengers comprehensively, then this would be time well spent.

In conclusion, passengers are legally required to be provided with safety information. This normally takes the form of a pre-departure briefing, supplemented by a safety card. In the event of an emergency, passengers stand a better chance of surviving, avoiding injury, and evacuating if they have paid attention to this information, and understood it. Exit row passengers are also better prepared to undertake safety-related duties if they have received a comprehensive briefing detailing exactly what will be required.

Pre-departure briefings, however delivered, should provide information that is consistent with what is actually required in an emergency, and with the commands that passengers expect to hear. Ideally, safety cards would be tested to ensure that they are comprehended by the largest possible proportion of the intended audience. Passengers assigned to exit rows should be given specific information on their responsibilities in an emergency situation.

All safety information should include specific detail on the emergency procedures and equipment for a particular aircraft type. It is exactly this type of detailed and specific information that is missed by people who do not pay attention to safety information (Johnson, 1979). Because they do not pay attention, there is no opportunity for them to correct the erroneous assumption that all safety briefings are the same. In disregarding safety information, passengers may be putting not only their own safety, but the survival of others at risk.

References

Air Navigation Order (ANO) (1997), 'Passenger Briefing by Commander', Article 39, paras 1–2.
Caird, J.K., Wheat, B., McIntosh, K.R. and Dewar, R.E. (1997), 'The Comprehensibility of Airline Safety Card Pictorials', *Proceedings of the Human Factors and Ergonomics Society 41st Annual Meeting, Human Factors Society*, Santa Monica, California, pp. 801–5.
Cobbett, A.M., Liston, P. and Muir, H.C. (2001), 'An Investigation into Methods of Briefing Passengers at Type III Exits', CAA Paper 2001/6, London: Civil Aviation Authority.
Cobbett, A.M. and Muir, H.C. (1996), 'The Influence of Cabin Crew during Emergency Evacuations at Floor Level Exits', CAA Paper 95006, London: Civil Aviation Authority.
Department of Transportation (1999), *Federal Aviation Regulations Part 121 – Operating requirements: Domestic, Flag and Supplemental Operations*, Washington, DC.

FAA (1999), 'Passenger Safety Information Briefing and Briefing Cards', Federal Aviation Administration Advisory Circular 121–24B, Issue 2/1/99.
Fennell, P.J. and Muir, H.C. (1992), 'Passenger Attitudes towards Airline Safety Information and Comprehension of Safety Briefings and Cards', CAA Paper 92015, London: Civil Aviation Authority.
ISO (2001) 'Graphical Symbols – Test Methods for Judged Comprehensibility and for Comprehension', *International Standard 9186*, 2nd edn, Switzerland: ISO.
Jentsch, F. (1996), 'Understanding of Aviation Safety Pictograms among Respondents from Europe and the US', *Proceedings of the Human Factors and Ergonomics Society 40th Annual Meeting, Human Factors Society*, Santa Monica, California, pp. 820–24.
Johnson, D.A. (1979), 'An Investigation of Factors Affecting Aircraft Passenger Attention to Safety Information Presentations', Report IRC–79–1 for the Federal Aviation Administration, Contract DOT–FA78WA–4095.
Johnson, D.A. (1980), 'The Design of Effective Safety Information Displays', in H.R. Poyday (ed.), *Proceedings of the Symposium: Human factors and industrial design in consumer products*, Medford, Massachusetts: Tufts University, pp. 314–28.
Johnson, D.A. (1998), 'Studies Reveal Passenger Misconceptions about Brace Commands and Brace Positions', *Cabin Crew Safety*, Vol. 33, No. 3, pp. 1–6.
Johnson, D.A and Altman, H.B. (1973), 'Effects of Briefing Card Information on Passenger Behavior during Aircraft Evacuation Demonstrations', *Proceedings of the Human Factors Society Convention, Human Factors Society*, Santa Monica, California, pp. 215–21.
King, D.F. (1988), 'Report on the Accident to Boeing 737–236 series 1, G–BGJL at Manchester International Airport on 22 August 1985', Air Accidents Investigation Branch, Department of Transport, HMSO, Aircraft Accident Report 8/88.
NTSB (1985), 'Airline Passenger Safety Education: A review of methods used to present safety information,' NTSB/SS–85/09, PB85–917014, Washington, DC.
NTSB (2000), 'Emergency Evacuation of Commercial Airplanes', NTSB/SS–00/01, PB2000–917002, Washington, DC.
NTSB (2001), 'Survivability of Accidents involving Part 121 US Air Carrier Operations, 1983 through 2000', NTSB/SR–01/01, PB2001–917001, Washington, DC.
SAE (1991), 'Passenger Safety Information Cards, ARP1384', issued 1976–08, revised 13 June, Revision B, Society of Automotive Engineers, Warrendale, Philadelphia.
Schmidt, J.K. and Kysor, K.P. (1987), 'Designing Airline Passenger Safety Cards', *Proceedings of the Human Factors Society 31st Annual Meeting*, Santa Monica, California, pp. 51–5.

Chapter 10

Passenger Behaviour in Emergency Situations

Ed Galea

Introduction

> I went to the end of my row of seats and waited to get into the aisle, ... The next thing I saw was thick black smoke coming from the front of the aircraft, I was sure it was coming from the front ... I got hold of my shirt and held it against my mouth to stop taking the smoke in, but I still took smoke in, it was burning my throat and I couldn't breathe. I couldn't get into the aisle, so I decided to go over the seats, the middle was flat and down so I climbed over them and made my way to the front right hand exit (Manchester, 1985, female, 18 years of age).

This graphic account from a survivor of the tragic Manchester Airport B737 fire of 1985 (King, 1988; Owen et al., 1998b) challenges a number of myths concerning survivability and human behaviour during aircraft emergency situations. The most commonly-held myth about aircraft emergencies is that they are non-survivable – if you are involved in an aircraft emergency you are as good as dead. This fatalistic view is often related to me by members of the travelling public, perplexed that these apparently non-survivable aircraft accidents involve opportunities to evacuate and hence to study.

The second most common myth, held by members of the travelling public and many aviation professionals – conditioned by the popular media – is that given an aircraft emergency situation, the most common behavioural response is for passengers to *panic*. In common parlance, the idea of panic has become synonymous with evacuation.

However, the picture that emerges from detailed research into aviation accidents is one not of hopelessness and panic, but one in which the passenger has a very good chance of surviving and in which the passenger behaves in a reasonable and thought-out manner and through this rational behaviour can help increase his or her chance of survival. In this chapter we will examine some of the findings of this research and develop a better understanding of the facts about human behaviour during aircraft emergencies.

Survival Rates

Throughout the world, the popular public perception concerning aviation accidents is that they are inherently non-survivable. This is both an incorrect and potentially dangerous view as this attitude can breed a disregard for issues concerning personal safety, such as paying attention to the pre-flight safety briefings, which can in turn diminish an individual's chance of surviving an accident. What is more, the truth of the situation is very different as statistics show that given an aviation accident, most people will survive and accidents involving the complete loss of life are relatively rare.

For many, the myth concerning accident survival is emotive and so deeply ingrained that it is difficult to dispel regardless of the statistical evidence. Indeed, it may be more precise to say despite the statistics, for the public are generally wary of statistics and treat them with suspicion, having for the most part adopted the position of Benjamin Disraeli, '... there are three kinds of lies – lies, damned lies and statistics'. Unfortunately, public perception is not shaped by an actuarial understanding of the statistics, but by the latest story on the evening news that graphically shows the aftermath of the latest tragic crash. However, to try and make sense of this complex issue, it is necessary to understand essentially two statistics, namely, what are your chances of being involved in an aviation accident and given that you are involved in such an incident, what are your chances of survival.

The European Transport Safety Council (ETSC) examined the survivability of aviation accidents worldwide and estimated that 90 per cent of aircraft accidents are survivable or technically survivable. The definition of a survivable accident was that no one was killed in the incident while technically survivable accidents are those accidents in which at least one person actually survives (ETSC, 1996). Furthermore, serious aviation accidents that result in the complete or near complete loss of life are very rare. The US National Transportation Safety Board (NTSB) regularly compiles detailed statistics on these types of events. The NTSB has compiled statistics of all civil aviation accidents in the US involving both scheduled and nonscheduled commercial flights for the period 1983 to 2000 inclusive (NTSB, 2001a). The NTSB classifies an accident as any incident associated with an aircraft that results in the death or serious injury of any person or in which the aircraft receives substantial damage. During this period there were 568 accidents equating to an average of 31.6 accidents per year.

In these 568 accidents, 95.7 per cent (51,207) of the occupants involved survived and 93 per cent (528) of the accidents achieved a survival rate of more than 80 per cent, while 6 per cent (34) achieved a survival rate of less than 20 per cent. Furthermore, 12.5 per cent (71) of the accidents resulted in at least one occupant fatality and only 1.4 per cent (8) of the accidents resulted in a fatality rate of at least 99 per cent (NTSB, 2001a). This data reinforces the position that the vast majority of aviation accidents are survivable and that accidents involving the loss of practically everyone on board are rare.

To put these numbers into perspective we can balance them with the total number of aircraft departures. Over this period there has been a steady growth in the number of departures per year with the total number of departures reaching 148,644,152 resulting in an average of 8,358,008 departures per year. Given the above accident record, this equates to one accident every 261,697 departures, accidents involving at least one fatality occurring every 2,093,579 departures and accidents involving the complete loss of everyone on board every 18,580,519 departures.

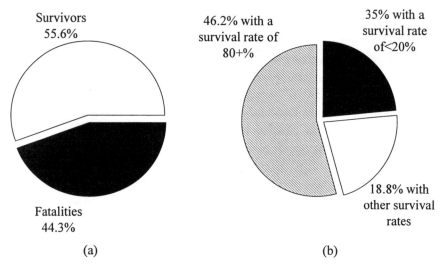

Figure 10.1 **Survival statistics as a function of all serious accidents in the US during the period 1983–2000: (a) overall survival rates and (b) specific survival rates**

Source: NTSB, 2001a.

It could be argued that this survival rate analysis is biased as the vast majority of the passengers involved in the 568 cited accidents were not involved in life-threatening situations, thus favouring an optimistic interpretation. Restricting the examination to only those accidents that can be classed as involving life-threatening conditions can lead to a clearer understanding of the issues associated with survivability. The NTSB defines serious accidents to be those accidents in which fire was present, at least one person sustained a serious injury or loss of life, and there was either substantial or complete destruction of the aircraft. In this period there were 26 accidents that meet this criterion involving 2,739 occupants of which 55.6 per cent (1,524) survived, 26.1 per cent (716) died from impact-related injuries, 4.8 per cent (131) died from exposure to fire/smoke and 13.4 per cent (368) died from other (e.g. drowning, mechanical asphyxia, etc.) or unknown causes (see Figure 10.1a). Furthermore, in 46.2 per cent (12) of the serious cases more than 80 per cent of the occupants survived, while in 35 per cent (9) of the serious cases less than 20 per cent survived (see Figure 10.1b). On average, life-threatening accidents are very rare, one such event occurring every 5,717,082 departures and an individuals chances of surviving such an event are good, being almost 56 per cent.

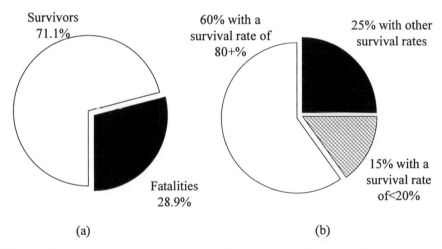

Figure 10.2 **Survival statistics as a function of all survivable serious accidents in the US during the period 1983–2000: (a) overall survival rates and (b) specific survival rates**

Source: NTSB, 2001a.

However, the above analysis still contains bias as it involves those accidents that are technically non-survivable and thus give the statistics a pessimistic bias. Of these 26 accidents, eight involved fatality rates of 99 per cent or more. If we further restrict the analysis to only those accidents which are technically survivable (i.e. at least one person survives) then during this period we have 20 serious but technically survivable accidents. These accidents involved 2,143 occupants of whom 71.1 per cent (1,524) survived, 21.6 per cent (460) died from impact, 6.1 per cent (131) died from fire/smoke, and 1.3 per cent (28) died from other (e.g. drowning, mechanical asphyxia, etc.) (see Figure 10.2a). Furthermore, in 60 per cent (12) of the serious but technically survivable cases more than 80 per cent of the occupants survived, while in 15 per cent (3) of the serious cases less than 20 per cent survived (see Figure 10.2b).

On average, a serious but technically survivable incident occurs every 7,432,208 departures and an individual has 71.1 per cent chance of surviving such an incident.

Table 10.1 Summary of serious accident statistics for the US

Category	Number of incidents	Million departures per incident	Number of incidents per million departures	Survival rate
1983–2000				
Serious but survivable	20	7.43	0.14	71.1%
Non-survivable	8	18.58	0.05	<1%
1983–2001				
Serious but survivable	21	7.58	0.13	71.5%
Non-survivable	13	12.24	0.08	<1%

Sources: based on NTSB 2001a and 2002a.

In summary, the statistics show that serious life threatening aviation accidents are rare events and that our chances of surviving such an incident are very good (see Table 10.1). On average, accidents involving total loss of life are very rare, only eight accidents being reported from 1983 to 2000 out of 148,644,152 departures. Over the same period, 20 serious life threatening but survivable accidents occurred resulting in a survival rate of better than 71 per cent, that is almost a three in four chance of survival. Even if the statistics from 2001 are included, the situation is not altered significantly.

Given that serious accidents are rare events and that the majority of people will survive, what type of human behaviour do we see in aviation accidents?

Human Behaviour

In emergency evacuations, no single behavioural response is likely to emerge from the evacuating throng. The evacuation process is complex and as varied as the people and circumstances they find themselves in. Once the passengers on board are placed in a situation were evacuation is required, there may be a variety of human responses including:

- *situational disorientation*: the passenger may remain seated in disbelief for a brief period of time;
- *anxiety behaviours*: when placed in unusual and high risk situations it can become increasingly difficult to deliver peak performance and even simple tasks such as releasing the seat restraint may be difficult;
- *social bonding behaviours*: passengers will attempt to reunite with separated travelling companions;
- *affiliative behaviour*: this can manifest itself as passenger movement towards the familiar, most commonly displayed as passengers collecting carry-on luggage and valuables prior to evacuating;
- *fear flight behaviour*: passengers immediately unbuckle their seat restraint and flee;
- *physiological disorientation*: in conditions of post-crash fire, passengers may be unable to locate exits due to smoke induced loss of visibility followed by intoxication effects brought on by inhalation of narcotic fire gases;
- *altruistic behaviour*: even under very severe conditions, passengers may attempt to assist fellow passengers, even at the risk of exposing themselves to potentially life-threatening situations;
- *behavioural inaction*: some passengers may remain frozen to the spot unable to move;
- *panic*: this is an irrational, asocial and potentially destructive behaviour such as fighting with fellow passengers.

Our knowledge of human behaviour during aviation emergencies is based on a combination of the study of past accidents, laboratory-based experimentation, experience from the industry standard 90 second evacuation certification trials (FAR, 1989), and worst of all, mythology. By mythology we mean the common practice of accepting a behaviour to be generally true when there is little or no convincing evidence to support this belief.

A commonly-held myth in aviation safety is that during an evacuation, passengers have a tendency to head for their most familiar exit, i.e. the boarding exit, thereby bypassing otherwise perfectly serviceable exits. This myth is a hangover from building evacuation research, where a considerable amount of evidence does support the hypothesis that occupants favour familiar exits. While this is believed – by some – to be true in aviation evacuations there is little convincing evidence to support this belief. Evidence superficially supporting this type of behaviour may be found in any one single accident (e.g. Manchester B737 incident); however, this does not make this apparent behaviour a global truth. Furthermore, if exit bypass does occur, when viewed within the context of the accident situation, there may be a rational explanation for this behaviour, rather than simply a desire to use a more familiar exit.

Another common myth is that when faced with a serious life-threatening situation, the majority of untrained, inexperienced people will panic and therefore act in an irrational and possibly self-destructive manner. Much of the discussion involving panic has taken place utilising only a layman's definition based largely on the assumption that people are not able to cope in situations of high stress where their lives may be at risk. This is derived from a 'commonsense' understanding of human behaviour rather than from rational scientific investigation. Most of the behaviour that we see in aviation evacuations, while possibly extreme, is a rational response to a rapidly changing situation. This is not to say that panic is not a behaviour that occurs during aviation emergencies. Indeed, panic *is* a feature of the evacuation process and cannot be ignored. However, panic is not necessarily the driving force behind the evacuation process. Furthermore, the general perception of what panic actually is is largely inaccurate and generally unhelpful in understanding evacuation behaviour. To the aviation safety specialist, the importance of identifying panic as a relatively rare behaviour is of paramount importance, for it justifies a more challenging and contemplative approach to understanding the causes of evacuation behaviour. Such an understanding must be capable of dealing with more than instinctive, irrational or even random actions.

In formulating our understanding of evacuation behaviour it is essential to separate the myth from the fact. We do this through the careful study of previous aviation accidents, laboratory experimentation and through the analysis of certification evacuation trials.

Accident Reports

The primary source of information concerning human behaviour in aircraft accidents is provided through aircraft accident human factors reports produced by national organisations such as the NTSB of the USA, Transport Safety

Board (TSB) of Canada and Air Accident Investigation Branch (AAIB) of the UK. These reports contain a wealth of information in the form of interviews with survivors (crew and passengers) and responses to questionnaires. The information is collected and documented to aid in the investigation of the accident. This information is invaluable, as on the whole, it represents the outcome of real world incidents that are impossible or impractical to replicate in controlled laboratory conditions for ethical, practical or financial reasons. Within the US alone, an evacuation of a scheduled flight occurs every 336,328 departures or 11 days based on 1998 figures (NTSB, 2001b).

While many national accident investigation authorities carry out accident investigations, the primary source of readily accessible information concerning human factors in aviation accidents is derived from the NTSB in the US (NTSB, 2002b). The NTSB is charged with investigating all US based aviation accidents involving a fatality or serious injury or in which the aircraft suffers serious damage.

A number of systematic studies (Snow et al., 1970; Schaeffer, 1994; TSB, 1995; Tomita, 1999; Hynes, 1999; NTSB, 2001b; Galea and Owen, 1998; Galea et al., 2000, 2002c) into human factors associated with aircraft accidents have been conducted based on findings from accident reports. For the most part, the information available in these studies is based on air accident investigation reports and the passenger and crew testimonies that they contain. This data tends to take the form of anecdotal evidence, sometimes with third party corroboration.

Early FAA study into passenger behaviour in aviation accidents One of the first systematic studies into human behaviour issues associated with aircraft evacuations was conducted by Snow et al. (1970). This seminal work, published in 1970, has influenced virtually all subsequent aircraft evacuation behavioural research, be it based on accident investigation, laboratory experimentation or computer simulation. The study was based on the investigation of three fatal crashes, involving, a DC-8 on 11 July 1961 with 114 passengers of whom 17 died, a B727 on 11 November 1965 with 85 passengers of whom 43 died, and a B707 on 23 November 1964 with 62 passengers of whom 45 passengers and five crew died. All three incidents involved fire.

Snow et al. were the first to elucidate the concept that four factors influence evacuation, namely, configurational, procedural, environmental and behavioural factors. Configurational considerations are those generally governed by the shape of the cabin geometry, and involve cabin layout, number of exits, exit type, travel distance, etc. In the event of fire, environmental aspects need to be considered. These include the likely debilitating effects on the passengers of heat, toxic and irritant gases and the impact of increasing smoke density on travel speeds and way-finding abilities. Procedural aspects cover the actions of crew, passenger prior knowledge of the cabin, emergency signage, etc. Finally, and possibly most importantly, the likely behavioural responses of the passengers must be considered. These include aspects such as the passengers' initial response to the call to evacuate, likely travel directions, family/group interactions etc. (Owen et al., 1996, 1998a).

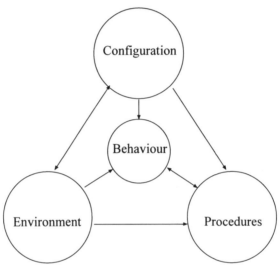

Figure 10.3 The four main interacting aspects that govern evacuation

Source: Owen et al., 1996, 1998a.

While this investigation must be viewed in the context of the standards prevalent at the time, a number of specific themes emerged from this study that are still relevant today. One of the central aspects of the study was an investigation of the exits used by survivors and the travel distance taken to those exits. Across the three accidents, on average, the survivors travelled 4.12 seat rows to an exit, whereas the average distance to their nearest exit was 2.94 seat rows (see Table 10.2). It is worth noting that the aircraft involved in these three accidents were built prior to the establishment of the regulation limiting exit separation to no more than 60 feet (FAR, 1989).

Their findings suggested that on average, survivors sat closer to potentially usable exits than fatalities, both survivors and fatalities tended to sacrifice some of their location advantage by ignoring nearby exits in favour of more distant exits, and the tendency towards less effective exit utilisation was more pronounced among the fatalities. The distance calculations were based on the number of seat rows between the passengers seat location and the exit. The information relating to fatalities was partially inferred from information relating to the body location.

Table 10.2 Average distance to exit as measured in units of seat rows, for survivors and fatalities

	Survivors	Fatalities
Seat-to-exit-used distance	4.12	6.40
Seat-to-nearest-usable-exit distance	2.94	3.99

Source: based on Snow et al., 1970.

Snow et al. noted the reasons some passengers gave for ignoring their nearest exits to be logical or understandable behaviour, namely;

- a given exit was blocked by fire or smoke;
- a given exit was unopened at the time;
- crowds around an exit made it unattractive;
- they were simply not aware of their nearest exit;
- they simply followed the crowd.

However, they also noted that some passengers, 'more or less automatically headed back in the direction from which they boarded' (Snow et al., 1970). Unfortunately, the number of passengers offering these various suggestions for their behaviour is not given. So while it is not clear how many people elected to use more distant exits simply because it was 'most familiar', this observation may reinforce the myth of the boarding exit as being most likely to attract passengers. Indeed, Snow et al. suggest that while some exiting decisions may have been rational, many were based on lack of familiarity with exit configuration or through panic.

Snow et al. also considered whether age and gender effects played a role in determining survival. They found that young males are the best survival risks and that adult females, elderly males and children are more prone to injury and likely to become fatalities. They also noted that age and gender effect was less apparent in less severe accident situations.

As a result of these findings, Snow et al. highlighted the importance of the pre-flight briefing and the need for positive involvement of the cabin crew in managing the evacuation. These sentiments are still relevant today.

Another issue raised by Snow et al. in their study was the issue of slide availability. In the three accidents they studied only 15 per cent of the passengers involved were able to use a fully-inflated and functioning slide. Several of the slides exploded after they were deployed. They raised the concern that the next generation of aircraft would be larger and hence require better technology to ensure that slides could cope with the increased number of passengers, higher sill heights and that they would be more reliable. With the dawn of the very large transport aircraft (VLTA) these issues are still relevant today, as will be discussed later.

Schaeffer study into exit usage during aviation emergencies The Schaeffer study (Schaeffer, 1994) involved 73 accidents to Western-manufactured aircraft over the period 1961 to 1993. The Schaeffer study was restricted to those incidents that were technically survivable and those in which a rapid evacuation was essential for survival, hence precautionary evacuations were excluded. The study focused on issues associated with the exits used by passengers. Schaeffer's main findings include:

- forward exits are used about five times out of 10 and by up to 50 per cent of the evacuees who use exits;
- over-wing exits are used about five to six times out of 10 and by about 30 per cent in wing-engined aircraft;
- exits just aft of the wing have a low usage rate with about 20 per cent of the evacuees who use exits make use of these exits, the extreme aft exits being used about four times out of 10 in wing-engined aircraft;
- in most cases involving external fire, exits are used on both sides of the aircraft, in only four out of 53 cases were all exits on one side used and three of these cases involved smaller aircraft.

Schaeffer suggested that a possible reason why passengers preferred the forward exits was because passengers had a tendency to use the door through which they boarded. However, the Schaeffer study did not take into consideration the starting location of the passengers and so did not consider which exits the passengers were closest to.

NTSB study into human behaviour during aviation emergencies Two recent studies have attempted to analyse evacuation behaviour over a wide range of different accidents (NTSB, 2001b; Galea and Owen, 1998; Galea et al., 2000, 2002c). The first is an NTSB study covering accidents from September 1997 to June 1999 involving 46 evacuations, 2,651 passengers and 18 different types of aircraft (NTSB, 2001b). All but one of the aircraft involved were narrow-bodied or regional aircraft and 30 of the incidents underwent detailed investigations, including passenger surveying via questionnaire. In total 457 passengers returned their questionnaires representing 18 of the 30 incidents. These evacuations were called for a variety of reasons, 18 of the 46 evacuations were for engine fires, three being suspected fires, eight were for suspected but not actual cargo hold fires, gear failure and smoke in the cabin lead to four evacuations each. Accident or evacuation related injuries occurred in 18 of the cases. Only one accident resulted in fatalities (11), five resulted in serious injuries, and 16 resulted in minor injuries. In four of the five accidents resulting in serious injuries, the injuries were evacuation related. The vast majority of these incidents are thus not considered serious and the conclusions concerning human behaviour should be viewed in this light.

The average age of the respondents was 43 and 45 per cent of these passengers were female. Unlike in the earlier Snow study (Snow et al., 1970), it was found that overall, older passengers were no more likely to sustain an injury than younger passengers. This is probably due to the difference in severity between the accidents considered in the NTSB and Snow studies. However, in line with the study by Snow et al., the injury rate amongst females (38 per cent) was higher than that reported by males (27 per cent).

On the whole, the passengers who responded to the questionnaire suggested that the evacuations were essentially cooperative (75 per cent agreed or strongly agreed with this statement while 13 per cent disagreed or strongly disagreed). The majority of the passengers who suggested the evacuations were uncooperative were involved in three evacuations, two of which involved fire and one that involved a runway overshoot. Significantly, the only fatal accident was not included in these three cases. The competitive behaviours reported included pushing, climbing over seats and disputes amongst passengers. Overall, 12.1 per cent of the responding passengers reported they climbed seats, the majority of these passengers (80 per cent) were involved in the fatal incident. Of all the passengers who responded, 18.7 per cent reported being pushed and slightly more than 10 per cent reported seeing passengers involved in disputes with other passengers.

140   *Passenger Behaviour*

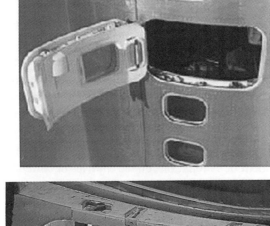
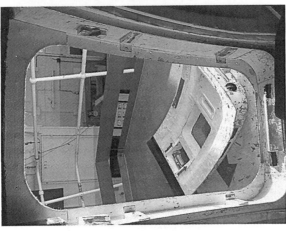

(a)

(b)

(c)

Figure 10.4   Over-wing Type-III emergency exits: (a) of the type typically found on aircraft that must be manually operated; (b) open Type-III with hatch thrown out; and (c) new hinged type found on Boeing new generation 737 aircraft

Sources: (a) photograph taken by E. Galea; (b) courtesy of Cranfield University; (c) courtesy of Boeing Commercial Aircraft Corporation.

While passengers can expect cabin crew to operate the majority of exits on board aircraft, the over-wing Type-III hatch is an exit that by design is intended to be operated by passengers. However, it is large, heavy and awkward to handle and is operated in a non-intuitive manner (see Figure 10.4). The vast majority of passengers will never have operated such a device, yet they are expected to operate it quickly and efficiently for the first time in high-stress, high-risk situations following an emergency. The Type-III hatch has a rectangular shape, not less than 20ins wide by 36ins high, with a step-up inside the aircraft of not more than 20 inches and with a step-down outside the aircraft of not more than 27 inches (FAR, 1989). The exit can weigh as much as 65lbs. To operate the exit, it is first necessary to pull the latch located at the top of the exit that releases the exit. The hatch is now free to move and if it has not fallen onto the unsuspecting passenger, it must be manoeuvred into the aircraft – a counterintuitive operation for most people. Once free, the hatch must be safely secured, preferably outside the aircraft, but there is a strong chance that the heavy hatch will be dumped inside the aircraft, potentially creating a hazard for evacuating passengers. These type of exits have received a considerable amount of research interest and have been the subject of a large number of experimental trials.

In total some 36 over-wing Type-III exits were used in 13 of the 46 evacuations. Specific information was only collected in six of the 13 evacuations and two of these used cabin crew to operate the exits. In one case two passengers indicated they had no problem in operating the exit while in the other three cases difficulties in operating the exits were reported. These included difficulties manoeuvring the hatch, difficulties in opening the hatch, and difficulties in understanding how to operate the hatch.

The need to select appropriate passengers to sit at exit rows and the importance of providing them with clear instructions is clear and the results from the NTSB accident study support this view. Two passengers seated by the emergency exit were over 70 years of age, one of which had difficulties in operating the exit while three passengers seated in exit rows did not speak the language in which the crew briefings were given. Furthermore, only nine of the 42 exit row passengers reported receiving a personal briefing from cabin crew and four of these passengers further reported examining the safety card. Twenty-four passengers reported receiving no briefing and only two of these passengers had examined the briefing card. The two briefed passengers who opened over-wing exits reported no difficulties. Four passengers who did not receive a briefing opened over-wing exits, two reported no difficulties while two others reported problems with operating the exit. However, in all cases, the hatches were eventually opened.

While the over-wing Type-III hatches did not appear to be a significant problem in these accidents, it is worth recalling the situation in the tragic Manchester Airport B737 incident of 1985 that claimed the lives of 55 passengers (King, 1988). In this incident, a female passenger located by the over-wing exit had difficulties in operating the exit, mistakenly pulling on the armrest of her seat rather than the lower hand grab of the exit. Eventually, a passenger located in the row behind the exit row, reached over and released the exit, which fell onto the exit row passenger. Eventually, the exit was cleared. However, the delay in operating the exit contributed to the severe nature of the incident. The recently developed over-wing exit for the new generation B737 series aircraft, which is hinged and outwardly opening, is intended to address these issues (see Figure 10.4). This exit should eliminate many of the passenger operation related problems associated with these type of exits.

Another issue addressed by the NTSB study concerns the transference of safety information through the crew safety briefing and the safety cards. Both these devices are intended to inform passengers of safety procedures and the location and operation of exits. Information that is vital in shaping the performance of passengers in emergency situations. However, the NTSB survey indicates that passengers do not generally listen to the briefings or study the safety cards and furthermore, do not consider them to be of much use. In the survey, 13 per cent of the 377 passengers who reported whether or not they watched the safety briefing, reported that they watched none of the briefing while, 48 per cent reported they watched at least 75 per cent of the briefing. The main reason reported by the passengers for ignoring the briefing was that they had seen it before. Passengers who had watched over half of the briefing were equally divided amongst those who thought the briefing was helpful and those that thought the briefing was unhelpful for their evacuation. Those in the former group felt that the briefing made them more aware of the exit locations. Of the 431 passengers who replied concerning the safety cards, 68 per cent indicated that they ignored the card and of these, 89 per cent suggested that they had read it before. Of the 399 passengers who responded to issues concerning the crew briefing and safety cards, a staggering 44 per cent reported that they neither examined the card nor listened to the briefing. The importance of the safety card and passenger briefing cannot be overestimated. The recent series of evacuation trials conducted by CAMI demonstrates the effectiveness of the briefing cards in instructing passengers on the correct operation of over-wing Type-III exits.

Passenger retrieval of carry-on baggage during emergency evacuations can compromise passenger safety. The passenger wastes valuable time retrieving their belongings and can also hinder the rapid evacuation of others. Furthermore, carrying baggage through over-wing exits or while jumping down slides can increase the chance of injury and contribute to slowing down the evacuation process. Carry-on baggage abandoned at or near exits also creates trip hazards for other passengers and again contributes to slowing down the entire evacuation process. The much-neglected safety briefing card is one way of indicating to passengers that carry-on baggage should be left behind. All but two of the safety cards reviewed by the NTSB indicated that carry-on baggage should be left behind during an emergency evacuation. In addition, during emergency evacuations, cabin crew issue the command to 'leave baggage'. In the survey, 33 of the 37 cabin crew indicated that they instructed passengers to leave carry-on behind during the evacuation. Of the 419 passengers who reported that they had carry-on baggage, nearly 50 per cent reported attempting to remove a bag during their evacuation. The primary reasons were to retrieve money, wallets, credit cards (53 per cent) or work-related items (31 per cent), keys (29 per cent), and medicines (25 per cent). Passengers exiting with carry-on baggage were the most frequently cited obstruction to evacuation and 70 passengers and eight cabin crew reported arguments between passengers and cabin crew over luggage.

Communication between crew and passengers is vital during emergencies. In the event of an emergency, it is essential that crew can communicate vital information regarding the nature of the rapidly developing situation to their colleagues. This could be information regarding the developing local cabin situation or the local situation just outside the cabin. This information may be key to deciding whether an evacuation is required and the nature of the evacuation that is required. Furthermore, crew who are obviously not in command of the situation or who are acting out of ignorance of the facts do not convey a feeling of confidence to the passengers and may instil in passengers a feeling that the crew are not in command. Sensing this, passengers may feel that they have to take control themselves. Equally important is the ability of the crew to communicate with passengers and issue commands that can be clearly and easily understood. When passengers receive clear information and instructions from the crew they are more likely to feel that the crew are in command and that they have the situation in control.

In a recent event not included in the NTSB survey, a Qantas B747–400 was involved in a runway overrun incident that resulted in the loss of the noise gear and subsequent loss of both the PA and cabin interphone systems

(ATSB Report, 2001). The flight deck and cabin crew communicated by cabin crew members acting as runners for more than 20 minutes before an evacuation was ordered. During the emergency, there were periods of time when two of the main cabin doors were unattended by cabin crew as they were performing other tasks such as relaying messages. During emergency situations, cabin crew should not be forced into situations that require them to abandon their exits, as this act in itself could jeopardise passenger safety. Had an evacuation been required, the passengers may have had to operate these doors, possibly delaying the evacuation or even resulting in the opening of a door that should have remained closed.

Needless to say, communication between the cabin crew and flight deck was slow and inefficient and the passengers noting this lack of communication grew increasingly nervous, with several passengers commenting:

> It felt like we were just waiting for this plane to burst into flames and our death.
>
> I just wanted to get off the plane ASAP and felt powerless and helpless just sitting there.
>
> We assumed the captain was seriously injured as we heard nothing from the flight deck, which was worrying.
>
> At one stage I was going to open the emergency exit myself because of my concern for my daughters and risk of fire (ATSB Report, 2001).

This incident highlights the importance of having a reliable communications system and the need for good communications both between crew and between crew and passengers.

Several examples in the NTSB study show the importance of good communications. In one pre-planned evacuation, the crew briefed the passengers on the correct brace position and location of exits. Furthermore, crew reseated passengers so that they were located close to exits and positioned crew by the over-wing exits so that they could be quickly and efficiently opened. The passengers praised the crew for the way they handled the situation. Crew in 24 of the studied evacuations responded to questions relating to communications equipment. In 18 of the 24 cases, crew indicated that the public address (PA) system was used to initiate the evacuation and nine cases in which the interphone system was used to prepare for the evacuation. In three evacuations the PA and interphone systems were inoperable due to crash-related damage and the cabin crew were forced to shout out commands.

Finally, as in the earlier Snow study (Snow et al., 1970), the NTSB study reported significant slide failure. They found that in 37 per cent of the evacuations with slide deployments, there were problems with at least one slide.

The AASK database The second large survey of accident data is part of an on-going UK CAA study undertaken by the Fire Safety Engineering Group (FSEG) of the University of Greenwich (Owen et al., 1998b; Galea et al., 2000; Galea and Owen, 1998; Galea et al., 2002c; Finney et al., 2002). This study has led to the development of the Aircraft Accident Statistics and Knowledge (AASK) database that is a repository of survivor accounts from aviation accidents. Its main purpose is to store observational and anecdotal data from the actual interviews of the occupants involved in aircraft accidents. The AASK concept has evolved into an on-line prototype system available over the Internet to selected users (http://fseg.gre.ac.uk/aask/index.html).

Data contained within AASK V3.0 consists of information derived from both passenger and cabin crew interviews, information concerning fatalities and basic accident details. Data entered into AASK was extracted from the transcripts supplied by the AAIB and the NTSB. Data imported into AASK V3.0 comprises information from accidents that occurred between April 1977 and March 1998 involving 55 accidents, 1,295 individual passenger records from survivors, 110 records referring to cabin crew interview transcripts, and 329 records of fatalities (passenger and crew).

Within the accidents in the database, the passenger reply rate varies from 2.63 per cent to 95.15 per cent with an average reply rate of 49.8 per cent. Thus data from approximately 30 per cent of the passengers that were on board these aircraft is available for analysis. Of the 1,295 individual passengers entered into the database, 905 survivors provided their age (see Figure 10.5). The average age of the respondents was 39.4 years (39.8 years of age for males and 39.3 years of age for the females), and 57 per cent of those that provided their gender (898) were male, which is similar to that found in the NTSB study.

One of the passenger behaviour issues that AASK has been used to study concerns the exit usage by survivors. As has already been described, many in the aviation safety community believe that passengers have a tendency to favour the exit through which they boarded the aircraft (see, for example, Snow et al., 1970; Schaeffer, 1994), thereby ignoring closer but unfamiliar emergency exits. Analysis using AASK (Owen et al., 1998b; Galea et al., 2002c) suggests that this is not the case and that overwhelmingly, passengers

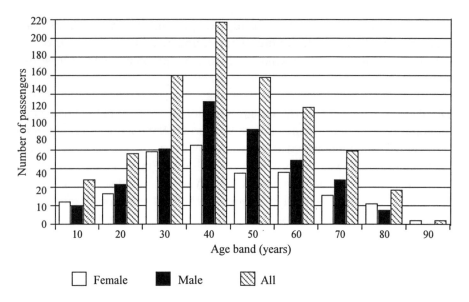

Figure 10.5 Age distribution of passengers in the AASK database

tend to use their nearest serviceable exit. The AASK analysis is based on passenger accounts that clearly state both the seating location and exit used by the passenger. However, in some cases either the seat location or exit used is not clearly stated by the passenger. In most of these cases, the missing information can be inferred from other information such as other passengers accounts. Both results are presented, values appearing after the '/' include inferred data. The results from AASK suggest that more than 70 per cent of passengers who report their exit usage make use of the nearest available exit (see Table 10.3).

Table 10.3 Passenger use of nearest exit

Category	Result
Passengers reporting exit usage	619/958
Passengers *not* using nearest available exit	179/304
% of passengers with reported exit usage not using nearest available exit	28.9% / 31.7%
Passengers *not* using actual nearest exit (available or not)	204/360

Note: values after the '/' include passengers where exit use and/or seat location is inferred.

Of the 179/304 passengers that did not use their nearest exit, 103/142 passengers supplied reasons for their actions. Examination of the explanations supplied by these passengers revealed the reasons given in Table 10.4. While by no means complete, this analysis suggests that an overwhelming 88 per cent of those passengers reporting their exit usage, either used or had a good reason not to use their *nearest exit*. The remaining 12 per cent/17 per cent did not supply any reason for not using their nearest exit, however, this is not to say that they did not have a reason.

Table 10.4 Reasons for exit choice given by those passengers NOT using nearest exit

Reason for exit choice	Number of passengers
No reason provided	75/160
Not applicable (e.g. rescued)	1/2
Nearest exit was/became unavailable	27/39
Followed attendant instructions	22/29
Followed other passenger	17/24
Shorter queue than other exits	11/14
Choice made before egress	9/11
Thought it was the nearest exit	7/7
Found exit during egress	7/10
Followed emergency lights	1/1
Only available exit	1/1
Followed companion	1/1
Helped through exit	0/5

Note: values after the '/' include passengers where exit use and/or seat location is inferred.

It is also interesting to consider the direction travelled by the passengers when evacuating. Table 10.5 shows that of the 619/958 passengers for which we know the direction of travel, 63 per cent/62 per cent travelled forward, 31 per cent/34 per cent travelled towards the rear while the remainder where situated within an exit row. This would seem to support the view of Schaeffer that the passengers have a propensity for travelling forward.

However, of those passengers choosing to travel forward, 70 per cent have selected their nearest exit, while for those choosing to travel towards the aft, 69 per cent have selected their nearest exit. This suggests that the overriding ambition of the passengers is to exit via their nearest exit, rather than to travel forward. In addition, this further supports the conjecture that passenger exit selection is based on a rational decision, at least for the survivors!

Table 10.5 Direction of travel and distance travelled in seat rows for passengers where starting locations and exit usage is known or inferred

Direction	# passengers	Min. distance	# passengers	Mean distance
Forward	391/596	True	273/385	4.3/4.6
		False	118/211	12.2/13.9
Aft	194/322	True	133/229	3.3/4.3
		False	61/93	11.5/13.6
Exit row	34/40	True	34/40	0

Note: values after the '/' include passengers where exit use and/or seat location is inferred.

The mean distance travelled (in terms of seat rows) by survivors in evacuating is 6.1 seat rows. Furthermore, those passengers who select their nearest exit travel on average approximately 3.7 seat rows, while those who do not travel towards their nearest exit travel 12 seat rows or at least three times as far. The mean travel distance for survivors determined by Snow et al. in his sample of three accidents was 4.1 seat rows. The difference between the average distance travelled by survivors could be due to a number of factors such as the small number of accidents in the Snow sample, the gradual increase in aircraft size since the earlier Snow study, improvements to survivability characteristics of aircraft since the Snow study, the severity of the conditions in the Snow study, etc.

As an extension to the previous analysis, it is possible to examine the exit usage in terms of exit location. This analysis is restricted to aircraft with three exit pairs (see Figure 10.6) where at least one exit from each pair was available. This was compared with the results from two equivalent aircraft evacuation certification trials. This analysis suggests that a bias in exit usage exists for the MID exits. The observed bias remains even if the last accident – which only has a passenger loading of 39 per cent – is removed from the sample. For aircraft with three exit pairs this is a disturbing trend as the MID exits are the smaller Type-III passenger operated hatch exits.

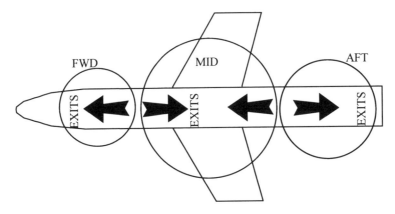

Figure 10.6 The division of the cabin into three general areas

Table 10.6 Exit usage in terms of percentage of passengers using each generalised exit position

Accident reference	Passenger loading	Fwd (%)	Mid (%)	Aft (%)
(43)	93.6%	19.2 [I]	61.5 [III]	19.2 [I]
(59)	96.6%	39.5 [I]	37.2 [III]	23.3 [I]
(7)	39.0%	44.7 [I]	50.0 [III]	5.3 [I]
Mean	–	34.5	49.6	15.9

Note: information in brackets identifies exit type.

Exit usage for two aircraft with three exit pairs, derived from actual 90-second certification trials, is presented in Table 10.7. Examination of the data for aircraft with three exit pairs suggests that the exit usage achieved in certification trials is quite different from that in actual accidents. In actual accidents, there appears to be a biased trend for exit usage in the midsections (i.e. the nearest exit for the majority of passengers) of the aircraft. Yet in the certification trials, the mean load on each exit pair is far more even and furthermore, fewer passengers use the midsection exits, the reverse of that seen in actual accidents.

The most probable reason for this lies in the behaviour of the passengers. Essentially, in a real accident the passengers have a higher motivation to escape and tend to do so by what they perceive to be the most direct method – their nearest exit. The cabin crew procedures used in these certification trials were designed to achieve a well-balanced evacuation with most of the exits working in an efficient manner, and in the conditions found in certification trials they tend to work well. However, in certification trials the passengers are working in a highly cooperative manner as opposed to the competitive behaviour likely to be exhibited by passengers in life threatening situations. This suggests that formulating cabin crew procedures solely on the basis of certification experience may be misleading in terms of their actual effectiveness.

In the previous two analyses, exit usage was examined from a passenger perspective. In this analysis, the exits that are actually available during the accident are examined for aircraft with potentially three and four exit pairs available. Accidents were restricted to situations in which the fuselage did not rupture and the aircraft was not partially or totally immersed in water. From the database five aircraft were found to be suitable with three exit pairs and 12 with four exit pairs.

Table 10.7 Generalised passenger exit usage for aircraft with three exit pairs in 90-second certification trials

Aircraft	Fwd %	Mid %	Aft %
1	40	20	40
2	27	37	36
Mean (%)	33.5	28.5	38

For the aircraft with three exit pairs, one aircraft had exactly 50 per cent of the exits available and one aircraft had less than 50 per cent of the exits available. For the aircraft with four exit pairs, two aircraft had exactly 50 per cent of the exits available and two aircraft had less than 50 per cent of the exits available. Thus out of the 17 accidents considered, six (i.e. 35 per cent) had half or less of the potentially available exits usable. Furthermore, of the 17 aircraft considered, 10 or 59 per cent had a cabin section in which no exits were available. No cases were found in which a single exit from an exit pair was available throughout the cabin. These results are similar to those found in the earlier Schaeffer study.

As part of the 90-second certification exercise (FAR, 1989), the trial criteria stipulate that only half of the available exits can be used. Without exception, where aircraft have exit pairs, only one exit of each pair is selected. Thus, the exit configuration used in the 90 second certification exercise does not correspond to the exit availability suggested in the sample of real accidents contained in AASK V3.0. Furthermore, the exit configuration actually used in the 90-second certification exercise is not a particularly onerous configuration as an exit is available in each cabin section. If the 90-second certification trial were to be more representative of accident scenarios, a more challenging exit combination should be selected. For example, in aircraft with three exit pairs, a more challenging exit combination that is also consistent with the observed exit availability – while maintaining the 50 per cent condition – would involve both forward exits and a single aft exit, or both mid exits and a single aft exit.

In aircraft evacuations the response time of passengers can be relatively short, as there is a high degree of apparent awareness of the seriousness of the incident. Excluding those passengers that attempt to retrieve carry-on baggage, some passengers, despite a short response time, are unable to commence their evacuation due to difficulties leaving their seat, either due to the aisle being heavily congested, or simply because they had difficulties releasing their seatbelt. The AASK database was queried to find those passengers who had mentioned difficulties with their seatbelts. In total some 81 passengers reported such difficulties.

Those passengers who reported being involved with seatbelt difficulties were placed into three categories: those passengers who helped others; those passengers who received assistance; and those passengers who managed alone. From this analysis it appears that males have fewer problems with seatbelts than females and that males are also more likely to render assistance to others than females. Furthermore, the number of males who rendered assistance or who managed alone is more than would be expected from the overall gender number mix. Similarly, the number of females who managed alone or who helped others is significantly less than would be expected from the overall gender mix. Finally, the number of males who received help is significantly less than would be expected from the overall gender mix while the number of females who received help is significantly greater.

It is also interesting to consider whether the occurrence of difficulties experienced by passengers in releasing the seat belt is related to the age of the passenger. In this analysis three categories of seatbelt difficulty were accepted for consideration. These were:

- *unfamiliar with buckle release mechanism*: e.g. 'He first thought it [the seatbelt] operated like the one in his car – a centre push button in the buckle to release';

- *environmental related complications excluding immersion in water*: e.g. 'could not release seatbelt due to smoke reduced visibility problems. Erroneously tugged on the buckle instead of undoing it';
- *buckle location*: e.g. 'thought seatbelt buckle was at side as in a car not in centre'.

Using these criteria, the number of passengers reporting experiencing difficulty with seatbelt release is reduced to 27. While the sample is too small to have statistical significance, the data does reveal that older passengers appear to be more likely to experience difficulties with seatbelts than younger passengers. While the numbers of passengers reporting difficulties with releasing seatbelts is small, it does highlight that some passengers, when under extreme stress, experience problems operating the seatbelt mechanism. It should also be remembered that these numbers simply refer to those passengers who have mentioned having difficulties on their questionnaires, not the actual number who may have experienced difficulties and so reflects a possible minimum incident rate.

These findings provide some additional evidence of the need to demonstrate the operation of the seatbelt in pre-flight briefings and safety briefing cards and of the need for passengers to pay attention to such briefings. Demonstrating the operation of the seatbelt is often seen as unnecessary as it is assumed most people have very little difficulty in operating such a simple device. However, for the vast majority of the public, seatbelts are routinely encountered in road vehicles, where the operation of the mechanism is very different to that found on aircraft. When forced to operate this device under conditions of high anxiety, as may be the case in an aviation accident, some passengers may automatically exhibit their learned behaviour, reverting to familiar behaviour patterns and attempt to 'press the button' to release the seatbelt. Perhaps as part of the pre-flight briefing, crew should reinforce that the release mechanism is different to that found in cars, and not merely demonstrate its operation.

An important aspect of behaviour that has been practically ignored in aviation safety research is the influence of social bonds on evacuation behaviour. The industry standard 90-second evacuation test assumes that each passenger is socially unconnected to other passengers, and the majority of experimental trails that have been conducted have also been based on individuals. Passenger behaviour during evacuation may be influenced by the presence of travelling companions and the nature of the social bond that exists between them. From the 1,295 passenger reports in AASK, 46 per cent (626) were entered into the database as travelling with a 'companion'. A companion could be a family member, friend, work colleague or other connections. However, the vast majority of the companion relationships were family related, with spouse being the most common form of companion. The size of the companion group also varies considerably, with groups being made up of two or more travelling companions (Finney et al., 2002). As with all data reported in AASK and other accident surveys, it should be noted that this data only corresponds to those passengers who have agreed to complete a survey. However, as this corresponds to approximately 30 per cent of the passengers, it suggests that we can expect an appreciable number of socially bonded passengers on aircraft.

As part of a study of human behaviour in severe life-threatening conditions occurring during building evacuation scenarios, Johnson et al. (1994) analysed in detail a fatal fire and evacuation from a large hotel/night club in which 165 people lost their lives. On the night of the fire there were 2,500 patrons dispersed in various rooms of the night club. In their analysis, Johnson et al. found that almost all the patrons were bound by social ties to others present – primarily spouses or dating couples – and many were embedded in networks with multiple bonds. From their analysis they concluded that the evacuation from the building was not individualistic, but that patrons fled as members of groups, often hesitating in their flight to ensure that others to whom they were socially bonded were also exiting. Furthermore, as the threat of entrapment increased, greater concern for group members was expressed. The results from this study suggest the importance of social bonds in determining behaviour during evacuation.

As AASK suggests that a significant number of social groupings are likely to exist on flights, it is essential to take this into consideration when determining likely behavioural responses of passengers. One such analysis considered family groups consisting of two adults and two children, 13 of which were found in the AASK database. These family units display a variety of evacuation behaviours. In some of these the male adult directs and leads the family, in others it is a joint operation. However, the most common behaviour is for each parent to assume responsibility of a child (often with the female adult carrying an infant). The analysis reveals that nine families stayed together while four family groups split. In each of the 13 cases, the family groups had a variety of viable exits available to them. In two cases, the male adult and one child went through one exit, while the female adult and the other child used the other exit of the exit pair. In a further two cases the family split so that one parent took both children through an exit whist the other adult went through the other exit in the exit pair. In one case it was a male leading; in the other it was the female who took the responsibility for the children.

Clearly, further data and analysis is needed to fully understand the response of family units and other social groupings. The results from this family analysis support the findings of Johnson et al. and suggest that the family should be treated most commonly as a unit staying and evacuating together. This has ramifications for crew procedures developed using 90-second certification analysis as a justification. One commonly practised procedure is that of crew initiated exit bypass, where crew members direct some passengers away from a functioning exit to another nearby functioning exit. While these procedures may be efficient under certification conditions – where social bonds play no significant role – in actual evacuations where social bonds become relevant, they may cause disruption leading to a slow down of the evacuation.

Evacuation Certification Trials

Regulators attempt to enforce and maintain safety standards through a set of essentially prescriptive rules that have evolved over time. In the USA the rules are known as the Federal Aviation Regulations or FAR (FAR, 1989), while in Europe they are know as Joint Aviation Regulations or JAR (JAR, 2001). Under these regulations aircraft manufacturers must demonstrate that new aircraft designs or seating configurations will allow a full load of passengers and crew to evacuate safely from the aircraft within 90 seconds. The accepted way of demonstrating this capability is to perform a single full-scale evacuation trial using the passenger compartment under question and an appropriate mix of passengers. The passenger age and gender mix used in the trials must conform to that specified in the regulations. This is selected to be representative of the travelling public. Half the normally available exits are used (usually along one side of the aircraft) and the demonstration is conducted in darkness. The passengers must evacuate to the ground and so the slides are fully deployed during the trial. As part of these trials a video record is made of the progress of the evacuation, showing the behaviour of passengers inside the cabin as they exit the cabin via the various exits and their behaviour on the slide.

By detailed study of video recordings from 90-second certification trials (see Figure 10.7), both qualitative and quantitative data can be generated relating to passenger behaviour. From the analysis of videos of 90-second certification trials it is possible to establish various behavioural traits common to *certification trials*. For example, passengers spend an insignificant amount of time in releasing seatbelts, very little aisle swapping occurs, passengers are very compliant to crew instructions, seat jumping is extremely rare,

Passenger Behaviour in Emergency Situations 155

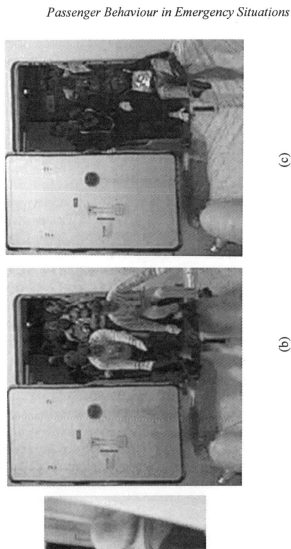

Figure 10.7 Images from certification type trials showing: (a) action of an assertive crew member making physical contact with passengers; (b) passengers jumping onto a Type-A slide; and (c) passengers sitting down onto a slide at a Type-A exit

Source: photographs of uncertain origin.

passengers hesitate at slide exits prior to committing to jump, etc. It is important to note that, while these behaviours are extremely relevant to certification trials, some of them may be irrelevant in real accident situations. An important aspect of data generated from certification trials is that it is possible to quantify passenger attributes using the video footage. For example, the flow rates and movement velocities of passengers in aisles, the passenger exit hesitation time for various exits types, time to traverse slides, time to open an exit, etc. can all be quantified.

It is, however, extremely difficult to obtain access to this type of information as aircraft manufacturers consider it to be valuable proprietary information. However, through a UK CAA project, through strict confidentiality agreements with all the major manufacturers (i.e. Airbus Industries, Boeing Commercial Airplane, British Aerospace and Douglas Aircraft Company Inc.) FSEG has access to a large amount of video footage from 90-second certification trials.

This information has been analysed by FSEG (Owen et al., 1999; Galea et al., 2002). In total, some 30 evacuation trials of 24 aircraft have been analysed, covering the period 1969 to 1996 and including commuter, single aisle, dual aisle and double deck aircraft. The data represents the evacuation of 68 flight crew, 194 cabin crew and 8,865 passenger participants. The data extracted concerns exiting behaviour of the passengers and crew on an aircraft by aircraft and exit-by-exit basis. From the data the following information was collated: cabin crew response times, exit opening times, slide inflation times, exit ready times, passenger exit use, passenger exit delay times, passenger escape slide/wing use 'off time', flow rates, efficiency measures and Type-A exit lane usage. This data is being used in the development of aircraft evacuation computer models such as the airEXODUS model (Galea and Galprarsoro, 1996; Galea et al., 1996; Owen et al., 1998a; Blake et al., 2002; Galea et al., 2002b).

One the most important parameters that can be derived from these studies is the passenger exit delay time. This phrase was coined by the author to represent the time spent by passengers in passing through an aircraft exit. When passing through doors typically found in buildings, people do not hesitate but pass through in a normal walking manner. Unlike doors found in buildings, when a passenger approaches an aircraft exit they are typically faced with a slide and the passenger must break their stride as they mount the slide, preferable by jumping onto the slide, but sometimes by sitting on the slide. In virtually all cases, passengers exhibit a momentary hesitation at the exit before proceeding through it. This is due to the passenger contemplating how to negotiate the exit. After this momentary pause, the passenger mounts the slide.

Passenger Behaviour in Emergency Situations 157

The mounting of the slide also incurs a slight delay, which can be quite small if the passengers jumps onto the slide or quite long if the passenger sits down onto the slide.

The passenger exit delay time incurred by a passenger at an aircraft exit is dependent upon a number of factors namely: *configurational*, i.e. dependent on the design of the exit and its approach; *procedural*, i.e. dependent on the presence and behaviour of crew; and *behavioural*, i.e. dependent on the physical characteristics of the passenger and their approach to exiting. From this analysis the most important factors are thought to be:

- *exit type* – each type of exit requires different styles of exiting techniques, for example passengers tend to crouch and climb out of Type-III exits, and jump out of Type-A exits;
- *exiting behaviour* – different behaviour traits can be exhibited by passengers, even for the same exit type. For example, some passengers jump through Type-A exits, whereas others sit on the sill and push off, some passengers step through Type-III exits while others stand on the sill and jump down;
- *passenger physical attributes* – the gender, age and physical size of the passengers will have an impact on the nature of the exiting behaviour likely to be exhibited at the exit, for example people of large girth take longer to pass through a Type-III exit than people of smaller girth, elderly people and women generally have a higher tendency to sit on slides than males;
- *presence of cabin attendants* – the presence (or absence) of cabin attendants at exits can enormously influence the behaviour exhibited by passengers at exits. Undirected passengers tend to take more time deciding how to use the exit, and indeed, which exit to use;
- *behaviour of cabin attendants* – when cabin attendants are present at an exit, the degree of assertiveness they display also influences the hesitation times. As the level of assertiveness increases, the range of slower hesitation times decreases, thus increasing the overall flow throughput of the exit.

Other factors may also have a bearing on passenger exit performance such as:

- *exit sill height* – the height of the exit above the ground may have an impact on the likely hesitation experienced by a passenger at the exit;
- *slide configuration* – the shape and configuration of the slide may have an impact on the passenger exit delay time, especially for very high exits.

While these last two factors are thought to have an impact on passenger performance, there is currently insufficient data to definitively determine the level of significance.

As an example of the analysis that has been conducted on passenger behaviour at exits, consider main deck Type-A exits with assertive cabin crew. Here, assertive cabin crew are taken to be crew who displayed a vocal and physical assertiveness during the majority of the passenger flow through their exit. Vocal assertiveness is taken to mean crew members who continuously yelled clear instructions to the passengers and physical assertiveness is represented by crew members who made physical contact with the passengers (see Figure 10.7).

From the FSEG analysis, suitable data from 11 previous certification tests involving Type-A exits with assertive cabin crew was found. The aircraft meeting these selection requirements were drawn from Boeing, Airbus and Douglas aircraft. It is also worth noting that three of these aircraft failed to meet the FAR Part 25.803 certification requirement. In total, passenger exit delay time data from 20 exits representing some 2,078 passengers was used to determine the passenger exit distribution. For each exit meeting the selection criteria (i.e. Type-A, main deck, assertive crew), a frequency distribution curve of passenger exit delay time can be generated. The shape of these distributions are remarkably similar, resembling an exponential/poisson distribution that peaks at the low end of the delay time distribution and tails off towards the higher end of the distribution. This suggests that the majority of the passengers display a short delay time (associated with a rapid jump onto the slide; see Figure 10.7b) while a sizeable number of passengers have a relatively long delay time (associated with sitters see Figure 10.7c). On the whole, the slowest passengers exit delay times are associated with personal attributes of being elderly and being female. From this data we note that the minimum delay time is approximately 0.2 seconds and the maximum delay time is 4.7 seconds. The typical distribution of delay times for main deck Type-A exits with assertive crew is depicted in Figure 10.8. The shape of the curve for unassertive crew is similar to that shown in Figure 10.8 with the fastest times being unaffected but with more passengers displaying the slower times.

Experiments

Whilst certification data and accident analysis provides much important information, these data sources do not completely satisfy our need for data concerning human behaviour in aviation emergencies.

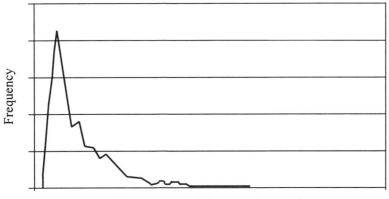

Figure 10.8 Passenger exit delay time distribution for main deck Type-A exits with assertive crew

While the certification trial is carried out in a controlled experimental environment, only a single trial is necessary to satisfy 90-second certification requirements. As a result, for some important behavioural parameters, it is not possible to develop a thorough understanding of the inherent variability in results. The need to perform repeated experiments should come as no surprise as, even under the most controlled experimental conditions, no evacuation exercise involving crowds of real people will produce identical results if the exercise is repeated – even if the same people are used (Galea, 1998). For any structure/population/environment combination, the evacuation performance of the combination is likely to follow some form of distribution.

Accident data also has certain limitations. Deriving definite time-scales of events from anecdotal evidence is difficult. As a consequence, important pieces of data such as the length of time taken to open exits, unbuckle seatbelts, etc. is difficult to obtain with any degree of certainty. The information is also reliant on the memories of the individuals involved. Furthermore, behavioural information is incomplete as not everyone undergoes an interview or completes a questionnaire. Finally, behavioural data concerning the fatalities can only be derived from secondary sources.

Due to the inherent limitations of certification trials and accident analysis, large-scale experiments and component tests offer an important additional source of information concerning human behaviour in aircraft emergencies. Since the mid-1960s a number of experiments have been carried out and have contributed much important information concerning our understanding of human behaviour in aviation emergency situations.

Early evacuation experiments One of the worlds first structured scientific investigations into cabin safety issues using a full-scale test facility was conducted in 1965 by CAMI researchers Garner and Blethrow (Garner and Blethrow, 1966). They used a cabin section from a Lockheed Constellation L-1649 that had recently crashed. Garner and Blethrow had part of the wreckage restored for use in their evacuation experiments. The test facility contained 50 passenger seats, 40 of which were in a five abreast configuration. The floor of the cabin section was at an angle as the aircraft had crashed onto a hill.

Four different experiments were conducted involving combinations of emergency lighting, dense white non-toxic smoke, outside flashing strobe lights, simulated debris, dolls representing children and an injured passenger. The evacuation tests also involved trained cabin crew performing their normal evacuation duties. Tests were conducted in night and day conditions and different passenger groups were used for each of the four experiments to ensure that subjects did not learn appropriate behaviours. As part of the experimental procedures, the passengers were subjected to taped take-off and landing noises, they received an 'in-flight' meal and the 'captain' made several announcements from the flight deck. The crew went through their normal duties, including the pre-flight briefing. Just prior to the emergency incident, the captain would announce an emergency landing would take place and the crew would then brief the passengers.

While the results from these trials were not statistically significant, as no repeat trials were undertaken, the results and the procedures developed were extremely important. For its time, this was an extremely innovative series of experiments. Many of the experimental procedures employed for the first time in these trials are still considered good experimental practice and followed today. Some of the findings from this work are also still relevant today. The main findings from this work include:

- elderly passengers had problems releasing their seatbelts, a similar observation to that found in the AASK analysis;
- seating of elderly or incapacitated passengers directly adjacent to an exit could delay the operation and use of the exit, an observation noted in the NTSB accident survey;
- passengers looked for and expected instructions from crew before taking action, highlighting the importance of good communications between crew and passengers;
- cabin crew can maintain control of an evacuation and instil a high degree of motivation through assertive voice commands;

- in terms of seeking their entrance route as the escape route, 6 per cent of the passengers in the night tests and 27 per cent of the passengers in the day tests claimed they sought their entrance route;
- additional lighting at exits to enhance exit location in conditions of poor visibility was suggested. Furthermore, a suggestion was made to investigate the possible use of sound to highlight exits in poor visibility conditions.

Following several experiments such as that conducted by Garner and Blethrow, it became clear that dedicated reusable experimental facilities were required to undertake a range of evacuation experiments. Today, there are two major facilities capable of undertaking large-scale aircraft evacuation experiments on a regular basis. These are located at the FAA Civil Aerospace Medical Institute (CAMI) in Oklahoma City, USA and Cranfield University in the UK. The primary purpose of these facilities has been to address operational or regulatory issues associated with aircraft evacuation.

CAMI experimental evacuation facility CAMI lead the world in developing a reusable large-scale test facility for evacuation analysis. The CAMI cabin simulator – built in 1968 – consists of a C124 fuselage section, 12ft wide and 77ft long, mounted on hydraulically controlled platforms so that various pitch and roll conditions can be simulated (Garner, 1966; Blethrow et al., 1977; FAA OAM website). The simulator provides a typical narrow body aircraft style six-abreast economy-class seating configuration with a 15in. wide central aisle and a maximum seating capacity of 80. The facility is restricted to studies involving narrow body aircraft and exit configurations consisting of Type-I and Type-III exits (see Figure 10.9). Some of the earliest studies to make use of the facility involved the investigation of the evacuation capabilities of disabled passengers from aircraft (Blethrow et al., 1977) and the impact of stairs on aircraft evacuation (Pollard et al., 1978). Over the past 30 years the CAMI facility has been extensively utilised to address issues concerning seating density, exit size, passenger flow rates through Type-I and Type-III exits, interaction of cabin crew with passenger during evacuation.

Cranfield experimental evacuation facility Cranfield University has two active cabin simulator facilities funded and supported by the UK CAA. The first is a B737 simulator capable of simulating narrow body aircraft evacuations, which has been in service since 1991, and the second, the very large evacuation simulator (VLES) was officially opened on 12 July 2001. In 1986, prior to the establishment of these two simulators, evacuation research at Cranfield

(a)

(b)

Figure 10.9 CAMI narrow body test facility: (a) passengers exiting a smoke filled simulator via a Type-I exit; and (b) internal passenger behaviour during a simulated evacuation

Source: courtesy of Civil Aerospace Medical Institute.

University was based on evacuation experiments conducted using a Trident Three aircraft cabin section to simulate narrow bodied aircraft evacuations. The Trident Three evacuation simulator has now been decommissioned following the construction of the B737 test simulator. The B737 simulator can accommodate up to 60 passengers and has two floor level Type-I exits (one with a functioning single lane slide) and a Type-III exit (see Figure 10.10).

Both narrow body facilities have been used to perform numerous experiments to understand human performance in evacuation situations better. Some trials have been performed under noncompetitive behaviour and so are similar in nature to the certification trial, while other trials have been performed under competitive behaviour – a technique pioneered by Cranfield University – in an attempt to simulate the conditions of real evacuation situations.

Results from experimental research Numerous experimental trials have been conducted at the CAMI, Cranfield and other facilities around the world. It is not possible to give a full description of all this work here. However, some of the major findings concerning human behaviour will be briefly discussed.

i) Evacuation performance of disabled passengers

The FAR 28.803 emergency demonstration does not require the inclusion of passengers with movement disabilities. As such, no information regarding the evacuation of disabled passengers is available from 90-second certification trials. While some information is available on the performance of disabled passengers in accident reports, this information provides no quantitative data on movement rates and performance capabilities.

In 1977, using their narrow body simulator, CAMI performed a series of trial evacuations using various categories of disabled passengers (Blethrow et al., 1977). To this day this experiment is unique and provides some of the only data available to the aviation industry on movement capabilities of disabled passengers. In total, 153 subjects were used, of whom 129 had some form of disability, both movement and cognitive. Disabilities included blindness and partial sight, deafness, being elderly, obesity, being in leg casts, arthritis, cerebral palsy, mental disability, multiple sclerosis, polio, paraplegia, quadriplegia, and being non-ambulant (via the use of anthropomorphic dummies). Useful quantitative data was generated concerning the extended response times of the disabled passengers, their slower movement speeds through aisles and seat rows and the significant increases in exit hesitation times. Results suggest that up to 50 per cent of the total travel time could be

164 *Passenger Behaviour*

(a)

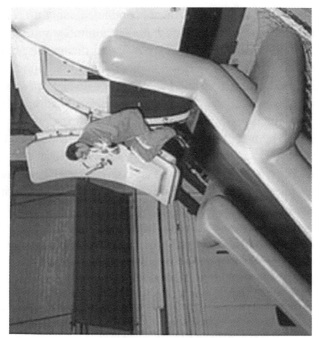

(b)

Figure 10.10 Cranfield B737 simulator: (a) interior view; and (b) Type-I exit in use

Source: courtesy of Cranfield University.

expended in moving from the window seat to the aisle in some cases. They further concluded that disabled passengers who were ambulatory could be seated anywhere in the cabin except in an exit row or a primary over-wing exit route. This was suggested as their location in these areas may impede the early stages of an evacuation. Those disabled passengers requiring assistance could be better assisted if seated away from heavily congested exit areas.

ii) The effects of aircraft attitude

Emergency evacuations are likely to occur under abnormal attitude conditions brought about by landing gear failure. However, the majority of evacuation research has concentrated on conditions of normal attitude (0° pitch and roll). The research of Garner and Blethrow (Garner and Blethrow, 1966) utilised a test facility in which the cabin had a pitch of 32°: perhaps somewhat surprisingly they concluded that slopes of this magnitude did not cause a great deal of difficulty for ambulant passengers. However, they did not repeat their experiments under normal conditions and so their conclusions were simply based on comments from the test subjects.

Using their narrow body test facility, CAMI undertook a series of trials to investigate the impact of landing gear failure, upon evacuation performance (Pollard et al., 1978). They considered attitudes consisting of combinations of 7° pitch and 12° roll (left and right) in order to approximate pitch and roll attitudes that may be encountered in nose and/or main gear collapse. Subjects were evacuating through spiral and straight-segmented staircases, passageways with seats on one side and without seats on both sides, both with and without simulated smoke. The simulated smoke was represented using light-obscuring goggles. In total CAMI performed 210 trials. A total of seven subject groups were used, each typically consisting of between 23–26 (depending upon attendance). The trials were run over a period of seven days, with each population performing 30 trials. Each subpopulation was subjected to a different series of scenarios on each day.

The findings from this work provide useful qualitative information into the performance of passengers under adverse conditions of attitude and visibility. They concluded that straight stairs provide more efficient movement between decks than spiral stairs and may also be safer to traverse. Changes in attitude and reduced visibility both reduced movement efficiency in all cases.

While important, these trials suffered a number of weaknesses. The use of goggles to represent smoke conditions, while simulating the reduction in visibility that may be encountered in a smoke-filled environment, does not induce the same level of psychological stress in the test subjects. Furthermore, the number of trials to which each passenger was subjected meant that learning effects could have had a major impact on the outcome of the results. Finally, volunteers were required to traverse the experimental apparatus in both directions, i.e. up and down the stairs and forward and aft of the passageway. Unfortunately, the published report does not present the results for each component but as a combination of both movement directions. It is thus impossible to separate out the effects and obtain a useful quantitative measure.

One of the areas touched upon by these experiments is that of staircase design. With the advent of aircraft with large upper decks such as the B747-400 and the A380, issues of staircase design and their impact on human performance during evacuation are very topical. Currently, the aviation regulations are silent on the issue of staircase design (e.g. FAR Part 25.807 Airworthiness Standards). While there are no specific rules addressing staircases, special conditions were specified for the certification of the B747. These conditions do not specify staircase design constraints but state objectives that should be meet by good staircase design, e.g. stairs must be safe, must work in adverse attitude conditions, etc. This omission could lead to the development of suboptimal conditions during an evacuation should the staircase be needed as a means of escape. As an example, the height of a stair riser and the depth of a stair tread are known to be important factors in determining the ease of use and efficiency of staircase design yet the regulations make no explicit mention concerning these issues. The work of Pollard and colleagues (Pollard et al., 1978) only considered single lane staircases with an effective width of 20ins. As such, the passengers evacuated in single file and used the handrails extensively. With the advent of the A380, these experiments are no longer relevant, as staircases are expected to accommodate two or more passengers simultaneously (see, for example, Figure 10.11).

Additionally, the requirement for handrails that separate a wide staircase into lanes has long been recognised as essential in building and marine regulations (Pauls, 1995; Life Safety Code Handbook, 1997). It is recognised that handrails enable passengers to use the entire width of the staircase during an emergency evacuation as opposed to 'hugging' the walls close to the handrails. Handrails are mandatory in building codes as they provide support to occupants and serve as guides for people whose vision may be impaired due to smoke and/or lighting failure (Life Safety Code Handbook, 1997). In addition, within building codes it is recognised that, to be effective, the handrails must be within reach of staircase users (ibid.). Therefore building codes mandate that handrails must be within 30ins of the 'natural path of

Passenger Behaviour in Emergency Situations 167

Figure 10.11 View down the main stair in the Cranfield VLES showing a possible dual lane stair configuration with central handrail

Source: photograph taken by E. Galea.

travel' (ibid.). On board marine vessels, the requirement for handrails is of even more importance as marine vessels are subject to dynamic and static changes in pitch and roll. Similar situations could develop on aircraft that have crashed and have gear failure.

While it is acknowledged that the stairs are not intended to be the primary means of escape for upper deck passengers, they cannot be ruled out as a viable means of egress in some circumstances. Their design must therefore take into account their use as a means of escape not only in ideal conditions as found in certification trials, but also in adverse attitude and visibility conditions. Research is currently being undertaken by Airbus Industries in this area (Lauber, 2002): it is, however, expected that this will continue to be the subject of research for years to come.

iii) Cranfield competitive evacuation procedure

Following the Manchester air disaster of 1985, and as part of a UK CAA-funded research programme, Professor Helen Muir and others from Cranfield University pioneered a new technique to simulate 'competitive behaviour' of the type reported in emergency evacuations (Muir et al., 1989). The technique involved giving £5 bonus payments to the first 50 per cent (later increased to 75 per cent in some experiments) of passengers to evacuate the test facility (a Trident aircraft fuselage).

For the bulkhead experiments, it was shown that, if the width of the bulkhead aperture was increased to at least 30ins, significant reductions in evacuation times could be achieved. Similarly, for Type-III exits, a vertical seat projection of 18ins would appear to be optimum. Furthermore, in the evacuations involving Type-III exits, evacuation times for competitive situations were considerably longer than for noncompetitive situations.

This research demonstrated that high motivation induced by financial rewards led to significant differences in performance to that observed under 'normal' experimental motivation levels. This study suggested that findings from experiments using 'normal' motivation levels were likely to be different from those using 'high' motivation levels. It was also found that human factor effects such as age and gender were highly influential on the experimental results, with young fit males being more likely to be amongst the first 50 per cent out of the aircraft, a result that was first suggested by Snow (Snow et al., 1970) some 20 years earlier.

This technique and its variations have become the standard testing procedure in aviation research. Using the cash incentive, trial subjects are motivated to exit the aircraft as quickly as possible, with test trials often displaying behaviour such as passengers struggling to get by each other, some climbing over seats and other participants within the cabin and at exits (see Figure 10.9b). It is argued that these types of condition are similar to those that occur in aircraft emergencies, in which the conditions rapidly deteriorate and become life threatening.

It should be recalled here that aviation accidents involving such conditions are extremely rare and that in the NTSB study of human behaviour, on the whole passengers reported essentially cooperative behaviour. Those passengers reporting uncooperative behaviour were restricted to only three evacuations, two of which involved fire. The competitive behaviours reported included pushing, climbing over seats and disputes amongst passengers – consistent with those observed in the Cranfield competitive trials. It should further be recalled that a significant number of passengers are socially bound to other passengers and that this is likely to have a significant effect on exiting behaviour. To date, the trials that have been conducted have focused on the behaviour of individuals. To be truly representative of aviation emergency situations, the competitive evacuation protocol must be extended to include couples and family groups. In such trials, the bonus would only be paid if all members of the group successfully evacuated.

Continuing this work, in 1992 and 1996 Muir analysed the impact of 'high' motivation when evacuating through bulkhead passageways and Type-III exits with and without smoke with different exit passageway widths (Muir et al., 1992; Muir, 1996b). This analysis further revealed that evacuation performance was significantly linked to passageway configurations. In addition, in conditions of smoke, gender was found to significantly affect egress time. However, other human factors such as height, weight and age did not appear to contribute to egress times.

The work of Cranfield has not been restricted to Type-III exits and bulkheads. The group has also studied the impact of cabin crew on passenger behaviour at Type-I exits (Muir et al., 1995; Muir and Cobbett, 1996; Muir, 1996a). This work has shown that the presence and motivation of assertive cabin crew tended to increase the flow rate of passengers through Type-I exits. This result is similar to the finding concerning passenger exit hesitation times based on the analysis of 90-second certification data for Type-I and Type-A exits (Owen et al., 1999; Galea et al., 2002).

These results are of great importance as they highlight the central role that cabin crew play in the evacuation process. Not only is it important to have crew present, but it is essential that the crew are well trained and able to be both vocally and physically assertive.

iv) CAMI trials

Following the Manchester accident, CAMI, like Cranfield, invested significant effort into examining the behaviour of passengers opening and exiting through Type-III exits. These experiments have concentrated on: exit hatch removal (Rasmussen et al., 1989); use of passenger smoke hoods during evacuation through Type-III exits (McLean et al., 1989); dual and single seating configurations adjacent to Type-III exits (McLean et al., 1992); high passenger motivation and seating configurations adjacent to Type-III exits (McLean et al., 1995); high passenger motivation and passenger physical attributes such as height, age, weight, waist size and gender on evacuation time through Type-

III exits (McLean and George, 1995); and passenger density or number on egress rate through Type-III exits (McLean et al., 1999). While these experiments have highlighted potential linkages between various factors and egress performance, these and similar experiments have suffered from a range of deficiencies including re-use of test subjects thereby introducing learning effects, small test groups and subject variability. Thus, it has been difficult to establish with any reliability definitive links between these parameters and evacuation efficiency (McLean, 2001).

In a bid to address some of the questions raised by these studies, CAMI have recently completed the most extensive series of aviation evacuation experiments concerning Type-III exits to date (McLean, 2002). The experiment involved 2,544 volunteers and required three months of experimentation. During the test programme 2.3 per cent of the participants (58 people) were injured, 11 seriously. In total, the series of experiments involved over 10,000 Type-III exit crossings as each participant was involved in four repeat trials. In total there were 48 naïve evacuations, i.e. evacuations involving participants experiencing the evacuation for the first time, and 192 participants were required to open the Type-III exit for the first time. The factors that were examined in this series of trials were: exit hatch removal; exit seating configuration and passenger density or number; passenger physical attributes such as height, age, weight, waist size and gender, all of which were examined under high and low passenger motivation. As in the earlier CAMI experiments, cabin crew were used to instruct passengers and direct passengers towards exits during the trials.

These trials have produced a massive amount of data that is only just beginning to be analysed. The initial analysis by CAMI suggests that it is the variability in physical parameters of the people passing through the Type-III exit that has the most profound impact on average flow rate through it. Of the factors investigated, girth, age and gender proved to be the most significant in determining average flow rate. Somewhat surprisingly, these factors were found to be more significant than group motivation, whether or not the hatch was disposed inside or outside the aircraft and the passageway width.

In combining this data and then separating out single factors, CAMI found that the mean egress time is about 14 per cent faster for males than females (1.49 seconds for males and 1.70 seconds for females). If the gender influence is considered with passageway width we find that for narrow passageway widths of around 10ins, the differences between males and females is small, being around 9.5 per cent, but that this difference increases as the passageway width grows to 20ins, producing a difference of about 23 per cent. At the smaller size passageways, the gender differences diminish as both genders are constrained by severe ergonomic effects.

If the age data is extracted, we find that as the test subjects get older, the mean egress time increases. For subjects in the 18–22 age group the mean egress time was 1.34 seconds, while for the 53–65 age group the mean egress time was 2.01 seconds, representing an increase of 50 per cent. If the girth data (as measured by waist size) is extracted, we find that, as the girth of the test subjects increases so does the mean egress time. For subjects in the 24–30in. waist size, the mean egress time was 1.35 seconds while for the 41–62in. waist size, the mean egress time was 1.96 seconds, representing an increase of 45 per cent.

By way of a comparison, the mean egress time was virtually unchanged whether the hatch was disposed in- or outside the aircraft (1.60 and 1.59 seconds respectively), whether low or high motivation methodologies were employed (1.64 and 1.55 seconds respectively), whether low or high group densities were used (1.56 and 1.60 seconds respectively) and whether a narrow or wide passageway was used (1.66 seconds for the 10in. approach and 1.50 seconds for the 20in. approach).

These factors appear to corroborate the earlier findings of Snow (Snow et al., 1970) and those of Muir (Muir et al., 1989) that young males make the best survivors. However, unlike the studies of Snow and Muir, which suggested that this trend was marked in high risk situations involving very severe fires, the CAMI results suggest that there is little significant difference between high and low motivation situations. However, this result could simply be down to the high level of motivation that the test subjects showed in the so-called 'low' motivation trials.

Another important factor noted in these trials relates to the use of safety briefing cards. Each participant who was required to operate the Type-III exit was also required to study the safety briefing card instructing them on the correct method for removal and disposal of the exit hatch. These cards were standard airline issued safety briefing cards and the participants received no additional instruction. As a result, the vast majority of the 192 naïve hatch openings were performed correctly.

The Future

There is still a wide array of data concerning human behaviour in aviation emergencies that requires collection and analysis. Perhaps the most significant factor missing in all of the analysis to date – both experimental and accident analysis – is the impact that social bonds may have on evacuation behaviour. In addition, as the recent CAMI trials have highlighted that passenger attributes play a significant role in determining egress capability, passenger cultural differences may also be an important factor and so should be examined both through accident analysis and in controlled experiments.

The importance of safety information has been highlighted and is recognised to play an important role in the success of evacuations. However, passengers have shown reluctance to view and study this information. In the future, new approaches to the passenger briefing should be explored. The advent of interactive seat-back entertainment systems offers a range of possibilities. For instance, a safety channel could be included in the in-flight programming. This could be used to provide continuous safety information. The programming could be designed so that it was both entertaining and informative. Information tailored to seating locations, such as showing the location of the nearest exits to each, seat could also be provided. By providing such information on demand and in interesting formats, the passenger would be more likely to view the material and, furthermore, they would be able to reacquaint themselves with the safety procedures prior to landing. Incentives could even be provided to passengers to view and study the material. Simple interactive questionnaires could be provided and, if correctly completed, the passenger would receive bonus miles on their loyalty card.

Communications between cabin crew is an area requiring further development and innovation – especially as our aircraft increase in size and number of passengers. In other crowd control situations such as in large public events, crowd control marshals have access to relevant information via headset communication devices. Such devices may also have a role to play in the management of aircraft emergencies. Cabin crew would be able to make use of such devices in emergency evacuation situations where they may need to redirect passengers to another viable exit or conversely attract passengers to a viable but under-utilised exit. If considered part of the uniform, such devices would also be useful in situations involving in-flight fire, disruptive passengers, in-flight medical emergencies and in hijack situations. The introduction of such devices would require the development of clear and easy to use operational procedures. These would need to cover issues associated with what information is conveyed, how and when it is conveyed and between which crew members communication would be restricted. It would also require the introduction of appropriate training to ensure that cabin crew could correctly and easily use such devices in emergency situations.

While much work still needs to be done to resolve many of the issues associated with human behaviour in narrow body aircraft, focus is shifting to wide body aircraft and VLTA. Both the CAA/Cranfield and the FAA/CAMI have invested heavily in acquiring flexible wide body test facilities, the former with their VLES simulator and the later with their B747 test fuselage.

Cranfield's VLES is 36ft wide (11m), 82ft long (25m) and 32.8ft (10m) high and has two decks, the upper deck has a sill height of 8m while the lower deck has a sill height of 5m (Greene and Muir, 2001). It is designed to accommodate up to 300 test subjects. The upper deck slide is 13m (42.5ft) long. The VLES is modular in construction allowing it to be configured into a number of different layouts. It is possible to change seat pitch, number of exits, width and number of aisles and the test can be undertaken with or without an internal staircase (see Figure 10.12).

The CAMI capabilities are also being extended with the introduction of a wide body test facility (see Figure 10.13). The main component of the facility is a retired B747 aircraft that will be used to enhance the study of evacuation problems encountered by larger aircraft with higher door sill heights (16ft) and multiple aisles. The aircraft was decommissioned and purchased by the FAA in 1997 and the facility has undergone a major refit to allow the installation of control and recording equipment, the rapid alteration of interior configuration making it possible to be used to simulate multiple interior layouts and the development of a zoned smoke system which allows the interior to be smoke filled in 30–45 seconds.

Both the CAMI and Cranfield wide body facilities will prove welcome additions to the aviation industries testing capabilities. For while wide body aircraft have been in commercial service since the late 1960s, there has been no dedicated test facility to study human behaviour in emergency situations involving these types of aircraft. Many questions remain to be studied, such as the impact of exit separation on evacuation, the nature of passenger aisle swapping during evacuation conditions, the influence that crew can exert on passengers at wide (Type-A) exits, the impact of increased passenger numbers on passenger behaviour during competitive situations, etc. In addition to the standard wide body aircraft, the advent of the VLTA pose additional questions regarding human behaviour. VLTA designs currently being considered are capable of carrying 800+ passengers with interiors consisting of two aisles and two full-length passenger decks. Other more radical concepts consist of a blended wing body (BWB) design, involving one or two decks with four or more aisles. Questions concerning seating arrangement, nature and design of recreational space, the number, design and location of internal staircases, the

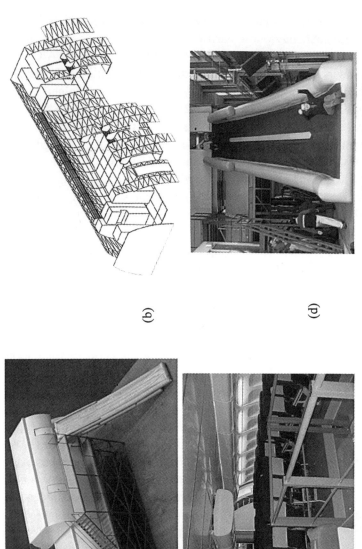

Figure 10.12 Cranfield VLES showing: (a) model view of the entire simulator with upper deck slide deployed; (b) modular nature of structure; (c) interior view of upper deck; and (d) upper deck slide in use

Source: courtesy of Cranfield University.

Figure 10.13 CAMI B747 facility: (a) aircraft exterior; and (b) artist's impression of completed facility

Source: courtesy of Civil Aerospace Medical Institute.

number, location and type of exits, the number of cabin crew required and the nature of the cabin crew emergency procedures are just some of the issues that may have an impact on human behaviour during emergency situations.

The massive increase in passenger capacity and aircraft size being suggested also challenges some of our preconceptions in equipment design and crew emergency procedures. For instance, in order to complete an evacuation efficiently, will it be necessary to extend emergency procedures to the marshalling of those passengers evacuated to the ground? Imagine a situation with 800 passengers on the ground, possibly on one side of the aircraft. What impact will they have on fire fighting and rescue operations? Who should take responsibility for the grounded passengers? Should evacuation procedures be developed that allow passengers to travel between decks before exiting the aircraft? How will crew communicate effectively to control such an evacuation on a single deck and between decks? Will the proximity of multiple emergency slides have a detrimental effect on evacuation efficiency and safety? Can exits be safely spaced further apart than the current arbitrary 60ft limit. What impact will this have on evacuation times and survivability?

If BWB aircraft become a reality, should designs incorporate continuous solid cabin partitions along the length of the aircraft? Should these cabins have cross-aisles linking each cabin section? How many and how wide should they be? Will it be sufficient to simply have exits in the forward and aft sections of the aircraft? Can the largest exits currently available cope with passenger flow arising from four or five main aisles? Do we need to consider new concepts in exit design, perhaps introducing three or four lane exits? How efficient can a three or four lane exit be in evacuating passengers? Should the main aisles be made wider to accommodate more passengers? How much time is actually required for safe egress from a BWB aircraft?

While there are currently no VLTA flying, the A380 has been labelled a VLTA by some. The A380, while physically the largest passenger aircraft currently planned, does not represent a massive increase in passenger capacity, at least for its standard configuration. The standard passenger seating capacity of the A380 is reported to be 550 passengers in a three class configuration (Learmount, 2001); however, significantly greater seating capacity options are possible, with 822 passengers being suggested for the single class configuration (Kingsley-Jones, 2001). This is compared with the B747-400 that carries 416 in a three class configuration with a reported maximum of 660 for the single class configuration (ibid.). Another feature of the A380 is that it has two passenger decks positioned one on top of the other. This in itself is not unusual or novel, as the B747 has flown with an upper deck for many years. While it may be debated whether the new Airbus A380 should be classified as a VLTA, the number of passengers that are seated on the upper deck make the A380 different to existing aircraft.

With the upper deck comes the need to evacuate passengers using the upper deck exits and slides. A feature of upper deck exits is that the exit slides are much longer than those of more 'standard' exits. For example, on the B747 the upper deck sill height is 7.8m and on the A380 it is set to be 7.9m above the ground (Lauber, 2002). One assumption concerning the use of high sill height exits is that passengers would hesitate longer at the upper deck exit before they jumped onto the slide, compared to lower height main deck exits. While there is very little data concerning the use of upper deck slides under certification evacuation conditions, what data that is available suggests that this is not the case, and that passenger exit hesitation delays, while slightly longer, are similar to those of more standard exits (Owen et al., 1999). The shape of the slide may also have an impact on passenger exit hesitation times. Slides that are designed to reduce the visual impact of the sill height may counteract any tendency for increased hesitation times. Clearly, more research in the form of component testing is required to generate the required data.

In addition to higher sill heights, longer exit slides and large numbers of passengers located on upper decks, VLTA double deck aircraft can possess one or more staircases. Again, in itself this is not a new concept, as the B747 has flown for many years with a staircase connecting the two decks. While evacuation procedures for VLTA may not require the use of the staircase(s) in order to pass an evacuation certification trial, it is desirable that staircase design be appropriate for evacuation situations. Emergency evacuation scenarios may develop where it is necessary or desirable to evacuate all or some passengers down the stairs and out the main deck exits rather than out the upper deck exits. While less likely, accident situations may also develop where it is necessary to move some passengers to the upper deck and out of the upper exits. Passengers on the upper deck may decide that they cannot exit from the upper deck and attempt to use the slides on the lower deck. While this may not be a problem for existing aircraft, the sheer number of passengers located on the upper deck of VLTA configurations makes this an issue worth investigating. Additional crew – located at the head and base of stairs – may be required to control the flow of passengers between decks. In such circumstances, crew communications devices such as the previously suggested headsets may prove invaluable in assisting the crew to optimally controlling the flow of passengers between decks.

Other more innovative devices may prove effective in assisting passengers in locating viable exits. Directional sound (Withington, 2002) is one such device. The principle behind directional sound is simple in concept and hinges on the use of auditory signals that guide passengers along a viable path to the nearest exit. However, unlike ordinary sound, which contains no directional component, directional sound contains 'directional' information enabling passengers to follow the sound – even through the thickest smoke – to a viable exit. If such systems can be shown to work effectively with crew and other on-board systems in a variety of accident scenarios, directional sound may prove a useful addition to the existing crew and vision-/light-based guidance systems for VLTA. Innovative uses of emergency lighting systems also offer promise. Rather than simply lighting the path to an exit – as is the current practice with floor level lighting – illuminating the entire perimeter of the exit with strip lighting could prove useful. This could be extended to illuminating the passageway created by cabin monuments located just in front of the exits in a similar manner. In this way, exits and approaches to exits would be marked by a halo of light, making them more attractive in low light and smoky environments.

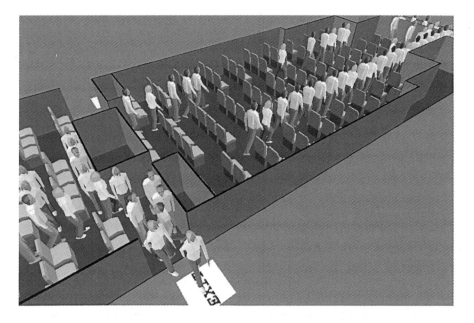

Figure 10.14 vrEXODUS generated scene from an airEXODUS evacuation simulation

In addition to the experimental work required to address these issues, computer-based movement and behaviour models capable of simulating the aviation evacuation process have a role to play. These models have been under development for the past 30 years and models such as airEXODUS (Blake et al., 2002; Galea and Gaprarsoro, 1993; Galea et al., 1997, 1996, 2002b; Owen et al., 1998a) have reached a level of sophistication that enables them correctly to predict the outcome of 90-second certification evacuation trials for both wide and narrow body aircraft (Galea et al., 2002b; Owen et al., 1998a). These models are also being used to simulate more realistic accident situations that are beyond the capabilities of experimental analysis, for instance, simulations involving the impact of fire, heat, smoke and toxic gases. For aircraft involving truly 'new' features it is expected that evacuation models in conjunction with experimental data resulting from component testing of the new features will be necessary. For the next generation of VLTA one of the areas requiring this form of collaboration concerns passenger exit hesitation times at upper deck exits. Computer-based aircraft evacuation models – together with reliable data – have the potential to make an already safe form of transportation safer by design.

References

Air Safety Week Report (2002), '"Fundamental Design Weakness" Revealed', *Air Safety Week*, Vol. 16, 13, 6–8, 1 April.

ATSB Report (2001), 'Boeing 747–438, VH-OJH Bangkok,Thailand, 23 September 1999', Australian Transport Safety Bureau, Investigation Report 199904538.

Blake, S., Galea, E., Gwynne, S., Lawrence, P. and Filippidis, L. (2002), 'Examining the Effect of Exit Separation on Aircraft Evacuation Performance during 90-second Certification Trials using Evacuation Modelling Techniques', *The Aeronautical Journal of the Royal Aeronautical Society*, Vol. 106, 1055, pp. 1–16.

Blethrow, J., Garner, J., Lowrey, D., Busby, D. and Chandler, R. (1977), *Emergency Escape of Handicapped Air Travellers*, DOT /FAA/AM/77–11, US Department of Transport, Federal Aviation Administration.

European Transport Safety Council (1996), *Increasing the Survival Rate in Aircraft Accidents: Impact protection, fire survivability, and evacuation*, Brussels: ETSC.

FAA OAM website, Office of Aerospace Medicine and Civil Aerospace Medical Institute, official websites, http://www.cami.jccbi.gov/.

FAR Part 25.807 Airworthiness Standards (1989), *Transport Category Airplanes*, including amendment 25–67 as published in the Federal Register on 16 June 1989, Washington, DC.

Finney, K., Galea, E., Dixon, A., Cooney, D. and Siddiqui, A. (2002), 'The AASK Database V3.0', University of Greenwich, paper in preparation.

Galea, E. (1998), 'A General Approach to Validating Evacuation Models with an Application to EXODUS', *Journal of Fire Sciences*, Vol. 16 (September/October), pp. 414–36.

Galea, E., Cooney, D., Dixon, A., Finney, K. and Siddiqui, A. (2000), 'The AASK DATABASE:Aircraft Accident Statistics and Knowledge. A Database to Record Human Experience of Evacuation in Aviation Accidents', Report for CAA Project 277/SRG/R+AD, April.

Galea, E., Blake, S. and Lawrence, P. (2002b), 'The airEXODUS Evacuation Model and its Application to Aircraft Safety', *Proceedings of the International Aircraft Fire and Cabin Safety Conference*, October 2001, Atlantic City, JAA–OSPAG–2002–1, CD-ROM.

Galea, E., Finney, K., Dixon, A., Cooney, D. and Siddiqui, A. (2002c), 'The AASK DATABASE V3.0: A database of human experience in evacuation derived from air accident reports', *Proceedings of the International Aircraft Fire and Cabin Safety Conference*, October 2001, Atlantic City, JAA–OSPAG–2002–1, CD-ROM.

Galea, E., Finney, K., Gwynne, S. and Dixon, A. (2002), 'Analysis of 90-second Certification Trial Data', CAA Report in preparation.

Galea, E. and Galprarsoro, J. (1993), 'EXODUS: An evacuation model for mass transport vehicles', Technical Report, UK CAA Paper 93006, ISBN 086039 543X.

Galea, E. and Owen, M. (1998), 'The AASK DATABASE: A database of human experience in evacuation derived from air accident reports', *Proceedings of the International Aircraft Fire and Cabin Safety Conference*, 16–20 November, Atlantic City, DOT/FAA/AR–99/68, CD-ROM.

Galea, E., Owen M., and Lawrence, P. (1996), 'Computer Modelling of Human Behaviour in Aircraft Fire Accidents', *Toxicology*, Vol. 115, Nos 1–3, pp. 63–78.

Galea, E., Owen, M. and Lawrence, P. (1997), 'The Role of Evacuation Modelling in the Development of Safer Air Travel', AGARD–CP–857, *Proceedings of AGARD PEP 88th Meeting on Aircraft Fire Safety*, Dresden, Vols 14–18 (October 1996), 36–1–36–13.

Garner, J. (1966), 'General Guidelines to Specifications for the Evacuation Simulator', unpublished report, CAMI.

Garner, J. and Blethrow, J. (1966), *Emergency Evacuation Tests of a Crashed L-1649*, Civil Aeromedical Institute, Federal Aviation Institute, DOT/FAA/AM–66/42.

Greene, G. and Muir, H. (2002), 'The Cranfield Large Cabin Evacuation Simulator', *Proceedings of the International Aircraft Fire and Cabin Safety Conference*, October 2001, Atlantic City, JAA–OSPAG–2002–1, CD-ROM.

Hynes, M. (1999), 'Human Factors Research on 519 Recent US Air Carrier Passenger Evacuation Events', *Proceedings of the International Aircraft Fire and Cabin Safety Conference*, 16–20 November, Atlantic City, DOT/FAA/AR–99/68, CD-ROM.

JAR Section 1 Part 25.807 Large Aeroplanes: Subpart D Design and Construction, as published in *Joint Aviation Requirements* (Change 15), 2001.

Johnson, N., Feinberg W. and Johnston, D. (1994), 'Microstructure and Panic: The impact of social bonds on individual action in collective flight from the Beverly Hills Supper Club Fire', in R. Dynes and K. Tierney (eds), *Disaster, Collective Behaviour and Social Organization*, Newark, Delaware: University of Delaware Press, pp. 168–89.

King D. (1988), Report on the Accident to Boeing 737–236 series 1, G–BGJL at Manchester International Airport on 22 August 1985', Aircraft Accident Report 8/88, London: HMSO.

Kingsley-Jones, M. (2001), 'Size or Speed', *Flight International*, 4–10 September, pp. 51–73.

Lauber, J. (2002), 'A380 Safety and Evacuation – Meeting the Challenge', presented at the Southern California Safety Institute 19th Annual Aircraft Cabin Safety Symposium, Los Angeles.

Learmount, D. (2001), 'Big on Safety', *Flight International* (June), pp. 12–18.

Life Safety Code Handbook (1997), 7th edn, ed. Ron Côte, P., Quincy, Massachusetts: National Fire Protection Association.

McLean, G. (2001), 'Access-to-egress: A meta-analysis of the factors that control emergency evacuation through the transport airplane Type-III overwing exit', DOT/FAA/AM–01/2, US Department of Transport, Federal Aviation Administration.

McLean, G. (2002), 'Access-to-egress: Factors influencing evacuation through a Type-III exit', presented at the Southern California Safety Institute 19th Annual Aircraft Cabin Safety Symposium, Los Angeles.

McLean, G., Chittum, C., Funkhouser, G., Fairlie, G. and Folk, E. (1992), 'Effects of Seating Configuration and Number of Type-III Exits on Emergency Aircraft Evacuation', DOT/FAA/AM–92–27, US Department of Transport, Federal Aviation Administration.

McLean, G. and George, M. (1995), 'Aircraft Evacuations through Type-III exits II: Effects of individual subject differences', DOT/FAA/AM–95/25, US Department of Transport, Federal Aviation Administration.

McLean, G., George, M., Chittum, C. and Funkhouser, G. (1995), 'Aircraft Evacuations through Type-III Exits I: Effects of seat placement at the exit', DOT/FAA/AM–95/22, US Department of Transport, Federal Aviation Administration.

McLean, G., Higgins, E., Lyne, P. and Vant, J. (1989), 'The Effects of Wearing Passenger Protective Breathing Equipment on Evacuation Times through Type–III and Type-IV Emergency Exits in Clear Air and Smoke', DOT/FAA/AM–89/12, US Department of Transport, Federal Aviation Administration.

Muir, H. (1996a), 'Research into the Factors Influencing Survival in Aircraft Accidents', *The Aeronautical Journal of the Royal Aeronautical Society* (May), pp. 177–82.

Muir, H. (1996b), 'The Effect on Aircraft Evacuations of Changes to the Vertical Projections between the Seat Rows Adjacent to the Overwing Exit From 399 to 69, 109 and 139' Cranfield University, CoA Report No. 9408.

Muir, H., Bottomley, D. and Hall, J. (1992), 'Aircraft Evacuations: Competitive evacuations in conditions of non-toxic smoke', Civil Aviation Authority UK, CAA Paper 92005.

Muir, H. and Cobbett, A.M. (1995), 'Cabin Crew Behaviour in Emergency Evacuations', Civil Aviation Authority/Federal Aviation Administration Paper DOT/FAA/CERTIFICATION TRIAL–95/16.

Muir, H. and Cobbett, A.M. (1996),'Cabin Crew Behaviour in Emergency Evacuations', Report for the Civil Aviation Authority (CAA), CAA Paper 95006: Part A (FAA No. DOT/FAA/AR–95/52), ISBN 0 86039 649 5 (Part A Only).

Muir, H., Marrison, C. and Evans, A. (1989), 'Aircraft Evacuations: The effect of passenger motivation and cabin configuration adjacent to the exit', CAA Paper 89019, Civil Aviation Authority.

National Transportation Safety Board (2001a), 'Survivability of Accidents involving Part 121 U.S. Air Carrier Operations, 1983 through 2000', Safety Report NTSB/SR–01/01, Washington, DC: NTSB.

National Transportation Safety Board (2001b), 'Safety Study, Emergency Evacuation of Commercial Airplanes', Safety Report NTSB/SS–00/01, Washington, DC: NTSB.

National Transportation Safety Board (2002a), 'Aviation Accident Statistics', NTSB website, http://www.ntsb.gov/aviation.

National Transportation Safety Board (2002b), 'Aviation Information', NTSB website, http://www.ntsb.gov/aviation.

Owen, M., Galea, E. and Dixon A. (1999), '90-second Certification Trial Data Archive Report', prepared for the UK CAA for Project 049/SRG/RandAD (March).

Owen, M., Galea, E. and Lawrence, P. (1996), 'The EXODUS Evacuation Model applied to Building Evacuation Scenarios', *Journal of Fire Protection Engineering*, Vol. 8, No. 2, pp. 65–86.

Owen, M., Galea, E., Lawrence, P. and Filippidis, L. (1998a), The Numerical Simulation of Aircraft Evacuation', *The Aeronautical Journal* (June/July), pp. 301–12.

Owen, M., Galea, E., Lawrence, P. and Filippidis, L. (1998b), 'AASK – Aircraft Accident Statistical Knowledge: A database of human experience in evacuation reports', *The Aeronautical Journal of the Royal Aeronautical Society* (August/September), pp. 353–63.

Pauls, J. (1995), *The SFPE Handbook of Fire Protection Engineering*, 2nd edn, Quincy, MA: National Fire Protection Association.

Pollard, D., Gerner, J., Blethrow, J. and Lowrey, D. (1978), 'Passenger Flow Rates between Compartments: Straight-segmented, spiral stairways, and passageways with restricted vision and changes of attitude' DOT/FAA/AM/78–3, US Department of Transport, Federal Aviation Administration.

Rasmussen, P. and Chittum, C. (1989), 'The Influence of Adjacent Seating Configurations on Egress through a Type-III Emergency Exit', DOT/FAA/AM–89/14, US Department of Transport, Federal Aviation Administration.

Schaeffer, F. (1994), 'Passenger Emergency Exit Usage in Actual Emergencies of Transport Aircraft', *Proceedings 11th Annual International Aircraft Cabin Safety Symposium and Technical Conference*, pp. 71–89.

Snow, C., Carroll, J. and Allgood, M. (1970), 'Survival in Emergency Escape from Passenger Aircraft', DOT/FAA/AM/70–16, Department of Transport, Federal Aviation Administration.

Tomita, H. (1999), 'For Less Injuries after Emergency Evacuations', *Proceedings, 1998 International Aircraft Fire and Cabin Safety Research Conference*, 16–20 November, Atlantic City, DOT/FAA/AR–99/68, CD-ROM.

Transportation Safety Board of Canada (1995), 'A Safety Study of Evacuations of Large, Passenger Carrying Aircraft', Report SA9501, Quebec: TSB.

Withington, D. (2002), 'The Use of Directional Sound to Aid Aircraft Evacuation', *Proceedings of the International Aircraft Fire and Cabin Safety Conference*, October, Atlantic City, JAA–OSPAG–2002–1, CD-ROM.

Chapter 11

The Psychological Impact of Aircraft Disasters

Man Cheung Chung

The occurrence of aircraft disasters can have devastating and traumatic ripple effects upon a whole range of people, including the passengers and aircrew on board, their families, relatives, close friends and colleagues, and on disaster personnel and, indeed, community residents living where the disaster has occurred. For example, on the basis of a non-fatal military aircraft accident which happened on the runway in Michigan in 1988, a study showed that people who were affected included the injured aircrew, their spouses, fellow squadron members and their spouses, fire-fighters, and control tower personnel on duty (those who watched the whole disaster and the rescue operation) during the accident. They showed a range of psychological symptoms including intrusive thoughts about the accident (68 per cent), avoidance behaviour (16 per cent), depression and anxiety (40 per cent), and post-traumatic stress symptoms (51 per cent) (Slagle et al., 1990).

Perhaps, recent research on the Gander aircraft disaster (in 1985, a chartered airliner, carrying eight aircrew and 248 US Army soldiers, took off from Gander, Newfoundland but crashed into the forest at the end of the runway, killing all on board) shows more clearly the range of people who can be traumatised by aircraft disasters. Five categories of people were identified. They were: 1) next of kin; 2) the bereaved; 3) service providers; 4) support providers; and 5) the infrastructure. The category of bereaved included next of kin of the deceased. It also included commanders who mourned the loss of their troops, and soldiers who returned safely on other flights. The category of service providers included police, fire-fighters, rescue recovery workers, rehabilitation personnel, chaplains and mental health workers. Other people included school personnel working with children affected by the disaster. The category of support providers included those who provided help, support, guidance, and logistical assistance to service providers. They also included families, friends and counsellors of the service providers. Finally, the category of infrastructure included members of some social organisations or authorities. These people helped to direct people and resources to the disaster site in order to support the work of service providers. They included personnel at the highest level in the military and the government (Wright, Ursano, Bartone and Ingraham, 1990).

Surviving Passengers

Given the foregoing broadly defined range of people affected by the traumatic ripple effects of aircraft disasters, let us turn our attention to literature which addresses the psychological reactions of some of the specific groups of people within this traumatic ripple. One of these groups is the passengers on the aircraft which crashed. However, systematic investigations into the traumatic psychological effects on passengers are few and far between, for the obvious reason that there is often a 100 per cent mortality rate with aircraft disasters. Nevertheless, anecdotal evidence is available which gives us a glimpse of the traumatic psychological effects of aircraft disasters on passengers.

For example, in 1977, a Tenerife jumbo jet collision occurred (a KLM 747 and a PanAm 747 collided), as a result of which 580 people died. Based on only eight of the 64 survivors on board, one study showed that they suffered from all or 75 per cent of the symptoms of a traumatic neurosis: uncontrollable emotions (particularly anxiety and rage), sleep disturbance and mental repetitions of the trauma in nightmares or daydreams. One year later, three suffered from a major physical illness, probably associated with the trauma, and psychic numbing, disbelief, phobias, mood swings, depression and psychosomatic problems (Perlberg, 1979).

In 1985, a Boeing 737 was waiting to take off on the runway at Manchester International Airport. Fire suddenly broke out in the aircraft, costing 54 lives. More than 80 survivors were sent to a nearby hospital (Lee, 1989). As the fire gradually consumed the aircraft, the behaviour of passengers trapped inside varied. While some were confused, extremely anxious and screaming hysterically, some were calm, and others stunned, dazed and bewildered. The latter group of passengers became submissive and dependent and needed to follow orders, even when the order might be inappropriate. For example, they followed an order telling them to stay in their seats with their seatbelts fastened. The passengers who were rescued were in severe shock, appeared to be sedated and seemed passively compliant and emotionless. They found it important to keep retelling what had happened, as if reliving the experience would help them to master the overwhelming experience. In fact, repeatedly talking to media and nursing staff about what had happened helped some survivors to become desensitised to the traumatic experience. Many survivors needed to find someone to blame, a scapegoat, and subsequently developed paranoid attitudes about, for example, those who asked them to stay in their seats. Some felt survivor guilt in that they had survived while others had died (Rawlins, 1985).

In 1997 an aircraft carrying French tourists crashed immediately after take-off and subsequently exploded on the ground, resulting in 23 dead and 29 seriously injured. Ten victims who were exposed to the loss of their loved ones, burned corpses and human remains were assessed. Four victims were diagnosed as suffering from acute stress disorder; two had peritraumatic dissociative symptoms; one experienced an intense feeling of numbness and derealisation and another reported depersonalisation with auditory hallucinations from the crash. One month later, of the four people with acute stress disorder, three now suffered from post-traumatic stress disorder; two suffered from major depression and displayed a high level of avoidance behaviour. Post-traumatic stress disorder was also associated with major depression (Birmes et al., 1999).

Fortunately, not all aircraft accidents incur such great costs in terms of human lives as those mentioned above. In some accidents passengers survived, having sustained no serious injuries, but nevertheless they experienced terror. In 1984, the East Tennessee State University basketball team and supportive personnel experienced a crash-landing at a small airport in rural Alabama. Thirty male survivors were assessed and the results showed that, 12 days after the accident, 93 per cent reported four or more of 12 symptoms of post-traumatic stress disorder. They experienced hyperalertness (82 per cent), decreased concentration or memory (79 per cent), intrusive thoughts (71 per cent), sleep disturbance (68 per cent), feeling detached or estranged (54 per cent) and dreams about the accident (50 per cent). They also reported frequent irritability (71 per cent) and a great deal of physical pain (65 per cent). One year later, three to five survivors still suffered from post-traumatic stress disorder. However, on the whole, the survivors as a group experienced a very high level of distress initially, which subsequently declined quickly and levelled off over time, in terms of the impact of the crash-landing accident, anxiety, depression, psychiatric symptoms and post-traumatic stress symptoms (Sloan, 1988).

Surviving Aircrew

Apart from passengers, aircrew are another group of people involved in the traumatic ripple effects of aircraft disasters. One would expect that their psychological reactions might well be different from those of passengers due to their experience and training. Indeed, research has revealed how helicopter aircrew managed to escape and survive a helicopter crash largely due to their previous accident training, which helped them not to give in to panic but to remain calm, relax, confident and in control (Hytten, 1989).

Research into aircrew's psychological reactions to aircraft disasters has focused on military aircrew's distressing experience of ejection, following an aircraft accident. Contrary to the above research on helicopter aircrew, many Royal Air Force ejectees did not find that their training had prepared them for the experiencing of ejection. In one study, 40 per cent of the 175 Royal Air Force ejectees revealed emotional reactions including prolonged fear, anger, apprehension, and anxiety which consequently affected their desire to return to flying. They also experienced transient confusional states, paranoid disturbance, nightmares, flashbacks of the accidents, and fear of being entangled in a crashed aircraft. They were intensely preoccupied with the accident and felt exhausted. Such a near-death experience led the ejectees to rethink about what was important in their lives. For several ejectees, family life became more important than service in the air force (Fowlie and Aveline, 1985; Aveline and Fowlie, 1987).

Bereaved Individuals

As was mentioned, aircraft disasters can affect not only those on board (i.e. passengers and aircrew) but also their families, relatives, close friends and colleagues, who form the group of bereaved individuals affected by aircraft disasters. However, despite the vast amount of literature on bereavement, little is known regarding aircraft disaster-related bereavement. After the Boston aircrash, which claimed all of the passengers' (n=89) lives, the bereaved relatives felt a strong sense of grief and anxiety about the future which was associated with apprehension about viewing and identifying the bodies of their loved ones. They also felt a strong sense of hostility, anger and bitterness towards the airline. This hostility and bitterness were related to issues of blame and negligence and the lengthy legal battle for compensation (Krell, 1974).

Focusing on the bereavement of colleagues, one study examined the bereavement reactions of 71 members of an Air Force community after the loss of seven aircrew and 1 passenger in a plane crash (in 1989, a C-141B Starlifter cargo jet from a US Air Force base crashed as it was preparing to land during a storm). It showed that 67 per cent of these members experienced a high severity of symptoms related to the impact of the crash, characterised by intrusive thoughts about the crash and avoidance behaviour. The intrusion and avoidance were associated with high levels of depressive symptoms, and closer community ties (i.e. the closer the community ties, the greater the intrusive, avoidance and depressive symptoms). The study also showed that people with perceived low social support from family and friends, low social networks, and low personality hardiness tended to report greater depression (Fullerton et al., 1999).

According to the above research, while social support was suggested to be important for the bereaved in moderating distress following aircraft disasters, providing formal professional support was also vital. In 1985, 137 passengers were killed when a Delta Airlines jet crashed at Dallas-Fort Worth International Airport. As the bereaved families arrived, they stayed in a secluded hotel where they waited for victims' bodies to be retrieved and identified. In this protected environment, the families received support from psychiatrists, nurses, hotel staff, airline representatives, and clergy. Under this protected, nurturing and supportive environment, the families were able to regress safely and to allow themselves to satisfy their basic yearning for an idealised caregiver who would fulfil all their needs. To establish such an environment is thought to be important and useful as an intervention strategy in future disasters with a high number of casualties (Black, 1987).

Disaster Personnel

It is beyond dispute that disaster personnel can experience the traumatic ripple effects caused by aircraft disasters, by exposing themselves to the disaster rescue operation in one way or another (Paton, 1989, 1990). Research suggests that by engaging in body handling and recovery, the risk of developing post-traumatic stress disorder during the six months following exposure to disasters is increased substantially (e.g. Hershisher and Quarantelli, 1976; Jones, 1985; Miles et al., 1984; Raphael, 1984).

Initially, following the 1979 Mount Erebus aircraft disaster (a DC10 aircraft crashed into the ice-covered slopes of Mount Erebus, killing the 257 on board), Taylor and Frazer (1982) showed that 53 per cent of the disaster personnel in their study who were involved with the recovery and identification of bodies experienced moderately severe intrusive thoughts, nightmares, sleep disturbance, withdrawal, tension, depression, somatisation, obsessive-compulsive symptoms, interpersonal sensitivity and anxiety. Twenty months after the disaster, although only a small minority (8 per cent) felt the need to talk about their involvement with the disaster and a large majority (80 per cent) thought that they had successfully overcome their problems, 15 per cent of the studied cohort still experienced occasional flashbacks of the accident, 5 per cent were still angry about the aircrash, and 4 per cent had marital problems which, they claimed, were related to the aircrash.

Returning to the Gander disaster mentioned previously, Bartone et al. (1989) examined the extent of psychological distress that family assistance officers experienced, following their involvement in the disaster. They found that six months after, family assistant officers reported such symptoms as headaches (40 per cent), feelings of nervousness or tenseness (33 per cent), sleeping difficulties (31 per cent), general aches and pains (29 per cent), common colds (25 per cent), depressed mood (21 per cent), and tiredness/ lack of energy (20 per cent). At one year follow-up, in general, twice as many symptoms were reported. For the body handlers, the police officers and fire personnel in the Gander aircraft disaster, exposing themselves to dead bodies and body parts – in particular, children's bodies – through viewing, smelling and touching was extremely distressing. Bodies which looked undamaged and did not show obvious cause of death were just as distressing as burned, mutilated and disfigured bodies. No matter how well these personnel prepared themselves prior to the disaster, what they were exposed to surprised and shocked them (Ursano and McCarroll, 1990).

To look further into the psychological reactions of disaster personnel exposed to disasters, McCarroll et al. (1993) examined the psychological reactions of disaster personnel before, during and after working with dead bodies in different disasters (the Gander aircraft crash in 1985, the United Airlines flight 232 crash in Sioux City, Iowa, in 1989 and a boat disaster, USS Iowa, in 1989). Before exposure, the personnel found the anticipation of their reaction to the dead and the lack of information on the nature of the tasks ahead stressful. They were nervous because they were unsure what to expect, what condition the bodies would be in or how difficult it would be to identify them. Some personnel thought that they should be told the worst before they handled the bodies so that they could minimise the surprises.

During the exposure, personnel tried to defend against the sensory stimuli of seeing burned and mutilated bodies, smelling them, and hearing the sounds which occurred during autopsy. The smell was thought to be the most difficult. Many personnel tried to cover the smell by burning coffee, smoking cigars, and using fragrances (e.g. peppermint oil and orange oil inside surgical masks). Most, however, reported that these strategies did not help because olfactory adaptation occurred. As was mentioned before, personnel found the bodies which bore very few visual signs of death very difficult; in fact, for some people these were more difficult than the damaged bodies, because the damaged bodies could be treated as nonhuman, while the undamaged ones could not. To these personnel, seeing a large number of bodies was overwhelming, and the stress from it could be reduced by taking frequent breaks or reducing visual contact with the bodies. Personnel tried to use humour, for example, to distance themselves emotionally from these bodies and tried not to identify any similarities between themselves and the bodies. Similarly, 30 per cent of the personnel involved in the Mount Erebus aircraft disaster distanced themselves emotionally from the bodies by considering them as some frozen objects or roasted meat, plane cargo, waxworks or scientific specimens (Taylor and Frazer, 1982).

After the exposure, many disaster personnel felt the need for a post-event debriefing and to ask questions about the disaster. They valued highly any statements of appreciation and recognition. Understandably, during this period, many personnel experienced feelings of fatigue and irritability, and felt the need for time off after work and a period of transition before returning to the real world. Interestingly, they thought that professional counselling or psychiatric help were unnecessary, the reason being that they were afraid of consequently being made unemployed and ridiculed by fellow workers. Social support from spouses was important but often was not available. Alcohol use was common among these personnel.

The investigation into the psychological reactions of disaster personnel during the three exposure periods revealed that many of those who were involved in disasters of mass casualties displayed specific cognitive reactions and behavioural responses, characterised by thinking in terms of similarity and identification, attribution of meaning and contagion of behaviour. With regard to thinking in terms of identification or similarity (Rosen, 1977), after having worked with the dead bodies for some time, the personnel began to think of the dead as being like or similar to themselves (Ursano et al., 1988). Body handlers, for example, may feel that a particular body represents themselves, a family member, or a friend, whereby they might say 'it could have been me or one of my family members'. Some body handlers in the Gander disaster felt that they knew the individual's family. One person reported that he was feeling anxious when he realised he was lying in bed in the same position as one of the bodies he had worked with (Ursano and Fullerton, 1990).

With respect to attribution of meaning, many of these disaster personnel found themselves wanting to create meaning through rituals, symbols, language and rumours (Dollinger, 1986; Green et al., 1985; Holloway and Ursano, 1984). For example, 10 days after the Gander aircraft crash, a drawing of the 'Screaming Eagle' with a tear was put on the wall of the mortuary, as a symbol of the people lost in the disaster (Ursano and Fullerton, 1990). Another example is the construction of meaning through rumours (Young et al., 1989). For example, following the Gander military aircraft crash, a rumour broke out claiming that the army was to blame for the crash, which was untrue (Ursano and Fullerton, 1990). Finally, very briefly, in terms of contagion of behaviour, disasters with mass casualties tend to affect and disrupt the organisation of the social system, the usual social organisers and directors of behaviour. Consequently, contagion of behaviour might increase. For example, five months after the Gander aircraft crash, a series of suicide attempts among adolescents occurred (Ursano and Fullerton, 1990).

Fortunately, many of these disaster personnel do eventually recover or adjust to collective traumatic loss. On the basis of the personnel from the Gander aircraft disaster, four relatively distinct psychosocial phases of recovery have been identified: 1) numb dedication; 2) anger betrayal; 3) stoic resolve; and 4) integration. During the first phase (1–6 weeks after the disaster), people often experience feelings of disbelief and denial. For example, several organisation officials refused to accept that the aircraft was one of theirs. Soldiers were asked to behave like soldiers and focus on the mission. In so doing, they detached themselves emotionally from the disaster. Nevertheless, some soldiers had difficulty sleeping due to disturbing dreams. They reported seeing soldiers appearing as ghosts. Soldiers also experienced post-traumatic stress symptoms including avoidance, hyperalertness, startle responses and survivor guilt. The latter was particularly severe and persistent among soldiers who had exchanged seats with other soldiers who in the end died in the crash.

The second phase (week 6–10), for these soldiers, was characterised by anger directed at the airline for safety violations, and at the army command for not checking the safety of military aircraft. Such anger was associated with betrayal. That is, they initially trusted the army to look after their safety and welfare but now felt that this trust had been violated. Disillusionment about the commitment of the organisation then followed. Some people managed to direct their anger constructively by, for example, caring for the dead and their bereaved families. Many soldiers, however, used tranquillisers and alcohol to cope with tension.

The third phase (week 10–20) involved a sense of relief among the soldiers when the last body had been identified. They felt that they could now put the disaster behind them and get on with their lives, instead of dwelling on their sadness and anger. The disaster itself then became a taboo. Nevertheless, at this stage, people still experienced sleeping problems and abused alcohol.

The last phase (week 20–30) was characterised by the soldiers having come to terms with the loss and integrated it into their life experience. Some saw the experience of the disaster as part of personal growth and learning. They now felt a renewed sense of hope, a sense of solidarity and brotherhood within the army and they felt they could now work with the new soldiers. They no longer saw the new soldiers as just replacements of the dead but saw them as members who could contribute to the army. Some still felt physically and emotionally exhausted (Bartone and Wright, 1990).

Community Residents

As previously mentioned, an aircraft disaster can have devastating and traumatic ripple effects upon the community in it occurs. Therefore, community residents can also be caught in this traumatic ripple. One could speculate that the psychological reactions of community residents may vary, partly depending on the way the aircraft disaster occurred, as demonstrated by the following: 1) aircraft that lose control and crash into housing in a community causing casualties among community residents; 2) aircraft that explode in mid-air, dropping wreckage onto housing in a community, also causing casualties among community residents; 3) aircraft that lose control and barely miss crashing into housing, causing a near-death experience among community residents.

Aircraft that Lose Control and Crash into Housing in a Community, Causing Casualties among Community Residents

In 1987, an Air Force jet fighter crashed into a Ramada Inn in Indianapolis, killing 10 people. Within four to six weeks of the disaster, 54 per cent of a cohort of 46 hotel employees fulfilled the criterion of a psychiatric disorder. Twenty-two per cent of the employees fulfilled the criteria for post-traumatic stress disorder. Twenty per cent had a tendency to abuse alcohol prior to the disaster, half of whom were actively abusing alcohol after the disaster. More than 40 per cent of the employees suffered from depression and 20 per cent suffered from generalised anxiety disorder, following the disaster. On the whole, employees who were on-site when the disaster occurred had more psychiatric symptoms than those who were off-site (Smith et al., 1990).

In 1992, the Bijlmermeer aircraft disaster occurred which resulted in 43 people being killed (including four people on board) and 400 households being evacuated (a Boeing cargo plane crashed into two high-rise blocks of flats in Bijlmermeer, Amsterdam). Initially, community residents went through an immediate shock phase (i.e. the first 24–26 hours) in which they felt numb about the disaster and found themselves wanting to talk about it. They went through the cry out phase a few days afterwards, in which the feelings of shock and numbness subsided and strong emotions arose. People tended to describe their devastating experiences repeatedly. Their feelings of helplessness became apparent and sometimes turned into anger and aggression towards responsible authorities. During this period, people tended to experience positive feelings derived from being close together which is sometimes called the 'honeymoon phase'. This phase lasted for about two weeks and then acute post-traumatic stress symptoms associated with depression, anxiety and agitation emerged. The final phase was called the intermediate post-traumatic period and it signalled the start of disillusionment. The positive feelings of being close together disappeared, and people continued to suffer from post-traumatic stress symptoms and face up to their losses and the effects of the trauma on their lives (Gersons and Carlier, 1993).

Six months after the Bijlmermeer disaster, one study showed that 26 per cent of community residents suffered from post-traumatic stress disorder associated with material damage and loss of loved ones or friends. They also reported emotional upset (52 per cent), hyperalertness (40 per cent) and intrusive thoughts (39 per cent). The study also showed that partial post-traumatic stress disorder (i.e. people only partially met the full set of diagnostic criteria for post-traumatic stress disorder) was 44 per cent. It is possible that at one time, these residents had fulfilled the full set of diagnostic criteria for post-traumatic stress disorder but currently only some of the symptoms were present (Carlier and Gersons, 1995, 1997).

Aircraft that Explode in Mid-air, Dropping Wreckage onto Housing in a Community and Causing Casualties among Community Residents

In 1988, PanAm Flight 103 exploded in mid-air and wreckage, burning aviation fuel and mutilated human bodies fell onto Lockerbie, Scotland, the town directly under the flight path. All people on board and 11 community residents in Lockerbie were consequently killed. Out of a cohort of 66 residents, 72 per cent had or had had post-traumatic stress disorder; 15 per cent, 12 per cent and 29 per cent had experienced panic disorder, anxiety disorder and major depression to varying degrees, respectively (Brooks and McKinlay, 1992). A longitudinal follow-up study (36 months after the disaster) informed us further on the long-term traumatic effects of these community residents. The initial 72 per cent of residents with post-traumatic stress disorder fell to 48 per cent at follow-up. However, the number of cases (7) with severe or moderate post-traumatic stress disorder at the initial assessment stayed the same at follow-up, suggesting that they had serious and persistent symptoms. Depression increased from 28 per cent at the initial assessment to 36 per cent at the follow-up assessment. Sixty-six per cent of the cases with post-traumatic stress disorder at follow-up also suffered from depression (Scott et al., 1995).

To ascertain the effect of age on psychological responses among the community residents in Lockerbie, comparisons were made between the elderly (n=31) and younger survivors (n=24) of the disaster. The elderly residents responded similarly to the younger residents. The majority were diagnosed as suffering from post-traumatic stress disorder in that both groups displayed similar levels of severity of intrusive thoughts about the disaster and avoidance behaviour. Property was lost or severely damaged among 64 per cent of the elderly and 71 per cent of the younger residents. One partner in five of the elderly residents, and one partner in eight of the younger residents was injured in the disaster. Twenty per cent of the elderly residents lost a friend, whereas almost 50 per cent of the younger residents lost a friend. Fifty-two per cent of the elderly residents witnessed human remains, whereas 40 per cent of the younger residents did so. The elderly were troubled by personal loss, injury to friends and the witnessing of human remains, all of which were correlated with post-traumatic stress disorder. This was not the case for the younger residents. Compared with the younger residents, the elderly had higher rates of major depression. For the elderly residents, material loss, personal loss or witnessing human remains were not associated with depression; however, significant material loss was associated with depression for the younger residents. The elderly residents were more socially dysfunctional than the younger residents (Livingston et al., 1992).

A longitudinal follow-up study (36 months after the disaster) was also carried out to examine the psychological reactions of some of the above elderly community residents (n=19). The results showed that there was no difference in terms of the proportion of psychiatric cases between year 1 and year 3 after the disaster. There were, however, significant improvements in somatic problems, anxiety and social dysfunction, but not severe depression. In three years, the traumatic impact of the disaster upon the elderly had diminished, compared to that of one year. Seventy-four per cent of the elderly suffered from post-traumatic stress disorder in year 1, which fell to 16 per cent at year 3. Post-traumatic stress in the third year was not associated with the witnessing of gruesome sights, loss of a partner or destruction of personal property, although these had been important correlates at the one year assessment (Livingston et al., 1994).

Aircraft that Lose Control and Barely Miss Crashing into Housing, Causing a Near-death Experience among Community Residents

One morning in 1994, a Boeing 737-2D6C was returning to Coventry, having unloaded a cargo of live animals in Amsterdam. It lost control, struck a pylon and began to descend on a community called Willenhall. It then clipped the roofs of two houses and finally crashed into a woodland area close to the edge of the community. Five people on board died, and hundreds of community residents narrowly escaped death (HMSO, 1996). There are features of this aircraft disaster which are markedly different from those mentioned previously. Firstly, the aircraft did not crash into the community. But, by chance, these residents could have been primary victims (i.e. those with maximal exposure to a disaster), also known as sesternary victims (Taylor and Frazer, 1981). This aircraft disaster nevertheless provoked a near-death experience for the residents. Secondly, the wreckage did not cause any damage to the residents' property, nor death or injury on the ground, apart from the two roofs which were clipped by the plane as it came down. Thirdly, the residents did not know the people on board which meant that there was no bereavement issue to deal with.

Six months after the disaster, we carried out research (Chung, Easthope, Eaton and McHugh, 1999; Chung, Easthope, Chung and Clark-Carter, 1999; Chung et al., 2000; Chung et al., 2001) looking at the traumatic effects of the disaster upon 82 community residents. We were interested in the degree of severity of post-traumatic stress symptoms among these residents, and in establishing associations between these symptoms and residents' death anxiety, personality factors and coping strategies.

We found that residents' experiences of the disaster were severe in impact (73 per cent), characterised by intrusive thoughts about the disaster and avoidance behaviour. The severity of residents' post-traumatic stress symptoms was similar to that of clinical populations exposed to other kinds of traumatic events. Residents also manifested health problems following the disaster. Anxiety was the most common problem for them, followed by somatic problems and social dysfunction. Fifty-seven per cent of the residents were thought to be psychiatric cases. Results of the study also revealed some significant associations between the impact of the aircraft disaster and health problems, in that residents with intrusive thoughts about the disaster and avoidance behaviour tended to experience somatic problems, anxiety, social dysfunction and depression.

We also measured the degree of death anxiety following the disaster. A large majority of the residents (80 per cent) were fearful of dying a painful death and over 70 per cent said that they often thought about how short life really was. Over 60 per cent said that it did make them feel nervous when people talked about death and that they were often distressed by the way time flies so rapidly. Over 50 per cent said that they were really scared of having a heart attack and that they shuddered when they heard people talking about a World War III. About 40 per cent said that they dreaded thinking about having to have an operation. The degree of severity of death anxiety among the residents was similar to that of ordinary non-clinical populations but was lower than clinical patients with high death anxiety.

Further analyses showed that there were significant relationships between the impact of the aircraft disaster, health problems and death anxiety. Those residents who were very much afraid to die, and who shuddered when they heard people talking about a World War III and found the sight of a dead body horrifying, tended to experience a high impact of the disaster and to suffer health problems.

We also investigated the kinds of coping strategies that residents endorsed. We found that the residents used distancing (e.g. they tried to forget the whole disaster) the most, followed by self-controlling (e.g. they tried to keep their feelings to themselves) and escape-avoidance (e.g. they avoided being with the residents who also experienced the disaster). We then established that residents who displayed avoidance behaviour tended to employ the escape-avoidance coping strategy, and that residents who experienced intrusive thoughts about the disaster tended to employ distancing and escape-avoidance coping strategies. We also established that residents who employed distancing and escape-avoidance coping strategies tended to report health problems. Finally, we also investigated the role that personality factors could play in the experience of traumatic effects. On the whole, the residents were somewhat introverted and less neurotic than the ordinary population. We then established that neurotic and introverted residents tended to report intrusive thoughts about the disaster or display avoidance behaviour.

Conclusion

What has been included in this chapter is by no means a comprehensive review of literature on the psychological effects of aircraft disasters upon people who have been exposed to the disasters in one way or another. It is beyond the scope of this chapter, for example, to review the research which indicates that the intrinsic factor of personality hardiness (Kobasa et al., 1982; Maddi and Kobasa, 1984) and the external factor of social support are beneficial factors for helping disaster personnel to buffer against the traumatic effects of aircraft disasters (Bartone et al., 1989).

It is also beyond the scope of this chapter to review how disaster personnel can be helped by means of psychological debriefing (Carlier et al., 1998; Fullerton et al., 2000). As a result of psychological debriefing, some research claims that the risk of developing chronic stress reactions can be reduced or prevented (e.g. Dunning, 1990; Dyregrov and Mitchell, 1992; Mitchell, 1983; Raphael, 1986; Shalev, 1994; Wright, Ursano, Ingraham and Bartone, 1990). However, the truth is that, despite its popularity, whether or not psychological debriefing is an effective treatment for trauma is still very much in question (e.g. Griffith, 1992; Hytten and Hasle, 1989; McFarlane, 1988). Systematic studies which evaluate the acute and long-term effectiveness of debriefing are very much in short supply (e.g. Avery et al., 1999; Gist et al., 1999; Matthews, 1998; Raphael et al., 1995).

Also, while the survey of research in this chapter thus far reveals the extent of suffering that people can experience as a result of aircraft disasters, attention has been paid increasingly to the phenomenon of perceived benefit (Thoits, 1995). That is, researchers are beginning to examine the extent to which people could grow or benefit, as a result of their traumatic experiences, in terms of, for example, changing their perception of themselves, life, relationship with others and coping skills (Schaefer and Moos, 1992; Tedeschi and Calhoun, 1995). Research evidence has suggested a positive association between perceived benefit and adjustment after trauma (e.g. Affleck et al., 1987; Affleck and Tennen, 1996; McMillen et al., 1997; Thompson, 1985), even though this association is still controversial at present (Lehman et al., 1993; Park et al., 1996).

References

Affleck, G., Tennen, H., Croog, S. and Levine, S (1987), 'Causal Attribution, Perceived Benefits, and Morbidity Following a Heart Attack', *Journal of Consulting and Clinical Psychology*, Vol. 55, pp. 29–35.

Affleck, G. and Tennen, H. (1996), 'Construing Benefits from Adversity: Adaptational significance and dispositional underpinnings', *Journal of Personality*, Vol. 64, pp. 899–922.

Aveline, M., and Fowlie, D. (1987), 'Surviving Ejection from Military Aircraft: Psychological reactions, modifying factors and intervention', *Stress Medicine*, Vol. 3, pp. 15–20.

Avery, A., King, S., Bretherton, R. and Orner, R. (1999), 'Deconstructing Psychological Debriefing and the Emergence of Calls for Evidence-based Practice', *Traumatic Stress Points*, Vol. 13, No. 2, pp. 6–8.

Bartone, P., Ursano, R., Wright, K. and Ingraham, L. (1989), 'The Impact of a Military Air Disaster on the Health of Assistance Workers', *Journal of Nervous and Mental Disease*, Vol. 177, No. 6, pp. 317–28.

Bartone, P. and Wright, K, (1990), 'Grief and Group Recovery Following a Military Air Disaster', *Journal of Traumatic Stress*, Vol. 3, No. 4, pp. 523–39.

Birmes, P., Arrieu, A., Payen, A., Warner, B. and Schmitt, L (1999), 'Traumatic Stress and Depression in a Group of Plane Crash Survivors', *Journal of Nervous and Mental Disease*, Vol. 187, No. 12, pp. 754–5.

Black, J. (1987), 'The Libidinal Cocoon: A nurturing retreat for the families of plane crash victims', *Hospital and Community Psychiatry*, Vol. 38, No. 12, pp. 1322–6.

Brooks, N. and McKinlay, W (1992), 'Mental Health Consequences of the Lockerbie Disaster', *Journal of Traumatic Stress*, Vol. 5, No. 4, pp. 527–43.

Carlier, I. and Gersons, B. (1995), 'Partial Post-traumatic Stress Disorder (PTSD): The issue of psychological scars and the occurrence of PTSD symptoms', *Journal of Nervous and Mental Disease*, Vol. 183, No. 2, pp. 107–9.

Carlier, I. and Gersons, B. (1997), 'Stress Reactions in Disaster Victims Following the Bijlmermeer Plane Crash', *Journal of Traumatic Stress*, Vol. 10, No. 2, pp. 329–35.

Carlier, I., Lamberts, R., van Uchelen, A. and Gersons, B. (1998), 'Disaster-related Post-traumatic Stress in Police Officers: A field study of the impact of debriefing', *Stress Medicine*, Vol. 14, pp. 143–8.

Chung, M., Easthope, Y., Eaton, B. and McHugh, C. (1999), 'Describing Traumatic Responses and Distress of Community Residents Directly and Indirectly Exposed to an Aircraft Crash', *Psychiatry: Interpersonal and Biological Processes*, Vol. 62, pp. 125–37.

Chung, M., Easthope, Y., Chung, C. and Clark-Carter, D. (1999), 'The Relationship between Trauma and Personality in Victims of the Boeing 737-2D6C Crash in Coventry', *Journal of Clinical Psychology*, Vol. 55, No. 5, pp. 617–29.

Chung, M., Chung, C. and Easthope, Y. (2000), 'Traumatic Stress and Death Anxiety among Community Residents exposed to an Aircraft Crash', *Death Studies*, Vol. 24, No. 8, pp. 689–704.

Chung, M., Easthope, Y., Chung, C. and Clark-Carter, D. (2001), 'Traumatic Stress and Coping Strategies of Sesternary Victims following an Aircraft Disaster in Coventry', *Stress and Health*, Vol. 17, pp. 67–75.

Dollinger, S. (1986), 'The Need for Meaning following Disaster: Attributions and emotional upset', *Personality and Social Psychology Bulletin*, Vol. 12, No. 3, pp. 300–10.

Dunning, C. (1990), 'Mental Health Sequelae in Disaster Workers: Prevention and intervention', *International Journal of Mental Health*, Vol. 19, pp. 91–103.

Dyregrov, A. and Mitchell, J. (1992), 'Work with Traumatized Children – Psychological Effects and Coping Strategies', *Journal of Traumatic Stress*, Vol. 5, pp. 5–17.

Fowlie, D. and Aveline, M. (1985), 'The Emotional Consequences of Ejection, Rescue and Rehabilitation in Royal Air Force Aircrew', *British Journal of Psychiatry*, Vol. 146, pp. 609–13.

Fullerton, C., Ursano, R., Kao, T. and Bharitya, V. (1999), 'Disaster-related Bereavement: Acute symptoms and subsequent depression', *Aviation, Space and Environmental Medicine*, Vol. 70, No. 9, pp. 902–9.

Fullerton, C., Ursano, R., Vance, K. and Wang, L. (2000), 'Debriefing following Trauma', *Psychiatric Quarterly*, Vol. 71, No. 3, pp. 259–76.

Gersons, B. and Carlier, I. (1993), 'Plane Crash Crisis Intervention: A preliminary report from the Bijlmermeer, Amsterdam', *Crisis*, Vol. 14, No. 3, pp. 109–16.

Gist, R., Lubin, B. and Redburn, B. (1999), 'Psychosocial, Ecological, and Community Perspectives on Disaster Response', in R. Gist. and B. Lubin (eds), *Response to Disaster: Psychosocial, community and ecological perspectives on disaster response*, Ann Arbor, Michigan: Braun-Brumfield.

Green, B., Wilson, J. and Lindy, J. (1985), 'Conceptualizing Post-traumatic Stress Disorder: A psychosocial framework', in C.R. Figley (ed.), *Trauma and its Wake: The study and treatment of post-traumatic stress disorder*, New York: Brunner/Mazel.

Griffith, W. (1992), *The Kempsy and Grafton Bus Crashes: The aftermath*, New South Wales: Lismore.

Hershisher, M. and Quarantelli, E. (1976), 'The Handling of the Dead in a Disaster', *Omega*, Vol. 7, No. 3, pp. 195–208.

HMSO (1996), 'Report on the Accident to Boeing 737-2D6C, 7T-VEE at Willenhall, Coventry, Warwickshire on 21 December 1994', London: HMSO.

Holloway, H. and Ursano, R. (1984), 'The Vietnam Veteran: Memory, social context and metaphor', *Psychiatry*, Vol. 47, pp. 103–8.

Hytten, K. (1989), 'Helicopter Crash in Water: Effects of simulator escape training', *Acta Psychiatrica Scandinavica*, Supplement 355, Vol. 80, pp. 73–8.

Hytten, K., and Hasle, A. (1989), 'Firefighters: A study of stress and coping', *Acta Psychiatrica Scandinavica*, Supplement 355, Vol. 80, pp. 50–55.

Jones, D. (1985), 'Secondary Disaster Victims: The emotional effects of recovery and identifying human remains', *American Journal of Psychiatry*, Vol. 142, No. 3, pp. 303–7.

Kobasa, S., Maddi, S. and Kahn, S. (1982), Hardiness and Health: A prospective study', *Journal of Personality and Social Psychology*, Vol. 42, pp. 168–77.

Krell, G. (1974), 'Support Services Aid Relatives of Victims', *Hospitals JAHA*, Vol. 48, pp. 56–9.

Lee, I. (1989), 'When an Aeroplane Catches Fire: The Manchester International Airport disaster, 1985', in M. Walsh (ed.), *Disasters: Current planning and recent experience*, London: Edward Arnold.

Lehman, D., Davis, C., DeLongis, A., Wortman, C., Bluck, S., Mandel, D. and Ellard, J. (1993), Positive and Negative Life Changes following Bereavement and their Relations to Adjustment', *Journal of Social and Clinical Psychology*, Vol. 12, pp. 90–112.

Livingston, H., Livingston, M., Brooks, N. and McKinlay, W. (1992), 'Elderly Survivors of the Lockerbie Air Disaster', *International Journal of Geriatric Psychiatry*, Vol. 7, pp. 725–9.

Livingston, H., Livingston, M. and Fell, S. (1994), 'The Lockerbie Disaster: A 3-year Follow-up of Elderly Victims', *International Journal of Geriatric Psychiatry*, Vol. 9, pp. 989–94.

Maddi, S. and Kobasa, S. (1984), *The Hardy Executive: Health under stress*, Homewood, Illinois: Dow Jones-Irwin.

Matthews, L.R. (1998), 'Effect of Staff Debriefing on Post-traumatic Stress Symptoms after Assaults by Community Housing Residents', *Psychiatric Services*, Vol. 49, pp. 207–12.

McCarroll, J., Ursano, R., Wright, K. and Fullerton, C. (1993), 'Handling Bodies after Violent Death: Strategies for coping', *American Journal of Orthopsychiatry*, Vol. 63, No. 2, pp. 209–14.

McFarlane, A. (1988), 'The Longitudinal Course of most Traumatic Morbidity. The Range of Outcomes and their Predictors', *Journal of Nervous and Mental Disease*, Vol. 176, pp. 30–39.

McMillen, J., Smith, E. and Fisher, R. (1997), 'Perceived Benefit and Mental Health after Three Types of Disaster', *Journal of Consulting and Clinical Psychology*, Vol. 65, No. 5, pp. 733–9.

Miles, M., Demi, A. and Mostyn-Aker, P. (1984), 'Rescue Workers' Reactions following the Hyatt Hotel Disaster', *Death Education*, Vol. 8, pp. 315–31.

Mitchell, J. (1983), 'When Disaster Strikes. The Critical Incident Stress Debriefing Process', *Journal of the Emergency Medical Services*, Vol. 8, pp. 36–9.

Park, C., Cohen, L. and Murch, R. (1996), 'Assessment and Prediction of Stress-related Growth', *Journal of Personality*, Vol. 64, pp. 71–105.

Paton, D. (1989), 'Disaster and Helpers: Psychological dynamics and implications for counselling', *Counselling Psychology Quarterly*, Vol. 2, No. 3, pp. 303–21.

Paton, D. (1990), 'Assessing the Impact of Disasters on Helpers', *Counselling Psychology Quarterly*, Vol. 3, No. 2, pp. 149–52.

Perlberg, M. (1979), 'Trauma at Tenerife: The psychic aftershocks of a jet disaster', *Human Behaviour*, Vol. 8, pp. 49–50.

Raphael, B. (1984), *The Anatomy of Bereavement*, London: Hutchinson.

Raphael, B. (1986), *When Disaster Strikes*, London: Hutchinson.

Raphael, B., Meldrum, L. and McFarlane, A.C. (1995), 'Does Debriefing after Psychological Trauma Work?', *British Medical Journal*, Vol. 310, pp. 1479–80.

Rawlins, T. (1985), 'Survivors', *Nursing Times*, November, Vol. 27, pp. 12–14.

Rosen, V. (1977), 'Disorders of Communication in Psychoanalysis', in V.H. Rosen (ed.), *Style, Character and Language*, New York: Jason Aaronson Inc.

Schaefer, J. and Moos, R. (1992), 'Life Crises and Personal Growth', in B. Carpenter (ed.), *Personal Coping: Theory, research and application*, Westport, Connecticut: Praeger.

Scott, R., Brooks, N. and McKinlay, W. (1995), 'Post-traumatic Morbidity in a Civilian Community of Litigants: A follow-up at 3 years', *Journal of Traumatic Stress*, Vol. 8, No. 3, pp. 403–17.

Shalev, A. (1994), 'Debriefing following Traumatic Exposure', in R.J. Ursano, B.G. McCaughey and C.S. Fullerton (eds), *Individual and Community Responses to Trauma and Disaster*, Cambridge: Cambridge University Press.

Slagle, D., Reichman, M., Rodenhauser, P., Knoedler, D. and Davis, C. (1990), 'Community Psychological Effects following a Non-fatal Aircraft Accident', *Aviation, Space and Environmental Medicine*, Vol. 61, No. 10, pp. 879–86.

Sloan, P. (1988), 'Post-traumatic Stress in Survivors of an Airplane Crash-landing: A clinical and exploratory research intervention', *Journal of Traumatic Stress*, Vol. 1, No. 2, pp. 211–29.

Smith, E., North, C., McCool, R. and Shea, J. (1990), 'Acute Post-disaster Psychiatric Disorders: Identification of persons at risk', *American Journal of Psychiatry*, Vol. 147, No. 2, pp. 202–6.

Taylor, A. and Frazer, A. (1981), 'Psychological Sequelae of Operation Overdue Following the DC10 Aircrash in Antarctica', *Victoria University of Wellington Publications in Psychology*, No. 27.

Taylor, A. and Frazer, A. (1982), 'The Stress of Post-disaster Body Handling and Victim Identification Work', *Journal of Human Stress*, Vol. 8, No. 4, pp. 4–12.

Tedeschi, R. and Calhoun, L. (1995), *Trauma and Transformation: Growing in the aftermath of suffering*, Thousand Oaks, California: Sage.

Thompson, S. (1985), 'Finding Positive Meaning in a Stressful Event and Coping', *Basic and Applied Social Psychology*, Vol. 6, pp. 279–95.

Thoits, P. (1995), 'Stress, Coping and Social Support Processes: Where are we? What next?', *Journal of Health and Social Behavior* (extra issue), pp. 53–79.

Ursano, R., Wright, K., Ingraham, L. and Bartone, P. (1988), 'Psychiatric Responses to Dead Bodies', *Proceedings of the American Psychiatric Association Annual Meeting*, Washington: American Psychiatric Press.

Ursano, R. and Fullerton, C. (1990), 'Cognitive and Behavioral Responses to Trauma', *Journal of Applied Social Psychology*, Vol. 20, pp. 1766–75.

Ursano, R. and McCarroll, J. (1990), 'The Nature of a Traumatic Stressor: Handling dead bodies', *Journal of Nervous and Mental Disease*, Vol. 78, No. 6, pp. 396–8.

Wright, K., Ursano, R., Bartone, P. and Ingraham, L. (1990), 'The Shared Experience of Catastrophe: An expanded classification of the disaster community', *American Journal of Orthopsychiatry*, Vol. 60, No. 1, pp. 35–42.

Wright, K., Ursano, R., Ingraham, L. and Bartone, P. (1990), 'Individual and Community Responses to an Aircraft Disaster', in M.E. Wolf and A.D. Mosnaim (eds), *Post-traumatic Stress Disorder: Etiology, phenomenology and treatment*, Washington: American Psychiatric Press, Inc.

Young, J., Ursano, R., Bally, R. and McMeill, D. (1989), 'Consultation to a Clinic following Suicide', *American Journal of Orthopsychiatry*, Vol. 59, No. 3, pp. 473–6.

Chapter 12

Hostage Behaviour in Aircraft Hijacking: A Script-based Analysis of Resistance Strategies

Margaret A. Wilson

Introduction

This chapter sets out to examine what happens in aircraft hijackings in terms of the behaviour of the passengers and crew. A great deal has been written about terrorism and a smaller, but not insubstantial amount, written on hostage-taking in general. However, few have focused specifically on aircraft hijackings. Nevertheless, much can be gleaned from research on hostage-taking in general. Wilson (2002) provides a general overview of the contributions made by psychological research to understanding terrorist hostage-taking. However, the present chapter addresses the hostages' response to incidents of hijacking, in particular the different parties' reactions, from compliance through to various forms of passive and active resistance.

Previous research on hostage-taking incidents has largely failed to consider what people actually do under such circumstances. Some researchers have studied the role that hostages play in these events, for example, as 'bargaining chips' in the negotiation process (e.g. Atkinson, Sandler and Tschirhart, 1987; Corsi, 1981; Lapan and Sandler 1988; Sandler and Scott, 1987). Those that have examined the passengers' individual responses to the incident have focused attention on the recovery process after the event (e.g. McDuff, 1992). One or two authors have presented accounts of their own experience of hijacking incidents, but these are subjective reports of specific incidents. For example, Jacobson (1973) has written from her own experience of being a hostage on board the 1970 Popular Front for the Liberation of Palestine (PFLP) hijacking of an American plane to the Jordanian desert. Her account details the behaviour of individuals and subgroups of passengers during almost a week of captivity. In terms of resistance strategies, St John (1991) presents an account of hijack responses, although his analysis examines the pilots' reactions alone. This research will be discussed later in the chapter.

The present analysis develops from the author's earlier consideration of people's behaviour in hostage-taking incidents (Wilson and Smith, 1999). However, where the previous research considered pro-social interactions between all parties in all forms of hostage-taking incident, the current analysis considers the resistance strategies employed specifically by hostages in aircraft hijacking incidents.

Scripted Behaviour

In order to understand people's behaviour in hostage-taking incidents, Wilson and Smith (1999) interpret what happens in terms of 'scripts' (Abelson, 1981). The notion of scripts suggests that people's behaviour follows predictable patterns that are governed by the social roles they occupy and the place rules applicable to the setting they are in. Social rules guide normal day to day interactions and place rules prescribe the use of environmental settings. Scripts are therefore predictable strings of behaviour that have been shown to exist in a variety of settings and interactions.

This approach has been used to interpret many aspects of people's behaviour. However, in the 1980s and early 1990s some very important findings emerged with respect to people's behaviour in emergencies. Sime (1990) pointed out that since most people have no prior experience of what actually happens in disasters such as major fires, they will behave according to what they think might happen and hence sometimes exhibit what might appear to be irrational behaviour under the circumstances. Furthermore, Sime (1990) points out that people's predictions, and subsequent behaviour, may be derived from media portrayals that are extremely inaccurate. These false social representations of what happens in incidents such as fires may help to explain counter-adaptive behaviour.

However, further evidence comes from researchers who have studied what people actually do in emergencies such as fires. Studying a number of major fires, researchers assert that the most frequent patterns of behaviour are far from the media portrayal of 'panic' (Canter, 1990a; Canter, Breaux and Sime, 1990; Donald and Canter, 1990, 1992). In the absence of scripts for novel situations people appear to revert to the normal social and place rules applicable to the setting they are in, even under life-threatening circumstances. For example, customers caught in a fire in the restaurant of a department store were still queuing up to pay at the cash desk (Canter, 1990a) and residents of a hotel fire went back to their rooms and called down to reception (Canter Breaux and Sime, 1990). Donald and Canter (1990, 1992) were able to piece together the movements of those who died in the King's Cross underground fire and found that in addition to following their usual route out of the underground station despite the fire, some people stopped to carry out everyday activities, for example to use the toilets.

Thus, there are two possible types of script-based behaviour for novel and even life-threatening situations. Firstly, it is likely that people will adopt the normal rules of social and environmental interactions. Secondly, it is possible that people will behave according invented scripts about how they think the situation is likely to unfold. It is possible that there may be an interaction between these two script forms. For example, an underestimation of the rate of development of a fire (false scripts) may lead a person to believe that they have long enough to carry out ordinary activities (everyday scripts).

Wilson and Smith (1999) take this notion of scripted behaviour and apply it to the players in hostage-taking situations. They argue that people typically behave according to their (invented) hostage-taking role and that this structure applies equally to all of the various parties involved; hostages should be passive and obedient, hostage takers should be dominant and controlling, and the authorities should negotiate. When any of the players digress from these roles the situation may move to a less predictable and increasingly dangerous structure. For example, not only are disobedient hostages likely to get themselves hurt, they are not likely to get any support from the other hostages as they are seen as destablising the situation and putting others at risk. Failed attempts at bluffing by any party can lead to poor outcomes. For example, when detected, trick destinations for hijacked planes can lead hostage takers to retaliate against the passengers and crew. Likewise, the perhaps good intentions of hostage takers who only pretend to have killed passengers can backfire with the authorities storming the plane. Nonadherence to the rules can have dangerous implications.

However, Wilson and Smith (1999) suggest that there are occasions when these prescribed roles break down and behaviours emerge that we do not perceive as being appropriate to hostage-taking incidents at all. However, because social representations of hostage-taking incidents involve fear and violence, unpredictable negative events do not seem 'inappropriate'. It is when positive interactions occur between the parties, that explanations are sought for these 'aberrations'. The most well known explanation for pro-social interactions in hostage-taking is the 'Stockholm syndrome'. Proponents of the Stockholm syndrome suggest that a bond may form between hostages and hostage takers that can be explained in terms of a clinical manifestation of dependency (Kulesnyk, 1984; Strentz, 1979, 1988; Turner, 1985). Although no empirical basis for the Stockholm syndrome exists, it is a widely accepted phenomenon and is drawn upon by negotiators in hostage-taking incidents to manipulate outcome (Wilson, 2002). However, Wilson and Smith (1999) argue that these positive interactions can be explained in terms of the breakdown of the 'hostage-taking script', to be replaced by those governing normal social interactions.

The purpose of this chapter is to extend this script-based theoretical position by examining the repertoires of behaviour exhibited in aircraft hijackings. Whilst the previous analysis focused on explanations for pro-social behaviour, the current analysis examines the full range of behaviour open to the hostages and the various script-based explanations that can be used to understand them.

A Hierarchy of Script-based Roles

The theoretical position taken allows for three possible types of script-related behaviour for the various parties involved in the incident, that is, the pilots and flight crew, cabin crew, passengers, and where applicable, security guards.

Firstly, it is possible that the hostages will adopt behaviour seen to be appropriate to their role as hostages. Since it is unlikely that people caught in hijacking incidents have been taken hostage previously, these scripts are socially constructed representations of the appropriate behaviour in the circumstances. St John (1991) reports that at the time of his analysis there were some 60,000 commercial pilots flying in the US, of whom only 2,000 'at most', had been involved in a hijacking incident. Therefore, while the crew are likely to have a more accurate understanding of the nature of hijacking incidents in general, the absence of realistic hostage-taking scripts can be hypothesised to be relevant also to the crew. Wilson and Smith (1999) propose that the appropriate behaviour for hostages is compliance, with no attempt to destabilise the situation. This predicts that both the passengers and crew will do what is asked of them by the hostage takers and await action by the authorities, be it negotiation or intervention.

Returning to the research on fires, one stable finding has been that people adhere to the behaviour appropriate to their occupational roles when caught in a disaster. Thus, for example, in a hospital fire, staff respond within the existing hierarchical structures of their occupational roles. While one might expect highly structured organisations like hospitals to have well-practiced roles, even in emergencies, this applies equally to other work role groups. For example, Canter (1990b) reports that during a fire in a major entertainment complex, waitresses played an important role in evacuating the restaurant, but only guided out the customers for whose tables they were responsible. Therefore, the second possible script that could be applied is adherence to behaviour governed by the existing social and environmental roles and rules in place at the time, predicting in this case, behaviour appropriate to people's role as passengers or various subgroups of crew members on board an aircraft.

The strength of occupational role in guiding emergency behaviour can therefore be hypothesised to play an important role in how people will behave on board a hijacked plane. The crew has an existing hierarchical structure and may look to the pilot in a role of command. The pilot may feel that he or she is ultimately responsible for the safety of the passengers and crew, and act accordingly. The cabin crew may be viewed as the 'buffer' between the flight deck and the passengers and would therefore be hypothesised to take responsibility for interactions with the passengers. The passengers themselves would still be predicted to do what they are told by the crew, as might be the case in any emergency. This therefore also suggests that the passengers would play a passive role in aircraft hijackings.

Whilst the occupational role of the flight and cabin crew may translate into an implicit defence role in the event of a hijack, the role of the security guards (where present) is quite explicit. Their purpose for being on the flight is to respond in the event of a security risk to the passengers and plane. Therefore it would not be surprising to find that they usually take some form of action. This position, then, suggests that we may see different patterns of behaviour between the passengers and the crew, and between different crew members fulfilling different occupational roles.

Finally, there is the possibility that owing to 'script breakdown', people will return to the normal scripts of interaction that would govern their behaviour in ordinary social circumstances, including the possibility of pro-social interactions.

These three possible script formations can be seen as a hierarchy, whereby at the global level, everyone on board has a common role as 'hostage' and may respond accordingly. However, at the level of 'occupational role', group differences may emerge relating to the person's position within the established role structure. Finally, at the individual level, each person has the potential to resort to the everyday rules of normal social interactions. Any or all of these roles may emerge during a hijacking incident.

The Hostages' Response

Two possible responses to the demands made by aircraft hijackers are compliance and resistance. Compliance would be associated with the 'hostage-taking script' for all of the hostages, passengers and crew alike. At the level of 'occupational role' compliance should be most likely in passengers and least likely in security guards with the crew falling somewhere in between. As discussed above, the 'script breakdown' hypothesis allows for the emergence of ordinary social interactions and may apply to any of the role groups. However, in terms of resistance, one might expect gender roles to influence behaviour.

There are a number of possible forms of resistance open to the hostages, both passive and active, verbal and non-verbal. St John (1991) presents a typology of three forms of resistance employed by pilots. His analysis was based on accounts of hijacking incidents from the Federal Aviation Administration hijack list of 1986. It is important to note that St John's typology is a typology of pilots, rather than responses. This is an important distinction. While a typology of responses allows for the same pilot to respond in different ways depending on the situation, characterising the person suggests consistency in response.

St John (1991) identifies the first type of pilot as 'movers and shakers'. These pilots are the most likely to respond to the situation with active resistance and often provoke the terrorist to respond violently. St John states that these pilots are 'almost all former military pilots, highly trained, very competitive, and usually extremely resentful of a terrorist trespassing on their domain' (ibid., p. 173). The second category of pilot, termed 'technicians', will defer to the terrorist while concentrating on flying and successfully landing the plane. For these individuals, St John claims that the passengers' safety is the central concern and they are unlikely to indulge in 'heroics'. Most pilots fall into this category. The final group of pilots is termed the 'diplomats', who St John sees as the most aware of the 'emotional dynamics' of the incident and who can cope with the loss of authority that the hijack brings. He states that these individuals will be well read on terrorist violence and are 'more in touch with their own feelings and tend to have good communication with the rest of the flight crew' (ibid., p. 174). It is these pilots who tend to get involved in negotiations with hijackers.

This chapter sets out to identify the types of resistance employed in aircraft hijackings and the role groups that use them. The intention is not to conduct an empirical analysis, but rather to develop an outline of the types of observed responses to hijacking incidents leading to a set of theoretically derived testable hypotheses. In order to establish the range of responses observed in hijacking incidents, accounts of hijacking incidents spanning four decades were content analysed. Reports of incidents occurring from the 1960s through to 1995 were taken from Mickolus and his colleagues' influential documentation of transnational terrorist incidents (Mickolus, 1980, 1993; Mickolus, Sandler and Murdock, 1989; Mickolus and Simmons, 1997). Each report was studied and highlighted if any form of hostage behaviour was mentioned, i.e. that of the passengers, crew or security guards. The behaviour of the hijackers themselves and the inherently predictable structure of hostage-taking incidents in general have been discussed elsewhere (Wilson, 2000; Wilson and Smith, 1999).

It is important to acknowledge the limitations of these data. The majority of incidents did not mention any action on the part of the hostages and it must be assumed that this indicates that they did nothing but comply with what was asked of them. However, just because retaliation was not mentioned in the account does not mean that nothing happened. Secondly, there are incidents that ended in destruction of the aircraft and the loss of all lives where we will never know what happened on board. Clearly, this represents an inevitable loss of information regarding incidents that ended with the worst possible outcome. The remaining accounts form the basis of this analysis of what the participants did in response to the hijacking incidents.

Compliance

Over the time period studied, 256 hijacking incidents were identified. In only 133 of these incidents is any mention made of anything that the passengers or crew did at all. Given the caveats of the accuracy of the data available, it must be assumed that the other 123 incidents represent full compliance by all parties and therefore 'hostage script' role behaviour by both the passengers and the crew.

Evidence of pro-social interactions between hostages and hostage takers has been presented elsewhere (Wilson and Smith, 1999). Nevertheless, some mention should be made again here in terms of compliance. While the majority of incidents appear to pass off without any behaviour of note, there are examples of compliance that go beyond our notions of simply following instructions. For example, it might initially seem surprising that at the end of the 1977 Japanese Red Army (JRA) hijacking, at the request of the hijackers, passengers completed and handed in a questionnaire evaluating the strengths and weaknesses of the operation (Strentz, 1988). However, according to the scripts of normal interaction people are accustomed to such compliance. Similarly, it might seem strange that the Kuwaiti hostages in the 1984 Tehran hijacking got themselves covered in ketchup to pose for photographs, implying that the hijackers had killed them. However, given that the hijackers had already genuinely killed two passengers, it certainly seems like a sensible alternative.

Passive Resistance

(a)   Noncompliance

Noncompliance with the hijackers' demands appears mainly on the part of the pilot, in the form of not altering the course of the plane. Sometimes this strategy works. For example, in July 1970 an attempted hijack in Mozambique ended peacefully after the pilot simply refused to divert the plane. Similarly, in July of 1984 a man attempted to hijack a Middle Eastern Airlines plane destined for Beirut back to its original starting point, armed only with an unidentified bottle of liquid, claiming it to be an explosive device. The pilot simply continued his flight to Beirut, where after some brief negotiations the hijacker gave himself up. The question that arises in these examples is the extent to which the pilot reveals that he or she is not actually following instructions, which is certainly not clear in the second example. In contrast, July 1986 saw a lone hijacker attempt to hijack a plane from Baghdad by passing the stewardess a note threatening to blow up the plane if it was not diverted to Israel. In this instance, rather than openly refusing to comply, the pilot announced that a hijack was in progress, yet maintained his course and flew on to his scheduled destination, where the mentally unstable hijacker was arrested.

The hijackers' response to noncompliance is clearly important, and in the above examples they did nothing. If the hijackers are aware that the pilot is not complying with their demands, perhaps the hijacker is thrown by this deviation from the expected 'script' and has not prepared for the eventuality. There are certainly examples of hijackers being ill-prepared for unexpected deviations from their plans (Wilson and Smith, 1999). It is also possible that there is limited action that can be taken against the pilot as the hijackers need someone to fly the plane. For example, in the September 1980 hijacking of an American plane, when the pilot refused to believe the hijackers' claim to have set an explosive device at Tampa Airport which would be detonated if they were not taken to Havana, they had little option but to continue to the scheduled destination. A similar judgement call was made by the pilot of a 1993 flight from Athens to London, when a man claimed to have a bomb in his briefcase. After 90 minutes of negotiation at Gatwick the man surrendered to the authorities. Nevertheless, if the hijacker does not retaliate against the pilots themselves they may attack others in the hope of gaining leverage for their demands. Furthermore, there does appear to be a small subset of hijackers who are prepared to shoot pilots, even at 30,000ft.

Refusal of the suggested destination seems more common in pilots being diverted to what they perceive as 'hostile' countries, usually where the hijackers are hoping to seek asylum. For example, a Polish plane flying from Warsaw to Brussels via East Berlin was hijacked to West Berlin by two East Germans armed with guns. When the pilot and the co-pilot refused to comply with their demands they were hit on the head with pistols causing slight injuries. The pilots then complied, and the hijackers surrendered to the authorities with the aim of seeking political asylum.

Interestingly, there is occasional negotiation of destination rather than outright refusal. In June 1984 two Iranian hijackers took over a domestic flight from Tehran threatening to blow up the plane unless it was diverted to Baghdad. The pilot declined Baghdad and so the hijackers suggested Qatar, to which the pilot agreed. Wilson (2000) reports an empirical association between hijackers with personally motivated demands and the tendency to release passengers unharmed on arrival at the desired destination. However, the analysis was again based on published accounts with their possible inaccuracies. Clearly, if substantiated with the most detailed data available, this finding has implications for hijacking policy.

As hypothesised, noncompliance was rarely found in passengers and cabin crew. However, this may be related to the fact that they are not often asked to do very much. Nevertheless, there are no reported cases of, for example, cabin crew not passing a note to the flight deck. In the much cited example of the June 1985 hijacking of a TWA flight from Athens, stewardess Uli Derickson is reported as having not identified Jewish and military passengers as requested (St John, 1991), and Jacobson (1973) reports having questioned the hijackers as to the reason for their asking for her passport. Interestingly she was met with demands from other passengers to comply and not to 'make trouble'. Partial compliance was demonstrated by stewardesses instructed to bind and gag the passengers of a 1995 Japanese domestic flight. Although they carried out the hijacker's instruction, they bound the passengers so lightly that many of them were able to free themselves.

(b) Deception

Attempts at deception again appear to be employed only by the flight crew. Two forms of deception account for the examples found, attempts to deceive the hijacker as to the destination and false claims of technical failure or the need for refuelling.

Destination deception Attempts to mislead the hijacker as to their destination/ location are perhaps the most interesting and range from the highly complex to the more simple. At its simplest the pilot may appear to be heading for the desired destination but actually be maintaining his or her course or altering it to a more friendly alternative. Clearly this overlaps with noncompliance, discussed above. For example, the pilot of a Brazilian plane hijacked to Cuba by four members of the Action for National Liberation (ALN) managed to return to Rio, despite having been shot, without alerting the hijackers to their actual destination.

The above example involved simply returning to the point of origin, but other attempts involve landing at a destination other than that specified, in an attempt to deceive the hijackers. The most complex example of this is in the 1970 Japanese Red Army hijacking where an attempt was made to mock up the South Korean airport to be North Korean. Kimpo Airport in Seoul was disguised, complete with a welcome committee, but the trick was detected when the hijackers noticed US planes parked on the runway (Mickolus, 1980).

Nevertheless, such a complex attempt at deception lies in the hands of the authorities and simpler versions are more common. Simple deception strategies have been used the fool Cuba-bound hijackers into thinking they have arrived at their desired destination. For example, landing in the Turks and Caicos Islands fooled the hijacker of a US bound flight from Puerto Rico long enough for him to be peacefully arrested. Similarly, in January of 1985 a hijacker carrying a harmless bottle of liquid managed to hijack a Miami-bound US flight. However, rather than landing in Cuba, the pilot landed at Orlando and parked the plane in a deserted area of the runway, announcing that they had arrived. In this incident the hijacker was overpowered by the co-pilot and one of the passengers.

The pilot of a US domestic flight from Chicago to Miami was faced with a poorly armed hijacker demanding to go to Cuba for a wedding. Although he changed his course down toward the Florida Keys, he circled back to Miami airport where the passengers joined in the attempted deception shouting 'Cuba, Cuba' on arrival. Passenger involvement in deception is very rare, beyond feigning illness in the hope of getting released. For example, in a personally motivated hijacking in Japan in 1970 a passenger feigned labour pains and the hijacker agreed that she be released. This also afforded the opportunity for the security forces to board the plane and successfully end the incident.

Most of the above incidents involved lone hijackers who were poorly armed and had personal motivations. These factors may have led to the decision to attempt deception. However, not all such attempts have ended successfully. On 9 November 1970, an Iranian aircraft was hijacked out of Dubai by a group of 'criminals' who were being sent back to Iran in the company of armed guards. The hijackers were armed with knives and pistols and demanded to be flown to Baghdad. The pilot attempted to fly to Iran anyway, enraging the hijackers, who threatened to destroy the plane. Likewise, in 1983, six hijackers armed with pistols attempted to hijack a Chinese domestic flight to Seoul. The pilot repeatedly tried to alter his course to return to China but his actions were discovered, provoking one of the hijackers to get very angry and the resulting struggle over the controls nearly crashed the plane.

Technical deception A more subtle, and arguably more effective, form of bluffing on the part of the pilot is to feign technical problems, for example technical faults or lack of fuel that necessitates landing at a destination other than that requested. For example, when a British West Indian Airways flight from Kingston, Jamaica to Miami was taken over by two men armed with pistols and knives, the pilot was able to convince them that a faulty oil pressure gauge necessitated landing in Havana, rather than flying on to Senegal, where a peaceful resolution was negotiated. Similarly, unnecessary refuelling stops may ground the plane long enough for the hijackers to be overpowered by the authorities or convinced to surrender. In the December 1982 hijacking of a plane on a short flight within California, the crew were able to convince the hijacker that there was not enough fuel to get to Washington State as he had requested, whereupon he backed down from his demands.

An attempt at both technical and location deception was made in 1988, when a USSR flight to Leningrad was hijacked by a group of armed men. Claiming that they needed to refuel in Finland, the crew landed at an airforce base in Leningrad where the resulting gun battle with the authorities left five hijackers, three passengers and one flight attendant dead and another 35 wounded.

Drawing on the role-rule analogy, technical deception would be predicted to be a more successful strategy, since it is unlikely that the hijackers will have specialist technical knowledge and it would be expected that they would defer to that of the pilots. That said, there does seem to be a small subset of irrational hijackers for whom no fuel, blown-out tyres and the like are no obstacle to flying. While 11 September 2001 saw the first political hijackers intending actually to fly the plane themselves, in 1992 Charles Lloyd Patterson, on prison leave in the US, hijacked, stole and flew a charter plane before vanishing somewhere in Texas. Remarkably, he managed to pull off this move again later that year, this time heading to Texas from Colorado, and was eventually arrested later that month.

Finally, there is one example of the crew successfully attempting deception. When the mentally disturbed hijacker on a 1969 US flight demanded the keys to the cockpit, the flight attendant gave him the wrong ones. When he discovered that he could not open the door he returned to his seat and was subdued by passengers and crew.

Active Resistance

(a) Banking the Plane

One form of nonviolent action that pilots may take is to bank the plane or otherwise try to throw the hijackers off balance. However, this is relatively rare and employed as a precursor to active action to disarm the hijacker. For example, in January 1970, although the lone hijacker was holding a knife to the stewardess' throat on the hijacked Delta Airlines Orlando to Atlanta run, the pilot deliberately made a bumpy scheduled landing in order to throw the hijacker off balance, allowing three of the passengers, assisted by the crew, to overpower him.

An Eastern Airlines flight in March 1970 on the New York to Boston run was taken over by a lone hijacker, this time, however, armed with a revolver, and demanding to be taken to an unspecified destination 'east'. Attempts at persuasion having failed, the pilot tried to throw the hijacker off balance by banking the plane, which led the hijacker to shoot the pilot in the arm. The co-pilot then attempted to disarm the hijacker, and was shot in the chest, later to die of his wounds. Nevertheless, the hijacker was also injured and both pilot and co-pilot were commended for heroism.

Later that year, October saw another such pilot response in the Soviet Union when a domestic flight with 51 passengers on board was hijacked by a man and his son demanding to be taken to Turkey. The pilot's attempt to throw the hijackers off balance by banking the plane failed and the resulting gunfire killed a flight attendant and injured the pilot, radio operator and one of the passengers. The co-pilot flew the plane to Turkey as requested, where the hijackers surrendered requesting political asylum.

A similar example occurred in 1981, when four armed hijackers attempted to hijack a Turkish Airlines flight out of Istanbul to Bulgaria. When two of the hijackers deplaned to hold a news conference, the pilot accelerated and braked suddenly throwing the remaining two hijackers off balance allowing the passengers to attempt to overpower them. However, the action once again resulted in shooting and five passengers were injured.

(b)   Persuasion

Persuasion tactics vary from simple statements to prolonged negotiations. The above analysis has already indicated that, on occasion, simply informing the hijacker that there is not enough fuel may be enough. Similarly, in the 1984 hijacking of an Air India flight to Bangalore, a passenger entered the cockpit and threatened to blow up the plane. The pilot simply asked him to go and sit down, which he did. Even if it does not actually persuade the hijacker to drop his demands, simple persuasion may be helpful in containing the situation, for example, by not alarming the passengers unduly. For instance, on a TWA flight on domestic run to New York, the hijacker approached the cockpit with a pistol and demanded to be flown to Havana. The pilot complied with the request but suggested that the hijacker remain in the cockpit for safety's sake. Likewise, on announcing a hijack in progress on a 1970 US domestic flight, one hijacker was convinced by a stewardess to keep his gun hidden to avoid alarming the passengers. Although this might have suggested that the hijacker was negotiable, later action by the flight crew in banking the plane and attempting to overpower the hijacker resulted in the death of the co-pilot and serious wounding of the pilot.

At the opposite end of the spectrum, pilots have been involved in quite lengthy negotiations with hijackers involving a considerable amount of diplomacy. For example, in the 1969 hijacking of a New York to Miami flight the pilot played a key role in the peaceful resolution of the incident by listening to the personal problems of a young couple armed with a knife. Mickolus and Simmons (1997) report that on 11 February 1993, in the first transatlantic hijacking for 16 years, a student hijacked a Lufthansa flight from Frankfurt, successfully diverting it to New York. The pilot was able to negotiate with the hijacker, eventually persuading him to hand over his gun in exchange for the pilot's sunglasses. The hijacker reciprocated by leaving the pilot his hat as a souvenir.

Here again, it appears to be the flight crew who get involved in negotiations with hijackers, if not directly, then often by playing a mediating role between the hijacker and the authorities once the negotiations are under way. St John (1991) claims that pilots should not be placed in this position as their own dependency on the outcome makes them poor negotiators. He goes on to praise the pilot of TWA flight 847 in June 1985 for handing over of responsibility to flight attendant Uli Derickson. She was able to employ a number of highly successful persuasion techniques owing to her linguistic skills and familiarity with the cultural and religious background of the terrorists. St John states that pilots have been reluctant to take the cabin crew seriously in management roles:

> perhaps they feel that flight attendants cannot manage stress as successfully as they can, or maybe pilots prefer to keep flight attendants in a buffer situation between themselves and the passengers. In moments of honesty, a number of pilots have admitted to sexist attitudes with regard to female flight and cabin crew (St John, 1991, p. 179).

(c) Physical Attack

Attempts to overpower the hijackers are the most common form of resistance, and it has been suggested that these attempts should decrease in frequency from the security guards through the crew to the passengers themselves.

Security guards There are no reported cases where security guards have been present and done nothing. The scale and outcome of the guards' actions, however, is variable. While in some cases the guards need only overpower and disarm the hijacker, in other cases they respond in a more extreme fashion. For example, in the 1984 hijacking of an Iraqi Airways flight from Cyprus to Baghdad, three hijackers were shot dead immediately by the security guards when they attempted to take over the plane. Similarly, a would-be hijacker on an Iranian flight in 1985 was killed outright, allowing the plane to land safely in Tehran. Five guards emerged from amongst the passengers when two Eritrean Liberation Front (ELF) hijackers attempted to take over an Ethiopian Airlines flight from Madrid to Addis Ababa. As the first hijacker headed for the cockpit, a guard grabbed the gun and turned it back on him, firing twice. The guard then fired another six shots from his own gun, while other guards shot dead another hijacker in the passenger section. On this occasion none of the passengers or crew were injured. However, with so much shooting going on it might be expected that others may sometimes get hurt.

The vast majority of violent action taken by the security guards is undertaken without assistance from any of the other players. This accords with the occupational role theory as, in the presence of guards, people may see it as unnecessary to get involved. However, it may be necessary for others to get involved if security guard themselves have been injured. For example, in the 1988 hijacking of a Pakistan International Airlines flight, a lone hijacker shot the security guard three times before being overwhelmed by the passengers.

Pilots With respect to the remaining crew it is often unclear from the accounts exactly who was involved in the action. However, there are clear examples where the pilots, St John's (1991) 'movers and shakers', take responsibility for attempting to overpower the hijackers. For example, in the 1971 hijacking of an Air Canada flight, a disturbed gunman demanding US$1.5 million and to be flown to Ireland was knocked unconscious by the pilot. Similarly, when a 1985 Turkish Airlines flight from Frankfurt to Istanbul was hijacked by a man holding a fire extinguisher, again the pilot seemed to have little trouble overpowering him. However, these incidents represent cases where there is only one hijacker with personal motivations. Where there are a number of hijackers, who are well armed, tackling the hijackers may not end so successfully.

For example, in 1983 six hijackers entered the cockpit of a Chinese aircraft and fired several shots. In trying to retaliate with axes, the radio operator and navigator were seriously injured. There are a number of instances where the pilot has killed the hijackers. For example, in 1983, an Aeroflot flight was taken over by eight hijackers demanding to be flown to Turkey. When the first man entered cockpit, the pilot shot him dead and locked the door. The eventual storming of the aircraft left one of the hijackers, one flight attendant, the pilot and co-pilot dead. Similarly, in 1983 a man attempted to divert a domestic flight in China to Taiwan. When he shot and killed the pilot, the navigator killed the hijacker with an axe.

Reports of action taken by the pilot or flight crew rarely refer to the involvement of any other parties. Only one instance of passengers coming to the pilot's aid was identified. Perhaps the pilots, like security guards, carry some kind of position of authority with respect to the passengers and cabin crew.

Cabin crew Specific reference to the cabin crew getting involved in physical attack on their own is unusual and, as hypothesised, gender roles appear to be important. More frequent is the involvement of the crew alongside passengers, which will be discussed below. Thus, while male cabin crew members may attempt to overpower the hijackers, female cabin crew taking action is rare, but not unheard of. For instance, in 1979 an Australian plane was hijacked by a mentally unstable man with a semiautomatic shotgun. A stewardess initially knocked the gun from his hands, after which three more stewardesses and two pilots overpowered him. Likewise, when a Somali airline on route to Saudi Arabia was hijacked by three men, a stewardess tried to grab the gun, resulting in another crew member being wounded.

Passengers The passengers' role has been hypothesised to be a passive one, both in terms of 'hostage-taking scripts' and in terms of 'occupational role' on board the plane. Nevertheless, there are numerous cases where passengers have got involved in trying to intervene in hijacking attempts, with various degrees of success. When passengers do get involved, they usually work alongside the crew members who are trying to overpower the hijacker. This behaviour suggests a return to the normal scripts of social behaviour, where a male passenger is unlikely to sit by while a (most likely female) flight attendant is grappling with a (most likely male) hijacker.

For example, when a lone hijacker on a 1983 Miami-bound US domestic flight diverted to Cuba grabbed a stewardess and held her at knife point, two passengers overpowered him and tied him up, allowing the plane to return to Miami as scheduled. Similarly, in another hijacking to Cuba in 1971, the hijacker held an ice pick to throat of a stewardess. Other crew members, aided by passengers, tried to disarm the man, resulting in injuries to the stewardess and her rescuers.

Passengers helping the crew to overpower the hijacker are therefore much more frequent than passengers coming to the aid of security guards or flight crew. However, there is another subset of interest. These are passengers who play some form of security role in their everyday lives and therefore feel qualified to take part despite their role as passenger.

For example, on a US domestic flight from Dallas to New York, a mentally unstable man tried to divert the plane to Cuba. He was disarmed by an FBI special agent amongst the passengers. An Ethiopian Airlines flight to French Somaliland was taken over by three well-armed hijackers associated with the Eritrean Liberation Front (ELF), who diverted the aircraft to South Yemen. Among the passengers was an Ethiopian secret police officer who shot one of the hijackers six times in the stomach and arms while the other two were overpowered. An attempt to hijack a Cuban plane to Miami in 1987 was thwarted when an off-duty police officer shot and killed the hijacker, but not before the hijacker had let off a grenade, injuring 13 passengers.

On occasion, passengers and crew who had considered acting to thwart the hijacking have explained their reasons for not doing so. For example, a professional wrestler on board a 1970 US domestic flight did not attempt an attack as the hijacker was holding a gun to the throat of a flight attendant and he feared for her safety. One pilot on another flight did not attempt to overpower a suicidal hijacker who was armed with a knife, a pistol and semiautomatic rifle and identified himself as a Vietnam veteran. He reasoned that since the hijacker had combat training it was best not attempted.

(d) Escape

The script-based hypotheses would not predict many attempts at escape at all, but where escape attempts do occur one would least expect it of the security guards and the flight crew. It is certainly the case that there were no reports of escaping security guards, and few involving the flight crew. Where this did happen, it took place after the cabin crew and passengers had already made their escape. For instance, in December 1971, a US domestic flight bound for Chicago was hijacked, with 29 passengers on board. The lone hijacker was armed with a revolver and demanded US$300,000 and two parachutes. On delivery of the money at Chicago he allowed all but two of the passengers to leave the aircraft. While the hijacker was counting the money, the flight deck crew escaped. Later, one of the flight attendants escaped while the hijacker was in the lavatory. Next, the remaining two flight attendants and one of the remaining passengers escaped, leaving the would-be hijacker with one passenger and no crew, whereupon he gave himself up. Thus, by the time the pilots left the plane, most of the other hostages had already been released.

More typically, the pilots will play a role in distracting the hijacker in order to afford the opportunity of escape to others on board. This then reflects the expectation that the pilots are in a role of command whereby their first obligation is to protect the passengers and cabin crew rather than themselves. For example, in the 1980 hijacking of a US flight to Cuba, the three pilots kept the armed hijacker talking while the passengers and remaining crew managed to escape down a food shaft by knotting blankets together. A similar incident was seen in 1987 on a US domestic flight where the pilot took distracting action whilst others escaped. In this case the lone hijacker was mentally ill and threatened to set fire to the plane unless he was allowed to see the Nation of Islam leader. Whilst the pilot talked to the man, all 45 passengers and five crew escaped unharmed.

Nevertheless, passengers do sometimes initiate an escape bid on their own. In April 1982, four politically-motivated terrorists took over a Honduran plane demanding US$1 million and the release of a large number of political prisoners. The escape attempt was led by a journalist among the passengers, after a lengthy period of being held hostage on board the plane. The ringleader, followed by 16 passengers and three crew members, leapt out of the emergency exit and through a glass window into the airport terminal to safety, despite sustaining inevitable injuries. In September 1984 two heavily-armed hijackers diverted an Iranian plane to Cairo where they falsely claimed that a number of passengers had been shot in order to appear to the authorities to be more committed. When a ladder was provided to remove the 'injured' through the rear door, 50 of the 114 passengers, along with two crew members, escaped. Here again, the flight crew remained to fly the plane on to Baghdad where the hijackers claimed political asylum.

In the above examples members of the cabin crew made their escape along with the passengers. Crew escaping without passengers appears to be very rare. Only one instance was identified, in the 1984 hijacking of an Air France flight from Frankfurt to Paris. Following refuelling in Geneva, the plane flew on to Beirut where a failed takeover attempt by the authorities led the plane to fly on and refuel again in Cyprus. Here, a male crew member escaped from the plane by jumping out of the door.

Conclusions

This chapter has presented a theoretically-based interpretation of what types of resistance are offered by hostages in aircraft hijackings and who is most likely to employ them. This, therefore, presents some testable hypotheses. Although some of these resistance strategies have been illustrated with anecdotal examples, there is clearly scope for empirical testing.

The various forms of resistance attempted may also be present in the same hijack and it would also be of interest to see in what order they are attempted. It is possible that, for example, people may start with passive resistance strategies and move to successively more active ones as each fails. Here again, detailed accounts would allow this hypothesis to be tested. Similarly, the accounts used in this analysis span several decades and it is possible that resistance strategies may change over time in line with changing scripts.

It would clearly be of importance to identify the likely success of various responses, in the context of the type of hijacking in progress. The number of successful instances of the passengers and crew overpowering the hijacker/s may give the impression that this is a strategy worth attempting. Nevertheless, there are numerous examples of where such action has resulted in injury and death, and as mentioned earlier, we have no way of knowing what precipitated incidents that led to the death of all on board. Before any conclusions can be drawn, it is essential to conduct an empirical study of the response of hijackers to various forms of intervention in order to establish the likely response. Further, such an analysis must take into account the type of hijacking in progress in terms of the motivations and resources of those involved (Wilson, 2000).

Recently there has been debate in the US as to whether pilots should be permitted to carry firearms to thwart hijackers. Whilst the pilots' union supported the call, a Senate Commerce Committee of the US government rejected the notion. The spokesman was quoted as saying: 'Pilots need to concentrate on flying the plane ... marshals are trained not only in the use of weapons but all the things that build up to that ... Misfiring of guns could bring planes down' (*Daily Telegraph*, 22 May 2002). The statement recommends that pilots remain locked in the cockpit and manoeuvre the plane to keep the hijackers off balance.

The media has been criticised by numerous authors for perpetuating hijacking incidents through contagion effects (Holden, 1986; Oots, 1986) and providing the publicity that terrorists seek (e.g. Martin, 1985; Rubin and Friedland, 1986). However, of more interest in the current context is the way in which the media operates in forming our 'hostage-taking scripts'. If people derive their invented hostage scripts from the media, whether news coverage of genuine events or fictional film representations, then it is possible that the way in which such events are reported or presented is important in determining the way people will react if faced with a real life incident. For example, primacy effects may lead people to remember scenes of murdered hostages being thrown onto the tarmac. On the other hand, no visual imagery accompanies successfully negotiated solutions. In fact, it is rare for hostages to be harmed in hostage-taking incidents, unless the authorities intervene (Wilson, Canter and Smith, 1995).

The events of 11 September 2001 will undoubtedly stand out in terms of both primacy and recency and raise the question as to whether what happened that day has changed hijacking scripts. The one or two aircraft that have crashed into buildings since 11 September have immediately drawn speculation of terrorist intent. The aircraft that missed its target on 11 September was not the first incident where passengers attempted to overpower the hijackers. Although subsequent intelligence has revealed a number of cases where the hijackers had intended to crash the plane, 11 September was perhaps the first time that passengers had an indication as to their fate if they did not act to overpower the hijackers. Importantly, it is the only record we have of passengers saying that they would attempt to overpower the hijackers at the time. If the real possibility of dying in a hijacked plane has become part of our collective scripts, then passengers may no longer be as prepared to play their role as passive hostages, preferring to tackle the hijackers as did those involved on 11 September.

It is also possible that the events of that day have altered hijackers' scripts as well. Following 11 September, the US government announced their intention to shoot down hijacked planes. It is questionable whether they would actually carry out this threat where bargaining and safe release may still be real options. However, if terrorists believe that this is a real possibility, perhaps this has had a deterrent effect on hijackers who would have taken aircraft for bargaining purposes. Analysis of the frequency of hijacking incidents in the 1990s showed that they were still increasing slightly each year (Wilson et al., 1995). Examination of references to hijacking incidents in quality British press in the 12 months up to 11 September identified 10 hijack incidents worldwide. The time period from 11 September to the time of writing (May 2002) identified only one such attempt. The question, therefore, is whether the events of 11 September have changed all of our scripts to the degree that the relatively well-scripted hijacking incidents of the last few decades are a thing of the past. Perhaps because of our new scripts, hijacking will become more dangerous and less predictable in the future.

Acknowledgement

The author would like to thank Nicola Mackenzie for her assistance with the research for this chapter.

References

Abelson, R. (1981), 'Psychological Status of the Script Concept', *American Psychologist*, Vol. 36, pp. 715–29.
Atkinson, S., Sandler, T. and Tschirhart, J., (1987), 'Terrorism in a Bargaining Framework', *Journal of Law and Economics*, Vol. 30, pp. 1–21.

Canter, D. (1990a), 'An Overview of Human Behaviour in Fires', in D. Canter (ed.), *Fires and Human Behaviour*, 2nd edn, London: David Fulton Publishers.

Canter, D. (1990b), 'Studying the Experience of Fires', in D. Canter (ed.), *Fires and Human Behaviour*, 2nd edn, London: David Fulton Publishers.

Canter, D., Breaux, J. and Sime, J. (1990), 'Domestic, Multiple Occupancy and Hospital Fires', in D. Canter (ed.), *Fires and Human Behaviour*, 2nd edn, London: David Fulton Publishers.

Corsi, J. (1981), Terrorism as a desperate game: fear, bargaining and communication in the terrorist event, Journal of Conflict Resolution, Vol. 25, No. 1, pp. 47–85.

Donald, I., and Canter, D. (1990), Behavioural aspects of the King's Cross fire', in D. Canter (ed.), *Fires and Human Behaviour*, 2nd edn, London: David Fulton Publishers.

Donald, I. and Canter, D. (1992), 'Intentionality and Fatality during the King's Cross Underground Fire', *European Journal of Social Psychology*, Vol. 22, No. 3, pp. 203–18.

Holden, R. (1986), 'The Contagiousness of Aircraft Hijacking', *American Journal of Sociology*, Vol. 91, No. 4, pp. 874–904.

Jacobson, S. (1973), 'Individual and Group Responses to Confinement in a Skyjacked Plane', *American Journal of Orthopsychiatry*, Vol. 43, No. 3, pp. 459–69.

Kuleshnyk, I. (1984), 'The Stockholm Syndrome: Toward an understanding', *Social Action and the Law*, Vol. 10, No. 2, pp. 37–42.

Lapan, H. and Sandler, T. (1988), 'The Political Economy of Terrorism: To bargain or not to bargain: that is the question', *AEA Papers and Proceedings*, Vol. 78, No. 2, pp. 16–21.

Martin, L. (1985), 'The Media's Role in International Terrorism', *Terrorism: An International Journal*, Vol. 8, No. 2, pp. 127–46.

McDuff, D. (1992), 'Social Issues in the Management of Released Hostages', *Hospital and Community Psychiatry*, Vol. 43, No. 8, pp. 825–8.

Mickolus, E. (1980), *Transnational Terrorism: A chronology of events. 1968–1979*, London: Greenwood Press.

Mickolus, E. (1993), *Terrorism 1988–1991: A chronology of events and a selectively annotated bibliography. 1968–1979*, London: Greenwood Press.

Mickolus, E., Sandler, T. and Murdoch, J. (1989), *International Terrorism in the 1980s: A chronology of events 1–2*, Iowa: Iowa State University Press.

Mickolus, E. and Simmons, S. (1997), *Terrorism, 1992–1995: A chronology of events and a selectively annotated bibliography*, London: Greenwood Press.

Oots, K. (1986), *A Political Organization Approach to Transnational Terrorism*, Westport, Connecticut: Greenwood Press.

Rubin, J. and Friedland, N. (1986), 'Theater of Terror', *Psychology Today*, Vol. 20, No. 3, pp. 18–28.

Sandler, T. and Scott, J. (1987), 'Terrorist Success in Hostage Taking Incidents: An empirical study', *Journal of Conflict Resolution*, Vol. 31, No. 1, pp. 35–53.

Sime, J. (1990), 'The Concept of Panic', in D. Canter (ed.), *Fires and Human Behaviour*, 2nd edn, London: David Fulton Publishers.

St John, O. (1991), 'Pilots and Pirates: Airline pilots and hijacking', in S. Deitz and W. Thoms (eds), *Pilots, Personality and Performance: Human behaviour and stress in the skies*, London: Quorum Books.

Strentz, T. (1979), 'The Stockholm Syndrome: Law enforcement policy and ego defenses of the hostage', *FBI Law Enforcement Bulletin*, Vol. 48, pp. 2–12.

Strentz, T. (1988), 'A Terrorist Psychosocial Profile: Past and present', *FBI Law Enforcement Bulletin*, Vol. 57, No. 4, pp. 13–18.

Turner, J. (1985), 'Factors Influencing the Development of Hostage Identification Syndrome', *Political Psychology*, Vol. 6, No. 4, pp. 705–11.

Wilson, M. (2000), 'Toward a Model of Terrorist Behaviour in Hostage Taking Incidents', *Journal of Conflict Resolution*, Vol. 44, pp. 403–24.

Wilson, M. (in press), 'The Psychology of Terrorist Hostage Taking', in Silke, A. (ed.), *Terrorists, Victims and Society: Psychological Perspectives on Terrorism and its Consequences*, Chichester: Wiley.

Wilson, M, and Smith, A. (1999), 'Roles and Rules in Terrorist Hostage Taking', in D.Canter and L. Alison (eds), *The Social Psychology of Crime: Groups, teams and networks*, Ashgate: Aldershot.

Wilson, M., Canter, D. and Smith, A. (1995), 'Modelling Terrorist Behavior', Final Report to the US Army Research Institute, Alexandra, Virginia: ARI.

Chapter 13

Physiology of Flying: Effects and Consequences of the Cabin Environment

Richard Dawood

'Safety is paramount in the airline industry, and nobody would wish it otherwise. Our concern is not that health is secondary to safety, but that it has been woefully neglected.' So begin the recommendations of the House of Lords Select Committee on Air Travel and Health, 2000. It is certainly true that health issues have been neglected, that opportunities to expand our knowledge have been missed, and that much more research now needs to be done. However, a considerable amount *is* known about the physiology of flying and the physical impact of the cabin environment upon the human body, enabling us to at least begin to speculate about the way such factors may influence passenger behaviour.

Among the physical and environmental factors to which air travellers are exposed, are the following, each of which will be considered in turn:

- reduced atmospheric pressure;
- reduced oxygen pressure;
- reduced air humidity;
- a perception of reduced air quality;
- aircraft motion;
- movement restriction/confined space;
- fluid shifts and dehydration;
- effects of alcohol;
- fatigue/sleep loss;
- effects of medication;
- interplay with stress, anxiety and psychosocial environment.

Reduced Atmospheric Pressure (Reduced Cabin Air Pressure)

Ascent to a cruising altitude in a typical, pressurised airliner results in a drop in cabin pressure from 760mm mercury (mm Hg) at sea-level to about 600mm Hg at 6000 feet. (Most aircraft cabins are 'pressurised' – their internal pressure is maintained at the equivalent of 6000–8000ft, even when cruising at 30,000–35,000 ft.)

The fall in atmospheric pressure has several consequences. One of the most obvious and immediate is expansion of gases in body cavities (in accordance with Boyle's Law) – typically by one-third. This translates into a feeling of bloating and vague discomfort that may persist throughout a flight, and that 'sets the scene' for the other bodily insults that follow. (In passengers with pre-existing medical problems, the consequences may be more serious – even catastrophic, in the case of some people recovering from abdominal thoracic or cranial surgery.) Contraction of gas during descent can bring additional problems – such as a painful middle ear or sinus 'squeeze' – notably in passengers with upper respiratory infection or sinus problems.

Reduced Oxygen Pressure

The most important direct consequence of the drop in total pressure is the proportionate reduction in *oxygen pressure*. For the vast majority of passengers, this generally seems to make little difference: haemoglobin in red blood cells absorbs oxygen with sufficient avidity to compensate.

In people with respiratory or cardiac problems, however, or in people who are anaemic or are suffering from a variety of other medical problems, the body's ability to cope with reduced oxygen pressure may be greatly diminished, and symptoms of hypoxia (reduced oxygen levels) rapidly appear (Harding, 2002). In this situation, it may be necessary to breathe supplemental oxygen.

Carbon monoxide can reduce haemoglobin's capacity for absorbing oxygen, which is one reason why heavy smokers may be more vulnerable to the effects of reduced oxygen pressure. (They may also be suffering from a smoking-related reduction in lung function, which may exacerbate the problem.)

The impact of hypoxia upon behaviour is poorly understood; it can certainly cause confusion, disorientation, and effects similar to those of alcoholic intoxication. It may also cause a reduction in concentration and mental performance. It is interesting to speculate upon whether 'air rage' incidents involving smokers may have hypoxia as a contributing factor – though a multitude of other factors may also be at play, such as the effects of nicotine withdrawal, for example.

It is difficult to know how many passengers experience subtle effects of hypoxia, and how significant such effects may be. Sleep, alcohol, medication, and anything that depresses the respiratory centre of the brain may each add to the problem of hypoxia. Babies and infants have an immature respiratory system and may be more susceptible to the effects of hypoxia than adults.

There is room for much more research on the extent to which passengers do experience hypoxia, and the relatively recent availability of miniaturised, battery-powered oximeters (devices for measuring oxygenation) should make such studies considerably easier to carry out.

Reduced Air Humidity

Cabin air is replaced by air drawn in from the aircraft's engines; however, the rarefied air outside the aircraft contains virtually no moisture. The humidity of the cabin air can therefore be as low as 1 or 2 per cent – any moisture within the air usually being derived from the passengers themselves.

The most direct consequence is rapid drying of moist body surfaces – notably the corneal and conjunctival surfaces of the eyes, and the mucosal surfaces of the nasal and upper respiratory passages.

This causes dryness and discomfort of the eyes, which may be considerably more severe in people who have a tendency towards dryness under normal conditions. Contact lens wearers may also be vulnerable, and may eventually sustain corneal abrasions or ulcers, especially if they do not use eye drops or are too fatigued or distracted to remove their lenses.

Dryness of the upper respiratory surfaces also causes discomfort. The film of moisture that normally lines these surfaces is considered to constitute an initial barrier to infection; it is uncertain to what extent loss of this film of moisture may contribute to an increased risk of airborne transmission of disease.

Dryness of the cabin air facilitates evaporation, and passengers may see practical evidence for this effect in hot weather or if they board the aircraft covered in perspiration from stress or exertion; once airborne, they quickly 'dry out'. However, this effect does not normally result in sufficient fluid loss to have any significant impact on hydration status (see below).

Perception of Reduced Air Quality

Amongst passengers, there is a widely-held sense that the airline industry has not adequately laid to rest issues relating to cabin air quality. Symptoms commonly attributed to reduced air quality include headache, dizziness, fatigue, abdominal discomfort, nausea, fever and respiratory infections. Anxieties exist in relation to such issues as recirculation of cabin air, the effectiveness of high efficiency particulate air (HEPA) filters, and the possible influence of chemical and particulate contaminants. It is very difficult to design scientific studies capable of distinguishing between such factors and those inherent in flight itself: reduced cabin pressure, reduced oxygen pressure, reduced humidity, jet lag, fatigue, noise, vibration, stress, and so on (Rayman, 2002).

Until such studies have been carried out to everyone's satisfaction, however, it is likely that passenger anxieties on this subject will remain.

Motion and Motion Sickness

Aircraft motion adds a further stressor, though modern aircraft design minimises the effects under normal flying conditions. Motion sickness is not a disorder, but a normal response when the brain receives an avalanche of mismatched signal. Conditions on board the aircraft – warmth, lack of ventilation, stuffiness, smells – can make matters worse. Nausea and vomiting may be accompanied by a dizzy, light-headed feeling, sweating, pale and clammy skin.

Several studies have indicated that there is relatively little to choose between the various remedies available, in terms of effectiveness; so sufferers should simply try to choose a remedy that is well tolerated and that does not cause troubling side-effects. (Common side-effects include such symptoms as drowsiness and a dry mouth.) Travellers who are prone to the condition should anticipate the problem and take medication in advance of the journey; once vomiting begins medication is seldom helpful. Other helpful strategies include choosing a seat close to the wings of the aircraft, where motion is likely to be least.

Movement Restriction/Confined Space

In the economy class cabin, the amount of space allocated to each passenger is usually quantified in term of 'seat pitch' – the distance from the back of one seat to the back of the seat in front. Present regulation of seat pitch is determined by safety considerations rather than by health: it is a safety requirement that the aircraft cabin should be capable of full evacuation within 90 seconds.

Current minimum seat pitch regulated by the Civil Aviation Authority is set at 26ins – a dimension that has to include the thickness of the seat back plus any material in seat-back pockets. Most seats on charter aircraft – the industry yardstick for discomfort – have a pitch of 28ins. The CAA is undertaking new research on the anthropomorphics of the modern airline passenger and will publish its conclusions shortly: the House of Lords committee called for the CAA to develop an unambiguous set of minimum seat dimensions and there is growing pressure for more generous standards to be drawn up and provided for in legislation.

Airlines debate the extent to which lack of space contributes to the risk of deep vein thrombosis (DVT), a medical condition involving the veins of the calf muscles and the lower leg. Under normal conditions, muscle contraction and leg movement helps keep blood flowing through the veins, forcing it up a system of one-way valves. Without muscle contraction, blood can stagnate and form clots; a variety of medical conditions and additional factors, from the contraceptive pill and HRT to cancer, can make this more likely to happen. Obstruction of the veins progresses to cause painful swelling of the leg, which can persist as a debilitating and long-term problem. The most dangerous, sometimes lethal, complication occurs if a clot from the leg breaks free and travels through the major veins, lodging in the heart and lungs (pulmonary embolism). Symptoms of DVT may take several days to appear, if they appear at all: there may be no swelling or pain, and even in clear-cut cases, pain typically takes five days to appear. Only the most dramatic cases of pulmonary embolism are lethal; many cases result in minor symptoms – cough and chest pains that can easily be mistaken for muscular aches. It is easy to see why even the most solid link between DVT and air travel might be difficult to establish. Symptoms might not seem important enough to mention to a doctor, or might be delayed to a point where the fact of having taken a flight might no longer seem relevant. And DVT is a relatively common condition anyway. It is for such reasons that the possibility of a link between DVT and air travel is one that has taken a long time to become established.

A prospective study of long-haul air travellers, using a sensitive scanning technique for detection of blood clots, found that one in 10 passengers developed symptomless clots in the veins of the lower leg – clots that dispersed spontaneously (Scurr, 2001). Individual risk of developing DVT in relation to flying probably requires the presence of additional predisposing factors, and in the UK – pending the outcome of continuing research studies – the Department of Health has published guidelines for passengers on its website (http://www.doh.gov.uk/dvt/index.htm).

Passengers are increasingly advised to move around the aircraft cabin, and to stretch and take gentle exercise during flight. The options for doing so may be severely limited by the amount of space allocated to each passenger, and by factors such as meal service (with table/trays obstructing escape from seats for prolonged periods at a time).

Improved management of aircraft payloads ensures that a high proportion of airline flights are filled to capacity, with available seats often sold at knockdown prices. This contributes increasingly to overcrowding and to passenger densities that may not have been fully allowed for in aircraft design. The impact of overcrowding on passenger behaviour has been insufficiently investigated.

Overcrowding, immobility and lack of space contribute to muscle stiffness and musculoskeletal problems that are commonplace among airline passengers, compounding any problems arising from carrying heavy luggage.

Immobility may be responsible for other important physiological effects on the body, notably fluid shifts that result in loss of fluid from the circulation, contributing to 'dehydration'.

Fluid Shifts and Dehydration

In one series of experiments, a medical team from the German airline Lufthansa used a mock-up of a Boeing 747 interior: they studied 12 volunteers in economy class seating on four simulated 12-hour flights (two daytime and two night-time), during which physiological tests were performed. The experiments were then repeated at 35,000ft, in a real 747 on a 10-hour flight, using the same volunteers; a total of 35,000 samples were taken and analysed.

Key observations included significant movement of fluid out of the bloodstream and into the tissues of the lower body – evident as the ankle swelling with which many air travellers are all too familiar. Volunteers' weight increased dramatically during the flights – some individuals gained as much as 2kg – an increase attributed almost entirely to the tissue fluid. There was remarkably little difference between the measurements in the air and those recorded from the 'passengers' who stayed on the ground, but there were significant differences between passengers who stayed in their seats and those who walked about the cabin or took exercise.

These findings suggest that the dehydration or fluid loss commonly associated with flying, and responsible for so many other symptoms, is in fact caused or made worse by sequestration of fluid in the tissues by gravity, during prolonged immobility in a seated position under cramped conditions. Other factors contributing to dehydration in the air include reduced/restricted fluid intake, reduced water content of any food consumed, and increased consumption of alcohol or caffeine-containing liquids.

Alcohol and Caffeine-containing Drinks

It is strange that alcohol and air travel should have become so closely identified with each other – they go together so badly. Duty-free alcohol should, on safety grounds, have been banned from the aircraft cabin long ago: is it really sensible for airline passengers to fly surrounded by hundreds of litres of inflammable liquid in glass bottles?

Alcohol has two main effects on the air traveller. The first and most insidious is dehydration. Staying well-hydrated during a flight – especially a long-haul one – is essential for comfort and health. At worst, dehydration increases the risk of life-threatening deep vein thrombosis (DVT); more often, it causes a hammering headache and a feeling of general discomfort. An intake of roughly one pint of water for every three hours in the air is essential for good hydration.

Alcohol is a diuretic. By suppressing secretion of the pituitary hormone ADH, it increases the amount of water lost from the body via the kidneys. The extent of the effect depends on how much alcohol is ingested and over what time frame. At best, even relatively dilute alcoholic drinks (like beer or some cocktails) are no better than 'neutral', in hydration terms: any extra water they contain is exactly balanced by the diuretic effect of their alcohol content. The thirst-quenching effect of such drinks is illusory, like drinking nothing at all. Tea and coffee the other drinks favoured by the airlines, are similarly diuretic or neutral; airline food contains very little water; and soft drinks are metered out in half-sized cans.

The intoxicating effect of alcohol on the brain is very similar to the effect from reduced oxygen pressure in the aircraft cabin, which is why this effect is enhanced whilst flying. This is most pronounced in smokers, because, as explained earlier, carbon monoxide from cigarette smoke reduces the oxygen-carrying capacity of the blood. People with lung disease are also more vulnerable, but so are we all, to a greater or lesser degree, especially when alcohol is taken in excess. Sleeping tablets, or indeed any medication that causes drowsiness or depresses the nervous system, can interact with alcohol and greatly exacerbate the problem.

Fatigue and Sleep Loss

Many air travellers confuse two quite distinct consequences of air travel that have an impact upon their sleep/wakefulness, performance and well-being. Movement across time zones at a rate that outstrips the body's ability to adapt results in 'jet lag', which is considered in greater detail elsewhere. In contrast, fatigue and sleep loss can commonly accompany any long journey, regardless of whether it traverses time zones. Travellers should choose flight times carefully, so as to keep sleep loss to a minimum, thereby improving mental ability and performance on arrival at their destination. Carefully-timed sleeping medication can sometimes help reduce fatigue and sleep loss.

Sleeping Medication

Sleeping medication does not speed up adaptation to a new time zone, but several studies suggest that taking medication results in better next-day performance, compared with sleep of questionable quality using no medication. Medication can be extremely useful in reducing fatigue arising from delayed or interrupted sleep during the nights after travel across time zones, and possibly in ensuring a good night's sleep during a flight that is long enough (though deep sleep in an awkward position may add to the risk of deep vein thrombosis).

Most sleeping tablets are intended to provide eight hours' sleep, so it is unwise to take medication for flights that are much shorter than this. Sleeping medication should generally not be used during a flight unless the traveller is able to stretch out in a horizontal position; it may otherwise contribute to immobility and restriction of the circulation, with a resulting increase in the risk of deep vein thrombosis.

Following eastbound travel, most people have difficulty falling asleep; a short-acting drug, such as zaleplon (Sonata), is most suitable – it works quickly and is rapidly eliminated from the body. For westbound travel, where the tendency is toward early waking, longer-lasting medication (such as temazepam) is more appropriate.

Alcohol and sleeping medication should never be taken together. In a recent, well-publicised case of 'air rage', the acquittal of an American rock star who blamed his violent rampage through the First Class cabin of a British Airways jet on an interaction between alcohol and a commonly-used sleeping tablet, set a dangerous precedent for the future.

Interplay with Stress and Anxiety

Modern air travel seems increasingly stressful. Travel is supposed to be pleasurable, but the agony columns of the travel press are filled with tales from travellers for whom it has proved otherwise, each giving a personal account of frustration and disappointment. Recurring problems are cancellations, delays, overbooking, lost baggage, rudeness, indifference, dishonesty, incompetence, and negligence; all, one must infer, occurring on a massive scale. There is a mismatch between the carefully cultivated image of comfort, speed and service, and a reality that is sometimes less appealing. A host of additional factors may further influence the context of a journey by air: security and safety concerns, phobias social and cultural issues, to name but some.

The physical and physiological factors described above do not take place in isolation, but against this background, and the complex interplay between all of these elements is one that demands much greater study and understanding.

References

Harding, R. (2002), 'Air Travel', in R. Dawood (ed.), *Travellers' Health: How to stay healthy abroad*, 4th edn, Oxford: Oxford University Press.

Rayman, R. (2002), 'Cabin Air Quality: An overview', *Aviation, Space and Environmental Medicine*, Vol. 73, pp. 211–15.

Scurr, J. (2001), 'Frequency and Prevention of Symptomless Deep-vein Thrombosis in Longhaul Flights: A randomised trial', *Lancet*, Vol. 357, pp. 1485–9.

Chapter 14

Health and Illness among Airline Passengers

Jane N. Zuckerman

The concept of travel has taken on a new meaning now that one can traverse more and more countries, borders and continents within ever-shortening periods. Approximately 2 billion people travel on commercial airlines per annum and there is now increasing awareness of the travel health needs and risks of those who travel by air (Gendreau and De John, 2002). While the discipline of travel medicine evolved initially from infectious diseases, tropical medicine and preventive medicine, and historically from quarantine and international health regulations, the subject encompasses the whole range of clinical and preventive medicine including care of travellers with special needs such as children, the elderly, pregnant women and the handicapped, and travellers with cardiovascular, respiratory, metabolic, renal, gastrointestinal, neurological, malignant diseases and others, including behavioural disorders. An important component of travel medicine includes not only vaccinations and prophylaxis against malaria but also advice on accident prevention, sexual health and guidance on contraception, safety of food and water, and hygienic and other precautions.

The discipline of travel medicine has evolved rapidly as a direct response to the needs of the travelling population worldwide. In recent years, approximately 50 million visits abroad have been made by UK residents per annum and this is set to increase in the future (Office of National Statistics, 1999). Between 1950 and 1999 the number of international arrivals grew from 25 million to 664 million (World Tourism Organisation, 2000). The World Tourist Organisation have predicted an 80 per cent increase in travel to long-haul destinations between 1995 and 2010 as more people will be travelling to increasingly more accessible destinations worldwide (World Tourism Organisation, 1998).

In addition, the dynamics of modern day tourism are also changing. International travel is no longer the domain of tourists from developed countries travelling to exotic destinations for a two-week holiday once a year.

Increasingly, journeys are more frequent and for shorter periods of time, with people travelling to countries with high endemicity for various infectious and tropical diseases as well as environmental hazards, resulting in considerable health risks (Zuckerman, 2001).

The development of travel medicine as a discipline is a recent advance in itself (Mardh, 2002). The importance of the need and consequential continued growth of the specialty has been recognised recently by the Department of Health in their future strategy for combating infectious disease in the United Kingdom, which confirms the need for specialists in travel medicine (Department of Health, 2002). During more recent years, a significant organisational development has been that of the establishment of dedicated specialist travel health clinics located in teaching hospitals, in primary care settings as well as those operated by independent commercial groups. Although much travel and travel health information may be available through the Internet, this is no substitute for a traveller receiving a travel health risk assessment in person; there is a defined need for travel health clinics, particularly as many people do not seek travel health advice before they set out (Stringer et al., 2002). The significance of the latter in terms of public health concerns is considerable, as increasing numbers of travellers could potentially result in an increased incidence of travel-related disease, as well as the subsequent possibility of importation of infection (Ipsos RSL, 1999).

In tandem with the recent development of the discipline of travel medicine, international and national societies of travel medicine have been established. The International Society of Travel Medicine (ISTM) and the British Travel Health Association (UK) provide information and support to travel medicine practitioners, including arranging scientific conferences. Information from ISTM is available on the web and also meets some of the needs of travellers, with the availability of a comprehensive and international listing of travel medicine specialists and travel health clinics. Guidelines and information relating to the discipline are made available from several other sources: the World Health Organisation, the Department of Health, the Centre for Disease Control as well as from a recently formed group, the European Travel Health Advisory Board (Zuckerman, 2001).

Travel medicine is often considered to be a component of infectious/ tropical medicine and general practice but it is becoming increasingly recognised as a distinct clinical and academic interdisciplinary specialty. Travel medicine practitioners consider varied and diverse aspects of travel-related health including fitness to travel, including understanding the potential risks to the travellers' health in relation to the presence of an underlying chronic disease e.g. diabetes mellitus, cardiopulmonary conditions, asplenia or the immuno-compromised; environmental hazards such as altitude including mountain sickness, climatic changes, psychological aspects, aviation medicine, e.g. deep vein thrombosis, diving medicine and decompression, jet lag, sun exposure, accidents and trauma, the health of migrant populations as well as exposure to a variety of infectious diseases including those in the returned traveller. Special consideration must also be made for travellers with special needs such as those who are pregnant, young children, the elderly and the disabled (Mileno et al., 2001).

Fitness to Travel

It is essential that travellers should receive accurate and appropriate advice before travelling in order to prevent travel-related illness. Such lack of awareness of the potential hazards may result in ill health for the unprepared traveller.

There are several different groups of travellers including:

- short-stay and frequent travellers, including business travellers, politicians and airline crew;
- package holiday makers;
- adventure or expedition tourists, including backpackers;
- expatriates, including embassy and government employees, missionaries, aid workers and business people;
- occupational groups, including healthcare workers, aid workers, missionaries and military staff;
- UK citizens returning to their native country.

These diverse groups are exposed to a variety of health risks which may vary and occasionally overlap according to their individual health needs, as well as with the purpose of their travel and the activities in which they will be involved while travelling. The epidemiology, demography and environment differ greatly from the country of origin to that of the destination including 'stop-overs'. The most significant risk of both morbidity and mortality occur when such contrasts are experienced. The very nature of travel itself exposes travellers to a variety of new hazards which may never have been previously encountered. The occurrence of illness has a multifactorial aetiology which includes the individual's age and health, the destination(s) being visited with the associated environment factors and potential exposure to infectious diseases. Different aspects of travel-related illness should be remembered, apart from those related to infectious disease. These include motion sickness, the stress of exposure to an altered climate and environment as well as the effects of the psychological aspects of the journey itself. Exacerbations of pre-existing diseases may be experienced by travellers exposed to a change of climate or altitude. Even unaccustomed exercise may result in ill health when abroad.

A travellers' fitness to travel is best determined by a trained travel medicine healthcare professional, who will undertake a travel health risk assessment for each individual traveller (Stringer et al., 2002). The risk assessment allows for the provision of the appropriate advice in accordance with the health of the traveller including consideration of the type of travel planned. Fitness to travel involves understanding the potential risks to the travellers' health in relation to the presence of an underlying chronic disease, e.g. diabetes mellitus, cardiopulmonary conditions, asplenia or being immunocompromised. Special consideration must also be made for travellers with special needs, as mentioned previously (Mileno et al., 2001).

In order to assess and reduce the risk of travel-related illness, it is recommended that a pre-travel health risk assessment be undertaken at least eight weeks prior to travel. Such a consultation should result in obtaining concise information concerning the travel arrangements so that appropriate and up-to-date advice concerning the prevalence of infectious disease and environmental hazards, including situations of civil unrest, is available. Immunisations, antimalarial and other preventive measures are considered.

The following points should be considered during a pre-travel health risk assessment:

- the geographic destination, particularly with regard to *all* the countries and the different areas of each country being visited. This is important with regard to the prevalence or re-emergence of infectious disease at the destination(s);
- the purpose of travel e.g. business, pleasure, aid work or expatriation. Occupational risk of exposure to disease will vary accordingly;
- the type of accommodation during travel, e.g. hotel, camping;
- exactly when the travel will occur and its duration;
- the mode of travel to arrive at, as well as within, the destination;
- special activities to be undertaken, e.g. trekking, diving;
- amount of contact with local population;

- the health status of the traveller both physical and psychological, including pregnancy, both actual and planned and the presence of any pre-existing health problems which may require special consideration, e.g. diabetes mellitus;
- previous immunisations and experience with antimalarial prophylaxis;
- previous experience travelling;
- any special needs necessary.

The pre-travel health risk assessment also presents an opportunity to discuss with the traveller other issues relating to the maintenance of healthy travel. This includes advice about general precautions with reference to avoiding common health problems such as:

- food and water hygiene – 'boil it, cook it, peel it or forget it';
- vector-borne diseases and the use of insect repellents and insecticide-impregnated nets as well as chemoprophylaxis;
- safe sexual practices and sexually transmitted diseases;
- transmission of blood-borne viruses;
- prevention of accidents – e.g. avoid motorcycles – and the provision of medical insurance and medical kits;
- environmental extremes, e.g. exposure to sun or high altitude;
- hazards associated with long-haul flights, e.g. DVT, jet lag;
- appropriate and protective clothing and footwear against agents of infectious diseases as well as trauma.

The provision of such education may also subsequently influence the behaviour of the traveller to their benefit.

There are many travellers who undertake short but frequent periods of travel as well as those who plan to travel for periods of long duration. Such travellers should also be considered to undergo a comprehensive medical examination including an ECG, CXR, dental and psychological assessment. Haematology, biochemistry and serological laboratory testing are useful to identify both past exposure to infectious diseases as well as blood group. Any specific health problems including allergies and any disabilities should be considered at this time too.

A significant number of European travellers do not seek travel health advice before travelling and this has been demonstrated clearly in a recent study in the United Kingdom conducted among approximately 4,000 travellers which showed that 67 per cent of those visiting high-risk destinations did not seek health advice before travel (Ipsos RSL, 1999). The significance of this in terms of public health concerns is considerable, as the increasing number of travellers could result potentially in an increased incidence of travel-related disease, as well as the subsequent possibility of importation of infection. The proportion of travellers who fall ill varies from 15–43 per cent, with gastrointestinal infections accounting for 50 per cent of health problems, followed by upper respiratory tract infections (14–30 per cent), fever (12–15 per cent), skin disorders (10–12 per cent) and sexually transmitted diseases (0.5–2 per cent) (Steffen et al., 1987).

Fitness to Fly

Travel by air has now become a readily acceptable, convenient, fast and comfortable way of travelling allowing for more far-flung destinations to become more easily accessible. However, consideration needs to be given to both the physiological as well as psychological aspects of air travel and fitness to fly. The environment found within a cabin of an aircraft may have physiological affects, as there are changes in the altitude while flying which has a consequent effect on the air pressure in the cabin. Other effects include those of temperature and humidity, with cabin air being relatively dry.

Air travel undertaken by a fit and healthy individual is normally uneventful but specific consideration of the effects of air travel should be given to those travelling with an underlying medical condition. An assessment of the fitness to undertake air travel has several objectives, including the provision of advice to the traveller and, where appropriate, to the airline, as well as the prevention of any delays or diversions as a result of an in-flight medical emergency.

Travellers are mainly unaware of the health risks associated with air travel and increasingly physicians, and in particular travel medicine specialists, are able to determine a traveller's fitness to fly. Airlines are able to meet the needs of passengers, including those with disabilities and those who have other requirements, e.g. the need for supplemental oxygen. It is recommended that the request is accompanied by a letter of explanation from the traveller's physician explaining the need and confirming the traveller's fitness to undertake air travel (Aerospace Medical Association, 1997). Since the dreadful events of 11 September 2001, travellers carrying any medical equipment, including needles and syringes and prescription medicines, must carry a certificate or document validating the necessity of these medical items (Department of Transportation, 2001). Advice on these aspects, as well as the actual fitness of a traveller to fly, are available from many of the larger commercial airlines (Bagshaw and Byrne, 1999).

There are many guidelines available regarding the fitness of travellers to travel by air who have either acute or chronic medical conditions (Harding and Mills, 1993; Bettes and McKenas, 1999). The guidelines available are based upon those published by the Aerospace Medical Association and a list of the contra-indications are listed in Table 14.1. Specific medical clearance to fly is required from an airline for fitness to travel due to an acute or chronic medical condition or if special services are required, e.g. oxygen, the use of a stretcher or accompanying medical equipment. This is facilitated through the completion of a recommended medical Information Form (MEDIF) published by the International Air Transport Association (IATA), which is used by both the travellers' doctor as well as the airline.

In general, air travel is contraindicated if the presence of a medical condition is adversely affected by hypoxia or changes in pressure which may lead to the expansion of trapped gases in anatomical compartments. Medical conditions of particular concern include those that affect the cardiovascular system (angina, myocardial infarction, congestive heart failure), deep vein thrombosis, respiratory disease (emphysema, asthma), surgical conditions, cerebrovascular accidents, epilepsy, psychiatric illness, diabetes and infectious disease. A useful measure of a traveller's fitness to fly includes whether he/ she can walk 50m or climb a flight of stairs without experiencing severe shortness of breath or chest pain (Bagshaw and Byrne, 2001).

Although the discipline of travel medicine has been established to maintain the health of travellers, illness may occur during the travelling period and advice may need to be sought before returning by air. For those travellers who are returning from their destination and are unwell with an infectious disease, guidelines are available concerning the infectivity period and rules with regard to travel. As expected, these rules are strictly adhered to worldwide and in the United Kingdom the port health authority is empowered to enforce disembarkation rules for an aircraft which is carrying a passenger suspected of having an infectious disease. The importance of having adequate travel insurance can never be emphasised enough, and for those with a chronic underlying medical condition insurance cover inclusive of repatriation is to be highly recommended.

Table 14.1 Guidelines for medical fitness to travel

Category	Do not accept	Remarks
Cardiovascular disorders	Uncomplicated myocardial infarction within 7 days Uncontrolled heart failure Open heart surgery within 10 days Angioplasty: no stenting 3 days with stenting 5 days	Myocardial infarction less than 21 days requires MEDIF assessment This includes CABG and valve surgery MEDIF Assessment required up to 21 days postoperatively Transpositions, ASD/VSD, transplants etc. will require discussion with airline medical advisor
Circulatory disorders	Active thrombophlebitis of lower limbs Bleeding/clotting conditions	Recently commenced anticoagulation therapy requires assessment
Blood disorders	Hb less than 7.5g dl d^{-1} History of sickling crisis within 10 days	MEDIF assessment required for Hb less than 10g dl^{-1}
Respiratory disorders	Pneumothorax which is not fully inflated, or within 14 days after full inflation Major chest surgery within 10 days If breathless after walking 50 metres on ground, or on continuous oxygen therapy on ground	MEDIF assessment required up to 21days post surgery Consider mobility and all aspects of total journey, interlining etc.

Table 14.1 cont'd

Category	Do not accept	Remarks
Gastrointestinal disorders	General surgery within 10 days	Laparoscopic investigation may travel after 24h if all gas absorbed. Laparoscopic surgery requires MEDIF up to 10 days
	GI tract bleeding within 24hrs	MEDIF required up to 10 days
CNS disorders	Stroke, including subarachnoid haemorrhage, within 3 days	Consider mobility/oxygenation aspects. MEDIF up to 10 days
	Epileptic fit (grand mal) within 24h	Petit mal or minor twitching – common sense prevails
	Brain surgery within 10 days	Cranium must be free from air
ENT disorders	Otitis media and sinusitis	
	Middle-ear surgery within 10 days	
	Tonsillectomy within 1 week	
	Wired jaw unless escorted and with wire cutters	If fitted with self quick-release wiring may be acceptable without escort
Eye disorders	Penetrating eye injury/intraocular surgery within 1 week	If gas in globe, total absorption necessary-may be up to 6 weeks, specialist check necessary
Psychiatric disorders	Unless escorted, with appropriate medication carried by escort, competent to administer such	MEDIF required. Medical, nursing or highly competent companion/relative escort
Pregnancy	After end of 36th week for single uncomplicated	Passenger advised to carry medical certificate
	After end of 32nd week for multiple uncomplicated	
Neonates	Within 48h	Accept after 48h if no complication present

Table 14.1 cont'd

Category	Do not accept	Remarks
Infectious disease	If in infective stage	As defined by American Public Health Association (Benenson, 1990)
Terminal illness	Until individual case assessed by airline medical advisor	Individual case assessment
Decompression	Symptomatic cases (bends, staggers, etc.) within 10 days	May need diving or aviation physician advice
Scuba diving	Within 24h	
Fractures in plaster	Within 48h unless splint bivalved	Extent, site and type of plaster may allow relaxation of guidelines. Exercise caution with fibreglass casts
Burns	Consult airline medical advisor	

Source: Reprinted with permission from Bagshaw, 2001.

Risk of Ill Health and Air Travel

Much attention has been given in recent months to the effects of air travel including the risk of infectious diseases, and particularly the risk of developing deep vein thrombosis. Clearly, a traveller with an infectious disease which may be at a contagious stage should not travel by air. The risk of transmission of an infectious disease during a flight is only restricted to those sitting in close proximity to the infected traveller, as the route of infection is by droplet spread and close contact, which occurs when people sit closely together. Concern has arisen regarding the risk of transmission of tuberculosis associated with air travel. To date, no case of active tuberculosis has been identified as a result of exposure during travel by air but there is some evidence that transmission of M tuberculosis may occur during flights of more than eight hours duration, as the risk of infection is related to the proximity and duration of exposure to the source patient (World Health Organisation, 2001). The concept that recirculated cabin air results in the transmission of respiratory borne disease is most unlikely, as there are filters in place which remove bacteria and viral particles.

Considerable attention has been given recently to the issues surrounding travel-related deep vein thrombosis (Geroulakos, 2001; Scurr et al., 2001). The House of Lords Select Committee undertook a comprehensive review of this subject in November 2000. The estimated risk of developing a DVT following a long-distance flight is between 0.1 and 0.4 per thousand of the general population. Attention has now been drawn to awareness and methods of prevention of DVT, including identification of travellers with predisposing risk factors (House of Lords, 2000). All passengers, regardless of their risk of DVT, should move around in their seat and in the aircraft cabin as much as possible during their journey. They should avoid alcohol and caffeine-containing drinks before and during the flight and drink water or soft drinks to reduce the effects of dehydration. Exercising the calf muscles while seated every half hour by spending a few minutes flexing and rotating the ankles is recommended, to reduce the effects of stasis. Debate currently ensues regarding the prophylactic use of aspirin and its efficacy in preventing DVT, with some advocating the use of subcutaneous heparin. Under the auspices of the World Health Organisation, studies are planned to evaluate the risk of DVT while travelling by air.

In-flight Medical Emergencies

Fortunately, in-flight medical emergencies are an uncommon event. During the period of 1999, British Airways carried 36.8 million passengers and there were 3,386 reported in-flight medical incidents – about one per 11,000 passengers (Dowdall, 2000). Three-quarters of these were managed by the cabin crew solely, while in almost 1,000 incidents, trained healthcare professionals were asked for their assistance. A range of medical equipment is available on board an aircraft to administer aid to a traveller. These include an emergency medical kit and extend to automated external defibrillators.

Many of the in-flight medical incidents are not serious in nature and include fainting and dizziness (Goodwin, 2000) (Table 14.2). The more serious causes include cardiovascular causes (angina, myocardial infarction), collapse (epilepsy, cardiac arrest), respiratory causes (asthma), epilepsy, psychiatric problems, gastrointestinal causes (diarrhoea, vomiting), diabetes, allergic reactions and obstetric and gynaecological emergencies (births, miscarriages). Although such events are uncommon, the consequences of an in-flight medical emergency may be considerable, including the possibility of having to divert an aircraft, inconvenience to the passengers and increased costs, as well as safety issues, when diversion has to be implemented.

Table 14.2 Common medical events aboard commercial aircraft*

Type of event	US 1989 (n=1107)†	US 2000 (n=1132)	UK 2000 (n=910)
		% of all incidents	
Vasovagal	4	22	8
Cardiac	20	20	10
Neurologic	8	12	9
Gastrointestinal	15	8	28
Respiratory	8	8	5
Traumatic	14	5	3

Notes

* Percentages do not total 100 because not all types of events are listed.
† Data shown represent in-flight cases only.

Source: adapted from Gendreau and De John, 2002.

Conclusion

Travel by aeroplane has become an easily available commodity and, as the travel industry continues to develop at an ever-increasing rate, so in tandem will the number of travellers traversing the world by air and other methods of travel. Consequently, there will be an increasing need to meet the health needs of all travellers to ensure their health and safety while travelling.

References

Aerospace Medical Association (1997), *Medical Guidelines for Airline Travel*, Alexandria, Virginia: Aerospace Medical Association.

Bagshaw, M. (2001), 'Aviation Medicine', in J.N. Zuckerman (ed.), *Principles and Practice of Travel Medicine*, Chichester: John Wiley & Sons.

Bagshaw, M. and Byrne, N. (1999), 'La santé des passagers, *Urgence Pratique*, Vol. 36, pp. 37–43.

Benenson, A.S. (ed.) (1990), *Control of Communicable Diseases in Man*, 15th edn, Washington, DC: American Public Health Association.

Bettes, T. and McKenas, D. (1999), 'Medical Advice for Commercial Air Travellers', *American Family Physician*, Vol. 60, pp. 801–10.

Department of Health of the United Kingdom (2002), *Getting Ahead of the Curve – A Strategy for Combating Infectious Diseases in the United Kingdom*, January, London: HMSO.

Department of Transportation, Aviation Consumer Protection Division (2001), 'Fact Sheet: Steps Taken to Ensure New Security Requirements Preserve and Respect the Civil Rights of People with Disabilities', 29 October, Washington, DC: Department of Transportation.

Dowdall, N. (2000), 'Is There a Doctor on the Aircraft? Top 10 In-flight Medical Emergencies', *British Medical Journal*, Vol. 321, pp. 1336–7.

Gendreau, M. and De John, C. (2002), 'Responding to Medical Events during Commercial Airline Events', *New England Journal of Medicine*, Vol. 346, No. 14, pp. 1067–73.

Geroulakos, G. (2001), 'The Risk of Venous Thromboembolism from Air Travel', *British Medical Journal*, Vol. 322, p. 188.

Goodwin, T. (2000), 'In-flight Medical Emergencies: An overview', *British Medical Journal*, Vol. 321, pp. 1338–41.

Harding, R. and Mills, F. (1993), 'Fitness to Travel by Air', in R. Harding and F. Mills (eds), *Aviation Medicine*, 3rd edn, London: BMJ Publishing, pp. 30–42.

House of Lords (2000), *The Select Committee on Science and Technology, Fifth Report*, London: HMSO.

Ipsos-RSL (1999), *Travellers' Omnibus Survey*, Harrow: Ipsos.

Mardh, P. (2002), 'What is Travel Medicine? Content, Current Position, Tools and Tasks', *Journal of Travel Medicine*, Vol. 9, pp. 34–47.

Mileno, M., Suh, K., Keystone, J. and Bia, F. (2001), 'Special High-risk Travel Group: Immunocompromised, older, disabled and chronically ill travellers', in J.N. Zuckerman (ed.), *Principles and Practice of Travel Medicine*, Chichester: John Wiley & Sons.

Office of National Statistics (1999), *UK International Passenger Survey*, London: HMSO.

Scurr, J., Machin, S., Bailey-King, S., Mackie, I., McDonald, S. and Coleridge Smith, P. (2001), 'Frequency and Prevention of Symptomless Deep-vein Thrombosis in Long-haul Flights: A randomised trial', *Lancet*, Vol. 357, pp. 1485–9.

Steffen, R., Rickenbach, M., Wilhelm, U., Helminger, A. and Schar, M. (1987), 'Health Problems after Travel to Developing Countries', *Journal of Infectious Diseases*, Vol. 156, pp. 84–91.

Stringer, C., Chiodini, J. and Zuckerman, J. (2002), 'Travel Health Risk Assessment', *Nursing Standard* (in press).

World Health Organisation (2001), *Tuberculosis and Air Travel*, July, Geneva: WHO.

World Tourism Organisation (1998), *Tourism Highlights*, Madrid: WTO.

World Tourism Organisation Statistics Service (2000), Madrid.

Zuckerman, J. (2001), 'Editorial – Reflections and Reactions: Shaping travel health and medicine for the future', *The Lancet Infectious Diseases*, Vol. 1, No. 5, pp. 296–7.

Chapter 15

Long-haul Flights, Travel Fatigue and Jet Lag

Jim Waterhouse, Thomas Reilly and Ben Edwards

For most long-haul travellers there are two problems associated with flying: 'travel fatigue', which arises because of the hassles associated with making a journey to a distant land and adapting one's lifestyle to it; and 'jet lag', which will affect those who travel long distances from their home country to the west or east, but not those who travel in a north-south direction. Both can be debilitating and distract travellers from performing at their best at a meeting or in a competition, or temporarily reduce their enjoyment in the new environment. The aim of this chapter is to explain the nature and cause of these two problems. A further aim is to give advice on how to reduce their negative effects.

Travel Fatigue

Travel fatigue is caused in part by the worry associated with preparations for the flights, the flights themselves, and becoming attuned to the new environment. Major fatigue factors during flights include boredom, a prolonged period spent in a cramped posture, sleep loss and the dry cabin air.

Advice to Combat Travel Fatigue

Before the flight Preparations for the flight include ensuring that: the passport is valid and that any visa requirements have been met; health advice (including any inoculations that might be required) has been sought and acted upon; the individual has sufficient funds and clothing for the trip and, if appropriate, any medication that might be required has been packed. Much of this preparation can be done well in advance so that problems do not arise if delays occur.

Preparations also include arranging the flight or flights, and it is here that often choices can be made about whether or not there should be a stop-over en route and whether to fly by day or by night. Advice on these issues depends partly upon how the individual plans to adjust to local time at the destination, a decision which requires a consideration of 'jet lag' (see below).

During the flight During the flight, several problems arise. The flight cabin is a cramped area and it provides only a very limited opportunity for movement. Being immobile for extended periods of time increases the risk of developing cramp and even, with air travel of more than four hours, deep vein thrombosis in susceptible individuals. Passengers are advised to walk around the cabin and to do some stretching exercises if there is opportunity. In addition, isometric exercises in the seat can liven up a sluggish circulation.

A further problem arises because the cabin air is very dry; this can cause lips to become sore and also lead to a general dehydration. Sore lips can be avoided by the use of lip salve and dehydration by increasing fluid intake. Alcoholic drinks, and even tea or coffee, are not ideal since they tend to cause further dehydration. Spring water, soft drinks and fruit juice are all more suitable ways of maintaining hydration status. Fluid loss can amount to 400 ml over a flight from Europe or South Africa to Australia; in replacing this loss, a further 200 ml should be added to account for urine production. Making a suitable drink part of the cabin luggage is a good precautionary measure.

For those who wear contact lenses, the eyes can become sore, and wearing spectacles instead is recommended.

There is always the problem of deciding how to pass the time on a long flight, and many travellers try to sleep or nap throughout it. If, as is likely to be the case, the naps or sleep are taking place at times coincident with night on the home time zone just left rather than with night on destination time, this will slow the process of adjustment to the new time zone. If it is daytime at the destination, therefore, the traveller should attempt to stay awake by reading, playing cards or investigating the in-flight entertainment, for example. A good piece of advice is to realise that, as soon as the plane has been boarded, 'home time' has been left behind and should be erased from the traveller's mind; instead, it is the time at the destination or stop-over point that now determines when things should be done. Changing one's watch immediately on boarding the plane should help in achieving this attitude of mind.

After the flight After arrival, there remain the problems of collecting baggage, clearing customs and finding land transport to the final destination, all of which take time and can cause aggravation, particularly if there are problems. When the destination is finally reached, the natural tendency is to sleep because of fatigue. This is a good idea if it is night-time, but this is not often the case. If it is daytime, then a recuperative nap of about 1 hour, followed by an invigorating shower and a relaxing drink, is recommended.

If local time differs from home time by only up to 2–3 hours, as would be the case after a short-haul flight or after a long-haul flight in a north-south direction, there should be little problem in staying awake until bedtime (by destination time), and then getting a refreshing night's sleep. By the next day, the effects of travel fatigue will have worn off, and the traveller can work well or enjoy the holiday.

The problems and advice are summarised in Table 15.1.

Table 15.1 Check list for travel fatigue

Symptoms
    Fatigue
    Disorientation
    Headaches
    'Travel weariness'

Causes
    Disruption of normal routine;
    Hassles associated with travel (checking in/baggage claim/customs clearance);
    Dehydration due to dry cabin air.

Advice
    Before the journey –
        plan the journey well in advance
        try to arrange for any stop-over to be comfortable
        make sure about documentation, inoculations, visas
        make arrangements at your destination

    On the plane –
        take some roughage (e.g. apples) to eat
        drink plenty of water or fruit juice (rather than tea/coffee/alcohol)

    On reaching the destination –
        relax with a nonalcoholic drink
        take a shower
        take a *brief* nap, if required

By contrast, if there has been a time-zone transition of four or more hours, particularly if it is in excess of eight hours, then a full sleep during the night at the destination will not be possible. Individuals will now begin the next day feeling unrefreshed and unable to work or enjoy themselves as effectively as hoped for. This is one of the symptoms of 'jet lag'.

Jet Lag

This is the term commonly applied to an assemblage of symptoms that include:

- feeling tired in the new local daytime, and yet unable to sleep at night;
- feeling less able to concentrate or to motivate oneself;
- decreased mental and physical performance;
- increased incidence of headaches and irritability;
- loss of appetite and general bowel irregularities.

These symptoms are not all experienced to the same extent by all individuals, age conferring an advantage, possibly because older individuals are better able to 'pace themselves'. Jet lag also tends to be worse as the number of time zones crossed increases, and after time-zone transitions to the east rather than to the west. The symptoms are transient and, as a rule of thumb, last about one day per time zone crossed. Until jet lag has disappeared completely, individuals are advised to avoid important meetings or physically demanding tasks where possible, and to accept that there will be a degree of under-achievement in what they do.

The problems encountered cannot be attributed to differences in climate or culture between the destination and the individual's home country. For example, they are likely to be marked for Europeans travelling to Australia, New Zealand or the west coast of America, but slight for travellers between Europe and Africa. They are due, instead, to a 'body clock' which is slow to adjust to the new time zone. To understand how this body clock accounts for the difficulties, it is necessary, first, to discuss the role which it normally plays and some of its properties.

The Rhythmic Body

In subjects living normally (asleep at night and active in the day), core temperature shows higher values in the day and lower values at night (Figure 15.1).

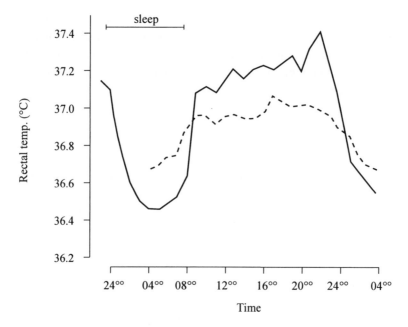

Figure 15.1 Mean circadian changes in core (rectal) temperature measured hourly in eight subjects: living normally and sleeping from 24:00 to 08:00h (solid line); and then woken at 04:00h and spending the next 24 hours on a 'constant routine' (dashed line)

Source: based on Reilly et al., 1997.

Many other variables, including heart rate, mental performance and several components of muscular performance, show rhythms that are timed similarly. By contrast, for many hormones – for instance, melatonin, a hormone released into the brain and blood stream from the pineal gland deep within the brain – the observed rhythm is the inverse, with nocturnal concentrations being higher than those in the daytime. Also, the perceived exertion associated with mental or physical tasks is higher at night than during the daytime.

These results might indicate that the body is responding to a day-orientated society, with opportunity at night for sleep and recuperation. Such an explanation is only partially correct, however, as can be deduced from studies of an individual during a 'constant routine'. In this, the subject is required to: stay awake and sedentary for at least 24 hours in an environment of constant temperature, humidity, and lighting; engage in similar activities throughout, generally reading or listening to music; and take identical meals at regularly-spaced intervals. In spite of the fact that this protocol means that any rhythmicity due to the environment and lifestyle has been removed, the rhythm of core temperature (and other variables that have been studied) persists, even though its amplitude is decreased (Figure 15.1). Three deductions can be made from this result:

1) The rhythm that remains must arise within the body; it is described as an endogenous rhythm and its generation is attributed to the 'body clock'.
2) Some effect of the environment and lifestyle is present, as can be deduced from the finding that the amplitude of the rhythm has decreased; this component of the rhythm is termed 'exogenous'. In the case of body temperature, it is raised by light and mental and physical activities during daytime waking, and decreased by darkness, sleep and inactivity during the night.
3) In subjects living a conventional lifestyle, these two components are in phase. This means that, during the daytime, the body temperature is raised by the body clock acting in synchrony with the environment and activity; and, during the night, the clock, environment and inactivity all act to reduce core temperature.

The site of the body clock and its circadian nature Humans have paired groups of cells in the base of the hypothalamus, a region of the brain closely associated with temperature regulation, the release of hormones, appetite for food, and sleep. These cells are called the suprachiasmatic nuclei (SCN). One piece of evidence (there are many others) that this is the site of the clock, is that slices of brain containing the SCN show rhythmicity in nerve activity when the slices are cultured *in vitro* in constant conditions; no other region of the brain shows autonomous activity in such circumstances.

When humans are studied in an environment in which there are no time cues – in an underground cave, for example – the daily rhythms of sleep and waking, body temperature, hormone release, and so on, continue. This fact confirms their endogenous origin, but it is observed that the period of such rhythms is closer to 25 than 24 hours. As a result of this, the subject becomes progressively more delayed with respect to the outside environment, and after about 3–4 weeks has actually 'lost' a whole day. For this reason, these clock-driven rhythms are called circadian (from the Latin for 'about a day').

Adjustment of the body clock Such circadian rhythmicity implies that the body clock needs to be continually adjusted for it to remain synchronised to a solar (24 hour) day. Synchrony is achieved by zeitgebers (German for 'time-giver'), rhythms resulting, directly or indirectly, from the environment. In different mammals, rhythms of the light-dark cycle, of food availability-unavailability, of activity-inactivity, and of social influences, act singly or in combination. In humans, a combination of these zeitgebers is normally present, although the most important are the light-dark cycle and the regular release at night of the hormone melatonin.

The effect of light depends on the time at which the individual is exposed to it. Pulses of bright light (that is, light of an intensity found outdoors rather than domestically) that are centred in the six hour 'window' immediately after the trough of the body temperature rhythm (the trough normally being 03:00–05:00h, see Figure 15.1) produce a phase advance; pulses centred in the six hour window before the temperature minimum, a phase delay; and those centred away from the trough by more than a few hours have little effect. Light pulses that are weaker (and similar in intensity to domestic lighting) also affect the clock and can produce smaller phase shifts. This is important, since most humans have very little exposure to natural daylight. In practice, therefore, exposure to light on waking in the morning, and even to light passing through our eyelids when asleep at this time, will cause a small advance of the body clock. This will result in the clock showing a period of 24 hours, synchronised to the solar day.

Melatonin ingestion has been shown to adjust the phase of the body clock; as with light exposure, melatonin can phase advance, phase delay or have no effect upon the body clock, according to the time at which it is ingested. The shifts produced at a particular time are in the opposite direction to those produced by light exposure at that time. Thus, melatonin in the afternoon and evening tends to advance the body clock, and in the morning tends to delay it. It is for this reason that melatonin is sometimes called an 'internal zeitgeber'. Receptors for melatonin are present in the SCN.

Since bright light also inhibits melatonin secretion, the phase-shifting effects of light and melatonin reinforce each other. Thus, bright light in the early morning, just after the temperature minimum, advances the phase of the body clock – not only directly but also indirectly, since it suppresses melatonin secretion and so prevents the phase-delaying effect that melatonin would have exerted at this time.

When light acts as a zeitgeber, information passes to the SCN from the eyes via a direct pathway, the retinohypothalamic tract. It seems that the retina contains a subgroup of receptors whose visual pigment is based on vitamin

B_2 (rather than the more conventional vitamin A-based opsins), and it is this subgroup that is responsible for the light signals going to the SCN.

The role of the body clock The body clock produces daily rhythms in core temperature, plasma hormone concentrations, the outflow of the sympathetic nervous system, and activity in the sleep centres of the brain, all of which exert effects throughout the body.

The effects of the clock are twofold. First, the body clock enables the 'ergotropic' actions of the body (those involving physical and mental activity and their associated biochemical and cardiovascular changes) to be promoted in the daytime, and for the 'trophotropic' actions (those involving recovery and restitution during a period of inactivity) to be promoted at night. The second role is to enable preparations to be made for the switches from the active to the sleeping state, and vice versa; individuals have to prepare biologically for going to sleep and for waking up. Such changes require an ordered reduction or increase in activity of a whole series of biochemical and physiological functions – and this has to be set in motion before the actual events of falling asleep or waking up take place.

To achieve the above aims, the body clock needs to be stable and robust, and not to respond to transient changes in the environment or lifestyle of the individual. For example, a clock that rapidly adjusted would compromise the phasing of the circadian rhythms of an animal during an eclipse, of an individual who woke transiently in the night, or of a person who took a nap in the daytime. The observation that the body clock is, in fact, slow to adjust to changes in lifestyle makes sound ecological sense, therefore.

However, such an intransigence becomes the bane of those who have to work at night or undergo time zone transitions since, before adjustment of the body clock to the changed sleep-wake pattern or local time has taken place, the normal synchrony between the endogenous and exogenous components of the circadian rhythms (see Figure 15.1) will have been lost. It is this lack of synchrony between the body clock and the outside world that causes these individuals to suffer the negative subjective and objective effects that are known, respectively, as 'shift workers malaise' and 'jet lag'.

Advice on Combating Jet Lag

If the stay in the new time zone is going to be for a few days only, then there will not be enough time for the body clock to adjust. In these cases, many travellers, including aircrew, continue to live as much as possible on home time. This means that, after a flight to the east, important activities should be undertaken in the afternoon or evening by local time in the new environment (coincident with daytime on home time), and the morning should be left free for relaxation or sleep (coincident with night on home time). If the flight is to the west, then important activities should be arranged for the morning, the afternoon and evening being for relaxation and sleep.

However, if the stay in the new time zone is for several days, then adjustment of the body clock and adherence to local time should be attempted. The following advice is the best currently available for reducing disruptions to sleeping and performing well in the new time zone to a minimum. It is important to realise that it applies particularly to the first day or so in the new time zone, that some of it applies as soon as the home time zone has been left behind, and some even when plans for the flights are being made. Thus, recent work indicates that the severity of jet lag, particularly fatigue, in the first day or so after arrival will be less if the flights are arranged such that the time that elapses between the last full sleep at night on home time and the first full sleep at night in the new time zone is made as short as flight schedules will allow. For example, less jet lag was experienced by subjects who flew from the UK to Australia leaving the UK in the morning and arriving (24 hours later) in the afternoon by local time than by subjects who left the UK in the evening and arrived (again, 24 hours later) in Australia early in the morning by local time. The first group had their first sleep in Australia about 30 hours after having woken up from their last sleep in the UK, whereas the second group had to wait a total of nearer to 50 hours. In spite of the fact that much of the flight for the second group was during the dark and more sleep was taken than was the case with the first group, this appears not to have made up for the large amount of time that elapsed between proper sleeps in a bed.

During the flight(s) and the first days in the new time zone one possibility is to use sleeping pills to promote sleep, since a disturbance of sleep will be one of the most unwanted corollaries of jet lag. Some travellers have used minor tranquillisers, such as temazepam and Zolpiden and other members of the diazepine group, in order to be refreshed for immediate activities on arrival. Even if the drug does help a person get to sleep, it does not guarantee a prolonged period of sleep, nor has it always been satisfactorily tested for subsequent residual effects on mental or physical performance. It is also important to realise that sleeping pills might be counterproductive if given at the incorrect time. A prolonged sleep at the time an individual feels drowsy, presumably when he or she would have been asleep in the time departure time zone, anchors the rhythms to this time zone and so operates against adjustment to the new time zone.

The use of melatonin as a hypnotic will be discussed separately below.

An alternative or additional approach is to use drugs which promote and maintain alertness. Such drugs include amphetamines, caffeine, Modafinil (an a-adrenoceptor antagonist) and Pemocline (with dopamine-like properties). Although these drugs improve performance in several tasks, they adversely affect the ability to initiate and sustain sleep (and so they could be counter-productive), and they might lead to addiction. Also, as with sleeping pills, their effects on physical performance have not been adequately addressed.

Promoting adjustment of the body clock The main advice is to aim at promoting adjustment of the body clock to the new time zone. Several methods have been suggested, differing in their practicality, the scientific evidence in support of them, and in potential side-effects. They include nutritional, environmental, and behavioural measures. In effect, they often amount to strengthening the zeitgebers that normally adjust the body clock. Attention here will be directed to the two methods that seem to be most effective, melatonin and bright light. Implementing the advice will not remove jet lag, but it will reduce it towards a minimum, a minimum that will depend upon the individual.

When attempting to promote adjustment of the body clock, it is essential to understand that this process can take place either by advancing or delaying it, and that each alternative requires a different timing of treatment. For time-zone transitions of up to eight hours to the east, a phase advance of the body clock should be promoted, and for time-zone transitions to the west, a phase delay. For journeys to the east through nine or more time zones, the position is more complex, since adjustment could be by advance or delay; in practice, delaying the phase of the body clock is sometimes easier, but this issue will have to be referred to again below.

Melatonin In normal circumstances, melatonin from the pineal gland is secreted into the bloodstream between about 21:00 and 07:00h, and can be regarded as a 'dark pulse' or 'internal zeitgeber' for the body clock. Melatonin capsules taken in the evening by local time in the new time zone reduce the symptoms of 'jet lag', the effect having been confirmed in both genders, after flights in either direction, and at whatever time the flight takes place. Even so, there are some caveats to the general advisability of taking melatonin:

- 'Jet lag', as defined in these studies, has concentrated on subjective symptoms and on the ability to sleep; it is not clear that there are always comparable improvements in mental and physical performance.

- It has not been established if the effects of melatonin are due to promoting the adjustment of the body clock or by increasing the ability to sleep. Melatonin has a hypnotic action, and this effect might be mediated by its lowering effect on body temperature. That is, taking melatonin in the evening on the new local time could directly help sleep and so reduce the amount of jet lag. However, whether the clock is advanced or delayed depends upon the time of ingestion of melatonin. No data have been published which indicate clearly whether or not the use of melatonin in the field adjusts the body clock.
- Melatonin is not widely available commercially, and then it is sometimes mixed with other substances.

In summary, more information is required before melatonin can be recommended unreservedly. In those cases where an individual has taken melatonin before, and has found it to be beneficial and with no adverse side-effects, there is, currently, no evidence against using it again. Nevertheless, medical advice should be sought. Results from studies with melatonin analogues – commercially-prepared derivatives of the natural molecule – are beginning to appear, and first results look promising.

Bright light exposure As described above, bright light can adjust the body clock, but the timing of the exposure to light is critical; bright light in a six hour 'window' before the temperature minimum delays the body clock, and in a six hour window after this minimum, advances it. In addition, light should be avoided at those times that produce a shift of the body clock in a direction opposite to that desired. Table 15.2 gives times when light should be sought or avoided on the first day after different time-zone transitions. After a couple of days, when partial adjustment of the body clock has occurred, the individual is then advised to alter the timings of light exposure and avoidance towards the local light-dark cycle by one hour per day. In this way, the traveller's exposure to light gradually becomes synchronised with that of the locals.

Adjusting as fully as possible to the lifestyle and habits in the new zone would seem intuitively to be the best remedy; and this intuition is borne out by the example of a westward flight through eight time zones. To delay the clock requires exposure to bright light at 21:00–03:00h *body time* and avoidance of it at 05:00–11:00h *body time* on the first day. By new local time (see Table 15.2), this becomes equal to 13:00–19:00h for bright light exposure and 21:00–03:00h for bright light avoidance, staying indoors in dim light. (On the second day in the new time zone, light exposure at 14:00–20:00h,

Table 15.2 The use of bright light to adjust the body clock after time-zone transitions

	Bad local times for exposure to bright light	Good local times for exposure to bright light
Time zones to the west		
4 h	01:00–07:00[a]	17:00–23:00[b]
8 h	21:00–03:00[a]	13:00–19:00[b]
12 h	17:00–23:00[a]	09:00–15:00[b]
16 h	13:00–19:00[a]	05:00–11:00[b]
Time zones to the east		
4 h	01:00–07:00[b]	09:00–15:00[a]
8 h	05:00–11:00[b]	13:00–19:00[a]
10–12 h	Treat these as 14–12 h to the west, respectively[c]	

Notes

a) This will advance the body clock.
b) This will delay the body clock.
c) This is because the body clock adjusts to large delays more easily than to large advances.

Source: based on Waterhouse et al., 1997.

and light avoidance 22:00–04:00, is required, and so on.) Exposure to the new local day-night cycle – by getting 'out and about' and mixing with the local people – would provide this.

However, immediately adopting the times of exposure to and avoidance of light in the new environment that are experienced by the local inhabitants can be the wrong approach. Consider, instead, a flight to the east through eight time zones, when a phase advance of the body clock is advised. This (see Table 15.2) requires bright light exposure at 05:00–11:00h body time (13:00–19:00h local time) and dim light (light avoidance) at 21:00–03:00h body time (05:00–11:00h local time). It also requires these times to be advanced by one hour per day. It can be seen from this requirement that morning light for the first day or so would be unhelpful and tend to make the clock adjust in the wrong direction – though afternoon and evening light are fine. Getting 'out and about' and mixing with local people needs to be modified in this case, therefore. This result is one explanation of why adjustment to phase advances is more difficult to achieve than is adjustment to phase delays.

As already mentioned, for flights to the east crossing more than nine time zones a choice exists with regard to whether one uses light exposure and avoidance to delay or to advance the body clock. For example, after a flight to the east coast of Australia from the UK (an eastward flight through 10 time zones), Table 15.2 can be used either by treating the flight as an eastward one across 10 time zones or a westward one through 14 time zones. The choice is up to individuals, but they must stick to one regimen throughout the process of adjustment, of course. They would be advised to select the light exposure-avoidance regimen that better fits in with their plans.

There are two other factors to bear in mind when considering whether to advance or delay the body clock after flights to the east across more than nine time zones. Again, these can be illustrated by using a flight from the UK to Australia as an example. First, on arrival, the time of minimum body temperature will be at about 15:00h local time. If a phase advance of the body clock is being attempted, then arrival in daylight in the morning by local time (which will be before the temperature minimum) will promote a phase delay of the body clock – unless the light is avoided and dark sunglasses are worn until the shelter of a dimly-lit hotel room is reached. By contrast, arrival in daylight in the local late afternoon or early evening (which will be after the temperature minimum) will promote a phase advance of the body clock, unless the bright light is avoided. Second, if a phase advance of the body clock is to be attempted, then the time of minimum body temperature (and, therefore, of minimum alertness and maximum fatigue) will advance through the afternoon and morning on subsequent days. The effects will be noticed more in this case than in the case where a delay is attempted, since, with a delay, the time of poorest performance will delay through the afternoon and evening, and fit in better with relaxing at these times.

The symptoms and advice relating to jet lag are summarised in Table 15.3.

Conclusion

The tendency to suffer from travel fatigue is a concomitant of all long-haul flights, and the additional problem of jet lag arises if the flight is across several times zones. The symptoms of both are inconvenient and can reduce temporarily travellers' enjoyment and performance at their destination. The causes are fairly well understood and so it is possible to give advice that will minimise these negative side-effects, even though it will not remove them completely.

Table 15.3 Check list for dealing with jet lag

1 Check if the journey is across sufficient time zones for jet lag to be a problem. If it is not, then it is necessary only to refer to advice on overcoming travel fatigue (Table 15.1).

2 If jet lag is likely, then consider if the stay is too short for adjustment of the body clock to take place (a stay of less than three days). If it is too short, then remain on home time, and attempt to arrange sleep and activities to coincide with this as much as possible.

3 If the stay is not too short (three days or more) and it is wished to promote adjustment, then consider ways of reducing jet lag. Advice relates to:
    before the flight;
    during the flight;
    after the flight.
The most important advice relates to after the flight.

4 Advice for promoting adjustment concentrates on:
    sleep and melatonin;
    exposure to, and avoidance of, bright light (Table 15.2).

Advice to deal with travel fatigue centres around the planning of the journey beforehand, and avoiding dehydration and getting some exercise during the flight.

For jet lag, the advice is concerned mainly with promoting sleep and the adjustment of the body clock. Melatonin capsules have been found to be useful for many travellers in reducing sleep problems, but these should only be taken after medical consultation. Promoting adjustment of the body clock is most easily achieved by the correct timing of exposure to, and avoidance of, bright light (especially of an intensity found outdoors) in the new time zone.

References

Akerstedt, T. and Ficca, G. (1997), 'Alertness-enhancing Drugs as a Countermeasure to Fatigue in Irregular Work Hours', *Chronobiology International*, Vol. 14, pp. 145–58.

Haimov, I. and Arendt, J. (1999), 'The Prevention and Treatment of Jet Lag', *Sleep Medicine Reviews*, Vol. 3, pp. 229–40.

Lewy, A., Bauer, V., Ahmed, S., Thomas, K., Cutler, N., Singer, C., Moffit, M. and Sack, R. (1998), 'The Human Phase Response Curve (PRC) to Melatonin is about 12 hours out of Phase with the PRC to Light', *Chronobiology International*, Vol. 15, pp. 71–83.

Reilly, T., Atkinson, G. and Waterhouse, J. (1997), *Biological Rhythms and Exercise*, Oxford: Oxford University Press.

Reilly, T., Maughan, R. and Budgett, R. (1998), 'Melatonin: A position statement of the British Olympic Association', *British Journal of Sports Medicine*, Vol. 32, pp. 99–100.

Waterhouse, J., Edwards, B., Nevill, A., Atkinson, G., Reilly, T., Davies, P. and Godfrey, R. (2000), 'Do Subjective Symptoms Predict our Perception of Jet Lag?', *Ergonomics*, Vol. 43, pp. 1514–27.

Waterhouse, J., Edwards, B., Nevill, A., Carvalho, S., Atkinson, G., Buckley, P., Reilly, T., Godfrey, R. and Ramsay, R. (2002), 'Identifying some Determinants of "jet lag" and its Symptoms: A study of athletes and other travellers', *British Journal of Sports Medicine*, Vol. 36, pp. 54–60.

Waterhouse, J., Reilly, T. and Atkinson, G. (1997), 'Jet-lag', *Lancet*, Vol. 350, pp. 1611–15.

Chapter 16

Appetite and In-flight Catering

Peter Jones and Margaret Lumbers

Introduction

Airline meals have always been part of the commercial travel experience. As early as 1914 meals accompanied by champagne were being served to passengers on Zeppelin airships. KLM claim to have begun the first ever commercial flights on 7 October 1919 and only four days later they were serving prepackaged meals on the London-Paris route (Wright, 1985). The flight took two hours and cream tea was served on the outward journey from England. On the return journey conditions were so turbulent that nothing was served (Franklin, 1980).

In this chapter we shall briefly consider why airlines serve meals on flights, consider how they go about this, and examine the effect meal consumption has on passengers. In some respects, the fact that passengers are fed at all is remarkable. Passenger aircraft travel at speeds in excess of 300 miles per hour, at around six miles above the ground. Serving up to 400 people with meals under these conditions is some undertaking. A fully-loaded, long-haul Boeing 747-400, the 'jumbo jet', has over 45,000 separate components, weighing 6.5 tonnes and occupying $60m^2$ of space, loaded in the 90 minutes it is at the gate prior to a flight (Jones and Kipps, 1995). These components include trolleys, 800 laid-up meal tray sets, food and drink commodities, and non-perishable items such as blankets, headsets and so on. In the flight catering industry there is an adage that the industry is '90 per cent logistics and 10 per cent catering'.

The Rationale for Serving Airline Meals

The nature of in-flight catering is fundamentally related to the airline, flight type and class of ticket. There are a number of different dimensions, which include the duration of flight – either long-haul or short-haul; the type of route – domestic or international; the type of flight – charter or scheduled; and class of service – budget/economy/tourist, club/business/executive, or first class.

Food service varies from a sold beverage and a pack of nuts or crackers on a short domestic flight to two or three meals served on china and accompanied by wines and liqueurs, as is found on a first class long-haul flight.

Historically, the food and beverage offer has closely reflected the expectations of each market segment served. Champagne was served on the very early flights simply because only the rich could afford to fly and champagne was what this class of passenger 'typically' imbibed. The philosophy of most airlines and flight caterers has always been to provide on-board an equivalent standard of product and service as the passenger might experience on the ground in an 'equivalent' style of catering operations.

Another of the original functions of meal service may have been to entertain and distract passengers from what could be a tedious or frightening experience, but this function has now, to a considerable extent, been superseded by in-flight entertainment systems. However, food and beverage service on aircraft has become a way of defining a unique characteristic of an airline – it is a means of product differentiation in what is otherwise a fairly standard way of covering long distances in a short period of time. Particularly where there is competition on a route, airlines may use the cabin service as a means of marketing their product.

Throughout the 1990s the nature of in-flight catering changed because of marketing, financial and operational pressures on airlines. Particularly in the case of short haul flights, where there is competition not only with other airlines but also with rail, airlines have responded to this pressure in different ways. Some airlines, such as easyJet and Ryanair, have chosen to compete on the basis of low costs and the fact that passengers need a simple and efficient journey from airport to airport. To this end, some airlines have reduced the cabin service to a simple cold snack or a trolley buffet service during the flight. On such 'no-frills' airlines, passengers pay for any food and beverage items they select.

With regards to full service carriers, there are two clear schools of thought in the airline catering industry, most clearly illustrated by the differences between the Asian and North American approaches. In Asia, many airlines have maintained direct control over on board provision and operate their own in-flight meal kitchens. For example, since 1980 Singapore Airline's catering operation (SATS) has continued to expand and renew their in-flight kitchens to meet the demand for finer meal service for their thousands of passengers. In the US, the birth of in-flight meal service is usually traced to the 1930s when J. Willard Marriott decided to sell boxed meals from one of his Hot Shoppes to passengers queued up for flights out of an adjacent airport (Romano,

1993). That side operation grew up to become Caterair, but in the decades that followed, the multi-billion-dollar market was largely left to contract operations that had the high-volume production techniques to provide in-flight meals for the few dollars that the airline allotted. In Europe many airlines did operate their own kitchens, especially at hub airports. Some have now divested themselves of these, notably British Airways and KLM, whereas others have deliberately grown their catering divisions, notably Lufthansa with LSG Sky Chef and Swissair, with Gate Gourmet (no longer part of the SAir Group).

Product Offering

Menu planning pays an important part in the process of providing airline meals. There are severe limitations on the service (tray size, etc.), on the technology (selecting foods and recipes which are tolerant of the time/ temperature process involved) and on the needs of captive and sedentary customers. Planned menus are converted to standard recipes which are used as the basis of the in-house or contract specification to control quantities, quality and cost. Photographs are often used to communicate precise information about both the meal and tray layout. Because of the importance of meal service as a means of breaking up the monotony of a long flight journey, particular emphasis must be placed on the appearance of the meal. Attention also needs to be paid to satisfying the requirements of specific groups such as vegetarian and vegan customers and those with particular ethnic requirements, such as kosher and halal meals. Medical diets are also catered for such as sugar- and salt-free. In total there are 22 special diets recognised in the international flight catering industry.

Menu items and dishes are also designed to take into account specific aspects of the flight experience. Both taste and appetite change when flying at altitude. Airlines attempt to recognise these changes in their provision of in-flight food and drinks. A variety of factors influence the enjoyment of airline food. For example, it has been found that the flavour of foods becomes less distinct at altitude and the aromas of wine are reduced. At high altitude many people react more strongly to alcohol and caffeine.

One of the effects of long-haul flights is dehydration, which has a variety of effects on the body, including ease of digestion. Combined with a restriction in the amount of movement and the opportunity for taking exercise, heavy foods and meals therefore are best avoided. In response a number of airlines offer a choice of light and easy to digest meals for their business and first class passengers; for example, British Airways have a 'Well-Being' menu choice on many flights. Although airlines have invested heavily in improving airline catering and service over the years, passengers still comment that 'all food tastes the same' (Kahn, 1995).

There are other effects of the cabin environment that produce physiological responses in people such as the reduced oxygen levels, altitude effects and dehydration, all of which affect appetite. Moreover, the timing and nature of cabin service is believed to play a part in countering jet lag. The meals served are designed in relation to the time of arrival so that the flight finishes with a meal that is appropriate for the time of day of the destination.

Production Processes

Once the on-board offer is specified, caterers have to produce and deliver this to the aircraft. Airlines may, in some circumstances, supply aircraft with enough supplies for both the outward and return leg of a flight ('backcatering'), but it is more common for aircraft to carry supplies for a single journey. Most national and international airports have a least one in-flight production kitchen. Often there is spare capacity, as airlines over the years have cut back on their level of on-board service. Kitchens vary in size depending on whether they cater specifically for one airline or have contracts to supply many. At London's Heathrow there are eight units: two Gate Gourmet kitchens, one supplying British Airways short haul, the other serving long-haul routes; two smaller units, one serving Japanese and Korean airlines, the other serving El Al; and four other kitchens of various sizes serving the remainder of airlines operating out of the airport. The number of meals they produce ranges from around 5,000 up to 25,000 per week.

Caterers prefer to have their kitchens built literally on the boundary of the airport, so that they have a 'land-side' to which goods are delivered by road, and an 'air-side', from which the caterer's lorries deliver trolleys for loading onto the aircraft. In the UK most units are not in this location, but are outside the airport boundary, normally on an adjacent industrial estate.

Flight kitchens are now being developed which have capacities in excess of 40,000 meals per day and service flights for up to 40 different airlines – for example, the facility provided by KLM at Schiphol airport. These modern in-flight kitchens are designed for year round, 24-hour per day operation (17 to 18 hours for production, four to five for cleaning and maintenance) and therefore employ up to 1,000 staff. The production units are divided into a number of departments, such as goods reception, central warehouse, preparation kitchens (meat, fish, vegetables), hot kitchen, cold kitchen, pastry/bakery, packing, tray assembly, trolley assembly, dispatch and waste disposal. In addition to these production areas, a number of ancillary areas are required, such as offices, changing rooms, product development kitchens and quality control laboratories

In all in-flight catering systems, hygiene plays an important part because of the use of high risk products, such as meat, fish and dairy products, which are stored at chilled temperatures for long periods of time. Strict quality control is required, based on the principles of risk assessment, precise time temperature control, microbiological testing of products and hygiene audits of all storage and production areas. In-flight production kitchens either have their own laboratory or send materials to a commercial laboratory for testing. This testing includes the quality of all raw materials and finished dishes and the hygiene standards of all production areas. Samples of all meals produced are kept until one week after the flight has ended, in case there have been any food-related illnesses or complaints reported.

Whether the service is provided by a subsidiary of the airline company or by a contractor, the basis of the production will be a detailed specification for each flight. Initial production planning is done one to two weeks before the flight, when an estimate is made of material requirements for each flight, to allow the ordering of materials. Four days before departure production plans are prepared for each department. Final adjustments are made on the day of the flight, when the detailed planning sequence is commenced. For each flight, there is a planned sequence of preparation of meals, assembly of materials and printing of labels for trolleys and containers. This includes all the special meal requirements and requirements for first class and VIP customers. An inventory list of all items required on the flight is printed out to allow inspectors to check for the correct assembly of items for each flight.

A computer system is used to link the production facility with information from reservations and check-in. Food items are produced to a schedule based on the estimated time of departure of the flight and on the projected number of passengers in each class. The majority of items are provided using a sophisticated cook-chill system.

Meal Preservation

In the early days of flight catering, systems depended on the warm-holding of foods in insulated containers. Warm-holding is most suited to situations where consumption takes place within a short time of production, i.e. where the delivery times are short. This is because with warm-holding over time the palatability, appearance and nutritional value of meals deteriorates rapidly. In terms of food safety the critical factor for these meals is that the food temperature should be maintained at over 63°C from cooking to final service to the consumer. For this reason insulated systems are usually limited to situations where meals can be loaded at a minimum temperature of 80°C and delivered within 30 minutes. Where these requirements cannot be met, heated delivery systems are necessary.

Preservation systems that extend the delivery/storage time are cook-chill and cook-freeze. Cook-chill systems are based on the rapid chilling of meals down to 3°C (within 90 minutes) and storage at between 0°C and 3°C. Under these conditions meals can be stored for up to five days, including the day of production and the day of service. Cook-freeze is based upon preservation through the blast freezing of meals down to below -18°C. Meals preserved in this way can be stored for several weeks, which gives much greater flexibility, and in their solid state are easily handled and transported. Regeneration can be either from the frozen state or after thawing. Cook-chill has been the predominant method used, although there is a trend towards the use of cook-freeze products, especially with regard to economy class meals.

Historically, flight kitchens processed raw materials, produced and chilled food all within the production unit at the airport. Increasingly, flight kitchens are doing less actual food production, outsourcing to food manufacturers cook-chill and cook-freeze meal components. Caterers predominantly 'add value' through their logistic capability – the assembly of tray sets and trolleys, along with their delivery to the aircraft at the specified time

The process of packing, assembly and loading begins a few hours before the flight is due to depart. Meals which are to be served hot are taken from chilled storage and packed into ovenproof containers, which may be foil, plastic or china. The foods are portioned into oven containers in accordance with the flight specification, which will lay down the weights of each components of the meal and the appearance of the meal. The oven containers are then loaded into oven racks and kept in chilled storage until they are required for assembly. Food assembly areas require control of temperature if hazardous foods remain in this area for any length of time out of refrigeration. Temperatures of 10°C or less are recommended.

The next stage is referred to as 'tray setting', which consists of assembling all of the items needed on a meal tray. For large operations a conveyor belt may be used to carry the trays past a series of assembly points. At the end of the conveyor, assembled trays are then placed into trolleys. There are many different sizes of trolleys used by the airlines and it is important that the correct trolleys are used to suit the type of aircraft used on a specific flight. Labels are placed on the outside of the trolley, indicating the flight number, the contents of the trolley and its location on the aircraft.

Two to three hours before a flight, all of the trolleys and containers are assembled in the dispatch bay. At this stage checks are made to ensure that all requirements are complete. These materials are then loaded into special delivery vehicles. The vehicles are designed to have pneumatic elevators to raise the height of the platform of the truck to that of the loading door on the aircraft – this is 9m above ground level in the case of a 747. At the last minute ice and newspapers are added to the load.

The truck's journey is planned to coincide with the requirements of the airline. Communications links are vital. Flight times are subject to delays and cancellations and there is often less than two hours to unload, clean and reload an aircraft. Before loading can begin, the used trolleys and containers must be removed from the aircraft into an empty truck and returned to the in-flight catering unit. To cope with last minute needs, the catering company will have a fleet of small vans which can be used to facilitate last minute changes which arise after the trucks have started their journey.

On-board Service

After they have been loaded onto the aircraft, materials and equipment are stowed in the galley areas. Small aircraft may have two galleys, whereas a 747-400 may have six. The precise configuration will be specified by the airline. All trolleys and containers must be stowed in the correct location in each of the galleys on the aircraft, so that cabin crew do not have to search through a number of trolleys before finding what they want. To this end, catering staff liaise with the cabin staff to check that all materials are on board and that materials are located in their correct storage areas. All equipment and supplies must be securely fastened ready for take-off.

At this stage, cabin crews have more to think about than just food and drink, since they need to ensure that all passengers are correctly seated, their cabin luggage securely stowed and that safety instructions are completed. However, even with all of these other activities taking place, cabin service may have started with the service of a complimentary drink to first and business class passengers while the aircraft is still on the ground. Also, the first meal to be served may be loaded into the on-board convection ovens, if it is to be served as soon as the flight is in the air.

The planned service of food and drink starts as soon as the plane is airborne. The exact sequence depends on the time and duration of the flight. A short domestic flight may have a full hot breakfast or dinner service in the short time that the aircraft is in the air. A charter flight may have only a beverage and chilled snack service. A long-haul flight may serve two or three hot meals during the flight, together with frequent drinks, to reduce the effects of dehydration and jet lag.

Whatever the nature of the flight, the sequence of service is similar. The pattern of service will be largely dictated by the configuration of the aircraft, taking into account factors such as the number of aisles and the number of seats in each section. Oven racks with pre-loaded hot meal containers are placed in the ovens 15 to 20 minutes before they are required for service. Cabin crew then start service according to a planned sequence, which will vary from one airline to another. For a given meal there may be one trolley for meal trays and hot meals and a second for beverage service. In addition to this, items such as bread rolls and hot beverages may be required. At the end of the meal, trays are returned to the trolleys which in turn are relocated in the appropriate galley storage area and made safe for landing.

When the aircraft has landed used trolleys and containers are transported to the local in-flight unit for sorting and cleaning. Conveyor belts are used to allow staff to separate glasses, china and cutlery from all of the waste material. There are now many initiatives to reduce the volume of waste and to maximise recycling of materials. In some operations this activity has been automated, with magnets used to remove cutlery and powerful water sprays to rinse off waste food, plastic materials and napkins. Large flight dishwashing machines are used to wash all of the glasses, china and trays. These are then returned to store until needed for the next flight. In order to service an aircraft, three sets of all equipment are required, one set on the aircraft, one off-loaded dirty set at the start of the flight and the other being prepared for loading at the destination.

Factors affecting Food Acceptability

In the light of what we know about menu design, food production, meal preservation and regeneration, and on-board service, it is of interest to explore in more detail those factors that influence the enjoyment of airline food. The following sections discuss the various factors that can affect food acceptability and how they are affected by high-altitude long-haul flights. The sensory model of food acceptance described by Cardello (1996) involves four aspects: physical, sensory, perceptual and hedonic. All foods have attributes of appearance (colour, presentation, etc.), texture (soft/hard, crisp, etc.), flavour (taste and smell), temperature, depending on their composition and preparation. These attributes dictate the impact on the above and hence the enjoyment or acceptability of food. In other words the human senses (taste, smell, texture and vision), singly or in combination, influence appetite and consumption of food.

Studies have demonstrated that flavour (taste and smell) is more important in terms of food acceptance than appearance or texture. However, the relationship varies between both types of food and individuals. When considering taste it should be noted that there are four basic tastes: salty, sweet, sour and bitter, although these may only be points along a continuous spectrum. A fifth taste quality has been suggested, termed 'umami', described as 'savoury'. Of course, taste and smell are not the only aspects of food and drink to affect its overall enjoyment.

The hedonic component (i.e. the pleasure of eating) is subject to previous experience and learned responses to food, the context, culture, expectations and physiological status (including appetite, hunger and thirst). A survey of the sources of pleasure when eating identified 'excellence of taste' as the most important factor for an affluent industrialised area of West Germany, whereas for a less affluent area in East Germany other factors, such as 'a pleasant atmosphere', were more important.

Airline catering must attempt to account for the influence of the cabin environment on each component of the sensory model – physical, sensory, perceptual and hedonic – for example, balancing such factors as the ambience and the taste of food, as well as the sociocultural contexts.

It is well known that the sense of taste and smell are affected by the cabin environment, potentially diminishing the enjoyment of meals. The low relative *humidity* of the cabin (less than 25 per cent) dries the mucous membranes lining the nasal cavity and reduces the sense of smell (Kahn, 1995). Similarly, dryness of mouth will affect the taste receptors. It is worth noting that odorants and the general aromas in the cabin will also contrive to mask or distort the experienced flavour of foods provided. The inhibition of taste and smell has a consequent effect on the digestion process that is stimulated by these senses.

To overcome this, airlines have made considerable efforts to modify dishes so that they have stronger and more robust flavours to improve enjoyment, possibly without a full appreciation of all the influential factors.

In-flight *atmospheric pressure* conditions in commercial jet aircraft approach altitude equivalents of 1500 to 2400m (Allemann et al., 1998). Hence the observations that have made regarding climbers at these altitudes apply to airline passengers. It has been observed that the mild oxygen lack suffered by individuals at high altitudes leads to weight loss, due to a change in water balance, reduced digestive efficiency and changes in attitudes to eating and drinking. Many individuals experience loss of appetite at altitude and have to be persuaded to eat (Westerterp-Plantenga et al., 1999). Another observation in climbers is that leptin values in the blood were found to be elevated (leptin is a discrete protein linked to the regulation of food intake). Hence the elevated leptin levels found in climbers may in part explain the decreased appetite. The lower cabin pressure and the associated mild lack of oxygen has been suggested as causing a sluggish effect on digestion and absorption of nutrients (Kahn, 1995).

In summary, the physiological effects of travelling at altitude are analogous to those observed in climbers and hence airlines should recognise and attempt to respond appropriately to maximise passenger satisfaction for example by:

- providing opportunities for smaller meals more frequently on demand;
- proactively addressing the water balance problem through passenger education and the availability/regular offering of drinking water;
- providing meals that are easy to digest and taste good.

Factors affecting Passenger Appetite, Mood and Behaviour

The cabin environment and on-board consumption affects not only the food perceptions of passengers, but also their appetite, mood and behaviour.

Appetite

A small region in the base of the brain, called the hypothalamus, in part acts as a regulator of appetite and thirst by producing hormones. The simplest model is of two centres in the hypothalamus, called the feeding and the satiety centres, regulate food intake. The 'feeding centre' is stimulated by hunger sensations from an empty stomach while the 'satiety' centre is stimulated when the stomach is full.

There are other compounding factors affecting appetite, including the:

- psychological state of the individual that may affect the production of hormones;
- activity level – the appetite control mechanism is less precise in those people who are sedentary;
- level of glucose and free fatty acids in the blood (chemical stimuli).

Digestive juices, which affect the utilisation and absorption of food, flow more freely when people are hungry, relaxed and attracted by the appearance and smell of food. Volatile food aromas play an important role in the stimulation of the olfactory receptors (located in the mucus membranes in the nasal cavity). Both olfactory and taste stimulation initiate what is known as the 'cephalic phase response'. The response brings about increased salivation and secretion of gastric and pancreatic juices in anticipation of eating. The extent of the response is thought to be associated with the overall acceptability of foods initiating the response. Learned responses also have a role in that most people have deeply ingrained ideas of what is regarded as acceptable to eat and what is unpleasant.

Another factor affecting the amount of food eaten is called 'specific satiety'. People can only eat a limited amount of the same food, whereas a greater amount can be consumed when there are several courses comprising a variety of foods. However, appetite, like taste, is not simply governed by biological factors.

Serious dehydration may also be overlooked by the unwary passenger. The causes of this on board aircraft are low humidity (due to the recycling of air in the cabin) and the consumption of both caffeine and alcohol. The need to drink plenty of fluids, ideally plain water, has reached wider public awareness since the publicity regarding long-haul flights and deep vein thrombosis.

Depression, anger, worry or apprehension can have a dramatic affect on appetite, ranging from complete suppression to the excessive consumption of familiar/comfort foods.

The success of in-flight catering in maximising passenger satisfaction will be achieved by addressing some of the discussed above factors, namely the:

- anxiety state of passengers;
- level of hunger – timing of service and previous meals;
- effects of the cabin environment on smell and taste;
- appearance and acceptability of food;
- level of dehydration.

Mood

Many aspects of eating and drinking affect mood and behaviour. Conversely, mood can influence eating and drinking patterns. There is a popular belief that missing breakfast makes people less alert and impairs cognitive efficiency. Heavy lunches are thought to give rise to a 'post-lunch dip'. However, studies tend to be rather inconclusive and in general cognitive performance is not thought to be affected by short-term fasting, although there is considerable variation observed between subjects (Rogers, 1996).

Starchy, carbohydrate-rich foods are thought to induce sleepiness (Wurtman et al., 1981). This could be due to a variety of mechanisms, including the stimulation of the release of a chemical in the brain – serotonin – high levels of which are associated with sleep inducement, sensory perception and temperature regulation. The converse is true for protein-rich meals that are thought to moderate serotonin production and hence make people more alert.

While most passengers do not choose food on the basis of the expected effects on mood, the overall enjoyment of the flight may include the quality of sleep, which can be influenced by the nature of the food provided.

Behaviour

In addition to the physiological effects described above, the two most likely factors to affect on-board behaviour are associated with the consumption of alcohol and caffeine.

Alcohol is offered on most flights and has become an expectation for most travellers. Airlines often appear to encourage alcohol consumption, for example, by supplying miniatures (which are more than a double measure) rather than using a standard optical measure.

Alcohol has a direct effect on the brain and changes behaviour to varying degrees depending on the amount consumed, the passenger's mood as well as individual tolerance levels. There are profound effects on judgement, emotional control, muscle coordination and vision. Recent studies show that people who binge drink could be causing rapid damage to their brain cells. Safe limits are 21 units for women and 28 units for men per week. A unit is equivalent to half a pint of beer, one measure of spirits, one glass of wine (120ml) or one glass of sherry or port. A typical consumption might be a spirit miniature (gin and tonic) followed by two glasses of wine (airline bottle size) with a meal followed possibly with a second spirit miniature (brandy) – amounting to probably more than six units, which is over the average limit for a day.

A general effect of alcohol is to depress appetite, although this varies according to the individual and the circumstances. The high calorific content of alcohol suppresses the appetite of the average person (Polivy and Herman, 1976). Such individuals become unaware that they are hungry, due to the satiating effects of the alcohol. However, alcohol may induce eating, particularly when anxiety is experienced. Further, for individuals who have eating problems (dieters, bingers, the obese) alcohol and anxiety can remove the self-imposed restraint leading to increased intakes/binging. It is also thought that the bitter flavours of some aperitifs such as vermouth and tonic water increase appetite.

Probably the majority of airline passengers experience some degree of stress and anxiety, to which the common response is to seek an alcoholic drink. Stress is reported to be high even among regular travellers (Joseph, 1990). The often cramped conditions, overcrowding and the sense of lack of control experienced during the flight are likely to increase the already raised level of stress associated with the process of checking-in and boarding. While passengers often use alcohol on board to relieve anxiety, it may not be appreciated that it also acts as a depressant.

Airlines usually offer passengers drinks early in the flight. If the passenger has not eaten for some time, the alcohol immediately diffuses through the walls of an empty stomach and reaches the brain within a minute of being swallowed, leading to intoxication. The increased potency of alcohol in the air is rarely communicated to passengers and has led to a number of disruptive episodes on planes, leading to high-profile court cases.

Another effect of alcohol is to increase urine output as it depresses the brain's production of antidiuretic hormone, causing increased thirst. This, in turn, aggravates the existing problem of dehydration, for which the only solution is to drink water. It is important, therefore, to make water readily available to passengers throughout the flight and, indeed, to encourage them to drink water. The use of ice and/or water to dilute drinks should be encouraged. It is also logical to avoid providing passengers with salty snacks and foods that increase thirst before offering alcoholic drinks.

Eating high carbohydrate and high fat snacks inhibits the absorption of alcohol by slowing peristalsis and keeps alcohol in the stomach for longer. Hence the provision of alcoholic drinks on airlines has multiple influences on appetite, mood, the ability to respond to a crisis and so on. Airlines can avoid some of the associated negative responses in various ways by:

- reducing the stress levels and hence the demand for alcoholic drinks;

- managing the quantities offered;
- avoiding thirst-inducing snacks prior to offering;
- providing water for rehydration;
- educating passengers about the adverse effects of in-flight alcohol consumption;
- perhaps encouraging passengers to take the miniature home to drink there!

Caffeine also has a major effect on passenger behaviour. Caffeine is the most popular psychoactive drug consumed worldwide (Harland, 2000). The main sources of caffeine are coffee and tea, but it is also found in cola drinks and other health and sports drinks, chocolate and some medications. Seventy-five per cent of caffeine taken daily comes from coffee; the remaining 25 per cent is equally divided between tea and coffee products. There is 50–70 per cent more caffeine in coffee than tea. Caffeine-containing drinks are in part often drunk for their potential psychoactive effects to improve alertness; conversely, coffee is avoided late in the evening. Caffeine is known to improve reaction time, concentration and alertness and energy. However, it may lead to increased anxiety, nervousness, irritability and headaches. As a true stimulant drug, caffeine increases breathing rate, heart rate, blood pressure and secretion of stress hormones. In higher doses it may lead to palpitations and cardiac arrhythmias.

In the context of commercial air travel the psychological and physiological effects of caffeine should be recognised, perhaps especially because of the concerns regarding deep vein thrombosis.

Simple measures that could be taken by airlines include:

- providing an alternative to decaffeinated drinks (which have lesser dehydration effect) such as herbal teas;
- ensuring the ready availability of water and encouraging its consumption;
- offering non-caffeine rich drinks before a sleep period.

Conclusion

The provision of food and drink on board passenger aircraft is highly challenging, attempting to meet a wide range of different objectives from multiple stakeholders. As far as possible, airlines and caterers have attempted to design systems and adopt technologies that make it possible to replicate in the air the type of meal provision and service that might be found on the ground. However, there are specific aspects of flying – notably air pressure, humidity and stress – that cause physiological changes in passengers that affect their experience of food and drink, their appetite, their mood and their behaviour. Passengers may be served very similar food and drink six miles high to that which they might be served in a restaurant, but how they respond to this is likely to be very different to the conventional meal experience.

References

Allemann, Y., Saner, H. and Meier, B. (1998), 'High Altitude Stay and Air Travel in Coronary Heart Disease', *Schweizerische Medizinische*, Vol. 128, No. 17, pp. 671–8.
Cardello, A. (1996), 'Food Choice, Acceptance and Consumption', in H.L. Meiselman and H.J.H. MacFie (eds), *Food Choice, Acceptance and Consumption*, London: Chapman and Hall.
Franklin, S. (1980), 'History of Inflight Catering: It all began in 1903 with Orville Wright', *Airline and Travel Foodservice*, September/October, Vol. 16, p. 21.
Harland, B. (2000), 'Caffeine and Nutrition', *Nutrition*, Vol. 16, pp. 522–6.
Jones, P. and Kipps, M. (1995), *Flight Catering*, London: Longman.
Joseph, R. (1990), 'Pie in the Sky 1990', *Airline Food and Wine Survey, Business Traveller*, April.
Kahn, F. (1995), 'Throw a Chicken in the Air ...', *Financial Times*, 21–22 October.
Polivy, R. and Herman, M. (1976), 'Effects of Alcohol on Eating Behaviour: Influences of mood and perceived intoxication', *Journal of Abnormal Psychology*, Vol. 85, pp. 601–6.
Rogers, P. (1996), 'Food Choice, Mood and Mental Performance: Some examples and some mechanisms', in H.L. Meiselman and H.J.H. MacFie (eds), *Food Choice, Acceptance and Consumption*, London: Chapman and Hall.
Richardson, G. and Tate, B. (2000), 'Hormonal and Pharmacological Manipulation of the Circadian Clock: Recent developments and future strategies', *Sleep*, Vol. 23, S77–S85.
Romano, M. (1993), 'Airline Food: Sky high', *Restaurant Business*, Vol. 92, No. 15, 10 October, pp. 66–8.
Romano, M. (1994), 'Who's Feeding them Now?', *Restaurant Business*, Vol. 93, No. 12, pp. 62, 64–69.
Westerterp-Plantenga, M., Westerterp, K., Rubbens, M., Verwegen, C., Richelet, J. and Gardette, B. (1999), 'Appetite at "High Altitude" [Operation Everest III(Comex-'97)]: A simulated ascent of Mount Everest', *Journal of Applied Physiology*, Vol. 87, No. 1, pp. 391–403.
Wright, C. (1985), *Tables in the Sky*, San Francisco: Allen.
Wurtman, R., Hefti, F. and Melamed, E. (1981), 'Precursor Control of Neurotransmitter Synthesis', *Pharmacological Reviews*, Vol. 32, pp. 315–35.

Chapter 17

Sex and International Travel: Behaviour, Health and Human Rights

Stephen Clift

Introduction

It may come as a surprise to find a chapter on sex and international travel in a book entitled *Passenger Behaviour*, and it is perhaps useful to start by explaining why this issue is an important one to consider. Many readers of this text may work within the travel industry, and may be frequent international travellers in the course of their work. They may also have direct experience of some of the issues discussed below by:

- coming into contact with groups of young people before, during or after being on holiday (especially organised by tour operators like Club 18–30);
- coming into contact with tourists, especially single male tourists, travelling to countries with a reputation for sex tourism;
- travelling, either on business or for a holiday, to countries known to have a significant sex industry catering for tourists;
- travelling to countries known to be a significant source of sex trafficking;
- coming into contact with young women and children entering the UK who have travelled from such countries (who may be being trafficked);
- being sexually active while away from home on business or on holiday.

This chapter aims to bring together material from recent reports and research studies addressing these kinds of issues, so that the reader can be better informed of the scope of connections between international travel and sexuality, and consider the issues these connections raise for health and human rights. Some of these issues may have a bearing on professional roles and responsibilities, and may also give pause for thought in relation to personal behaviour as travellers.

Clift and Carter (2000), in their recent analysis of the literature on travel and sex, argue that the interconnections between tourism and sex have been approached from social scientific, public health and human rights perspectives, each with their own distinctive concerns and discourses. From a social science perspective empirical investigations are carried out in order to further knowledge and understanding the varied phenomena of sexuality connected with travel and tourism, and attempts are made to interpret data gathered within more general theoretical frameworks within social scientific disciplines (particularly sociology and psychology). Through their methods of research, social scientists seek to establish and explain patterns of social organisation and individual behaviours in a relatively dispassionate and objective fashion. In relation to sex and travel they have sought to address questions such as the following:

- why has sex tourism arisen in certain destinations and how does it continue to operate;
- what are the motivations and characteristics of tourists (predominantly men, but some women) who pay for sex with money or goods;
- how common is the 'Shirley Valentine' scenario and what are the outcomes of holiday romances;
- what difference does 'being away from home' make to the sexual behaviour of individuals;
- how common is sex activity among different groups of professional travellers (e.g. business men who travel frequently, airline pilots and crew, members of the armed forces stationed overseas, volunteers working for charitable agencies abroad)?

Closely associated with the social science perspective, but more specifically focused on issues of sexual risk-taking and its consequences, is the public health perspective. Travel in its diverse forms is an essential factor in the geographic spread of sexual infections, as they can only be transmitted through intimate personal contact and move through space as people move. A developing body of research has therefore examined the extent to which travellers engage in risky, unprotected sexual intercourse with new partners, and the factors that may be associated with a failure to use condoms when sexually active away from home. It is important to establish the extent of sexual risk behaviour during the travel and the factors associated with it, as a basis, hopefully, for the development of health promotion interventions (see Mulhall, 1996; Clift and Grabowski, 1997; Clift, Luongo and Callister, 2002).

A third answer to why tourism and sex attracts research and public interest draws explicitly on a moral and legal framework, with an emphasis on the human rights implications of sex tourism and trafficking. As Ryan (2000) has made clear, there are many ways in which travel/tourism and sex interact. Some of these connections, involving children, bonded labour or the trafficking of women, clearly constitute severe forms of exploitation and abuse. Much work in relation to sex tourism and trafficking is motivated, therefore, not by a dispassionate interest in theoretical understandings of cultural values, social organisation or the factors influencing individual behaviour, but by a commitment to eradicate serious assaults on fundamental human rights motivated purely by the selfish pursuit of physical pleasure and by financial gain. This is particularly so where investigative journalists attempt to expose the scale of abuse associated with international mobility of various kinds and the trafficking of women. A recent significant example is the *Correspondent* (BBC, 2002) investigation of the growth of a sex industry and trafficking in Bosnia to service international peacekeepers and police.

The Growth of International Travel and Tourism

It is something of a cliché to say that the world has become a smaller place. Advances in communication technology and increased levels of international travel, have enhanced levels of global interconnectedness to a degree unimagined even a few decades ago, and this is a critical factor in any discussion of sex and travel and the emergence of a globalised sex industry.

Statistics compiled by the World Tourism Organisation (WTO, 2002) show a steady increase in international arrivals from an estimate of approximately 25 million in 1950, to a staggering figure of 697 million in 2000. While arrivals figures showed a slight decline to an estimated 689 million in 2001 due to the terrorist attacks on the United States on 11 September that year, the WTO predicts that the upward trend in numbers of people travelling across international borders will continue into the foreseeable future. The WTO's *Tourism 2020 Vision* forecasts that international arrivals are expected to reach over 1.56 billion by the year 2020. The large majority of international arrivals occur by air travel, and of course the WTO figures underestimate the total volume of air travellers, as passengers on domestic flights are not included.

With increased travel has come increased opportunities for sexual activity 'away from home' – especially among the large numbers of men unaccompanied by their partners travelling for a wide variety of reasons around the globe. The last 10 years have seen a significant growth in research on travel and sexual activity and a number of significant texts addressing various aspects of sex and travel have also appeared in the last few years (e.g. Clift and Carter, 2000; Oppermann, 1998; Ryan and Hall, 2001 and Clift, Luongo and Callister, 2002).

The focus of such research has been on sexual activity in destinations away from home and, as far as the author is aware, no research attention has been given to sexual behaviour during travel itself. Almost as an aside, however, it is of interest initially to consider what is known about sexual activity during travel itself.

Sex on board aircraft, ferries and trains may take place legitimately and in private, where sleeping accommodation is provided for passengers (e.g. Virgin Atlantic have recently introduce double sleeping accommodation on their flights, and have advertised the fact in clearly suggestive ways!). However, sexual incidents of a more illicit nature certainly happen during air travel, and judging by the cases that have received press coverage recently (see Box 17.1), such activity may be more common on flights into London! No systematic research appears to have been done on this issue, however, either among passengers, or more importantly among employees who might be faced with a situation that is potentially embarrassing, at the very least. This may indicate that the incidence of such activity is probably quite rare, and that where it does happen is undertaken discreetly with few obvious signs.

Perhaps of greater significance for staff, however, are cases of sexual harassment – one form of a wider problem of passenger misconduct or unruly behaviour, which appears to have increased in recent years. According to *Japan Economic Newswire* (1 July 2001):

> Twelve domestic airlines jointly launched a campaign Sunday to stop passenger misconduct such as violence and sexual harassment, airline officials said. Flight attendants distributed leaflets on the campaign at Narita, Naneda and Kansai airports, calling for passengers to behave properly aboard planes. The number of acts of misconduct on planes operated by Japan Airlines (JAL), All Nippon Airways and Japan Air System last year came to 570, a more than sevenfold rise over four years earlier, a survey by the three firms showed.

Sexually Transmitted Infections: The Global Picture

Much of the recent work on travel and sexual activity has been stimulated by the emergence of HIV/AIDS and the contribution of travel to the development of the AIDS pandemic. HIV/AIDS is only one of a large number of sexually transmitted infections, however, and before considering the findings from

> **Box 17.1 Reports of sexual incidents in the course of air travel**
>
> In-flight *in flagrante delicto* is the hottest trend in air travel since frequent flier miles, says the staid old *Wall Street Journal*. One-third of the cases of 'unruly behaviour' aboard Singapore Airlines last year, for example, were cases involving sexual misconduct. Aboard a South African Airways jet bound from Johannesburg to London recently, 'a couple in business class disrobed from the waist down and began having sex in the a seat in full view of other passengers.' This was stopped only after the captain was called in, yelling at the couple that the plane was 'not a shag house' (*San Francisco Chronicle*, 24 June 1998).
>
> Two strangers who shocked passengers with a drunken sexual encounter on a transatlantic plane were fined a total of £2,250 yesterday. Amanda Holt, 37, and David Machin, 40, both married, admitted being drunk on an American Airlines flight from Dallas to Manchester. Both have lost well-paid jobs. Holt was seen in various stages of undress in the business class section as the lights dimmed for a film, Manchester Crown Court heart. Judge Harold Singer said that a woman across the aisle had been 'offended and outraged' (*Daily Telegraph*, 6 April 2000).
>
> Two business-class passengers on a British airways jumbo jet have been 'mildly rebuked' after their sexual escapade in a plane toilet caused a stir among fellow passengers. The couple – a man wearing a dark business suit and a woman dressed in an expensive blue dress – did not know each other when they boarded flight BA 212 in Boston, bound for London's Heathrow Airport. But as flight attendants served drinks after take-off, the two passengers, who were seated next to each other, struck up a conversation. One hour into the night flight, passengers noticed the woman got up and went into a toilet. Two minutes later, the man followed her. Shortly afterwards passengers started to hear groaning and thumping noises coming from the toilet. The noises continued until, 30 minutes later, one passenger complained to a flight attendant (*Straits Times Singapore*, 25 February 2001).

some recent studies of sexual behaviour among travellers/tourists, it is important to look at what is known currently about global patterns of sexual health. Taken together, sexually transmitted infections represent a major global cause of acute illness, infertility, long-term disability and death, with severe medical and psychological consequences for millions and men, women and infants.

There are more that 20 pathogens that are transmissible during sexual intercourse. Many of them are curable by appropriate antimicrobial treatment. However, despite the availability of effective treatments, bacterial STIs are still a major public health concern in both industrialised and developing countries. In developing countries, STIs and their complications are amongst the top five disease categories for which adults seek health care. In women of childbearing age, STIs (excluding HIV) are second only to maternal factors as causes of disease, death and healthy life lost.

The estimated number of new sexual infections worldwide during 1999 is over a third of a billion (World Health Organisation, 2001a). The scale of the problem of sexual infections varies from region to region around the world, but the most severely affected areas are the countries of Sub-Saharan Africa and South America and the Caribbean. In Sub-Saharan Africa, for example, more than one in 10 of the population of 15–49 years olds are estimated, at any given time, to have some form of sexual infection. It is important to remember in considering such figures that they relate only to curable infections – and many potentially serious and life-threatening viral infections, including genital wart virus and HIV – are not included in these estimates.

Not only are sexually transmitted infections highly prevalent throughout the world, the scale of the problem is increasing, and this has been true in recent years even in many affluent countries with good healthcare facilities. In England and Wales, for example, between 1995–97, male cases of gonorrhoea increased by 35 per cent and female cases by 32 per cent. Such increases, however, pale into insignificance compared with the dramatic increase in cases of syphilis in the Baltic states and other countries of the former Soviet Union, since the early 1990s. Syphilis has increased from 5–15 per 100,000 in 1990 to as high as 200–270 per 100,000 in the late 1990s (World Health Organisation, 1999).

Epidemiological data on the prevalence of sexually transmitted diseases and their dramatic rates of increase in some areas of the world are of particular significance in considering the sexual health implications of sexual activity in the context of travel. Clearly, an individual travelling from a region of relatively low prevalence to one of much higher prevalence, who is sexually active with locals in that region, especially if this is unprotected sex with prostitutes, is likely to be at considerably enhanced risk of acquiring a sexual infection. It is not surprising, therefore, to find increasing cases of imported sexually transmitted infections around the world, especially in affluent tourist sending countries. Perhaps the most dramatic documented example of this phenomenon occurred in Finland in 1995 (see Box 17.2).

> **Box 17.2 Imported syphilis in Finland**
>
> In the early 1990s only 30 to 40 new cases of syphilis were reported annually in Finland. Since 1993, however the incidence of syphilis has increased. In 1994 there were 63 cases, and this jumped to a total of 118 cases in 1995. Thirty-seven per cent of patients in 1995 were female, and 77 per cent had been infected in Finland. In contrast, 63 per cent were male, and 65 per cent of them were infected abroad (just over half in Russia). Most of the cases in 1995 were found in southern Finland or in the southeast near the Russian border. One cluster of 30 cases occurred in the city of Tampere. The origins of this local outbreak were three males, who acquired the infection in Russia.
>
> Travel to St Petersburg and to neighbouring areas for business and for pleasure has increased remarkably since the Soviet Union collapsed. In 1995, the incidence of syphilis in Russia was 86 times higher (172/100,000) than in Finland (2/100,000) and is increasing. In St Petersburg in particular, the incidence of syphilis is among the highest in Russian administrative territories (318/100,000).
>
> *Source*: HiltunenBack et al. (1996).

The Global HIV/AIDS Pandemic

Since the first reported cases of AIDS in the United States in the late 1970s, HIV/AIDS has become a global pandemic of extraordinary proportions. Currently, HIV/AIDS is an increasing problem throughout the world, and there is little sign, even in many affluent countries, that the huge investments in research and prevention initiatives have succeeded in stabilising, let alone reducing, the year-on-year increase in new HIV infections. The most recent estimates of the global HIV/AIDS problem were published by the World Health Organisation on World AIDS Day (1 December) 2001. The total number of people living with HIV/AIDS was estimated to be 40 million, with a total of 5 million new infections with HIV in the course of 2001 (World Health Organisation, 2001b). Sub-Saharan Africa continues to the most severely affected region globally, but rapidly increasing rates of new infections were reported, particularly in the countries of the former Soviet Union.

The significance of population mobility for the geographic spread of HIV infection is undeniable. A substantial contribution to an understanding of the role of different forms of mobility in the global spread of HIV has been made by Quinn (1994). In the African context, for example, major human movements have occurred over the last 20 years due to economically motivated migration from rural to urban areas, natural disasters, political instability and armed conflicts. Such large-scale movements are heavily implicated in the development of the HIV/AIDS epidemic across the continent. More specifically, with reference to the situation in Uganda, Quinn notes that three principal hypotheses have been proposed to account for the patterns of distribution of infection throughout the country. First the 'truck town' hypothesis suggests that the geographic dispersal of infection reflects the pattern of major roads in the country, which 'act as principal corridors of virus spread between urban areas and other proximal settlements'. Truck drivers along these routes and commercial sex workers who offer their services to drivers at rest sites are the principal actors in this process. Second, the 'migrant labour' hypothesis suggests that HIV has moved from 'areas of labour demand in urban areas to areas of labour supply in rural districts through a process of return migration'. And a third hypothesis is that the diffusion of HIV throughout Uganda reflected ethnic patterns of recruitment into the Ugandan National Liberation Army, after the overthrow of Idi Amin in 1979. Quinn notes that probably all three hypotheses together help to explain the spread of HIV within Uganda.

Various forms of international mobility are also important in the movement of HIV infection across national borders. In the UK, for instance, approximately three quarters of all cases of heterosexually acquired HIV infection in the UK by December 2001, were 'acquired abroad'. The majority of these cases are among members of ethnic minority communities who have immigrated into the UK, and are a direct consequence of the epidemic elsewhere in the world, particularly sub Saharan Africa. In addition, however, international sex tourism has also had an impact on the UK epidemic, with approximately one hundred cases of HIV infection among heterosexual men associated with sexual activity in Thailand (Public Health Laboratory Service, personal communication, February 2002).

Recent Research on the Sexual Behaviour of Travellers

The last 10 years has seen a significant growth in research on the sexual behaviour of international travellers and tourists. Space precludes a detailed review of this research here (see Clift and Carter, 2000; Mulhall, 1996), but Table 17.1 summaries a number of recent British studies in this field. These studies give a sense of the range of methods employed in researching this sensitive subject and some of the findings that have emerged.

Table 17.1 Details of six recent British studies on sexual behaviour and risk among travellers/tourists

Authors/date	Sample	Methods	Sexual activity	Sexual intercourse	Unprotected sex	Variables associated with sex
Bloor et al., 1988, 2000	5675 18–34 yr-olds who had been abroad unaccompanied by a sexual partner during previous two years, surveyed to identify 400 sexually active abroad and 568 nonactive controls	Sample identified initially through routine opinion polling procedures. Followed up by structured computer assisted telephone interview	11% of total sample reported involvement in a romantic or sexual relationship while abroad. Only 0.2% of encounters were homosexual and 0.3% commercial	7% of the total sample reported sexual intercourse. Substantial sex difference apparent with 10% of men having intercourse compared with 4% of women	25% of those engaging in sexual intercourse reported unprotected sex	*Sexual intercourse*: men, being single, being drunk abroad, experience of casual sex at home *Unsafe sex*: higher number of sexual partners abroad, didn't take condoms abroad, condoms not used at home
Clift and Forrest, 1999, 2000	562 gay men in southern England surveyed in August 1996. 391 reported at least one holiday in 1996 up to the time of the survey	Men recruited in gay venues in Brighton and through a local gay and lesbian magazine. Self completion questionnaire used to gather information on sexual activity on holiday	48% of men were sexually active with a new partner on holiday. 30% of sexually active men reported as many or more partners during a single holiday than during the year up to the survey at home	29% of the total sample reported anal intercourse. 23% reported insertive anal intercourse and 18% receptive intercourse	21% of men reporting receptive anal intercourse did not use condoms consistently. 10% of men engaging in insertive anal intercourse reported unsafe sex	*Sexual activity*: higher number of sexual partners at home, on holiday alone or with friends *Sexual intercourse*: Not in a relationship, more sexual partners at home, taking condoms and lubricant on holiday *Unsafe sex*: didn't take condoms on holiday, uncertain or positive HIV status
Hawkes et al., 1995	All attendees at a central London GUM clinic (March to June 1993) who had travelled abroad within the previous three months: 462 eligible patients (18% of attendees), of whom 386 participated (83%). 54% women, 46% men, mean age 30 years	Self completion questionnaire used to gather information on sexual behaviour before and during trip abroad	No distinction drawn between sexual activity and sexual intercourse	24% of those who had travelled abroad in last three months reported sexual activity: 18% of the women, 25% of the heterosexual men, and 44% of the gay men	Among those sexually active abroad, 69% reported unprotected sex. Estimated that 12% of sexually transmitted diseases treated in the clinic acquired from sexual activity abroad	*Sexual activity*: no current regular partner, abroad alone, new casual partners since returning

Table 17.1 cont'd

Authors/date	Sample	Methods	Sexual activity	Sexual intercourse	Unprotected sex	Variables associated with sex
Carter et al., 1997	Attendees at two Glasgow GUM clinics during two three month periods who had travelled abroad during the previous three months. 325 participated out of those eligible (87% response)	Self completion questionnaire to gather data on sexual activity abroad and during a three month period prior to travel	No distinction drawn between sexual activity and sexual intercourse	28% of those who had travelled abroad in last three months reported sexual activity: 20% of the women, 31% of the heterosexual men, and 42% of the gay men. Number of partners on average 2–3 times greater on holiday than at home	50% of the women and 59% of the heterosexual men reported unprotected intercourse. No figures given for homosexual men	*Sexual activity*: men more sexually active than women abroad. *Unprotected sex*: more likely the longer the trip abroad, those reporting unsafe sex at home were more likely to report unsafe sex abroad
Elliott et al., 1998	160 young people travelling from Scotland to Ibiza in September 1995 for a dance holiday. Some of the young people travelled with their partners. 90 young people attending a reunion in November 1995 (47 of whom travelled to Ibiza)	Self-completion questionnaires at the end of the holiday and during the reunion. 30 interviews conducted during the holiday and young people observed	No distinction drawn between sexual activity and sexual intercourse	27% reported sex with a known partner on holiday, compared with 49% over the same period at home. 17% reported sex with an unknown partner on holiday, compared with 26% at home	85% reported unprotected sex with a known partner on holiday, compared with 76% over the same period at home. 53% reported unprotected sex with an unknown partner on holiday, compared with 44% at home	No statistically significant differences were found in levels of reported sexual activity and unsafe sex on holiday and at home. Authors note that there was wide spread disinterest in sex among both men and women whilst on holiday. Young people more interested in dancing, alcohol and drugs
Thomas, 2000	35 women who had travelled abroad without a partner in the last two years	A qualitative study involving focus group discussion and in-depth interviews	19 women interviewed reported a romantic or sexual relationship during a holiday abroad	11 of the 19 women	Condom use not addressed	A number of themes associated with the occurrence or not of sexual intercourse identified from women's accounts: sexual desire/pleasure; relationship status and history; alcohol use; space and privacy; emotional involvement; anonymity

The studies by Bloor et al. (2000) and Clift and Forrest (1999), for example, made use of survey techniques to gather data on sexual activity abroad among broadly representative samples of young people travelling alone and gay men respectively. The most interesting finding to emerge from the Bloor study, which remains the largest and most systematic investigation in this field, is that a relatively small proportion of young people claimed to be sexually active with new partners abroad (but more men than women did so). Gay men, in contrast, studied by Clift and Forrest, were much more likely to report being sexually active with new partners while abroad. Evidence also emerged from both surveys that patterns of sexual activity abroad, including whether safer sex was practiced, tended to reflect patterns of sexual activity at home.

The studies by Hawkes et al. (1995) and Carter et al. (1997) were undertaken in the context of genitourinary medicine clinics in London and Glasgow, and show that patients attending such clinics report a relatively high level of sexual activity abroad, with substantial levels of unprotected sex. Clearly, this group of sexually active people is a particularly important target group for sexual health interventions.

Finally, the studies by Elliott et al. (1998) and Thomas (2000) are examples of more qualitative research in which the details of the context and quality of sexual encounters on holiday are explored. The Elliott et al. study is important in that it is one of the few that looks at sexual activity among young people in the context of alcohol and drug use, and makes direct comparisons between sexual behaviour at home and abroad. It is striking that the young people investigated appeared to be less sexually active while on holiday, and this probably reflects both their high levels of substance use and the fact that they were primarily motivated by enjoying themselves clubbing and dancing. Thomas's study is also of interest in highlighting that factors that may facilitate sexual activity on holiday can also serve to render it less likely (e.g. higher levels of alcohol consumption can reduce inhibitions, but can also lead to sleep rather than sex!).

Tourism, Sex Industries and Prostitution

Global travel and tourism have undoubtedly supported the development of sex industries and prostitution in most major urban centres around the world. The development of tourism in 'exotic' destinations in poor tropical countries has also encouraged the growth of more informal systems of prostitution in and around many resort areas. The development of the Internet has also fuelled these developments, enabling the rapid compilation of reports from travellers around the world of information on sexual opportunities in different destinations. 'Sex tourism' is primarily a phenomenon involving single men travelling from relatively affluent parts of the world to less affluent destinations, with a goal of sexual gratification from women in mind (primarily though not exclusively, as women may also travel for sex, see below). Male travellers may not think of themselves as 'sex tourists' and may indeed be travelling for purposes other than leisure, nor do the women involved in providing sexual services necessarily regard themselves as 'prostitutes.' Nevertheless, the fact remains that large numbers of men take advantage of the opportunities provided by international travel to engage in sex with disadvantaged, impoverished or exploited women in return for money or services. A good insight into sex tourism from the point of view of male 'consumers' and the number and geographic spread of 'sex tourism' destinations can be gained from consulting the main websites established to provide information for men about opportunities for 'adult travel' (see Box 17.3).

Sex tourism and prostitution in tourist destinations has been the focus of much academic study and space precludes a detailed review (see sources listed above). A particular focus of recent research, however, has been the Caribbean, and in particular the Dominican Republic, and a selection of such studies can serve to highlight some of the key issues associated with sex tourism across the globe. Indeed, Wonders and Michalowski (2001), in their recent comparison of sex tourism in Amsterdam and Havana, argue that while these two cities are very different, patterns of sex tourism in each locale are increasingly overdetermined by global economic forces, connecting the practice of sex work in both cities with the broader phenomenon of globalized sex tourism. A major reason for this being so is that the vast majority of prostitutes working in the sex industry in Amsterdam, as in most other major European cities, are not local women, but women trafficked from the Third World and Eastern Europe.

Sex Tourism in the Dominican Republic

Forsythe, Hasbun and de Lister (1998) report a wide-ranging study in which information was gathered from tourists, hotel workers and commercial sex workers in the Dominican Republic. The focus of their work was on assessing the potential interactions between the HIV/AIDS epidemic and tourism in the island – how HIV/AIDS may affect tourism and how tourism may affect its spread. Their survey of over 700 tourists prior to their departure from the island highlights, as one might expect, that the vast majority of tourists travelled

> **Box 17.3 Two sex tourism websites**
>
> *The World Sex Guide* (www.worldsexguide.org)
>
> This is the oldest sex travel website established in 1994 in the United States. It describes its purpose in a brash 'in your face' mission statement: 'This is the *World Sex Guide*. Our mission is simple: Finding women and getting laid. If you are offended by stuff like this, I don't care.' The site includes Report Archives, which give 'the best of all the reports we've received over the years, edited down to provide you with an historical perspective of what's been the scene in every state and every country'. It also has a Discussion Board, which 'contains thousands of first-hand reports from the United States and every country in the world'.
>
> *Travel and the Single Male* (www.tsmtravel.com)
>
> This site is run by the publishers of the book with the same title by Bruce Cassirer. It boasts 'over 3500 photos from our women of the world travel collection', 'over 3000 articles covering 71 countries' (the first 10 listed being Cambodia, Vietnam, Norway, Latvia, Iceland, Australia, France, Holland, Chile and German), a new 'Java chat room where you can discuss all your thoughts, plans or just ask away', 'Fifty-one multi-media newsletters' (which include 'erotic Phuket, mischievous Cuba, steamy Cancun, deviant Negril, racy Pattaya etc.), and finally 'A private message board and travel forum, just for members' where 'you can post messages, ask questions and receive answers to your most personal adult travel questions'.

with partners and families and were unlikely to have engaged in sexual activity with local residents. However, 12 per cent of visitors were on holiday alone and they were more likely to view themselves as being at greater risk of becoming infected with HIV on holiday than at home, when compared to all other tourists (53 per cent *vs* 38 per cent). Of greater interest, however, in terms of sex tourism, were the findings from interviews with sex and hotel workers. Just under 400 sex workers were interviewed and the authors sum up their circumstances as follows:

> About 80% of the CSWs were under 30 years old, with more of the women under 25 years old. In terms of education, more that three-quarters of the women had fewer than nine years of education. Early sexual initiation, abuse and child

prostitution appear to have been fairly common among the Dominican CSWs. Twenty per cent of the women began to sell sex prior to their 18th birthday, with 16 of the women interviewed admitting that they had started before their 12th birthday (p. 283).

It was also found that most of the CSWs preferred foreign clients, primarily because they were willing to pay more. Foreign tourists were also more willing to accept using condoms, although this varied by nationality, as German men were much more likely to want to use a condom than men from Spain or Italy.

Over 200 hotel workers were also surveyed, 17 per cent of whom reported sexual relations with tourists (29 per cent of male hotel workers and 5 per cent of female workers). The males who were sexually active with tourists were primarily male entertainers working in the hotels (see below for a more detailed account of female sex tourism in the Dominican Republic).

Brennan (2001) provides a detailed account of the nature of sex tourism operating in the small town of Sosua in the Dominican Republic, which she argues has become 'a transnational sexual meeting ground, a sexscape of sorts, for two groups of individuals between whom there is a vast disparity in power' (p. 622). Most of the Dominican sex workers in Sosua have migrated to the town from rural areas of the island, are young and have dependent children. Brennan argues that their migration is motivated by a fantasy of entering into a relationship with a foreign man who will treat her better than local Dominican men, and offer her an escape route from the island and poverty. The town is a popular holiday destination for German tourists, and male sex tourists also seek to play out their fantasies of finding a dark-skinned, sexually exciting and compliant Dominican girl who is the mirror image of demanding German women:

> Just as Dominican women look to German men to be better providers than Dominican men, German men too, compare Dominican women to German women. They imagine Dominican women as more sexual, more compliant, and having fewer commodity needs and desires. In fact, as Dominican women hope (but do not expect) German men to break with traditional assumptions about gender role, German men expect Dominican women to adhere to very traditional – and regressive – understandings of gender roles (p. 642).

Unfortunately, the fantasies on either side are generally unfulfilled, and the greater disadvantage and powerlessness of the Dominican women means that they rarely gain economically or in terms of increased security for themselves or their children, from liaisons with German men:

> In this economy of desire, some dreams are realised, while others prove hollow. White, middle-class and lower-middle class European visitors and residents are much better positioned to secure from 'above' what they want in Sosua then poor, black Dominican sex workers and other Dominican migrants who are likely to be disillusioned by Sosua, tourism and tourists (p. 654).

Brennan constructs her account of sex tourism in Sosua on the basis of extensive fieldwork and interviews with sex workers and men, but also draws illustrative material from the websites given in Box 17.3 to demonstrate the racialised and gendered fantasies held by the sex tourists. A similar range of methods is adopted by O'Connell Davidson (2001) in her remarkable study of the social networks and subcultures among 'hardcore' sex tourists – those for whom sex with multiples of prostitutes is 'a conscious and explicit part of the motivation to travel', and 'sexpatriates' – men who find 'the pleasures associated with a particular destination so great that they eventually decide to migrate and settle permanently in their chosen "sexual paradise"'. These sexpatriates have worked to build up an infrastructure to support sex tourism in major Dominican resorts:

> Many of the hotels, restaurants and bars that facilitate prostitute use by tourists in Boca Chica, Puerto Plata and in Sosua (the country's three main sex tourist destinations) are owned or managed by North American or European expatriates. The more entrepreneurial of them have discovered that the internet offers excellent marketing opportunities, and their hotels and bars now feature on several websites that promote sex tourism (p. 7).

Through interviews with 31 sexpatriates and 30 hardcore sex tourists, and well as through reference to the messages posted on the *Travel and the Single Male* website, O'Connell Davidson is able to paint a graphic picture of the 'aggressively heterosexist, deeply misogynist and profoundly racist' mentality of these men. They see themselves as escaping from a Western context in which the superiority of white men over women and other racial groups has been eroded, to the setting in which they can exert a sense of legitimate masculine power at the top of an economic, racial and sexual hierarchy:

> Hardcore sex tourists and sexpatriates see the Dominican Republic as a lawless and corrupt place ('There is no law here' they say), but it is simultaneously described as a place where 'natural laws' operate. Thus, white men are feared, revered and obeyed by their 'racial' and gender subordinates, while 'naturally'

promiscuous Dominican women and girls are available to meet white man's 'needs' uninhibited by European/North American codes of sexual morality (p. 14).

And not surprisingly, the greater power and sexual voraciousness of such men, 'has grave consequences for the safety, health and well-being of local women and girl children' in this so-called 'tourist paradise'.

While sex tourism is primarily a male phenomenon, it is important to recognise that forms of female sex tourism also exist. This issue has been researched recently by Sanchez Taylor (2001) who gathered information by questionnaire from 240 female tourists in three resorts: Negril in Jamaica, and Boca Chica and Sosua in the Dominican Republic. The women were single or were travelling alone without their partner/spouse, and ranged in age from late teens to 60s. Almost a third of the women had experienced sexual relationships with local men during their holiday; in most cases they reported only one partner, but 30 per cent of the sexually active women reported two or more partners. Almost all of these were on return visits and following Albuquerque (1999), Sanchez Taylor suggests that they may be described as 'veteran female sex tourists'.

Interestingly, about a quarter of the women surveyed reported being approached by a male 'prostitute' with an offer of sex for payment, but none of them admitted to accepting the offer. This suggests that the women did not see their sexual encounters with men as 'prostitute-client transactions' despite the fact that 60 per cent of sexually active women did report giving their partners cash, gifts or buying them meals. Consistent with these findings, a majority of the sexually active women described their relationship in emotional terms as either a 'holiday romance' (39 per cent), 'real love' (22 per cent) or 'both physical and holiday romance' (12 per cent), and few admitted to their contacts with local men being 'purely physical' (3 per cent). These perceptions of the relationship appeared to influence condom use, as those who described their relationships with local men as 'real love' tended to report taking no precautions against the risk of STDs.

Sanchez Taylor provides further insights into the phenomenon of female sex tourism by considering the roles of economic power, racism and gender as organising forces in the nature of sexual contacts between female tourists and local men – and usefully explores both the similarities and differences between male and female sex tourism. As with male sex tourists, women entering into sexual relationships with local men, gain a sense of affirmation:

> Like male sex tourists, being able to command 'fit' and sexually desirable bodies which would otherwise be denied to them reaffirms female tourists' sense of their own privilege as 'First World' citizens ... White women, in particular, explained that they felt valued in the Caribbean in ways in which they are not back home. Their economic power and their whiteness means that they are not treated as local women but respected and protected. Their bodies are valued over local women's bodies and they are offered a stage upon which they can simultaneously affirm their femininity through their ability to command local men and reject the white men who have rejected them (p. 760).

Sanchez Taylor acknowledges, however, that 'there are important respects in which patterns of sexual interaction between tourist women and local men differ from patterns of sexual interaction between tourist men and women'. Thus, men make use of organised prostitution in Jamaica and the Dominican Republic in which women offer specific sexual services for a set fee. There is no system of organised male prostitution, which caters for female tourists in the same way. In addition, local prostitute women are vulnerable to being cheated, physically assaulted and raped by male tourists, and are also subject to harassment and prosecution from local police. Local men who involve themselves in sexual encounters with female tourists are not vulnerable in the same ways.

Sex Tourism and Mainstream Travel and Tourism Businesses

O'Connell Davidson (1998/9) makes a striking claim which should give pause for thought for everyone involved in travel and tourism businesses. The 'prime beneficiaries of sex tourism' she suggests, 'are probably the airlines which transport prostitute users half way around the globe, the hotels (many of which are owned by international conglomerates) in which they stay, and the travel agents which arrange their flights and accommodation.' She illustrates her point by citing the case of one 'habitual British sex tourist' she interviewed, who goes to Pattaya for a three-week holiday every year:

> His holiday is organised by a respectable ABTA-bonded tour operator and booked through an ordinary high-street travel agent; he pays just over £900 for his flights, transfer and accommodation. He allows himself a budget of £300 for meals and drinks and £300 for purposes of sexual exploitation during his trip. Because he is a seasoned sex tourist and knows how to get 'value for money' (mainly by using young and inexperienced prostitutes and visiting cheaper brothels outside the tourist centre), this sum allows him to live handsomely and to 'go through about thirty or forty girls' on each trip. A large proportion of the

total cost of his trip, then, goes to enrich Western-owned travel conglomerates, while the multiples of women and children he exploits probably retain less than 10 per cent between them (p. 17).

In support of the claim that ordinary high street travel businesses benefit from sex tourism, here is an extract from a 2001 Thomas Cook *Holidays Worldwide* brochure giving details of holidays in Pattaya:

MAKING THE MOST OF PATTAYA
Just two and half hours from Bangkok, Pattaya is the playground of the Orient, offering every form of fun devised by man. Its busy beach boasts a wealth of watersports from silent scuba diving, to skilled water-skiing and rowdy rides. The surrounding countryside offers unmissable golf courses, go karting, horse riding and archery. An excellent selection of hotels, shops, bars and restaurants cover an area inland from the shoreline, whilst at the southern tip of the bay is 'The Strip' – a brash bawdy jungle of outrageous entertainment. It is here you will find go-go bars, risqué cabarets and night long discos. Here 'sanuk' or 'have fun' is the keyword and the air of unbridled enjoyment is as intoxicating for the people watcher as for the pleasure seeker (p. 54).

Child Sex Tourism and the International Trafficking of Women and Children for Sexual Purposes

Without doubt, the most disturbing and pernicious connections between sexuality and international travel/tourism are the problems of child sex tourism and the illegal trafficking of women and children for purposes of sexual exploitation. In recent years, considerable attention has been focused on these problems by intergovernmental organisations (UN, WTO, ILO, EU), national governments, international aid organisations, campaign groups (notably ECPAT (End Child Prostitution, Pornography and Trafficking) and academic researchers. The sexual exploitation of children worldwide has also been the subject of two major international conferences (Stockholm in 1996 and Yokohama in 2001). The links between international trafficking, prostitution and sex tourism are well documented, as many women and girls available for sex in major cities throughout the world, and well known sex tourism resorts, are not from local communities or from the same country, but have been trafficked into the destination, often over considerable distances. Globally, much of this trafficking involves illicit smuggling over land by road and sea, but trafficking over long distances occurs by air via commercial airlines and through international airports.

Hecht (2001), in a specially commissioned theme paper for the Yokohama conference, provides a valuable overview of the significance of three areas of private commercial business in both facilitating and combating the commercial sexual exploitation of children worldwide. These are travel and tourism, the media (photography, television, film etc.) and the new technologies (particularly Internet service providers). In the context of the present chapter, Hecht's discussion of the role of travel and tourism businesses in addressing the problem of child sex tourism is particularly important. The vast majority of these businesses undoubtedly have no direct involvement in promoting any form of sex tourism involving prostitution or sexual exploitation of minors. But clearly such businesses provide the wherewithal for large numbers of people to travel to destinations where commercial sex tourism of various kinds takes place, and increasingly over the last 10 years they have shown a willingness to take a stand against commercial sex tourism, especially where this may involve the exploitation of minors. Hecht (2001, p. 2) writes:

> The five years following the first World Congress against Commercial Sexual Exploitation of Children (CSEC) have seen remarkable advancements in initiatives taken by the private sector to undermine CSEC. In this respect the travel and tourism industries have taken a lead role. A number of high profile agreements and resolutions have been made at the international level. A particularly notable initiative was the recent adoption by the WTO General Assembly of a new Global Code of *Ethics for Tourism*. Many travel-related agencies, at international, regional and national levels, have also taken measures to help prevent CSEC, including the promulgation of codes, training programmes for employees, and campaigns for public education through projects such as messaged luggage tags.

Trafficking for sexual purposes is a growing phenomenon throughout the world, and important work has been undertaken to document the nature and scale of this horrific trade. Two recent publications are of particular interest as they report on what is known about the trafficking of women and children into and through the UK. According to Kelly and Regan (2000), in a report commissioned by the Home Office as part of their Police Research Series, between 142 and 1,420 women have been trafficked into the UK each year since 1998. While Kelly and Regan's information on trafficking was gained from 36 police forces in the UK, they suggest that 'the majority of police forces have limited knowledge of, and thus give limited attention to, trafficking and there is a danger that this unintentionally creates a climate of tolerance for trafficking of women into and with the UK'. However, those forces that were able to provide information indicated that the first signs of trafficking were detected about 10 years ago in Triad-controlled brothels in London. Since then, women from Thailand and Central and Eastern Europe countries are most likely to be trafficked into the UK.

Kelly and Regan detail the movement of the trafficker and their 'cargo' into the UK. They point out that women rarely enter the UK by illegal means, such as being smuggled in lorries. These women enter on legitimate or illegitimate documents and are accompanied by the trafficker or an English speaking man who poses as her husband or boyfriend. Some women arrive by plane, especially if they are from Thailand or Africa, although sometimes, the trafficker and victim fly into another European country, and travel by Eurostar train into the UK. Once in the UK, the woman is taken to a brothel, where her false papers and passport are confiscated by the trafficker. For many of the women, the reality of their situation is only perceived at this point. Any protests are followed by threats from the trafficker to hurt her or her family.

While this study gives some insight into the trafficking of women into the UK, of particular significance is the overall lack of police awareness of the issue. Apart from the work of the Clubs and Vice Police Unit in London, very little attention is given to the trafficking of women by other police forces.

A second important study by Somerset (2001) addresses what various professionals know about the trafficking of children into, and through, the UK for sexual purposes.

In September 2000, ECPAT groups from Belgium, Finland, France, Germany, Italy, the Netherlands, Norway and the UK, started research into the trafficking of children (minors under the age of 18) from Eastern Europe to their respective countries. With respect to the UK, the work undertaken was the first of its kind, as up until then no research had been carried out into the trafficking of children into the UK for sexual purposes. Somerset contacted 50 people regarding the issue of trafficking of children into the UK, and 24 interviews were carried out involving members of organisations in three categories: officials (Immigration and police), nongovernmental organisations (child care and refugee organisations, HIV service providers) and observers (academics, journalists, lawyers).

Of particular significance in her investigation was the information provided from West Sussex Social Services, who care for any unaccompanied minors seeking asylum on arrival at Gatwick airport. Since September 1995, a total of 66 children (18 of whom were boys, and many under the age of 16, from Nigeria, Liberia, Sierra Leone, Gabon, Ghana, Sudan, Kenya and China), have gone missing after being taken into care. Somerset provides the following account of one train of events, that can unfold, based on a police investigation of missing Nigerian girls (Operation Newbridge):

> On arrival at Gatwick Airport, in the county of Sussex, the majority of girls declare themselves to immigration as asylum seekers, and unaccompanied minors. Many of these girls have used false passports in order to leave Africa but these are often destroyed on the plane ... Once they have been identified by Immigration, Social Services are contacted ... Those referred to West Sussex Social Services are taken in under Section 20 of the Children Act 1989. They are then placed in the safe house set up to take in girls thought to be at risk of being trafficked ... children go missing from one day to six months after they are admitted, although some never go missing at all. Those that do go missing are taken to London, and then driven or flown to Europe, with the main destination being Italy.
>
> The numbers of children known to West Sussex Social Services who have gone missing, and presumed to be victims of trafficking, peaked at 23 in 1999, and has since declined, with 4 children going missing during 2001. Somerset suggests that this 'may be due to the traffickers realising the police, Immigration and Social Services are aware of their movements, and causing the traffickers to stop using Gatwick airport as an entry point (p. 8).

As of July 2000, West Sussex Social Services put together an 'at risk profile' which was circulated to the police and the Immigration Service. This profile applies to children entering the country, and declaring themselves asylum seekers and unaccompanied minors, to ensure they are taken into Social Services (see Box 17.4).

Final Thoughts

The links between travel and sexual licence have been known for centuries, but it is only recently that this connection has been the subject of systematic investigation and research. This chapter does not claim to have provided a comprehensive or even adequate overview of the issues raised by this area nor the work undertaken. But it is hoped that it has raised awareness of these issues and provided useful leads for those readers who wish to learn more.

Everyone travels for a purpose, be it a holiday, on business, to visit family, or to mark life-stage transitions. Those who work in the travel industries should be aware that travel is also a means to sexual exploration and entertainment for some travellers and that risky sexual behaviour (whether due to the risk of

> **Box 17.4 At risk profile for unaccompanied minors arriving in the UK and seeking asylum (West Sussex Social Services)**
> - Male or female.
> - Aged 12–28.
> - May maintain to Immigration Service that they are older than they appear.
> - Come from West Africa or from China.
> - May have documentation which is not West African.
> - Anxious/distressed.
> - May have been drugged or held captive prior to flight.
> - Girls may wear wigs.
> - Girls often wear 'old style' clothes, but have modern, Westernised, skimpy clothes in their luggage, often with British labels.
> - Girls are submissive and cowed, uncommunicative and tense, and often fail to make eye contact, although it is recognised that this is a cultural norm for some. However, this may be the case even when the social worker and carers have known them for some time.
> - Interest shown by suspected perpetrators.
> - On arrival a solicitor or legal representative has been informed by a third party of their arrival and attempts to make contact with Immigration or Social Services.
> - Some of the young people who fit the profile are known to be accomplices of the perpetrators.

infections or the legal consequences of illicit behaviour) may, for a variety of reasons, be more likely when people are away from home. This may also be true of some who work within the travel industry itself.

References

Albuquerque, K. (1999), 'Sex, Beach Boys and Female Tourists in the Caribbean', in B.M. Dank and R. Refinetti (eds), *Sex Work and Sex Workers: Sexuality and culture, Vol. 2*, New Brunswick, NJ: Transactions Books.

BBC (2002), 'Boys will be Boys', *Correspondent*, 14 June 2002, see www.news.bbc.co.uk/hi/english/audiovisual/programmes/correspondent.

Bloor, M., Thomas, M., Abeni, D., Goujon, C., Hausser, D., Hubert, M., Klieber, D. and Nieto, J. A. (1998), 'Differences in Sexual Risk Behaviour between Young Men and Women Travelling Sbroad from the UK', *The Lancet*, Vol. 352, No. 21, pp. 1664–8.

Bloor, M., Thomas, M., Abeni, D., Goujon, C., Hausser, D., Hubert, M., Klieber, D. and Nieto, J.A. (2000), 'Sexual Risk Behaviour in a Sample of 5676 Young, Unaccompanied

Travellers', in S. Clift and S. Carter (eds), *Tourism and Sex: Culture, Commerce and Coercion*, London: Continuum.

Brennan, D. (2001), 'Tourism in Transnational Places: Dominican sex workers and German sex tourists imagine one another', *Identities*, Vol. 7, No. 4, pp. 621–63.

Carter, S., Horn, K., Hart, G., Dunbar, M., Scoular, A. and MacIntyre, S. (1997), 'The Sexual Behaviour of International Travellers at Two Glasgow GUM Clinics', *International Journal of STD and AIDS*, Vol. 8, pp. 336–8.

Clift, S. and Carter, S. (eds) (2000), *Tourism and Sex: Culture, Commerce and Coercion*, London: Continuum.

Clift, S. and Forrest, S. (1999), 'Factors Associated with Gay Men's Sexual Behaviour and Risk on Holiday', *AIDS Care*, Vol. 11, pp. 281–95.

Clift, S. and Forrest, S. (2000), 'Tourism and the Sexual Ecology of Gay Men', in S. Clift and S. Carter (eds), *Tourism and Sex: Culture, Commerce and Coercion*, London: Continuum.

Clift, S. and Grabowski, P. (eds) (1997), *Tourism and Health: Risks, Research and Responses*, London: Pinter.

Clift, S., Luongo, M. and Callister, C. (eds) (2002), *Gay Tourism: Culture, Identity and Sex*, London: Continuum.

Elliott, L., Morrison, A., Ditton, J., Farrall, S., Short, E., Cowan, L. and Gruer, L. (1998), 'Alcohol, Drug Use, and Sexual Behaviour of Young Adults on a Mediterranean Dance Holiday', *Addiction Research*, Vol. 6, No. 4, pp. 319–40.

Forsythe, S., Hasbun, J. and de Lister, M.B. (1998), 'Protecting Paradise: Tourism and AIDS in the Dominican Republic', *Health Policy and Planning*, Vol. 13, No. 3, pp. 277–86.

Hart, G. and Hawkes, S. (2000), 'International Travel and the Social Context of Sexual Risk', in S. Clift and S. Carter (eds), *Tourism and Sex: Culture, Commerce and Coercion*, London: Continuum.

Hawkes, S., Hart, G.J., Bletsoe, E., Shergold, C and Johnson, A.M. (1995), 'Risk Behaviour and STD Acquisition in Genitourinary Medicine Clinic Attenders who have Travelled', *Genitourinary Medicine*, Vol. 71, pp. 351–4.

Hecht, M.E. (2001), 'The Role and Involvement of the Private Sector', theme paper prepared for the *Second World Congress against Commercial Sexual Exploitation of Children*, Yokohama, Japan, 17–20 December (see www.focalpointngo.org/yokohama/themepapers).

HiltunenBack, E., Haikala, O., Koskela, P. and Reunala, T. (1996), 'Increase of Syphilis in Finland Related to the Russian Epidemic', *Eurosurveillance*, Vol. 1, p. 1.

Kelly, L. and Regan, L. (2000), 'Stopping Traffic: Exploring the extent and responses to, trafficking of women for sexual exploitation in the UK', *Police Research Series, Paper 125*, London: Home Office.

Mulhall, B. (1996), 'Sex and Travel: Studies of sexual behaviour, disease and health promotion in international travellers – a global review', *International Journal of STD and AIDS*, Vol. 7, No. 7, pp. 455–65.

O'Connell Davidson, J. (1998/9), 'Doing the Hustle', *Tourism in Focus*, Vol. 30, pp. 7–8.

O'Connell Davidson, J. (2001), 'The Sex Tourist, the Expatriate, his Ex-wife and Her "other": The politics of loss, difference and desire', *Sexualities*, Vol. 4, No. 1, pp. 5–24.

Oppermann, M. (ed.) (1998), *Sex Tourism and Prostitution: Aspects of leisure, recreation and work*, New York: Cognizant Press.

Quinn, T.C. (1994), 'Population Migration and the Spread of Types 1 and 2 Human Immunodeficiency viruses', *Proceedings of the National Academy of Sciences USA*, Vol. 91, pp. 2407–2414.

Ryan, C. (2000), 'Sex Tourism: Paradigms of Confusion?', in S. Clift and S. Carter (eds), *Tourism and Sex: Culture, commerce and coercion*, London: Continuum.

Ryan, C. and Hall, C.M. (2001), *Sex Tourism: Marginal People and Liminalities*, London: Routledge.

Sanchez Taylor, J. (2001), 'Dollars are a Girl's Best Friend? Female Tourists' Sexual Behaviour in the Caribbean', *Sociology*, Vol. 35, No. 3, pp. 749–64.

Somerset, C. (2001), *What the Professionals Know: The trafficking of children into, and through, the UK for sexual purposes*, London: UKPAT UK

Thomas, M. (2000), 'Exploring the Contexts and Meanings of Women's Experiences of Sexual Intercourse on Holiday', in S. Clift and S. Carter (eds), *Tourism and Sex: Culture, Commerce and Coercion*, London: Continuum.

Wonders, N.A. and Michalowski, R. (2001), 'Bodies, Borders, and Sex Tourism in a Globalized World: A tale of two cities – Amsterdam and Havana', *Social Problems*, Vol. 48, No. 4, pp. 545–71.

World Health Organisation (1999), 'Task Force for the Urgent Response to the Epidemics of Sexually Transmitted Infections in Eastern Europe and Central Asia', Report on the Third Meeting, Copenhagen 1–2 June, Copenhagen: World Health Organisation.

World Health Organisation (2001a), *Global Prevalence and Incidence of Selected Curable Sexually Transmitted Infections: Overview and estimates*, Geneva: World Health Organisation.

World Health Organisation (2001b), *AIDS Epidemic Update: December 2001*, Geneva: World Health Organisation.

World Tourism Organisation (1999), 'Global Code of Ethics for Tourism' (see http://www.world-tourism.org/omt/sextorui/wto-a.htm).

World Tourism Organisation (2002), *World Tourism Trends 2001*, Madrid: WTO.

Chapter 18

Civil Aviation?

Simon Calder

> Summer should be a season for celebration, yet on a Saturday morning in August at Britain's fastest-growing airport it is a mix of drudgery, gloom and histrionics. At Stansted Airport, the only people who are smiling are the retailers, cashing in on the most captive of markets: thousands of passengers whose delayed flights are being blamed on air traffic control delays. They have nothing to do but eat, drink and shop. Hordes of fractious children are being dragged around the seemingly endless glass and steel corridors by despairing parents. 'It's like herding cats', complains one frowning father to his stressed partner as they try to steer their brood towards gate 45.
>
> When they reach the departure gate, comfortably before the deadline laid down by the airline, they join a crowd of people scanning the horizon for the essential component for the next stage of the complex journey: an aircraft. They have done what is required of them: paid in advance for transportation from A to B, at a fare well above the 'headline' bargains trumpeted by the new breed of low-cost airlines; presented themselves at the airport in good time; and surmounted the series of hurdles that checking in for a flight involves these days. Now, in the no-man's-land beyond security control, there is nothing to do except get angry with the hapless woman at the desk who feels powerless to do anything but repeat the fibs that her managers are telling her about when the absent aeroplane might appear.

Patterns of air passenger behaviour in the twenty-first century have their roots in the tangled growth of twentieth-century flying. When civil aviation began in the aftermath of World War I, the immense relative cost meant that only the very rich could afford to fly. Consequently, the stresses that derive from constraints on capacity – at airports and in the skies – did not exist. Airlines functioned more like air-taxi services, with upper-class passengers calling the shots. In return, they accepted a high degree of risk. On the bumpy, uncomfortable and dangerous journey between Croydon and Amsterdam there was no option for passengers but to keep quiet and hope for the best.

By 1936, when Gatwick opened as the first modern, purpose-built airport terminal, the customer base for aviation had broadened. At the same time, the glamour of aviation was arguably at a peak. Passengers could leave central London by train, glide through a tunnel from Gatwick Airport station into a stunning terminal building and be on board within two minutes. The centres of London and Paris were less than three hours apart – an achievement no longer feasible by air, and only just within the capabilities of Eurostar trains. Airports were seen as conduits in which passengers should spend the absolute minimum of time.

A lifetime later, the airport comprises an obstacle course. Some obstacles, like the rigorous security checks, enjoy a consensus about the need to diminish risk. But others are created by the airport owner as an essential commercial element of business. Anyone entering the departure area at Britain's two largest airports, Gatwick and Heathrow, will be forgiven for thinking that they have strayed into a shopping mall rather than a transport hub. The traveller has to run a retail gauntlet before seeing anything resembling a plane, or at least a departure gate. Major airports make more money from passengers during the extensive 'dwell time' involved in twenty-first century aviation than they do from charges to airlines.

Collectively, passengers are induced to spend freely to subsidise the airlines' activities. Some travellers limit their purchases to last-minute essentials, but many others will be persuaded to indulge in entirely inappropriate consumption: eating fatty food and drinking alcohol, neither of which will enhance their enjoyment of the subsequent journey. A few airports, such as Singapore, offer the sorts of facilities that enable travellers to prepare well for a flight, such as a swim in the rooftop pool or a workout at the gym. But they are rare exceptions to the rule that airports are retail emporia with runways attached.

When aviation was the exclusive preserve of the wealthy, there was no such distorted economics – in return for spending the equivalent of the nation's average earning, the passenger could expect a smooth, cosseted journey – except during World War II, when normal service was suspended.

Democratisation of air travel grew from the ashes of the global conflict. Servicemen returned to 'a land fit for heroes' with a desire to see more of the world in peacetime, while the families of those who never came home wished to visit the graves where their loved ones lay. But a stronger dynamic was rising: disposable incomes – coupled with a large number of surplus aircraft that were searching for a role.

For three years after hostilities ceased, demand was stifled by the UK government's ban on leisure travel abroad. Even after restrictions were lifted, a return flight to the south of France cost £70 – the equivalent of £1,400 today. But a bright young Russian expatriate named Vladimir Raitz opened up the world for British tourists in 1950, when he unveiled the first package holiday: flights from Gatwick to Corsica and back, plus a fortnight of full board at a holiday camp, costing just £32.10 shillings (£32.50, or £650 at today's prices). The seeds were sown for the astonishing growth in package holidays, which today sees close on 20 million British people claiming their place in the sun each year.

> At the moment, a large proportion of those travellers appear to be grounded at Stansted Airport, which – like much of the nation's aviation infrastructure – is straining to cope with the public's demand for air travel. But at gate 45, an aircraft has finally turned up. A swarm of workers surround the Boeing and begin to set about the plane as though it were a beached whale, plundering the baggage from its belly while a line of passengers oozes out of each end. This is a one-class aircraft – besides everyone being equally late, everyone has received the same level of service.

That was how it always was for the first few decades of civil aviation. Until 1952, there was only one class: first, with passengers served by an implausible number of flight attendants whose uniforms were as clean and crisp as the white tablecloths on which ambitious gourmet feasts were served. But on May Day of that year the American carrier Trans World Airways unveiled the first economy class. TWA coined the term 'tourist class' for the second-rate space behind the curtain. The name was telling; then, as now, the word 'tourist' had a faintly pejorative tone, with the implication that any serious starlet or executive would never condescend to travel in anything but first.

In 2001, the pioneering airline was taken over by the world's largest carrier, American Airlines, which promptly erased the brand; TWA is dead, but tourist class is thriving. From the outset, it proved a huge success in attracting a stratum of travellers who had previously been excluded from aviation. In an industry where bright ideas tend to be copied about 10 minutes later by everyone else, other airlines soon followed suit. Even so, the market was not exactly flooded with bargains; fares were still high enough to confine the masses to railways or buses. Airlines were mostly run by governments for the benefit of an unholy trinity: national prestige, foreign policy and airline staff.

High fares prevailed, and with the state coffers obliged to meet any deficit there was little incentive for efficiency. A web of anti-competitive restrictions meant the private sector struggled to survive. The great entrepreneur Freddie Laker spent seven years fighting a series of legal battles to get his Skytrain transatlantic service aloft, to break the assumption that aviation was a club for the wealthy. Yet when I began working for his airline in the late 1970s, the perception among passengers was that they were, indeed, lucky to be able to fly – and even when squashed aboard a Laker Skytrain flight across the Atlantic, they were correct to infer that jetsetting endowed them with a certain glamour. When people believe that the activity in which they are participating is one that many others would yearn to experience, then they are more likely to be compliant consumers.

In one large part of the world, the USSR, flying was almost classless (though, naturally, special treatment was reserved for party apparatchiks). Air travel allowed Soviet citizens to travel across the planet's largest country for fares that, in Western terms, were implausibly low; as the USSR was on the point of collapse, I paid £2 to fly between Leningrad (now St Petersburg) and Moscow, and less than £1 for the hop between Minsk and Kiev. It was, predictably, a dismal experience but, in a federation where the state held the monopoly on everything, my fellow passengers took the delays and offensive in-flight catering in their weary stride.

> At Stansted, the most recently-promised departure time has been and gone, but at the gate there is at last some sign of activity: and tense, whispered discussions are taking place among the staff about the risk of missing a precious slot. Eventually, families with babies and young children are invited to board. This is an interesting arrangement, under which small children – the passengers least suited to an extended spell aboard an overheated aircraft stuck on the airport apron – are the ones who have to endure it for the longest. There will be tears before take-off.

Many airlines have wept buckets about the way they have had to cut costs and become leaner organisations, consequently with fewer resources and less flexibility to recover when things go wrong. But they, like their customers, have become more honest. Even in the 1980s, the passenger who wanted to cut the cost of flying had to behave badly, or at least illegally, to save. I take no pride in confessing that I have in the past done all of the following: stayed on board for one stop longer than I should have (luckily, the ticket inspector did not come round); used a student card 10 years after finishing my education, at the suggestion, and with the connivance, of the travel agent; impersonated my friend Lawrence Hourahane to use a ticket made out in his name; and pretended to own property in Italy and Greece to circumvent the tiresome rules designed to protect scheduled carriers from the reprehensible practice of charter airlines selling seat-only deals to eager travellers. But at the time, these were essential tactics for anyone wanting to save money.

By the end of the 1980s, even the European Community had noticed that the travel industry was taking unfair advantage and began to outlaw restrictions and encourage competition. Today, in Europe at least, airline-imposed constrictions on aviation have dwindled, and anyone with access to the Internet can get access to a range of fares without ludicrous conditions. Yet while you can purchase almost any other product on-line and be reasonably certain that it will be supplied as promised, that does not apply to aviation. Back at Stansted, there is no news of the likely departure time of the flight, but the public address system chimes with a litany of delay announcements for other travellers.

During the 1990s, the British consumer experienced a dramatic rise in self-confidence. The BBC-TV programme *Watchdog* pursued traders who failed to deliver what they promised, and holiday companies almost topped the list – narrowly beaten by Internet service providers. The adversarial presenter, Anne Robinson, ended each programme with the incitement 'Complain, complain, complain'. At the travel desk of *The Independent* the number of grievances I received from travellers increased sharply, with many of the letters marked 'cc. *Watchdog*'. Most were valid – though a few suggested that expectations among airline passengers were way ahead of the prevalent service levels in aviation.

Or perhaps the new generation of travellers was simply unimpressed by the old excuse of 'operational difficulties', which airlines had come to depend on as a catch-all defence. By now, flying was no longer a privilege of the few, but the right of the many. When Stelios Haji-Ioannou launched easyJet between Luton and Scotland in 1995, he promised a flight for the price of a pair of jeans; when easyJet spread to France in 2002, potential customers were offered the choice between 'deux steack frites ou un vol' – steak-and-chips twice, or a flight. A socioeconomic group that had been excluded from aviation quickly found it could take its place in the check-in queue.

All sorts of people are flying these days: one in 20 of Stansted's passengers is classified by BAA (which owns the airport) as belonging to socioeconomic class DE. One in 10 is classed C2. One in five is a business traveller. In Britain, the world centre of cheap aviation, anyone who earns the average annual wage can save enough to fly to Australia and back with just eight days' labour. And 50 new no-frills routes opened from Britain in 2002 alone.

With the dramatic increase in access has come a profound change in the way that flying is regarded, and consequent modifications in behaviour. Air travel has now acquired many of the attributes of a commodity: one size fits all (though none too comfortably), and consumers are becoming experienced at shopping around for a seat at the right price. Most airlines are packing similar numbers of people into the same tubes of aluminium; the average traveller cares less about the name on the side of the plane and more about the thing leaving and arriving on time.

> Punctuality is not the strong suit at Stansted this morning. With no clue about why we are waiting, some travellers seek solace, to calm their agitation and soothe their anxieties about flying, from the obvious source: swigging, illegally, at the booze they bought at the airport.

When competition in aviation was minimal, and airlines fixed inflated fares between themselves, they would use some of their surplus earnings to soothe passengers with meals or overnight accommodation in the event of long delays. Stelios prided himself on a customer-care policy of 'under-promising and overdelivering', and easyJet's management of delays is usually excellent, but the trend among airlines is to promise nothing – and deliver it. But two low-cost airlines – Ryanair and MyTravelLite – specify that they will never offer such frills. Other market entrants look set to follow suit. Increased competition conventionally leads to lower prices and higher standards; in short-haul aviation, while fares are falling fast, so too are standards.

> The ground staff look relieved as the stampede for general boarding begins, as this signifies the angry passengers are about to become someone else's problem. On board, the cabin crew have the advantage that everyone is (or is supposed to be) strapped in. The aviation system treats everyone age 24 months or over as an adult – yet with a degree of condescension that would be out of place even in a primary school. The safety briefing given by a jaded Northwest Airlines flight attendant between Minneapolis and Orlando hit the right note: 'For those of you who have not been in a car for 25 years, this is how to fasten your seat belt.'

Americans were the first nation to regard aviation as nothing more exceptional than getting on a bus. Perhaps this helps to explain why, in my experience, they tend to be more accepting of inconvenience, and more docile in stressful situations. Or it could be that alcohol features less in the journey of an average American flyer. Unlike on international flights, economy class passengers on US domestic flights are obliged to pay for their drinks. Many of the most notorious episodes of disruption among American passengers are those in premium classes, where free drink flows generously.

> Aboard this particular flight, bound only as far as France, some passengers have already begun to mix the fiery cocktail of fear, frustration and alcohol. And things are about to get worse. 'We've been given a departure time 35 minutes from now', explains the captain, blaming National Air Traffic Services but adding 'I'm quietly confident we'll get an improvement on that.' Three-quarters of an hour later, everyone is still waiting, and speculating about the pilot's interpretation of 'improvement' and what else he might be 'quietly confident' about.
>
> Compared with the hours of stress and delay that preceded it, the flight itself is quiet and uneventful. The early drinkers swig furtively from their dwindling cut-price bottles, confident that the overworked cabin crew will be too busy to notice. On a 90-minute flight there is hardly time for frustration to mutate into full-blown fury. Almost everyone is going on holiday, and in the context of fortnight's vacation, a two-hour delay is merely an unwelcome dent.

For the business flyers on a short trip, such a delay can jeopardise the whole purpose of a journey, and – perhaps more significantly – cause embarrassment to the travelling executive in the eyes of his clients and colleagues. Since 11 September 2001 the pressure on business travellers to cut costs yet achieve more has risen sharply, and inversely to tolerance of delays or diversions.

Violent or aggressive behaviour by passengers can never be justified, but the reasons for it can be understood, and steps taken to reduce the causes of disruption. Almost unbelievably, the standard conditions of contract for international aviation are based on the 1929 Warsaw Convention, a time when flying was fraught with difficulties and uncertainties of a different magnitude to today. When aviation was young, airlines needed the flexibility to send passengers from A to B via C, and strictly to limit liability in the event of difficulty or disaster. In the twenty-first century, the consumer has the right to be treated with probity and respect, and knows it.

Index

AASK (Aircraft Accident Statistics and Knowledge) database 145–54
accidents
   AASK database 145–54
   and bereaved individuals 186–7
   and panic 128, 134
   psychological effects 183–96
   reports 134–5
   statistics 129–32
   survivability 119, 128
   survival rates 129–32
   see also emergencies
AIDS *see* HIV/AIDS
air hostesses *see* flight attendants
air humidity, cabin environment 225
air marshal programme, and September 11 events 98
Air Navigation Order (2000), passenger behaviour 12–13
air quality, cabin environment, perception 225–6
air rage
   and alcohol 26, 64, 110
   and cabin crew 104
   and cabin environment 41
   dimensions 109–11
   gender differences 64
   incidents 64, 112
   and personality disorders 63–4
   prevention 7, 64–5
   and psychiatric problems 63
   research 65
   and smoking 26
air safety
   cost 95–6
   staff problems 97

air travel
   attachment
      behaviour 6, 67
      theory 71–4
   and Chernobyl 47
   commodification 305
   companies, advice 78–9
   consequences 1–2
   developmental theory 74
   DVT 26, 227, 242
   and family life 68–9
   fitness for 237–8
   guidelines 239–41
   Gulf War 47
   health risks 23, 234–6
   homesickness 81–93
   and illness 8, 242
   jet aircraft 35–7
   mass 37, 233, 278
   medical emergencies 60–1
   and package holidays 302
   propellor-based aircraft 33–5
   psychiatric problems 6, 62–3
   psychological problems 60–1
   and relationships 66–8
      beliefs 74–5
      case histories 71, 72, 75, 77
      coping strategies 77–9
      gender differences 75–7
   research issues 9
   risk, perceived 47–8
   and September 11 events 6, 26, 47, 70, 95
   and sexual activity 8, 76–7
      key issues 277
      studies 283–6

and sexual infections 277, 281
sleeping medication 230, 254
smoking 16, 39, 229
stress 3, 6, 20–1, 231
systems theory 69–70
theories 69–77
and Tripoli bombing (1986) 47
air travellers
  growth 9, 17, 42, 46–7
  health fears 26–7
  powerlessness 20–1
  problems 2–3
  profile 40–1
  see also passenger behaviour; passengers
Airbus A380 56, 176
aircraft
  altitude, evacuation experiments 165–7
  jet 35–7
  propellor-based 33–5
aircrew, accidents, psychological effects 185–6
airEXODUS, evacuation experiments 178–9
airline fares, and consumer pressure 303–4
airline industry
  changing patterns 41–4
  development 2, 300–1
  services 38–9
airline meals
  and cabin environment 269
  evolution 36, 40
  flight kitchens 264–5
  food acceptability 268–70
  hygiene 265
  in-flight service 8, 267–8
  market segmentation 262
  meal preservation 265–7
  origins 261
  production processes 264–5

rationale for serving 261–3
success factors 271
variety 263–4
airport security
  breaches 101–2
  passenger screening 98–9
  perceptions of 97–8
airports, and shopping 301
alcohol
  and air rage 26, 64, 110
  and anxiety 28
  and appetite 273–4
  and dehydration 229, 273–4
  and passenger behaviour 272
ALN (Action for National Liberation), hijackings 210
American Airlines Flight 63, 'shoe bomber' 104–5
American Psychiatric Association, *Diagnostic and Statistical Manual of Mental Disorders* 48
anxiety
  and alcohol 28
  cognitive/physical symptoms 61–2
  factors 19–20
  in-flight 24–5
    gender differences 61
  nature of 17
  pre-flight 21–2
  reduction 25–6, 28–9
  treatment 27–8
  see also fear of flying; stress; stressors
appetite
  and alcohol 273–4
  and emotions 271
  factors influencing 270–1
  loss of, and atmospheric pressure 270
assertiveness, cabin crew, emergencies 158
atmospheric pressure
  cabin environment 223–4, 270
  and loss of appetite 270

Index

attachment
  behaviour, and air travel 6, 67
  theory, air travel 71–4
Aviation Security Act (1982) 12

baggage, carry-on, retrieval, during evacuation 143
baggage-checking systems, cost 96
beliefs, air travel 74–5
bereaved individuals, accidents, psychological effects 186–7
body, temperature changes 249–50
body clock
  adjustment 251–3, 255
  and light 252, 256–8
  role 253
  and SCN 251, 252–3
  site 251
  synchrony 252
body rhythms 249–51
  and melatonin 250, 252
Boeing 707 35, 36
Boeing 737 accident, Manchester (1985) 124, 128, 142, 168, 184
Boeing 737-2D6C crash (1994) 194–5
Boeing 747, introduction 36
Boeing 747-400 incident 143–4
boredom, cabin environment 247
British Travel Health Association (UK) 233

cabin crew
  and air rage 104
  conditions of service 40
  emergencies 120
    assertiveness 158
  flight deck, communication 144
  hijackings
    noncompliance 209
    physical attack by 215–16
  leadership 114
  passengers, communication 143, 172
  passengers' views on 119–20
  qualifications 36
  role, post-September 11 103–8, 113–16
  selection 106
  service delivery 115
  training 108–11, 113–14
cabin environment
  air humidity 225
  air quality, perception 225–6
  and air rage 41
  airline meals 269
  atmospheric pressure 223–4, 270
  body fluid shifts 228
  boredom 247
  conditions 41, 61
  dehydration 228–9, 247, 271
  design factors 176
  health factors 223
  motion sickness 226
  movement restriction 226–8
  oxygen pressure 224–5
  physiological factors 223–31
  space restriction 226–8, 247
cabin security 104–5
  and quality service 107–8
cabin simulators
  evacuation experiments 161, 163, 173
    photographs 162, 164, 174–5, 178
caffeine
  and dehydration 229
  effects 274
CAMI, evacuation experiments 169–71
Canadian Air Transportation Security Authority (CATSA) 96
Carriage by Air Act (1961) 11
case histories
  in-flight sexual activity 280
  panic attacks 19, 70

relationships, and air travel 71, 72, 75, 77
stress 23, 25
syphilis, Finland 282
catering *see* airline meals
certification trials
    evacuations 154, 156–8
        photographs 156
charter airlines 39
Chernobyl, and air travel 47
children
    sex tourism 293–4
        studies 293–4
    trafficking, UK 295–6
circadian rhythms *see* body rhythms
Civil Aviation Act (1982) 12
Civil Aviation (Amendment) Act (1996) 12
civil rights, and passenger screening 99–101
cognitive behaviour therapy, fear of flying 53
cognitive/physical symptoms, anxiety 61–2
Comet aircraft 35
commodification, air travel 305
community residents, accidents, psychological effects 191–5
companies, air travel, advice 78–9
comprehension, safety cards 123
Concorde aircraft 36
consumer pressure, and airline fares 303–4
control, loss of
    air travellers 20–1
    and homesickness 87–8
coping strategies
    fear of flying 46
    homesickness 90–2, 92–3
    relationships, and air travel 77–9
    stress 25–7

cost
    air safety 95–6
    baggage-checking systems 96
Cranfield University, evacuation experiments 168–9

DC-3 aircraft 33
DC10 crash (1979) 36, 187–8
dehydration
    and alcohol 229, 273–4
    and the cabin environment 228–9, 247, 271
    and caffeine 229
    and DVT 229
deregulation, US 36
design criteria, safety cards 124
developmental theory, air travel 74
disabled passengers, evacuation experiments 163, 165
disaster personnel, accidents, psychological effects 187–91
distance, and intimacy 73
Dominican Republic
    sex tourism 287–92
    sex workers 288–9
DVT (Deep Vein Thrombosis)
    air travel 26, 227, 242
    and dehydration 229
    and space restriction 227

EAA (European Airline Association) 47
ECPAT (End Child Prostitution, Pornography and Trafficking) 293, 295
ELF (Eritrean Liberation Front), hijacking 214, 216
emergencies
    cabin crew 120
        assertiveness 158
    fires, behaviour 202–3
    NTSB study 139, 141–3
    passenger behaviour 133–45
    see also accidents

emotions, and appetite 271
escapes, hijackings 217–18
ETSC (European Transport Safety Council) 129
European Travel Health Advisory Board 233
evacuations
  carry-on baggage, retrieval 143
  certification trials 154, 156–8
    photographs 155
  exit delay time 156–8
  experiments 158–71
    aircraft altitude 165–7
    airEXODUS simulator 178–9
    cabin simulators 161–4, 173, 174–5, 178
    Cranfield University 168–9
    disabled passengers 163, 165
    findings 160–1
    staircase design 166–7
    Type III exit hatch 169–71
  factors influencing 135–6
  post-exit actions 176
  recommendations 176–8
  response time 151
  and safety briefing 124–6
  seat belt problems 151–2
  slide use 138, 145
  and social bonding 152–4, 172
  VLTA aircraft 176–8
exit delay time, evacuations 156–8
exit proximity, and passenger behaviour 136–8, 145–51

FAA (Federal Aviation Administration), safety briefing, recommendations 121
familiarity, and homesickness 89–90
family life
  and air travel 68–9
  and jet lag 68
fear of flying
  causes 51–2

  cognitive behaviour therapy 53
  components 49–51
  consequences 27, 45–6
  coping strategies 46
  cost 46
  gender differences 51
  and other phobias 49, 50–1
  and perceived risk 47–8
  prevalence 6, 18, 46
  psychodynamic psychotherapy 53
  treatments 52–6
    comparative studies 55
    efficacy 55–6
  virtual reality treatment 54
Finland, syphilis, increase 282
fires
  King's Cross underground 203
  scripted behaviour 202–3, 204–5
fitness
  for air travel 237–8
    guidelines 239–41
  for travel 234–7
Flight Anxiety Situations questionnaire 28
flight attendants *see* cabin crew
flight deck, cabin crew, communication 144
flight kitchens, airline meals 264–5
fluid shifts, bodily, cabin environment 228
food
  acceptability, airline meals 268–70
  and air travel 36
  intake, and jet lag 264
  and mood 272

gender differences
  air rage 64
  air travel, and relationships 75–7
  and attention to safety information 119
  fear of flying 51

in-flight anxiety 61
sex tourism 291–2
grief, and homesickness 86–7
Gulf War, and air travel 47

Hague Convention (1970) 12
health factors, cabin environment 223
health fears, air travellers 26–7
health risks, air travel 23, 234–6
hijackings
  ALN 210
  cabin crew
    noncompliance 209
    physical attack by 215–16
  ELF 214, 216
  escapes 217–18
  hostages
    compliance 206, 207–8
    resistance 206
    response 206–7
    studies 201–2, 207
  Japanese Red Army 207
  passengers
    attitudes 102
    behaviour 201–20
    intervention 102–6
    physical attack by 216–17
  persuasion 213–14
  physical attack 214–15
  pilots
    deception 210–12
    noncompliance 208–9
    physical attack by 215
    resistance 212–13
  scripted behaviour 203–5
    testing 219
  security guards, action by 214–15
  and September 11 events 7, 219–20
  'Stockholm syndrome' 203–4
  Teheran (1984) 208
  United Airlines Flight 93 (2001) 102

HIV/AIDS
  and mobility 282–3
  prevalence 282
  and tourism 287–8
homesickness
  causes 85–9
  coping strategies 90–2, 92–3
  effects 84–5
  and familiarity 89–90
  and grief 86–7
  and interruption in routine 88
  and loss of control 87–8
  meaning 82–3
  prevalence 83–4
  and role change 88–9
  sufferers 90, 92
  symptoms 82
hostages
  hijackings
    compliance 206, 207–8
    resistance 206
    response 7, 206–7
    studies 201–2, 207
human rights, and sex tourism 278
hygiene, airline meals 265
hyperventilation 19
hypnotherapy, and stress reduction 26
hypoxia 19
  effects on passenger behaviour 224–5

IATA Resolution 724 13
IATA Resolution RRP 1724, right to refuse carriage 13–15
illness, and air travel 8, 242
information content, safety cards 122–3
Internet, and sex tourism 286–7, 288
intimacy, and distance 73
ISTM (International Society of Travel Medicine) 233

Japanese Red Army, hijackings 207

jet lag 8, 22–3, 230
  and family life 68
  and food intake 264
  meaning 249
  prevention 253–8
    check list 259
  sleep disturbance 254–5
  see also travel fatigue

King's Cross underground, fire 203

Laker, Freddie 303
law
  and passenger behaviour 6, 11–16
  see also regulations
leadership, cabin crew 114
light, and the body clock 252, 256–8
Lockerbie air disaster 192–4
Lockheed L1011 36
low-cost carriers 39, 304–5

Maritime Security Act (1990) 12
market segmentation, airline meals 262
meal preservation, airline meals 265–7
medical emergencies
  air travel 60–1
  in-flight 243
medication, for stress 26
Medlink 60–1
melatonin
  and body rhythms 250, 252
  use, advice 255–6
mobility, and HIV/AIDS 282–3
Montreal Convention (1999) 11
mood, and food 272
motion sickness, cabin environment 226
movement restriction, cabin environment 226–8
myths, passenger behaviour 133–4

NTSB (National Transportation Safety Board) 118, 120, 122
  accident statistics 129–32
  emergencies, study 139, 141–3
  safety card research 122

occupational role, and scripted behaviour 205
oxygen pressure, cabin environment 224–5

package holidays, and air travel 302
PanAm Clippers 33
PanAm Flight 103 (1988) disaster, Lockerbie 192–3
panic, and accidents 128, 134
panic attacks
  case histories 19, 70
  characteristics 18
passenger behaviour
  and Air Navigation Order (2000) 12–13
  and alcohol 272
  Boeing 737 accident 184–5
  changing patterns 41–2
  in emergencies 133–45
  and exit proximity 136–8, 145–51
  factors 3–5
  hijackings 201–20
  hypoxia effects 224–5
  law 6, 11–16
  myths about 133–4
  sanctions 15–16
  and September 11 events 44 n.1
passengers
  accidents, psychological effects 184–5
  cabin crew
    communication 143, 172
    views on 119–20
  disabled, evacuation experiments 163, 165

hijackings
    attitudes 102
    intervention 102–6
    physical attack by 216–17
post-evacuation, marshalling
    procedures 176
quality service, perceptions 107
safety briefing, views on 119, 120–1
safety information
    attention to 118–26, 142, 172
    gender differences 119
screening
    airport security 98–9
    and civil rights 99–101
see also passenger behaviour
Pattaya, sex tourism 292–3
People's Express 37, 38
personality disorders, and air rage 63–4
phobias
    classification 51, 55
    and fear of flying 49
physiology, factors, cabin environment 223–31
pictograms
    safety cards 122
    evaluation 123
pilots
    hijackings
        deception 210–12
        noncompliance 208–9
        physical attacks by 215
        resistance 212–13
psychiatric problems
    and air rage 63
    and air travel 6, 62–3
psychodynamic psychotherapy, fear of flying 53
psychological effects
    accidents 183–96
        aircrew 185–6
        bereaved individuals 186–7
        community residents 191–5

disaster personnel 187–91
passengers 184–5
psychological problems, and air travel 60–1

Raitz, Vladimir 302
regulations
    Air Navigation Order (2000) 12–13
    Aviation Security Act (1982) 12
    Carriage by Air Act (1961) 11
    Chicago Convention (1944) 11
    Civil Aviation Act (1982) 12
    Civil Aviation (Amendment) Act (1996) 12
    Hague Convention (1970) 12
    IATA Resolution 724 13
    IATA Resolution RRP 1724 13
    Maritime Security Act (1990) 12
    Montreal Convention (1999) 11
    Tokyo Convention (1963) 11–12
    Warsaw Convention (1929) 11, 306
relationships
    air travel 66–8
        case histories 71, 72, 77
        coping strategies 77–9
risk
    perceived
        and air travel 47–8
        and fear of flying 47–8
role change, and homesickness 88–9
routine, interruption in, and homesickness 88

SAE (Society of Automotive Engineers), safety cards, information content 122
safety briefing
    content 121
    and evacuation 124–6
    FAA recommendations 121
    Passengers' views 119, 120–1
    safety cards 121–2

video use 121
safety cards
    comprehension 123
    design criteria 124
    information content 122–3
    pictograms 122
        evaluation 123
    research 122, 171
    safety briefing 121–2
    text, evaluation 123–4
safety information, passengers'
    attention to 118–26, 142, 172
sanctions, passenger behaviour 15–16
SCN (Suprachiasmatic Nuclei), and
    body clock 251, 252–3
scripted behaviour
    fires 202–3, 204–5
    hijackings 203–5
    and occupational role 205
seat belt problems, evacuations 151–2
security *see* airport security; cabin
    security
security guards, hijackings, action by
    214–15
September 11 events
    and air marshal programme 98
    and air travel 6, 26, 47, 70, 95
    cabin crew role 103–8, 113–16
    and hijackings 7, 219–20
    and passenger behaviour 44 n.1
service
    delivery, cabin crew 115
    quality
        and cabin security 107–8
        passenger perceptions 107
sex tourism 8
    characteristics 287
    children 293–4
    Dominican Republic 287–92
    gender differences 291–2
    and human rights 278
    and the Internet 286–7, 288

Pattaya 292–3
    studies 287, 293–4
    and travel agents 292–3
sex workers, Dominican Republic
    288–9
sexual activity
    and air travel 8, 76–7
        key issues 277
        studies 283–6
    in-flight 77, 279, 280
sexual harassment, in-flight 279
sexual infections
    and air travel 277, 281
    prevalence 281
    see also HIV/AIDS
'shoe bomber', American Airlines
    Flight 63 104–5
shopping, and airports 301
simulators *see* cabin simulators
Skytrain service 303
sleep disturbance, jet lag 254–5
sleeping medication, air travel 230,
    254
slides
    use
        and evacuation 138, 145
        photographs 155
smoking
    air rage 26
    air travel 16, 39, 229
    and stress 26
social bonding, and evacuations 152–4,
    172
space restriction
    cabin environment 226–8, 247
    and DVT 227
staff problems, air safety 97
staircase design, evacuation experi-
    ments 166–7
statistics
    accidents 129–32
    travel 278

'Stockholm syndrome', hijackings
  203–4
stress
  air travel 3, 6, 20–1, 231
  case histories 23, 25
  coping strategies 25–7
  medication for 26
  reduction
    hypnotherapy 26
    smoking 26
  see also anxiety
stressors
  advice on 27
  management of 23–5
  see also anxiety
survivability, accidents 119, 128
survival rates, accidents 129–32
synchrony, body clock 252
syphilis, Finland, increase 282
systems theory, air travel 69–70

Teheran hijacking (1984) 208
Tenerife accident (1977) 184
terrorism see hijackings; September 11
  events
text, safety cards, evaluation 123–4
Tokyo Convention (1963) 11–12
tourism, and HIV/AIDS 287–8
trafficking
  children, UK 295–6
  profile, at risk minors 297
  women, UK 294–5
training, cabin crew 108–11, 113–14
travel, fitness for 234–7
travel agents, and sex tourism 292–3
travel fatigue
  causes 246
  check list 248–9
  prevention
    in-flight 247

post-flight 247–8
pre-flight 246–7
see also jet lag
travel medicine
  components 233–4
  development 233
  organizations 233
travel statistics, WTO 278
Tripoli bombing (1986), and air travel
  47
TSA (Transportation Security
  Administration) 98
Twin Towers disaster see September
  11 events
Type A exit hatch 155, 158, 173
Type I exit hatch 169
Type III exit hatch 124–6, 141–2
  experiments 169–71
  photographs 140

UK
  trafficking
    children 295–6
    women 294–5
United Airlines Flight 93 (2001),
  hijacking 102
US, deregulation 36

video, use in safety briefing 121
virtual reality treatment, fear of flying 54
VLTA (Very Large Transport Aircraft),
  evacuations 176–8

Warsaw Convention (1929) 11, 306
West Sussex Social Services, at risk
  minors, profile 297
Wright brothers 2
Write Partnership Ltd 63, 64
WTO (World Tourism Organisation),
  travel statistics 278